ARIS & PHILLIPS CLASSICAL TEXTS

OVID

Amores II

Edited with an Introduction, Translation and Commentary by

Joan Booth

Aris & Phillips is an imprint of
Oxbow Books, Park End Place, Oxford OX1 1HN

First published 1991. Reprinted with addendum 1999, 2007.

ISBN 0-85668-175-X
ISBN 978-0-85668-175-2

A CIP record for this book is available from the British Library

Front cover illustration: Terracotta Arretine bowl stamp (40–20 B.C.) held in the Staatliche Museum, Berlin.

Printed in Great Britain
by CPI Antony Rowe, Eastbourne

Contents

Preface

I first began to read Ovid's *Amores* some twenty years ago as an undergraduate in the University of London. And, conditioned as I was by this poet's prevailing reputation as a lightweight, I thought I would not be long detained or entertained. I was wrong. I discovered a text full of puzzles and delights, but equipped only with ageing or perfunctory commentaries and, astonishingly, with none whatsoever in English. Now, of course, professional scholars are being provided with an invaluable aid to the close reading I believe the three books of *Amores* deserve in James McKeown's monumental edition (timing, and not lack of appreciation, is responsible for the paucity of my own references to Vol. II, the commentary on Book i), but little which is appropriately detailed has so far been offered to the less experienced Latinist and the ever-increasing number of classical enthusiasts with no Latin at all. The present edition of Book ii has therefore been produced with their needs especially in mind, though I hope that more advanced scholars may also find it of some use and interest.

The unconventional format is largely due to this possibly foolhardy attempt to offer 'something for everyone'. If it proves to please no one, I ask my readers' sympathy at least for the intention. The Latinless and near-Latinless user will find the text and parallel translation of each poem or pair of poems followed by a general 'Discussion' (with select bibliography; see p. v) in which Latin is included only where unavoidable and then is usually translated (as is all Greek). The commentary, which is presented separately and to which the reader of the 'Discussions' is occasionally referred, offers the linguistically competent further philologically based criticism, textual notes and help with the Latin. It is not exhaustive, either in terms of factual information or of critical interpretation; in particular, I have not attempted to take on the 'French' school of radical literary theorists. I have been persuaded to allow the apparatus criticus, for technical and economic reasons, to be printed *en bloc* rather than in its normal position at the foot of each page of text; I hope that the placing will not seriously inconvenience the more traditional user.

This book has been far too long in gestation for very personal reasons with which I shall not bore the reader. Most gladly, however, I record my gratitude to all those, within and without the groves of academe, whose store of knowledge I have plundered and whose good nature I have imposed upon during the writing of it. I hope they will forgive me if I do not name them all, for they are so many, but of some I must make special mention. The late Professor F.R.D. Goodyear, teacher, friend and counsellor, without whom this book would never have been begun; Professor Niall Rudd, generous reader of almost the entire manuscript at various stages and source of countless improvements, without whom it would never have been finished; Professor J.B. Hall, who supervised with kindly patience the doctoral thesis out of which the present edition grew; Professor E.J. Kenney, who examined it, and subsequently made numerous helpful comments and suggestions; Mr A.G. Lee, who gave me his valuable reactions to several radical ideas; and Mr Ceri Davies, my immediate colleague, who unstintingly provided practical help and support at a crucial time. These friends and scholars have saved me from many errors of fact and judgement; where I have persisted with my own view against theirs, I shall no doubt regret it, and for such *bêtises* as remain the responsibility is entirely my own. I should also like to register my gratitude to the late Mr John Aris, *homini humanissimo*, to Mr Adrian Phillips and his editorial staff, to the University College of Swansea for granting me one term's sabbatical leave to work on this book, to the Warden and Fellows of Robinson College, Cambridge, for electing me to a Bye-Fellowship for the duration of my leave, and to the Wolfson Foundation for a grant towards expenses. Finally, to David Hunt for his sympathetic ear and moral support over many years and to my father for his uncomplaining tolerance (especially in the project's latter stages) of what in a dog would be called 'uncertain temper' I offer my warmest thanks. Now, at long last, *i, libelle*!

J.B.
Swansea, 1991

Addendum 1999

A limited amount of bibliographical updating and revision has been possible in the corrected reprint. It may be supplemented from J.C. McKeown, *Ovid, Amores*. Vol. III, *A Commentary on Book II, ARCA* 36 (Leeds, 1998), ix-xxxii. A second edition of Kenney's OCT (see p. vi) appeared in 1994 (corrected 1995) and an edition with German translation by M. von Albrecht (*Ovid: Amores. Liebesgedichte*, Stuttgart) in 1997. An edition with new German translation by N. Holzberg in the Tusculum series (Zurich-Düsseldorf) is due in 1999-2000.

Abbreviations

The following abbreviations are used throughout this book:

ALL = *Archiv für lateinische Lexikographie und Grammatik* (Leipzig, 1884–1908)
ANRW = *Aufstieg und Niedergang der römischen Welt*, edd. H. Temporini and W. Haase (Berlin, 1972–)
CHCL = *The Cambridge History of Classical Literature*, Vol. II, edd. E.J. Kenney and W.V. Clausen (Cambridge, 1982)
CIL = *Corpus Inscriptionum Latinarum* (Berlin, 1862–)
CLE = *Carmina Latina Epigraphica* (= *Anthologia Latina* II, ed. F. Bücheler, Parts I and II (Leipzig, 1921 and 1897))
Hofmann-Szantyr = J.B. Hofmann, *Lateinische Syntax und Stilistik,* rev. by A. Szantyr (Munich, 1965)
Housman, *Classical Papers* = *The Classical Papers of A.E. Housman*, edd. J. Diggle and F.R.D. Goodyear (Cambridge, 1972)
Kühner-Stegmann = R. Kühner and C. Stegmann, *Ausführliche Grammatik der lateinischen Sprache*: *Satzlehre*, 3rd edn., rev. by A. Thierfelder (Darmstadt, 1955)
Nisbet-Hubbard = R.G.M. Nisbet and M. Hubbard, *A Commentary on Horace*: *Odes Book I* (Oxford, 1970), *Odes Book II* (Oxford, 1978)
OLD = *The Oxford Latin Dictionary* (Oxford, 1968–82)
Ovidiana = *Ovidiana. Recherches sur Ovide*, ed. N.I. Herescu (Paris, 1958)
RE = Pauly-Wissowa, *Real-Encyclopädie der classischen Altertumswisssenschaft* (Stuttgart, 1893–1978)
ThLL = *Thesaurus Linguae Latinae* (Leipzig, 1900–)

Latin authors and works are generally abbreviated as in *The Oxford Latin Dictionary* and Greek authors and works as in H.G. Liddell, R. Scott, H. Stuart-Jones and R. McKenzie *A Greek-English Lexicon,* (9th edn. with supplement, Oxford, 1968); more explicit references are occasionally given for the sake of clarity. The works of Ovid are normally cited without the author's name. References are as far as possible to the Oxford Classical Text, and elsewhere to the Teubner or other specified edition. All references to Callimachus are to the edition of R. Pfeiffer (Oxford, 1949–53). Figures for occurrences of a particular word in Ovid are based on the *Concordance of Ovid* by R.J. Deferrari, I. Barry and R.P. McGuire (Washington, 1939) and exclude spurious works. The abbreviations 'p.' and 'pp.' normally refer to the pages of this book.

A select bibliography follows each of my 'Discussions' of individual poems or pairs of poems; * marks treatments substantially different from mine in conclusion or emphasis. For further select bibliography of the *Amores* and Ovid in general see J.A. Barsby, *Ovid. Greece & Rome New Surveys in the Classics* 12 (Oxford, 1978) with my own bibliographical update in the new edition (1991).

Works cited

(A) Editions, Commentaries and Translations

Only those editions etc. cited in this book are included here; for a more complete list see Munari xlix–xl. These works are normally referred to by editor's or translator's name alone.

Bertini = *P. Ovidio Nasone Amori*, a cura di F. Bertini (Milan, 1983).

Bornecque = *Ovide: les Amours.* Texte établi et traduit par H. Bornecque (Budé edn., Paris, 1930).

Brandt = *P. Ouidi Nasonis Amorum Libri Tres*, erklärt von P. Brandt (Leipzig, 1911).

Burman = *P. Ouidii Nasonis opera omnia,* cum integris Micylli, Ciofani, et D. Heinsii notis et N. Heinsii curis secundis, cura et studio P. Burmanni (Amsterdam, 1727). *Amores* Vol. I, 231ff.

Ehwald = *P. Ouidius Naso, Amores, Epistulae, Medic. Fac. Fem., Ars Amat., Remedia Amoris*, ex R. Merkelii recognitione edidit R. Ehwald (Teubner edn., Leipzig, 1888).

Goold: see Showerman.

Green = *Ovid: The Erotic Poems*, translated with an introduction and notes by P. Green (Penguin edn., Harmondsworth, 1982).

Harder-Marg = *P. Ovidius Naso, Liebesgedichte. Amores*, lateinisch und deutsch von W. Marg und R. Harder (Munich, 1956, 6th edn., 1984).

Heinsius = *Operum P. Ovidii Nasonis editio noua.* Nic. Heinsius Dan. f. recensuit ac notas addidit (Amsterdam, 1661). *Amores* Vol. I. 119ff., notes 193ff.

Kenney = *P. Ouidi Nasonis Amores, Medicamina Faciei Femineae, Ars Amatoria, Remedia Amoris*, edidit breuique adnotatione critica instruxit E.J. Kenney (OCT, Oxford, 1961, corrected 1965).

Lee = *Ovid's Amores.* English translation by G. Lee with Latin text (London, 1968).

Lenz = *Ovid, Die Liebeselegien*, lateinisch und deutsch von F.W. Lenz (Berlin, 1965, 3rd edn., 1976).

McKeown = *Ovid: Amores in 4 vols,* edited by J.C. McKeown. Vol. I *Text and Prolegomena* (*ARCA 20*, Liverpool, 1987), Vol. II *A Commentary on Book I* (*ARCA* 22, Leeds, 1989).

Melville = *Ovid. The Love Poems*, translated by A.D. Melville, with an introduction and notes by E.J. Kenney (World's Classics edn., Oxford, 1989).

Munari = *P. Ouidi Nasonis Amores*: testo, introduzione, traduzione e note di F. Munari (Florence, 1951, 5th edn., 1970).

Némethy = *P. Ouidii Nasonis Amores*, edidit adnotationibus exegeticis et criticis instruxit G. Némethy (Budapest, 1907).

Showerman = *Ovid, Heroides and Amores* with an English translation by G. Showerman (Loeb edn., London-Cambridge, Mass., 1914, 2nd edn., revised by G.P. Goold, 1977).

(B) Other Works

The list below is not intended as a full or even a select bibliography, but simply as an index of secondary works (excluding well-known commentaries on Greek and Latin texts) normally cited by author's name alone or author-date. The full reference is given at the time of citation for all works (again excluding well-known commentaries) cited once only within this book. References to periodicals follow the system of *L'Année Philologique.*

Adams, J.N. (1973). 'Two Latin words for "kill"', *Glotta* 51, 280–92.

—— (1982). *The Latin Sexual Vocabulary* (London).

André, J. *Étude sur les termes de couleur dans la langue latine* (Paris, 1949).

Axelson, B. *Unpoetische Wörter* (Lund, 1945).

Balsdon, J.P.V.D. *Roman Women* (London, 1962).

Barsby, J.A. 'Ovid's *Amores* and Roman Comedy', *PLLS* 9 (1996), 135-57.

Berger, A. *An Encyclopaedic Dictionary of Roman Law, TAPhS* 43, Part 2 (1953).

Booth, J. (1981). 'Aspects of Ovid's language', *ANRW* II. 31. 4, 2686–700.

—— (1982). 'Two notes on the text of Ovid's *Amores*', *CQ* n.s. 32, 156–8.

Booth, J. and Lee, G. *Catullus to Ovid: Reading Latin Love Elegy* (Bristol) (forthcoming, 1999).
Boyd, B.W. *Ovid's Literary Loves. Influence and Innovation in the Amores* (Ann Arbor, 1997).
Bright, D.F. *Haec mihi fingebam: Tibullus in his world* (*Cincinnati Classical Studies* 3, Leiden, 1978).
Brunt, P.A. *Italian Manpower 225 B.C.–A.D. 14* (Oxford, 1971).
Büchner, K. (1970). *Studien zur römischen Literatur* VIII (Wiesbaden).
Buchan, M. '*Ovidius imperamator*: beginnings and endings of love poems and empire in the *Amores*', *Arethusa* 28 (1995), 53-85.
Burck, E. 'Römische Wesenzüge der augusteischen Liebeselegie', *Hermes* 80 (1952), 163–200 [= *Vom Menschenbild in der römischen Literatur* (Heidelberg, 1966), 191–237].
Bürger, R. *De Ouidi carminum amatoriorum inuentione et arte* (Diss. Göttingen, 1901).
Cahoon, L. 'The bed as battlefield: erotic conquest and military metaphor in Ovid's *Amores*', *TAPhA* 118 (1988), 293–307.
Cairns, F. *Generic Composition in Greek and Roman Poetry* (Edinburgh, 1972).
Cameron, A. (1968). 'The first edition of Ovid's *Amores*', *CQ* n.s. 18, 320–33.
—— (1995) *Callimachus and his Critics* (Princeton).
Connor, P.J. 'His dupes and accomplices: a study of Ovid the illusionist in the *Amores*', *Ramus* 3 (1974), 18–40.
Damon, C. 'Poem division, paired poems and *Amores* ii. 9 and iii. 11', *TAPhA* 120 (1990), 269–90.
D'Arcy Thompson, W. *A Glossary of Greek Birds* (2nd edn., Oxford, 1936).
Daremberg, C. and Saglio, E. *Dictionnaire des antiquités grecques et romaines d'après les textes et les monuments* (Paris, 1887–1919).
Daube, D. 'No kissing or else ...' in *The Classical Tradition: Literary and Historical Studies in Honor of H. Caplan*, ed. L. Wallach (New York, 1966), 222–31.
Davis, J.T. (1977). *Dramatic Pairings in the Elegies of Propertius and Ovid.* (*Noctes Romanae* 15, Berne-Stuttgart).
—— (1981). '*Risit Amor*: Aspects of literary burlesque in Ovid's *Amores*', *ANRW* II. 31. 4, 2460–506.
—— (1989). *Fictus Adulter: Poet as Actor in the Amores* (Amsterdam).
Day, A.A. *The Origins of Latin Love Elegy* (Oxford, 1938).
D'Elia, S. *Ovidio* (Naples, 1959).
Donnet, D. 'Ovide, Properce et l'élégie latine', *LEC* 33 (1965), 253–79.
Due, O.S. 'Amores und Abtreibung', *C & M* 32 (1980), 133–50.
Du Quesnay, I.M. Le M. 'The *Amores*' in *Ovid*, ed. J.W. Binns (London, 1973), 1–48.
Eck, W. 'Senatorial self-representation: developments in the Augustan period' in *Caesar Augustus: Seven Aspects*, edd. F. Millar and E. Segal (Oxford, 1984), 129–67.
Fantham, E. *Comparative Studies in Republican Latin Imagery* (Toronto, 1972).
Fränkel, H. *Ovid: A Poet between two Worlds* (Berkeley-Los Angeles, 1945).
Frécaut, J.-M. *L'esprit et l'humeur chez Ovide* (Grenoble, 1972).
Galinsky, G.K. (1969). 'The triumph theme in the Augustan elegy', *WS* 82, 75–107.
—— (1996). *Augustan Culture. An Interpretive Introduction* (Princeton).
Gauly, B.M. *Liebeserfahrungen. Zur Rolle des elegischen Ich in Ovids Amores* (Frankfurt am Main, 1990).
Giangrande, G. 'Hellenistic topoi in Ovid's *Amores*', *MPhL* 4 (1981), 25–51.
Goold, G.P. (1965a). '*Amatoria Critica*', *HSPh* 69, 1–107.
—— (1965b). Review of Kenney's edition, *AJPh* 86, 89–92.
Greene, E.S. *The Erotics of Domination. Male Desire and the Mistress in Latin Love Poetry* (Baltimore-London, 1998).
Griffin, J. (1984). 'Augustus and the poets: *Caesar qui cogere posset*' in *Caesar Augustus* (see Eck above), 189-218.
—— (1985). *Latin Poets and Roman Life* (London).
Hand, F. *Tursellinus seu de particulis latinis commentarii* (Leipzig, 1829–45).
Hardie, P.R. *Virgil's Aeneid: Cosmos and Imperium* (Oxford, 1986).
Hau, P. *De casuum usu Ouidiano* (Diss. Münster, 1884).

Hiltbrunner, O. (1970). 'Ovids Gedicht von Siegelring und ein anonymes Epigramm aus Pompei', *Gymnasium* 77 (1970), 283–99.
Hinds, S.E. (1987). 'Generalising about Ovid', *Ramus* 16, 4–31.
—— (1998). *Allusion and Intertext. Dynamics of Appropriation in Roman Poetry* (Cambridge).
Heyob, S.K. *The Cult of Isis among Women in the Greco-Roman World* (Leiden, 1975).
Hofmann, J.B. *Lateinische Umgangssprache* (3rd edn., Heidelberg, 1951).
Holzberg, N. (1997a). *Ovid. Dichter und Werk* (Munich, 2nd edn., 1998).
—— (1997b). 'Playing with his life: Ovid's "autobiographical" reference', *Lampas* 30, 4-19.
Jacobson, H. *Ovid's Heroides* (Princeton, 1974).
Jäger, K. *Zweigliedrige Gedichte und Gedichtpaare bei Properz und in Ovids Amores* (Diss. Tübingen, 1967).
Jäkel, S. 'Beobachtungen zur dramatischen Komposition von Ovids *Amores', A & A* 16 (1970), 12–28.
Keith, A.M. '*Corpus eroticum*: elegiac poetics and elegiac *puellae* in Ovid's *Amores*', *CW* 88 (1994-5), 27-40.
Kennedy, D.F. *The Arts of Love. Five Studies in the Discourse of Roman Love Elegy* (Cambridge, 1993).
Kenney, E.J. (1955). 'The tradition of Ovid's *Amores*', *CR* n.s. 5, 13–14.
—— (1958a). 'Notes on Ovid', *CQ* n.s. 8, 54–66.
—— (1958b). '*Nequitiae poeta*', *Ovidiana* 201–9.
—— (1959). 'Notes on Ovid II', *CQ* n.s. 9, 240–60.
—— (1962). 'The manuscript tradition of Ovid's *Amores, Ars Amatoria* and *Remedia Amoris*', *CQ* n.s. 12, 1–31.
—— (1966). 'First thoughts on the *Hamiltonensis*', *CR* n.s. 16, 267–71.
—— (1969). 'Ovid and the Law', *YCIS* 21, 243–63.
Keul, M. *Liebe im Widerstreit: Interpretationen zu Ovids Amores und ihrem literarischen Hintergrund* (Frankfurt am Main, 1989).
Knox, P.E. *Ovid's Metamorphoses and the Traditions of Augustan Poetry* (*PCPhS Suppl.* 11, Cambridge, 1986).
Krenkel, W. 'Der Abortus in der Antike', *Erotica* I, *Wissenschaftliche Zeitschrift der Universität Rostock* 20 (1971), 443–51.
Kroll, W. *Studien zum Verständnis der römischen Literatur* (Stuttgart, 1924).
Labate, M. 'Tradizione elegiaca e società galante negli *Amores*', *SCO* 27 (1977), 283–339.
La Penna, A. 'Note sul linguaggio erotico dell' elegia latina', *Maia* 4 (1957), 187–209.
Lattimore, R. *Themes in Greek and Latin Epitaphs* (*Illinois Studies in Language and Literature* 28, Urbana, 1942).
Lee, A.G. (1962). '*Tenerorum lusor Amorum*' in *Critical Essays on Roman Literature*: *Elegy and Lyric*, ed. J.P. Sullivan (London, 1962), 149–79.
Lenz, F.W. (1959). 'Io ed il paese di Sulmona' in *Atti del convegno internationale ouidiano, Sulmona 1958* (2 vols., Rome) Vol. II, 59–68.
—— (1962). 'Noch einmal "io ed il paese di Sulmona" ', *RCCM* 4, 150–53.
Leumann, M. 'Die lateinische Dichtersprache', *MH* 4 (1947), 116–39 [= *id., Kleine Schriften* (Zurich-Stuttgart, 1959), 131–56].
Lilja, S. *The Roman Elegists' Attitude to Women* (Helsinki, 1965).
Lloyd-Jones, H. and Parsons P.J. (edd.) *Supplementum Hellenisticum* (Berlin-New York, 1983).
Löfstedt, E. *Syntactica: Studien und Beiträge zur historischen Syntax des Lateins*, Vol. I (2nd edn., Lund, 1942), Vol. II (Lund, 1933).
Lörcher, G. *Der Aufbau der drei Bücher von Ovids Amores* (*Heuremata* 3, Amsterdam, 1975).
Luck, G. (1969). *The Latin Love Elegy* (2nd edn., London).
—— (1970). 'Der Dichter zwischen Elegie und Epos' in *Antike Lyrik*, ed. W. Eisenhut (Darmstadt), 464–79.
—— (1974). 'The woman's role in Latin love poetry' in *Perspectives of Roman Poetry*, ed. G.K. Galinsky (Austin, Texas), 17–31.
Lyne, R.O.A.M. (1979). '*Seruitium amoris*', *CQ* n.s. 29, 117–30.
—— (1980). *The Latin Love Poets from Catullus to Horace* (Oxford).

McKeown, J.C. (1979). 'Augustan elegy and mime', *PCPhS* n.s. 25, 71–84.

McKie, D.S. 'Ovid's *Amores*: the prime sources for the text', *CQ* n.s. 36 (1986), 219–38.

Morgan, K. *Ovid's Art of Imitation: Propertius in the Amores*, (*Mnemosyne Suppl.* 47, Leiden, 1977).

Murgatroyd, P. (1984). 'Genre and themes in Ovid, *Amores* ii. 15', *EMC* 28, 15–22.

Murgia, C.E. (1986a). 'The date of Ovid's *Ars Amatoria* iii', *AJPh* 107, 74–94.

——— (1986b). 'Influence of Ovid's *Remedia Amoris* on *Ars Amatoria* iii and *Amores* iii', *CPh* 81, 203–20.

Neue, F. and Wagener, C. *Formenlehre der lateinischen Sprache* (3rd edn., Berlin, 1892–1905).

Neumann, R. *Qua ratione Ouidius in Amoribus scribendis Properti elegiis usus sit* (Diss. Göttingen, 1919).

Oliver, R.P. (1958). 'Ovid in his ring (*Am.* ii. 15. 9–26)', *CPh* 53, 103–5.

——— (1969). 'The text of Ovid's *Amores*' in *Classical Studies presented to B.E. Perry* (*Illinois Studies in Language and Literature* 58, Urbana) 138–64.

Opelt, I. *Die lateinische Schimpfwörter* (Heidelberg, 1965).

Otis, B. 'Ovid and the Augustans', *TAPhA* 69 (1938), 188–229 (German version of 194–211 in *Ovid,* edd. M. von Albrecht and E. Zinn (*Wege der Forschung* 92, Darmstadt, 1968), 233–544).

Otto, A. *Die Sprichwörter und sprichwörtlichen Redensarten der Römer* (Leipzig, 1890) with *Nachträge*, ed. R. Haüssler (Darmstadt, 1968).

Pichon, R. *Index Verborum Amatoriorum* (Hildesheim, 1966) [= *De sermone amatorio apud latinos elegiarum scriptores* (Diss., Paris, 1902), 75–303].

Platnauer, M. *Latin Elegiac Verse. A Study of the Metrical Uses of Tibullus, Propertius and Ovid* (Cambridge, 1951).

Pokrowskij, M. 'Neue Beiträge zur Characteristik Ovids', *Philologus, Suppl.* 11 (1907–10), 351–404.

Pomeroy, S.B. *Goddesses, Whores, Wives and Slaves* (New York, 1975).

Pöschl, V. 'Ovid und Horaz', *RCCM* 1 (1959), 15–25.

Quinn, K. 'Persistence of a theme: the Propempticon' in *id., Latin Explorations* (London, 1963), 239–73.

Reitzenstein, E. 'Das neue Kunstwollen in den *Amores* Ovids', *RhM* 84 (1935), 62–88 [= *Wege der Forschung* 92 (see Otis above), 206–32].

Sabot, A.-F. *Ovide, poète de l'amour dans ses oeuvres de jeunesse* (Paris, 1976).

Scivoletto, N. *Musa Iocosa: studio sulla poesia giovanile di Ovidio* (Rome, 1976).

Shackleton Bailey, D.R. *Propertiana* (Cambridge, 1955).

Sittl, C. *Die Gebärden der Griechen und Römer* (Leipzig, 1890).

Snowden, F.M. *Blacks in Antiquity: Ethiopians in the Greco-Roman Experience* (Cambridge, Mass., 1970).

Spies, A. *Militat omnis amans. Ein Beitrag zur Bildersprache der antiken Erotik* (Diss. Tübingen, 1930).

Stahl, H.-P. *Propertius: 'Love' and 'War'. Individual and State under Augustus* (Berkeley-Los Angeles, 1985).

Stirrup, B.E. 'Structure and Separation: a comparative analysis of Ovid, *Am.* ii. 11 and ii. 16', *Eranos* 74 (1976), 32–52.

Stroh, W. (1971). *Die römische Liebeselegie als werbende Dichtung* (Amsterdam).

——— (1979). 'Ovids Liebeskunst und die Ehegesetze des Augustus', *Gymnasium* 86 (1979), 323–52.

Syme, R. (1939). *The Roman Revolution* (Oxford).

——— (1978). *History in Ovid* (Oxford).

Thomas, E. (1964). 'Variations on a military theme in Ovid's *Amores*', *G & R* n.s. 11, 151–65.

Tränkle, H. *Die Sprachkunst des Properz und die Tradition der lateinischen Dichtersprache*, (*Hermes Einzelschr.* 15, Wiesbaden, 1960).

Tremoli, P. *Influssi retorici e ispirazione poetica negli Amores di Ovidio* (*Fac. di Lett., Ist. di Filol. Class* I, Trieste, 1965).

Tupet, A.-M. *La magie dans la poésie latine 1: des origines à la fin du règne d'Auguste* (Paris, 1976).

Veyne, P. *Roman Erotic Elegy. Love, Poetry and the West*, translated by D. Pellauer (Chicago-London, 1988).

Watson, P.A. 'Axelson revisited: the selection of vocabulary in Latin poetry', *CQ* n.s. 35 (1985), 430–48.

Watts, W.J. 'Ovid, the law and Roman Society on abortion', *AClass* 16 (1973), 89–101.

West, M.L. *Studies in Greek Elegy and Iambus (Untersuchungen zur antiken Literatur und Geschichte* 14, Berlin-New York, 1974).

Wilhelm, F. 'Zur Elegie', *RhM* 71 (1916), 136–42.

Wilkinson, L.P. (1955). *Ovid Recalled* (Cambridge).

—— (1963). *Golden Latin Artistry* (Cambridge).

Williams, G. (1968). *Tradition and Originality in Roman Poetry* (Oxford).

—— (1978). *Change and Decline: Roman Literature in the Early Empire* (Berkeley-Los Angeles).

Wills, J. *Repetition in Latin Poetry: Figures of Allusion* (Oxford, 1996).

Wimmel, W. *Kallimachos in Rom. Die Nachfolge seines apologetischen Dichtens in Augusteerzeit.* (*Hermes Einzelschr.* 16, Wiesbaden, 1960).

Witt, R.E. *Isis in the Greco-Roman World* (London, 1971).

Woodcock, E.C. *A New Latin Syntax* (London, 1959).

Woytek, E. 'Die unlauteren Absichten eines Ehrenmannes (Zur Doppelbödigkeit von Ovid, *Amores* i. 3)', *WS* 110 (1995), 417-38.

Wyke, M. 'Reading female flesh: *Amores* iii. 1' in *History as Text*, ed. Averil Cameron (London, 1989), 111-43.

Yardley, J.C. (1977). 'The Roman elegists, sick girls and the *soteria*', *CQ* n.s. 27, 394–401.

—— (1987). 'Propertius iv. 5, Ovid, *Amores* i. 6 and Roman Comedy,' *PCPhS* n.s. 33, 179–89.

Zanker, P. *The Power of Images in the Age of Augustus*, translated by A. Shapiro (Michigan, 1988).

Zingerle, A. *Ovidius und sein Verhältnis zu den Vorgängern und gleichzeitigen römischen Dichtern*, 3 vols. (Innsbruck, 1869–71).

INTRODUCTION

I. 'THE GLORY OF THE PAELIGNIAN PEOPLE'[1]: OVID AND HIS POETIC CAREER

We have done well out of the all-but-indecent self-confidence of Publius Ovidius Naso;[2] for his belief in the enduring appeal of his writing and the subsequent curiosity of future generations about its author led him to leave us his own full account of his life in *Tristia* iv. 10, written in A.D. 10 or 11 from his place of exile, Tomis on the Black Sea in present-day Romania. Though it is doubtless as carefully contrived as an entry in *Who's Who*,[3] there is no reason to dispute the essential information offered. Ovid was born on 20 March, 43 B.C. in the Paelignian town of Sulmo[4] into a family of long-established equestrian rank (vv. 1-8). He and his brother, his elder by one year and coincidentally sharing his birthday (9-14), were sent to Rome to be schooled in the art of public speaking (i.e. rhetoric – the traditional education for the sons of the propertied classes). His brother gave early promise of progressing towards a conventionally respectable oratorical career, presumably in law or politics (15-18), but young Publius – our Ovid – was much more interested in writing poetry, which exasperated his father because he thought there was no money in it (19-22). Ovid made a token effort to do better, and he and his exemplary brother at the age of sixteen or so assumed the toga with the 'broad purple stripe', which marked them out as candidates for the sequence of magistracies (*cursus honorum*) leading to admission to the senate (23-30; from elsewhere we learn that Ovid also went to Athens to study and travelled abroad with his friend, the poet Macer[5]). After the death of his brother at twenty, Ovid did hold minor office as a *triumuir,* i.e. one of a three-man legal tribunal (and this was not in fact his only public service[6]), but he then 'narrowed his purple stripe', in other words, gave up public life and all prospect of senatorial rank, to devote himself to his first love, poetry (31-40). On his own admission, he hung around all the well-known poets of the time, including Tibullus, Propertius and Horace (and eventually acquired the patronage of Tibullus' sponsor, Messalla Corvinus[7]); the awesome Virgil he 'only saw' (42-56). He gave recitations of his own youthful poetry, he says, 'when his beard had been cut once or twice', and his

1 *Paeligni dicar gloria gentis ego*: Ovid on himself (*Am.* iii. 15. 8).

2 For Ovid's name see 1. 2n. *Naso.*

3 For its possible literary models and ulterior motives see J. Fairweather, 'Ovid's autobiographical poem, *Tristia* iv. 10', *CQ* n.s. 37 (1987), 181-96, B. R. Fredericks, '*Tristia* iv. 10: Poet's autobiography and poetic autobiography', *TAPhA* 106 (1976), 139-54 (with further bibliography), Holzberg (1997a) 31-7, *id.* (1997b) 4-10.

4 See 16. 1n.

5 *Tr.* i. 2. 77, *Pont.* ii. 10, *Fast.* vi. 421-4; see also 18. 3n.

6 He also acted as a *decemuir slitibus iudicandis* (*Fast.* iv. 383-4), a *centumuir* (*Tr.* ii. 93-4) and a *iudex priuatus* (*Tr.* ii. 95-6); see further Kenney (1969) 244-9.

7 *Pont.* ii. 3. 75-8; see further Williams (1978) 65-70.

inspiration was a woman he called Corinna (57-60). He was married three times, the first time disastrously, the second uneventfully and the last to a paragon who stood by him in his exile,[8] and he had one daughter who gave him two grandchildren (69-76). Both his parents – mercifully, he says – died before the day of his 'punishment' (i.e. his exile[9] in A.D. 8), which was caused not by a crime, but a 'mistake' (77-90). Resigned to ending his life in Tomis (according to St Jerome he died in A.D. 17), he found his poetry and the prospect of immortality as a result of it his only consolation (109-32).

Despite endless investigation,[10] the cause of Ovid's exile remains a mystery. He himself claims that a poem, the *Ars Amatoria*, as well as a mistake was to blame,[11] the specific charge against the *Ars* being that it incited women to adultery.[12] Technically, of course, it did not, for married women were specifically excluded from Ovid's invited audience.[13] But so directly counter in spirit did it run to the Augustan legislation designed to strengthen marriage and the family[14] that it would not be surprising, if Augustus – rather like those who, illogically but understandably, suspect television violence of encouraging violence in real life – had considered it at the very least a bad influence when his own daughter Julia committed adultery in 2 B.C., probably the same year as the first two books of the *Ars* were published.[15] Ovid's card, so to speak, may well have been marked at this time; and then his *error* – its nature remains obscure, but it seems likely to have been some indiscretion connected with the adultery of the *younger* Julia, Augustus' granddaughter, in A.D. 8 -- may have provided Augustus with the pretext he needed for venting his personal spleen against the outstanding poet of the time.

The *Amores* is the only one of Ovid's works which he mentions in *Tr.* iv. 10, and then in a way which does not allow us to establish when either of the two editions of the collected poems was published – the poet tells us in his prefatory epigram to the surviving collection that he has reduced the original five-book edition to one of three. The existence of the epigram points to the simultaneous publication of the three books of

8 See M. Helzle, 'Mr and Mrs Ovid', *G & R* n.s. 36 (1989), 183-93.

9 Ovid's punishment, strictly speaking, was *relegatio*, and not exile proper, which would have deprived him of his property as well as banishing him.

10 See J.C. Thibault, *The Mystery of Ovid's Exile* (Berkeley-Los Angeles, 1964); see also F. Norwood, *CPh* 58 (1963), 150-63, Hollis' edition of *Ars* i, introduction xii-xvii, Syme (1978) 251ff., T. D. Barnes, 'Julia's child', *Phoenix* 35 (1981), 362-3, R. G. M. Nisbet, '"Great and Lesser Bear" (Ovid, *Tristia* iv. 3)', *JRS* 72 (1982), 49-56, G. P. Goold, 'The cause of Ovid's exile', *ICS* 8 (1983), 94-107, Murgia (1986a) 86, R. Verdière, *Le secret du voltigeur d'amour ou le mystère de la relégation d'Ovide* (Brussels, 1992). A.D. Fitton-Brown ('The unreality of Ovid's Tomitan exile', *LCM* 10 (1985), 18-22) suggests that the experience of Tomis was all in the poet's mind.

11 *Tr.* ii. 207 *perdiderunt me duo crimina, carmen et error.*

12 *Tr.* ii. 211-12.

13 *Ars* i. 31-4; cf. *Ars* iii. 57-8.

14 See 2. 47-60, 14. 9-12nn.

15 This date for *Ars* i-ii (published separately from *Ars* iii, which was only added as an afterthought) is suggested by Ovid's allusion (i. 171) to Augustus' mock naval battle of 2 B.C. as a recent event and his presentation of the departure of Gaius Caesar for Parthia, which took place in 1 B.C., as imminent (i. 177-212). Syme ((1978) 13-19), however, has argued (without convincing me) for a first edition as early as 7 (or even 9) B.C.

the second edition, but the opening announcement of *Am.* ii. 1 points to the five books of the first edition circulating separately (it is excessively heavy-handed as a connection with a previous book published at the same time). If the 'youthful poems' to which Ovid refers at *Tr.* iv. 10. 57-8 were poems of the *Amores* (which seems almost certain, given the subsequent mention of Corinna), and if he is to be taken literally when he says that he began reciting after his 'beard had been cut once or twice', he must have started writing these poems (though not necessarily publishing them in book-form) around 25 B.C. But his claim may be the equivalent of saying that he began when he was 'wet behind the ears', i.e. very immature, and point to no particular date. At the other end of the time-scale, the second edition of the *Amores* must ante-date the completion of *Ars* iii, which most scholars place in A.D. 1 or 2,[16] since *Ars* iii. 343-4 refer to the *Amores* as a three-volume work.[17] The earliest datable allusion in the collection is to the death of Tibullus in 19 B.C. (iii. 9) and the latest which is relatively uncontentious to the defeat of the Sygambri, a German tribe (i. 14. 45-50), either in 11 B.C., when Drusus won an ovation for his campaign against them, or, if the reference to their being 'triumphed over' (v. 46) is to be taken literally, in 8 B.C. when Tiberius was awarded a triumph for crushing them finally. ii. 18, however, was probably composed later than this. Vv. 21-6 allude to the 'single' heroines' *Epistles* and 19-20 most probably to the *Ars Amatoria*[18] as Ovid's current work; admittedly, these remarks allow no certainty about the state of completion of either the *Ars* or the *Epistles*, but it seems unlikely that Ovid was working on both of these and on the *Amores* simultaneously, and what he says perhaps points more plausibly to a stage when some *Epistles* (which may initially have circulated individually) and *Ars* i-ii had already been published and other *Epistles* and *Ars* iii were still to come.[19] If this *is* the indication, *Am.* ii. 18 may be dated as late as 2 B.C. A maximum time-span of 8-11 years (19 to 11 or 8 B.C.) for the publication of five separate books of *Amores,* containing, say, 30 poems each, is just about credible, if somewhat luxurious, but a maximum of 17 years (19-2 B.C.) very much less so. The obvious inference is that ii. 18 was composed for the second edition.[20] Other factors also point to this: (a) if any single poem was written specially for a new edition,[21] it is surely likely to have been one which brought the reader up to date with the author's latest work; and (b) if, as I believe, the reference at ii. 18. 13-14 is to Ovid's lost *Medea*, substantially advanced but as yet incomplete,[22] ii. 18 may have been inserted not least to

16 Since Gaius Caesar at *Rem.* 155-6 is in Parthia and does not appear to have met the Parthian king Phraataces, as we know he did in the spring of A.D. 2, it is generally assumed that the *Remedia* was complete by that date and that *Ars* iii preceded it. Murgia (1986a), however, has proposed a date of A.D. 8 for *Ars* iii.

17 The text is disputed at *Ars* iii. 343, but I follow Kenney and most scholars in reading *deue tribus*.

18 See 18. 19-20n.

19 See 18. 19n. *profitemur*.

20 Might not the immediate success of *Ars* i and ii even have been the impetus for a new edition of the *Amores*?

21 Though a number of the *Amores* poems have been suspected of being of relatively late composition (see Murgia (1986a) 91-4, (1986b) 209-10), only in the case of ii. 18 is this virtually certain.

22 See n. *ad loc.*

explain why the tragedy promised in *Am.* iii. 1 and 15 (both of which probably already stood in the first edition) had still not appeared (where to place it, of course, if Ovid was to retain iii. 1 and 15 in the second edition as the opener and epilogue of his final book, would have presented a problem; see pp. 10-11). Moreover, if ii. 18 was written not just for inclusion in the second edition, but, along with the prefatory epigram, specifically to mark its publication, that edition must have appeared almost immediately after its composition, i.e. probably about 2 B.C.

So, while stressing that precision is impossible,[23] I would tentatively suggest the following chronology for Ovid's works before the *Fasti, Metamorphoses, Tristia, Ex Ponto* and *Ibis* (all these in their surviving form belong to the exile period, though the *Fasti* and *Metamorphoses* were started much earlier): 19 to 11 or even 8 B.C. – the five books of the first edition of the *Amores*; in a period perhaps overlapping with this at the start and extending to 2 B.C. at the latest – the *Medea* (begun but not completed), some or all of the 'single' *Epistles*, *Ars* i and ii (perhaps preceded by the *Medicamina Faciei*), and the second edition of *Amores*; between A.D. 1 and 8 – *Ars* iii and the *Remedia Amoris*, the 'double' (and perhaps more 'single') *Epistles*, and the completion of the *Medea*. The aborted *Gigantomachia* is almost certainly a fiction.[24]

But, to return finally to *Tr.* iv. 10, it is noteworthy that at the end of his life and work Ovid still identified himself as 'the playful poet of the tender *Amores*'; perhaps this, his only personal love-elegy, was always his most popular work.

II. 'POEMS A LASS WOULD LIKE TO HEAR'[25]: LOVE ELEGY

'Love-elegy' designates the Latin poetry in elegiac couplets (see p. 14) and on amatory themes written during the relatively brief period of the principate of Augustus by Tibullus, Propertius and Ovid.[26] Love featured *inter alia* in Greek poetry written in the elegiac metre as early as the 7th century B.C. by Mimnermus, but whether he treated it 'subjectively', i.e. whether the love was supposed to be his own, and whether it was for a named woman, it is impossible to tell from the extant fragments.[27] The Hellenistic

---

23 The large number of different conclusions arrived at on the same evidence is itself an indication of the complexity of the problem. The most commendably rigorous investigations are those of Jacobson (300-18), Murgia (1986a), (1986b), and now McKeown (I. 74-89). For further useful discussions see H. Emonds, *Zweite Auflage im Altertum* (Leipzig,1941), 236-48, Cameron (1968), Sabot 49-99 (with copious bibliography of earlier work at 14-16), Knox 2-4, Holzberg (1997a) 41-8, *id.* (1997b) 10-15. See also pp. 10-12 on the arrangement of the *Amores* poems.

24 See 1. 11-16n.

25 *quod quaeuis nosse puella uelit* (Prop. i. 9. 14). For my updated overview of the nature, development and context of Latin love elegy see Booth and Lee, 'Introduction: the Genre'; also N. Holzberg, *Die römische Liebeselegie: eine Einführung* (Darmstadt, 1990), 1-17.

26 Under Tibullus' name have also come down to us 6 elegies by an Augustan woman, Sulpicia ([Tib.] iii. 13-18). Those by 'Lygdamus' ([Tib.] iii. 1-6) may or may not be Augustan; see 5. 36-8n.

27 Translations and discussion in A. W. H. Adkins, *Poetic Craft in the Early Greek Elegists* (Chicago, 1985), 93-106. Subjective but exclusively homosexual love features in the brief 5th-century (or earlier) elegiac pieces attributed to Theognis; see West 41ff.

period (3rd to 1st century B.C.) also saw much writing of Greek poetry in elegiacs, but all that survives of a clearly subjective erotic nature is in the form of epigrams (collected mainly in Books v and xii of the *Greek Anthology* (*Anthologia Palatina*), rarely more than 10 lines long, detached or ironical in tone, and witty in execution.[28] Longer Greek poems in elegiacs written in the Hellenistic period also dealt with love; but in all the surviving (very fragmentary) examples it is apparently of an 'objective' nature, i.e. it concerns not the poets' own love but that of mythological characters.[29] The Latin poets' subjective treatment of love in longer elegiac compositions seems to be new.[30]

Some scholars have always been reluctant to believe that any Roman writer ever originated anything,[31] and the similarity of material in both Greek and Roman New Comedy and in late Greek erotic epistolography to that of Latin love-elegy has been taken to point to a common source for all three in a lost corpus of subjective Hellenistic love-elegy.[32] But in all probability such a corpus never existed,[33] and there is no reason why the Latin elegists should not have drawn on New Comedy directly for any material which attracted them, nor why either the comic dramatists or the erotic epistolographers should in turn be denied inventiveness.[34] For all this, however, Augustan love-elegy did not spring up towards the end of the 1st century B.C. without immediate roots. We first see subjective love treated in Latin elegiacs in a few epigrams in the Hellenistic manner from c. 100 B.C.,[35] but it is in Catullus that the earliest elegiac pieces appear in which the poet attempts to present in all its anguished complexity his own romantic (i.e.

---

28 Samples (some homosexual) are translated and discussed in D. H. Garrison, *Mild Frenzy. A reading of Hellenistic Love Epigram, Hermes Einzelschr.* 41 (Wiesbaden, 1978).

29 See Callimachus' *Aetia* and the fragments of Euphorion, Hermesianax, Phanocles and Philetas in J. U. Powell, *Collectanea Alexandrina* (Oxford, 1925), with the concise discussion in Luck (1969) 38-42; more recent discoveries of these poets are published in Lloyd-Jones and Parsons. Antimachus' *Lyde*, a 5th-century B.C. extended mythological poem in elegiacs, may have influenced them; see West 18.

30 This is not, of course, to deny completely the influence of the above-mentioned erotic literature on the Roman poets; see e.g. p. 53.

31 The Romans themselves must bear some responsibility for this; notice e.g. Quintilian's famous understatement *à propos* of elegy at *Inst.* x. 1. 93 *elegia quoque nos Graecos prouocamus* ('In elegy we too challenge the Greeks').

32 The suggestion first came from F. Leo, *Plautinische Forschungen* (2nd edn., Berlin, 1912), 140-57. Cf. Wilhelm 137-42.

33 See the seminal refutation of F. Jacoby, 'Zur Entstehung der römischen Elegie', *RhM* 60 (1905), 38-105; also (a concise summary of arguments) H. E. Butler and E. A. Barber, *The Elegies of Propertius* (Oxford, 1933), xlviii-l, Day 1-36. The view that subjective love-elegy was written in the Hellenistic period is cautiously restated by F. Cairns (*Tibullus: A Hellenistic Poet at Rome* (Cambridge, 1979), 214ff.).

34 See Day 37-58, 85-101. Luck ((1969) 42-56) denies the influence of any New Comedy on elegy. R. F. Thomas, 'New Comedy, Callimachus and Roman Poetry', *HSPh* 83 (1979), 179-206, postulates the influence of Menander, partly via Callimachus. Griffin ((1985) 198-210) and Yardley (1987) argue convincingly for the direct influence of *Roman* comedy on elegy (cf. pp. 31-2); *contra*, Barsby. Mime probably also contributed ideas; see 5. 13-32n. and p. 49.

35 Valerius Aedituus, fr. 1-2, Porcius Licinus, fr. 6, Q. Lutatius Catulus, fr. 1-2 Büchner.

spiritual as well as physical, and all-consuming[36]) attraction to a particular beloved ('Lesbia') – one of them (76) is significantly longer than the average epigram; and in Catullus too we see the first attempts to illustrate subjective love with extended mythological allusion (68). Perhaps the most influential trail-blazer for the Augustans, however, was the poet the Romans themselves catalogue as the first elegist:[37] Cornelius Gallus (69-26 B.C.), soldier-poet and friend of Virgil, disgraced under Augustus apparently for his self-aggrandizement as prefect of Egypt. The nature of his four elegiac books of *Amores* concerning his love for the actress Cytheris, whom he calls 'Lycoris', and particularly their role in fusing elements of the Hellenistic narrative elegiac tradition with the developing Latin one of subjective love, we mainly have to surmise from what Virgil says about him at *Ecl.* 6. 64-73 and in *Ecl.* 10. Nothing can be gleaned from the one line of Gallus' own poetry which was all that survived until 1978,[38] and though many intriguing questions are raised by the further 10 lines almost certainly his which were then discovered on a papyrus from the Nubian desert,[39] they offer no advance on existing conjecture about his importance in the history of love-elegy.[40]

In the two elegiac books of Tibullus (born c. 55/48 and died in 19 B.C.) and the first three of Propertius (born c. 57/48 and died c. 2 B.C.), we begin to see the development of certain conventions in respect of material, form and manner. At the risk of over-simplification, I will outline the most important. The poet is in love with a beautiful, intelligent and artistically accomplished woman[41] (Tibullus with first Delia then Nemesis, and Propertius with Cynthia – all invented names[42]) to whom he does not have free access. This may be because she is married, because she is co-habiting with a kind of common-law husband (the Latin *uir* covers both a husband proper and a mere 'partner'), or because she is controlled by a brothel-mistress or 'madam' (*lena*); certainly the poet himself never contemplates marrying her – theirs is by definition an extra-marital relationship. Inconsistencies in presentation make it impossible to identify the poet's mistress as an adulterous wife, a freedwoman-courtesan, or a common prostitute. But it does not greatly matter, for even in real life 'the dividing line [between them] may not have been as easy to draw as in theory, perhaps, it should have been'.[43] Moreover, if

---

36 I use the term 'romantic' of love throughout this book in a sense which approximates to that defined by N. Rudd, 'Romantic love in classical times', *Ramus* 10 (1981), 140-55. Readers of Lyne (1980) should be warned that my usage of the word differs from his.

37 See *Tr.* iv. 10. 53, Quint. *Inst.* x. 1. 93, Diomedes the grammarian I. 484 Keil.

38 Fr. 1 Büchner.

39 The text is published in R. D. Anderson, P. J. Parsons and R. G. M. Nisbet, 'Elegiacs by Gallus from Qaṣr Ibrîm', *JRS* 69 (1979), 125-55. For samples of the discussion generated by the discovery see the articles by S. Hinds, '*Carmina digna:* Gallus *P. Qaṣr Ibrîm* 6-7 metamorphosed', *PLLS* 4 (1983), 43-54, J. Fairweather, 'The Gallus Papyrus: a new interpretation', *CQ* n.s. 34 (1984), 167-74. Updated bibliography in R. G. M. Nisbet, *Collected Papers on Latin Literature*, ed. S. J. Harrison (Oxford, 1995), 432.

40 On this see D. O. Ross, *Backgrounds to Augustan Poetry: Gallus, Elegy and Rome* (Cambridge, 1975) and cf. pp. 60, 78

41 Tibullus, however, also has a boy-lover, Marathus, in i. 4, 8 and 9.

42 Apuleius' attempt (*Apol.* 10) to match the names of Delia and Cynthia with real women may be regarded with some scepticism. See Bright 99ff.

43 Griffin (1985) 28. Griffin conveniently documents at this point a wide range of conflicting scholarly opinion on the endlessly debated issue of the elegiac mistress' social status. For a different approach see J. P. Hallett, 'The role of women in Roman elegy: counter-cultural

with us the same woman may be a wife, a girl-friend, a fiancée or a housekeeper (to name but a few), depending on who wants to know (neighbours, peers, parents, the tax inspector, and so on), a Latin poet's beloved may surely vary in status according to what particular aspect of a relationship he wants to write about[44] – and that need not be restricted to what he has actually experienced.[45] The mistress herself often treats her poet-lover badly, with mercenary demands, repulses and infidelities. He is prepared to overlook some peccadilloes, but in general her unfaithfulness grieves him, because he is romantically (see pp. 5-6) attracted to her. For his own part he (usually!) professes absolute fidelity and subservience (the metaphor of the lover as a slave is developed to convey this[46]). And he looks to his poetry to assist him in winning her exclusive love and devotion. Tibullus' *oeuvre* shows a growing general disillusion with love, and Propertius gradually moves from depiction of his total subjection to Cynthia in Book i to his final emancipation from her in Book iii; in Book iii and, especially, Book iv his interest shifts markedly to so-called 'aetiological' poetry, i.e. that which purports to account for the existence of latter-day stories, practices or artefacts.

The individual elegies of Tibullus and Propertius take diverse forms. The staples are simple narrative, soliloquy and direct address, but Tibullus is particularly given to the reverie (i.e. a poem in which he ranges freely over past, present and future and/or between imagination and reality, e.g. i. 1, 5, 6), and both poets sometimes attempt dramatic monologue (i.e. a poem in the form of a direct speech to one or more other characters whose presence, and sometimes reactions, are obliquely indicated *en passant*; e.g. Tib. i. 8, Prop. iii. 6[47]). 'Set-piece' poems are popular; by this I mean those dealing with recurrent themes and situations through a stock range of sub-motifs and procedures. The (mostly Greek) labels which modern scholars tend to attach to such poems (e.g. *propempticon, epicedion, paraklausithyron*; *recusatio* is a coined Latin term of the same kind) are useful as broadly descriptive terms, but they do not fix the limits of interpretation. And, though it would be unrealistic to deny altogether the influence of rhetorical education (see p. 1) on Latin writing, the use of these and similar labels by late Greek rhetorical theorists to describe the prose set-pieces for which they lay down

feminism', *Arethusa* 6 (1973), 103-24, Veyne 67-84, B. Feichtinger, '*Casta matrona — puella fallax*. Zum literarischen Frauenbild der römischen Elegie', *SO* 68 (1993), 40-68; see also next n.

44 I do not mean to imply, however, that Delia, Nemesis and Cynthia were necessarily completely fictitious (so Veyne 58-64, M. Wyke, 'The elegiac woman at Rome', *PCPhS* n.s. 33 (1987), 153-78, and 'Written women: Propertius' *Scripta Puella', JRS* 77 (1987), 47-61); Ovid's Corinna is another matter (see p. 8).

45 This would seem self-evident, but it has had to be stated fairly frequently in respect of Latin love-elegy; see e.g. A. W. Allen, 'Elegy and the classical attitude towards love', *YClS* 7 (1950), 255-77, *id.*, 'Sincerity and the Roman elegists', *CPh* 45 (1958), 145-60, J. P. Sullivan, *TAPhA* 92 (1961), 522-8, and now, approaching from a different direction but arriving at much the same conclusion, Veyne *passim*, Kennedy, *passim*. Ovid warns us that poets are not to be taken at their word (e.g. *Am.* iii. 12. 19-20, 41-4, *Tr.* ii. 355-6); but the claim is itself a cliché, and, of course, if taken literally, self-defeating.

46 See p. 82

47 See further Williams (1968) 220-21, Nisbet-Hubbard I. 310-11.

compositional rules does not justify the assumption that the Romans were primarily guided by such prescriptions in their writing of verse.[48]

In scale, technique and outlook Tibullan and Propertian love-elegy is perceptibly 'Alexandrian' – modest (in comparison with e.g. Homeric epic), refined, learned and emotional. This was the manner championed by that doyen of literary individualists, Callimachus (c.305 – c.240 B.C.).[49] But the Augustan setting lends the elegists' rejection of the material and the style of the most ambitious poetic genre a political dimension. For in opting to celebrate the private pleasures and sorrows of extra-marital love in elegy rather than Roman military prowess in epic (the metaphor of love as a kind of substitute soldiering was developed to highlight the incompatibility of the two[50]), they effectively, though for the most part discreetly, dissociated themselves from the policies of Augustus – glorification of militarism, measures to support marriage and the family, and encouragement of nationalistic literature.[51]

It would be wrong, however, to suggest that the elegies of Tibullus and Propertius were unrelievedly solemn and circumspect. Both are able to regard the antics of the lover with humorous irony,[52] and Propertius is not above making a joke of his un-Augustan attitudes.[53] But they left plenty of scope for an Ovid.

III. 'FRIVOLOUS MUSE'[54]: THE *AMORES*

Ovid is different. Different from his predecessors in his attitude to almost all the elegiac conventions. And to none more so than the mistress. In the *Amores* a woman of much the usual kind is there – but not immediately. A tussle with Cupid opens the collection in i. 1 and 2,[55] and not until i. 3 does any particular beloved appear; leading-lady Corinna is not named until i. 5 (recall that Tibullus' Delia appeared in the first poem of his *oeuvre* and Propertius' Cynthia in the first word). And, while the other elegists' mistresses are just hard to place (see pp. 6-7), Ovid actively encourages us to wonder whether Corinna really exists or not. *Am.* iii. 12, in which he complains that he has lost her as a result of publicising her charms in his poetry, suggests that she was indeed a single, real woman rather than a fictitious or composite figure (the fictitiousness of her *name* need not trouble us[56]), but *Am.* ii. 17 makes it clear that her identity was as obscure

48 This theory was advanced by Francis Cairns in *Generic Composition in Greek and Roman Poetry* (1972). For a forceful refutation see Griffin (1985) 48-64 (with R. G. M. Nisbet's review in *JRS* 77 (1987), 185-6).

49 See p. 24. Propertius explicitly claims Callimachus as a model at iii. 1.1. Cameron (1995) now challenges much received opinion on Callimachus.

50 See pp. 53–4.

51 See J. P. Sullivan, 'The politics of elegy', *Arethusa* 5 (1972), 17-34, Stahl 139-71. A different view in Galinsky (1996) 269-79.

52 See e.g. Tib. i. 2. 55-60, 6. 5-14, Prop. i. 16. 17-44.

53 See Prop. iii. 4. 15-22.

54 *Musa iocosa* (*Tr.* ii. 354).

55 For Cupid's role in the *Amores* see p. 53.

56 To this Ovid freely admits (*Tr.* iv. 10. 60) and we could have guessed it anyway, for the use of a pseudonym is conventional (see p. 6, with n. 42). 'Corinna' is the name of a 3rd- (or 5th-) century B.C. Greek lyric poetess (and also of a prostitute at Lucian, *DMeretr.* 6); cf. J. G. Randall, *LCM* 4 (1979), 34-5.

to Ovid's contemporary readers as it is to us.[57] 'There, that's got you guessing, hasn't it?', Ovid says in effect in that poem, '– and what's more, I'm not going to tell!'. Nor does he, ever.[58] And there, I think, the matter should probably rest.[59]

Almost never in the *Amores* does Ovid value women for anything other than their sex-appeal, and his own interests far outweigh theirs (in Book ii see especially 8, 10, 12, 15 and 19; even in the apparent exception, ii. 13, his attitude is perhaps more egocentric than has generally been supposed[60]). He himself rarely professes exclusive love,[61] but rather advertises his own promiscuity (in Book ii see especially 4, 8 and 10), and when his mistress is unfaithful, he consciously resorts to the simple expedient of self-deception (see e.g. i. 4. 66-70, ii. 11. 53-4 and – the *locus classicus* – iii. 14). Trickery delights him, rejection stimulates him, and obstruction is a challenge he cannot live without.[62] Not only is love itself de-mystified, but the conventional power of love-poetry, too, is cynically explained and exploited;[63] moreover, he does not even *pretend* to be presenting personal truth (see ii. 1. 5, and cf. p. 25). Romance (see p. 5) has gone, and in its place is a robust and shameless humour.[64] But it is as well to recall that Tibullus and Propertius are not invariably poker-faced (see p. 8): the difference in Ovid is sometimes one of degree – where their humour is muted and elusive, his is full-blooded, ostentatious and occasionally *risqué*.

Form and structure are also involved in Ovid's frivolous approach. The reverie (see p. 7) is developed as a vehicle for self-mockery (e.g. ii. 5, 11 and 16), and the dramatic monologue (see p. 7) is honed to comic perfection (e.g. i. 6, 7, 14, iii. 2[65]); the emotion-deflating ending becomes almost a trademark (e.g. ii. 5. 61-2, 11. 53-6, 15. 27-8[66]). A particularly striking, and on one occasion (ii. 7 and 8) scandalously comic, innovation is what I have called the 'dramatic diptych' – a pair of dramatically related poems which derive special impact from juxtaposition.[67] 'Set-pieces' (see p. 7) are subjected to humorous treatment too: in Book ii the *recusatio* (1), *epicedion* (6), *propempticon*, (11) gift-poem (15) and (arguably) *paraklausithyron* (19). And much of the humour stems from the sheer ingenuity with which Ovid adapts, varies and inverts the stock motifs.

His tendency towards systematic and exhaustive treatment of one theme per poem, his liking for multiplying examples and his inability to resist the clever twist of argument and the witty turn of phrase (see pp. 16-17) have been attributed to the overriding

57 See p. 83 and 17. 29-30n.
58 This has not prevented some wild speculation: Sidonius Apollinaris in the 5th century A.D. identified the girl with Augustus' daughter Julia (see M. Przychocki, '*De Ouidii Caesarea puella*', *WS* 35 (1914), 340-42). A periodically popular modern theory is that 'Corinna' = Ovid's love poetry; see e.g. G. Luck, *Die römische Liebeselegie* (Heidelberg, 1961), Keith 29-33.
59 Those who wish to pursue it should start with McKeown I. 19-24.
60 See pp. 70-73.
61 His promise at *Am.* i. 3. 13-16 is subverted by the mischievous *si qua fides* in v. 16 and three suspect *exempla* in vv. 21-4. Woytek considers possible motives for this.
62 See p. 90.
63 See pp. 25, 82-3, 87.
64 This aspect of the *Amores* was first appreciated by Reitzenstein in 1935.
65 See further V. A. Tracy, 'Dramatic elements in Ovid's *Amores*', *Latomus* 36 (1977), 496-500, J. T. Davis, 'Dramatic and comic devices in *Amores* iii. 2', *Hermes* 107 (1979), 51-69.
66 See D. Parker, 'The Ovidian coda', *Arion* 8 (1969), 80-97.
67 See p. 30.

influence of his formal rhetorical training.[68] But probably unjustly, for Seneca the Elder implies that for school purposes Ovid actually had to *curb* that natural ingenuity to which he gave free rein in his poetry.[69] Nor is it entirely fair to label him 'rhetorical'[70] in the wider modern sense, for his elaboration is by no means always otiose,[71] and in his work wit and intellectual subtlety are not mutually exclusive.[72]

The combined effect of Ovid's exuberant inventiveness and nonconformist temperament is never more obvious than in the attitude he adopts towards the Augustan régime. His lack of sympathy with its ideology is much more marked and open than his predecessors': instead of merely distancing himself from it, he positively makes fun at its expense,[73] and he will have no truck with pussy-footing excuses for not deferring to Augustus' tastes in literature.[74] But this does not indicate serious political disaffection.[75] Ovid was not so much anti-Augustan as anti-traditionalist; anything and everything remotely 'established', from poetic pretension to romantic love, was fair game for his deflating humour. Since, however, Augustus had harnessed tradition to his cause and was sensitive about his public image, he and Ovid were clearly on a collision course and the catastrophe of A.D. 8 (see p. 2) only a matter of time.

So much for the content of the *Amores* poems; what of their arrangement within the collection? The three books as transmitted consist of 15, 19 and 15 poems respectively, and, given the Augustan liking for books of poems in multiples of 10 (Virgil, *Ecl.* (10), Horace *S.* i (10), *Carm.* ii (20) and iii (30), *Ep.* i (10), Tibullus i (10)), it seems almost certain that Ovid intended 15, 20, 15; the retention of 2 and 3 as separate poems and the division of 9 into two, both of which I favour on internal grounds,[76] would produce the

---

68 See e.g. C. Brück, *De Ouidio scholasticarum declamationum imitatore* (Diss. Giessen, 1909), Day 71ff., Tremoli *passim,* Sabot 218ff. Further bibliography on the question at Donnet 254.

69 *uerbis minime licenter usus est nisi in carminibus* (*Con.* ii. 2. 12). T. F. Higham's 'Ovid and rhetoric', *Ovidiana* 32-48, is still the most judicious discussion of the matter. Cf. now Holzberg (1997a) 31.

70 Fränkel (167-9) usefully analyses the varying implications of this term.

71 See e.g. 5. 25-8, 35-42nn. and p. 71.

72 Ovid has always suffered from the somewhat stuffy strictures of his ancient critics, who obviously thought him too clever for comfort. See e.g. *Sen. Con.* ii. 2. 12 *non ignorauit sua uitia sed amauit*, ix. 5. 17 *nescit quod bene cessit relinquere,* Quint. *Inst.* x. 1. 88 *nimium amator ingenii sui*; cf. x. 1. 98. Some of the moderns still tend to echo them; see e.g. R. Whittaker, *Myth and Personal Experience in Roman Love Elegy, Hypomnemata* 76 (Göttingen, 1983), 133-66. Others, led by Hinds (1987) now contend that, far from being showy but shallow, Ovid is a poet of quite formidable complexity. They overstate the case perhaps (see also Hinds' monograph, *The Metamorphosis of Persephone* (Cambridge, 1987)), but some redressing of the balance through close attention to the text was long overdue.

73 See 2. 47-60, 14. 9-12nn. and pp. 53-5, 64-5, 71; also Otis *passim.*

74 See pp. 24-5, 86-7.

75 Nor is it likely that Ovid was under-appreciative of the benefits of Augustanism because he was too young to have known anything else; see J. C. McKeown in *Poetry and Politics in the Age of Augustus,* edd. A. J. Woodman and D. A. West (Cambridge, 1984), 238, n. 21.

76 See pp. 30-31, 52-3.

desirable number in Book ii.[77] Each of the three books opens with an obviously programmatic poem, i.e. one in which the poet indicates his poetic intentions, and Books i and iii close with one too. There is no reason to suppose that any of these did not stand in the original five-book edition as opening and epilogue pieces.[78] Obviously that edition must have contained two more opening and three more epilogue pieces (ii. 19 may or may not have been one of the latter), and the present i. 2 was once suggested as one of the original openers.[79] That suggestion has generally been rejected on the grounds that i. 1-3 form a coherent sequence. So they do, but need they have been *written* as a coherent sequence? Could Ovid not have concocted it from all the poems at his disposal when he came to assemble the second edition? And furthermore, could not i. 3 also be one of the original openers? This seems especially likely because of its very close relationship with ii. 17, which might so easily have provided a complementary epilogue for the same original book.[80] As it is, these poems still seem to have some sort of programmatic function as a pair, for i. 3 stands third from the beginning and ii. 17 third from the end of Books i-ii, which form a unit as the Corinna-orientated part of the *Amores* (Ovid's depiction of his affair very generally follows the pattern of Prop. i.-iii: in *Amores* iii Corinna, like Cynthia in Prop. iii, has left the centre-stage). ii. 18, however, does not, as might be expected, 'match' i. 2 (or ii. 2, for that matter); if anything, it matches i. 1 and ii. 1[81] and in fact seems an obvious candidate for epilogue to Book ii. ii. 19, on the other hand, does not, at first sight, seem so suitable for that position[82] and certainly does not match i. 1, though it has some links with ii. 1 and many with ii. 2. The inevitable suspicion is that it is occupying the place Ovid originally intended for ii. 18. Why? Ovid may well have considered the end of his central book a good place to insert the clearly programmatic poem (the present ii. 18) which he had possibly written specially for his second edition to explain non-completion of his *Medea* (see pp. 3-4), but on realising that it would then stand immediately before a poem in which he gives no indication of having even started anything of the kind (iii. 1), he perhaps relegated it to the penultimate place and advanced 19, an at least passable epilogue poem,[83] to the end instead. But if this did happen, the rearrangement has not quite come off, for, in attempting to remedy one element of awkwardness, Ovid has created another.[84]

Apart from the placing of these programmatic poems and the juxtaposing of the two constituent elegies of the dramatic diptychs, the basis of arrangement is 'artful disorder',[85] totally unconnected poems often being juxtaposed and some which are

---

77 I reserve judgement on Book iii, where the authenticity of 5 is in doubt (see E. J. Kenney, 'On the *Somnium* attributed to Ovid', *Agon* 3 (1969), 1-14) and 11 may be two poems rather than one.

78 See Murgia (1986a) 93.

79 See Cameron (1968) 322-7.

80 See p. 83.

81 See pp. 86-7.

82 See p. 92.

83 See p. 92.

84 See 18. 20n.

85 I.e. *uariatio*; the felicitous English term is Kenney's in his introduction to Melville's translation, p. xviii. On this feature in books of Augustan poetry see W. Port, 'Die Anordnung in Gedichtbüchern augusteischer Zeit', *Philologus* 81 (1926), 283-308, 427-68,

linked by contrast widely separated (e.g. i. 4 and ii. 5, ii. 6 and iii. 9, ii. 19 and iii. 4). At the same time many poems have multiple connections with others; e.g. ii. 10 has thematic material in common with both ii. 9 and ii. 4, but ii. 4 also contrasts with i. 3, and ii. 9 finds an echo in iii. 11; ii. 12 is related loosely to ii. 11 through Propertian reminiscence, but to ii. 13 by the contrast of its tone and material, and ii. 11 is related also to ii. 16 by its theme and form.

As in content, so in arrangement, then, the watchwords are ingenuity, inventiveness and surprise.[86]

IV. WHAT CAME NATURALLY[87]: OVID'S ELEGIAC STYLE[88]

The distinctively Ovidian Latin of the *Amores* is both the delight and the despair of a translator: limpid, elegant and mellifluous, but impossible to render without some loss of nuance or sparkle.[89] Yet it is in many respects remarkably ordinary.[90] The vocabulary is, for the most part, standard Augustan lyric/elegiac – less grandiloquent than that of epic and more so than that of comedy, satire and epigram. Ovid does introduce some words previously rare or unattested in verse, and one of the bolder elements in his vocabulary is his admission of notably more legal and legalistic terms than any other poet before him.[91] But there are many features in the diction of the *Amores* common to Latin poetry of all types and periods: e.g. the allusive and/or ornamental epithet;[92] metonymy, i.e. the use of an adjunct or characteristic of something

---

J. Michelfeit, 'Das augusteische Gedichtbuch', *RhM* 112 (1969), 347-70. Attempts to discover precise geometrical patterning in the *Amores* are totally unconvincing; see e.g. Jäkel, Lörcher. Further bibliography at McKeown I. 90, n. 1. Holzberg ((1997a) 55-7; cf. *id.*, (1997b) 12-13) argues that the *Amores* poems are arranged to form an 'erotic novel' (*Liebesroman*). Buchan posits an elaborate metaliterary sequence in Book 1. 1-5; Woytek takes a similar line.

86 For further general appreciation of the *Amores* see Wilkinson (1955) 44-82, Lee (1962), Du Quesnay, Lyne (1980), 239-87, S. Mack, *Ovid* (New Haven-London, 1988), 53-69, Boyd, *passim*.

87 Cf. *Tr.* iv. 10. 25 *sponte sua carmen numeros ueniebat ad aptos.*

88 I define 'style' for the purposes of this discussion as the element of choice in expression and attempt to treat only linguistic and metrical matters; all examples are taken from *Amores* ii. Frécaut offers a broader study of Ovid's style.

89 For the principles guiding this translator's attempt at the impossible see p. 19.

90 I hope the following brief analysis will help those who may be unfamiliar with some terms of philological criticism used in the commentary. Though perhaps mildly distasteful in a concentrated dose, once understood, they circumvent a good deal of rigmarole.

91 See Kenney (1969), and cf. 5. 29-32n. Possibly, as Kenney suggests, Ovid's own brief juristic experience (see p. 1) was what made him aware of the literary potential of these expressions; but none of those which he uses demonstrates specialist knowledge (I am indebted here to Professor Alan Watson for making available to me an unpublished paper on legalisms in Roman elegy).

92 E.g. 1. 32 *Haemoniis*, 6. 35 *armiferae*, 8. 20 *Carpathium,* 11. 29 *fecundae*, 14. 35 *Armeniis*, 17. 32 *frigidus, populifer.*

to refer to the thing itself;[93] synecdoche, i.e. a part of something standing for the whole;[94] and litotes, i.e. negative for positive.[95] Words Ovid appears to have coined, though sometimes striking in themselves, are manufactured in the traditional manner by attaching standard prefixes, such as prepositions or negative *in-*, and suffixes, such as *-fer* and *-ger,* to a wide variety of stems[96] (uncommon compounds he admits fairly freely[97]). Like other poets, he will often use compound for simple, and vice versa, sometimes for metrical convenience and sometimes for special effect.[98]

The syntax of the *Amores*, too, is marked by standard poeticisms, some metrically convenient (present subjunctive for imperative,[99] dative of agent with passive verbs,[100] and perfect infinitive for present[101]), and some fashionable mannerisms (adverbial accusative,[102] ablative of comparison,[103] ablative of gerund[104] and epexegetic infinitive[105]). And Ovid is also in line with other poets in admitting or excluding prepositions largely to suit the demands of his metre.[106] Word-order is often subject to the small dislocations which are generally common, again either for metrical convenience or as a matter of stylistic fashion: postponement of connectives, subordinating conjunctions and correlatives,[107] anastrophe, i.e. inversion of normal order,[108] and separation of prepositions from their noun or pronoun.[109] 'Hysteron proteron', i.e. 'cart-before-horse' expression, is frequent enough in the poets too.[110]

---

93 E.g. 5. 35 *Tithoni coniuge* = dawn, 7. 21 *Veneris* = sweetheart, 8. 8 *Veneris* = love, 9A. 21 *pinum* = ship, 11. 49 *Lyaeo* = wine, 14. 3, 18. 36 *Marte* = war.

94 E.g. 4. 8, *puppis* (literally 'stern') = ship, 11. 24 *carina* (literally 'keel') = ship.

95 E.g. 1. 5 *non frigida = ardens,* 8. 3 *non rustica = culta,* 16. 22 *non aequis = iniquis.*

96 The most felicitous coinages in *Am.* ii are *subrubere* (5. 36) and *indesertus* (9B. 53); see nn. *ad loc.*, and cf. Booth (1981) 2696-8. For a full list of words appearing first or only in Ovid see E. Linse, *De P. Ouidi Nasone uocabulorum inuentore* (Diss. Tübingen, 1891), 8ff.

97 E. J. Kenney in *Ovid* ed. J. W. Binns (London, 1973), 121-3 has some interesting observations on this phenomenon in the *Metamorphoses*; see also Knox 40-42.

98 See e.g. 11. 6, 27, 13. 8, 14. 39, 16. 26nn., Bömer on *Met.* v. 188, Brink on Hor. *Ars* 40.

99 E.g. 1. 19, 5. 1, 8. 19, 11. 41, 15. 3.

100 E.g. 5. 12, 8. 12.

101 See 4. 22n.

102 See 4. 25n.

103 See 1. 20n.

104 See 1. 31n.

105 See 7. 17n.

106 Arguments that the presence or absence of a preposition is generally justified by some underlying sense (see e.g. Tränkle 87ff., K. Guttman, *Sogennantes instrumentales 'ab' bei Ovid* (Diss. Dortmund, 1890)) fail to convince. It is hardly reasonable to contend e.g. that *ab* is used with *causa ... omni* at 4. 31 because a 'stimulus' (*causa*), though technically inanimate, here issues from an animate source, and then turn the same argument on its head to explain *utraque* without *ab* 4 lines later.

107 E.g. 1. 32, 3. 2, 8. 2, 11. 25, 15. 16; see further Platnauer 96, Norden on Verg. *A.* vi, 'Anhang' III, p. 403.

108 E.g. 6. 57, 11. 26, and see Bömer on *Met.* i. 18.

109 E.g. 6. 9, 29, 13. 10, and see Platnauer 103.

110 See 5. 9-10, 15. 11nn.

For variation or ornament or to heighten emotion, Ovid resorts to the fashionable Alexandrian devices of apostrophe, i.e. brief, interjected direct address,[111] anaphora, i.e. repetition of the initial word or words in successive clauses,[112] and epanalepsis, i.e. repetition of any word or words purely for emotive effect.[113] Like all poets, he is alive to the potential of alliteration and assonance.[114] And for amatory imagery he turns to time-honoured universal metaphors[115] and to the specifically elegiac figures of soldiering and slavery.[116]

So what is it that makes Ovid's elegiacs unmistakably his? Two things, I think: (i) fluency – the '*cantabile* manner'[117] of the writing; and (ii) wit – the verbal virtuosity which embellishes almost every line. Both of these effects are bound up with Ovid's handling of his metre, the elegiac couplet.[118] Like all classical Latin metres, this is based on a rhythmical pattern arising essentially from varying length of syllables (quantity), and not, as in English, on a pattern arising essentially from syllable-stress within words. It consists of a hexameter, i.e. a line made up of six rhythmical units ('feet'), which (with the exception of the last two) can be either spondees (i.e. two long syllables, marked – –) or dactyls (one long and two short syllables, marked – ∪ ∪), and a pentameter, i.e. a line which falls into two halves, each of two and half feet, with a strong rhythmical break, 'caesura' (= 'cutting') at the half-way point; the first two full feet may be dactyls or spondees, but the second two are always dactyls, and the two half-feet are always single long syllables. The pattern, then, looks like this:

— ⏕ | — ⏕ | — ⏕ | — ⏕ | – ⏑⏑ | – ⏓ hexameter

— ⏕ | — ⏕ | — ‖ — ⏑⏑ | — ⏑⏑ | – pentameter

The relatively fixed rhythm of the pentameter, with the second half's near or exact repetition of the first (basically *tum ti-ti, tum ti-ti, tum // tum ti-ti, tum ti-ti, tum*), is particularly satisfying. Two methods of enhancing this are already found in Ovid's elegiac predecessors: (i) the ending of each half with words in grammatical agreement and often with rhyming inflection:

e.g. Tib. i. 3. 4

abstineas auid<u>as</u> Mors modo nigra man<u>us</u>

Prop. i. 1. 12

ibat et hirsut<u>as</u> ille uidere fer<u>as</u>,

---

111 E.g. 4. 17-18, 33-4, 8. 19-20, 9B. 41-2, 10. 11-14, 12. 22, 18. 22.

112 E.g. 6. 17-20, 8. 8, 11. 11, 12. 3, 19. 11-13; see Wills 175-7, 353-71, 397-414.

113 E.g. 6. 2-3, 43-4, 59, 8. 19, 10. 1. Wills (124-86) includes this in his broader category of 'expanded gemination'.

114 See e.g. 6. 3, 49, 8. 27-8, 19. 9-10nn.

115 See e.g. 1. 8n. (on heat and fire imagery), 9B. 29-32n. (on sailing imagery).

116 See pp. 53-4, p. 82.

117 Lee (1962) 167.

118 I aim here only to give the reader – and especially the reader with little or no Latin – a general impression of how the elegiac couplet works and sounds. For a thorough analysis of metrical technique in the *Amores* see McKeown I. 108-23. For briefer discussions see Wilkinson (1955) 27-43, W. F. Jackson Knight, 'Ovid's metre and rhythm', *Ovidiana* 106-20.

and (ii), increasingly in Propertius, the ending of the second half with a disyllabic word, so that the natural word-stress and the strong beat at the beginning of the penultimate foot coincide to produce a perfect cadence. In Ovid (i) is even more common, while (ii) is virtually invariable, and this above anything is what gives his couplets their easy fluency (a high proportion of dactyls, too, makes for a general rapidity). A further refinement (found also in the hexameter) is the symmetrical arrangement of words within the line in the basic pattern of adjective (or noun) A, adjective (or noun) B, noun (or adjective) B, noun (or adjective) A,[119]

e.g. ii. 1. 14
ardua (A) deuexum (B) Pelion (B) Ossa (A) tulit[120]

The couplet or the line is the normal sense-unit in Ovid. He himself describes the couplet's movement as 'rising' in the hexameter and 'sinking back' in the pentameter,[121] and this is apt enough in a non-technical way, when he uses the pentameter somehow to 'resolve' the sentiment in the hexameter,

e.g. ii. 1. 1
Hoc quoque composui Paelignis natus aquosis,
 ille ego nequitiae Naso poeta meae.

But there are various other types of relationship between the two lines, and necessarily so, if monotony is to be avoided. Sometimes the pentameter simply completes the thought of the hexameter,

e.g. ii. i. 15-16
in manibus nimbos et cum Ioue fulmen habebam,
 quod bene pro caelo mitteret ille suo,

sometimes almost restates it,

e.g. ii. 9A. 9-10
uenator sequitur fugientia, capta relinquit,
 semper et inuentis ulteriora petit.

and sometimes contrasts with it,

e.g. ii. 9A. 5-6
cur tua fax urit, figit tuus arcus amicos?
 gloria pugnantes uincere maior erat.

And occasionally Ovid achieves surprise and special effects by not observing his usual sense-pause at the end of the hexameter (this is called 'enjambement'),

e.g. ii. 2. 63-4
non scelus aggredimur, non ad miscenda coimus
 toxica.[122]

The two halves of the pentameter frequently echo, complement or contrast with each other, and the relationship is sometimes emphasised by repetition such as anaphora (see p. 14),

---

119 A variation on the so-called 'golden line', which follows this chiastic (i.e. ABBA) pattern, but has the verb in the centre.

120 Cf. 6. 50, 7. 20, and for slight variations on this pattern, 1. 6, 4. 27, 30, 8. 20, 11. 4, 14. 9, 24, 15. 17, 16. 10, 36, 19. 22.

121 *Am.* i. 1. 27 *sex mihi surgat opus numeris, in quinque residat.*

122 See n. *ad loc.*, and cf. 2. 43-4, 5. 49-50, 12. 12nn.

e.g. ii. 5. 44
maesta erat in uultu: maesta decenter erat
ii. 10. 8
et magis haec nobis, et magis illa placet,

and polyptoton, i.e. different forms of the same word (e.g. cases of a noun or persons of a verb) in close proximity,

e.g. ii. 11. 36
Nereidesque deae Nereidumque pater
ii. 18. 24
Hippolytique parens Hippolytusque legant

These and other forms of repetition[123] often ornament the hexameter as well, or help to link hexameter and pentameter. Though Ovid is capable of mild to severe hyperbaton (i.e. the intertwining of one clause – and in Ovid's case especially a relative clause – with another or others, resulting in very dislocated word-order),[124] the overall effect of his elegiacs is one of smoothness and symmetry. They show more of the grace of Tibullus than the angularity of Propertius, and yet there is a jauntiness about them which is all Ovid's own.

This brings us to his love of verbal wit, which has often been held against him (see pp. 9-10). Linguistic cleverness is obviously involved in most of the devices discussed above, but it takes many other forms too. A few examples will have to suffice here. Opposites are often ingeniously juxtaposed, either for pure decoration (e.g. ii. 4. 41, *niuea pulli*), or to underline a contrast (e.g. ii. 17. 14 *magnis inferiora*), or to point some irony (e.g. ii. 6. 51 *fides dubiis*).[125] Sense is sometimes cleverly reflected in word-order,

e.g. ii. 1. 23
mollierunt duras lenia uerba fores

(note the 'pressure' exerted on *duras* by *mollierunt* on one side and *lenia* on the other), or in construction,

e.g. ii. 10. 7
pulchrior hac illa est, haec est quoque pulchrior illa

(note the juggling with the pronominal inflections), or through a combination of both,

e.g. ii. 5. 58
lingua tua est nostris, nostra recepta tuis

(polyptoton is thrown in here too!).[126]

Paratactical sentence structure, i.e. non-subordination and non-connection of clauses, combined with polyptoton or other repetition often points the cynicism of Ovid's thought,

e.g. ii. 2. 20

---

123 See e.g. 4. 49, 5. 43, 45, 19. 5, 50; in general, G. Howe, 'A type of verbal repetition in Ovid's elegy', *SPhNC* 13 (1916), 81-94, and now Wills, *passim*.

124 Different scholars define the term in different ways, but I use it in much the same way as Platnauer at 104-8. The most violent examples of hyperbaton in *Am.* ii are at 5. 38 and 14. 11-12.

125 On this trick see E. Moser, *Die Entsprechung benachbarter Wörter und Begriffe in der Sprache der römischen Elegie* (Diss. Munich, 1935).

126 Cf. 5. 31, 15. 5, 16. 29, 17. 17; on this in general see Wills 222-68.

uenerit ignotus: postmodo notus erit
ii. 4. 21-2
est etiam quae me uatem et mea carmina culpet:
culpantis cupiam sustinuisse femur.

And puns and *double entendres* abound.[127] They are often *risqué,*[128] but never indelicate; there are no 'four-letter' words in Ovid.

Fluency and wit: perhaps the following two brief but supreme examples of both can be left, finally, to illustrate the quintessential Ovid:

ii. 16. 41
ulmus amat uitem, uitis non deserit ulmum,
ii. 11. 10
et gelidum Borean egelidumque Notum.

If 'the style is the man', we are in contact with a scintillating personality.

V. THE TEXT [129]

The *Amores* have been transmitted in two main groups of MSS, both almost certainly descended from a single source (the 'archetype') dating from the 8th or early 9th century.[130] One group consists of the oldest MSS, (*antiquiores*): the 9th-century *R* (Paris Bibl. Nat. Lat. 7311, 'Regius'), the 9th- or 10th-century *P*, and the 11th-century *S* and *Y* (full details of *PSY* appear in the *sigla* on p. 93). What distinguishes these MSS as a group, however, is not just their greater antiquity but the fact that they, and only they, omit some genuine lines preserved in the rest of the tradition (see 2. 18-27n.); this indicates that they all descend from from one and the same ancestor, the 'hyparchetype' which Kenney designates α.[131] *R* contains the whole of the *Ars* and *Remedia* but everything after i. 2. 50 of the *Amores* has been torn away and lost. *P*, as it happens, begins at i. 2. 51, but was probably copied independently from α, and not from the lost portion of *R*, as at first sight seems likely.[132] *Y*'s membership of the α group was not discovered until 1963; it had previously been miscatalogued in the Berlin Staatsbibliothek as 14th-century.[133] The other group consists of over seventy later MSS ranging from the 12th to the 15th century (the *recentiores*); they are too heavily 'contaminated' (i.e. each of them admits readings from a variety of sources rather than

---

127 E.g. 1. 15, 17, 20, 27-8, 4. 48, 9A. 24, 11. 44, 14. 16, 16. 32; see nn. *ad loca*.

128 E.g. 3. 5-12, 8. 4, 9B. 48, 10. 24-8, 35-6, 15. 5-7, 25-6, 19. 16.

129 This discussion is intended as an introduction to the history of the text for the curious but inexpert reader. Any whose curiosity grows should consult McKie for the best and most recent detailed examination of the MS tradition. The articles by Kenney (1962) and Goold (1965a) are also seminal.

130 So McKie 237, Goold (1965b) 89; *contra,* Kenney (1962) 26. The single archetype postulated was not necessarily the only MS which survived the Dark Ages; see McKie 238.

131 'Not greatly older than *R* and *P*' (McKie 230), i.e. probably dating from the early 9th century.

132 See McKie 219-28.

133 On 'discovery', it was collated by Munari. His collations are published in F. Munari, *Il codice Hamilton 471 di Ovidio* (Rome, 1965); cf. Kenney (1966).

following a single exemplar) and 'interpolated' (i.e. they contain unacknowledged conjectures by their copyists) for their provenance and interrelationship to be precisely determined, but (a) their inclusion of the lines which *PSY* omit, and (b) their common ignorance of the title *Amores*,[134] suggest that they derive from a common hyparchetype, which can be designated β.[135]

PSY as a group contain more sound readings than the *recc.* *S* has little independent value, for it is much contaminated from the β branch of the tradition[136] and offers the truth in isolation (and perhaps then by interpolation) only once (at *Am.* ii. 8. 7). *Y*, however, being more faithful to α than *S*, offers valuable testimony where *P* is obviously in error, and it sometimes supports later conjecture; the true reading *licenda* at *Am.* i. 10. 30 it alone preserves. None of the contaminated *recc.* carries independent weight, even though some, notably *D* and *M*, the latter (my *siglum*) now identified as the 'Arondelianus' used by Heinsius,[137] show closer affinities with the α tradition than the others. But as a class they are valuable. In some cases their readings which differ from those of *PSY* result from interpolation; this is especially so in the 14th- and 15th-century MSS of the Italian renaissance, but even the 12th- and 13th-century MSS (produced during the first vogue for Ovid's poetry since antiquity) are not immune. Some different – and true – readings, however, must stem from the hyparchetype β, unknown to the MSS descended from α, and from the variants which it probably contained. *P*, *Y* and some MSS of the β branch are equipped with 'corrections' added by a different hand; the value of these is equivalent to that of any of the *recc.*[138] A few poems are also preserved in collections of miscellaneous extracts (*florilegia* and *excerpta*),[139] and these too may be classed with the *recc.*

Any editor of the *Amores*, while recognising the generally greater reliability of *PSY*, especially in consensus, has to be alive to the possibility of a true reading surviving only – and anywhere – in the *recc.* The value of an eclectic use of the MSS was recognised by the first great editor of the collection, Nicolaus Heinsius, and the wisdom and sensibility of his 1661 edition continue to guide his successors. Outstanding among these are Munari and Kenney, whose respective critical editions of 1951 and 1961 (corrected edn. 1965) are based on meticulous collation of both groups of MSS. The subsequent unmasking of *Y* and *M*, however, means that their documentation is now incomplete. McKeown's 1987 text brings us up to date (see now p. v, 'Addendum').

The present edition of *Amores* ii does not claim to be a new recension of the text. Like McKeown, and for the same reasons,[140] I have not embarked on any systematic re-reading of MSS; I have, however, exercised independent critical judgement to produce

---

134 See Oliver (1969), 148-52, McKie 233-6. The collection circulated as 'Ovid without a title' (*Ouidius sine titulo*) in this branch of the tradition.

135 See McKie 236, Goold (1965b) 90; *contra*, Kenney (1962), 25 (cf. *id.*, *The Classical Text* (Berkeley-Los Angeles-London, 1974), 134).

136 McKie (232) suggests that the source of the contamination may be the 11th-century hyparchetype β.

137 See M. D. Reeve, 'Heinsius' MSS of Ovid', *RhM* 117 (1974), 133-66, *id.* *RhM* 119 (1976) 65-78.

138 See Kenney (1962) 10.

139 See Kenney (1962) 29-31.

140 See his preface, Vol. I, p. viii.

the text I believe to be closest to Ovid's original. My generously selective apparatus criticus (pp. 93-8) is based on Kenney's corrected edition of 1965 (I have adopted his signification ω for a majority of the *recc.* and ς or a minority, and the term *Itali* to indicate readings drawn from renaissance MSS [141]); for additional documentation I have relied on the collations of *Y* and *M* by Munari and Reeve.[142] The abbreviations *eras.* and *in ras.* indicate respectively places where the original reading of the MS has been erased and something inserted in its place. I have standardised the spelling by adopting assimilated forms (e.g. *composui*, not *conposui*; *tranasset*, not *transnasset*) throughout.[143]

A traditional critical apparatus, albeit untraditionally located (cf. p. iv), may be thought to be a luxury in an edition of this kind, but I have found it still the most economical way of showing the enquiring reader where the text is based on an undisputed MS reading, where on editorial choice between variants, and where on scholarly conjecture; moreover, obvious errors and interpolations can at times assist interpretation. And for even the reader working mainly from the translation, the physical presence of an apparatus may perhaps, in the age of the photocopier and other processes of easy and mass reproduction, serve as a timely reminder of the mediaeval monk in his technology-deprived scriptorium who has played an essential part in putting the text of Ovid's *Amores* before our eyes today.

VI. THE TRANSLATION

The prose translation I offer is close, but not literal. Where I have departed radically from the Latin, or I think the English requires further explanation, I refer the reader to the commentary. I have tried to follow Ovid's own word-order as far as possible within the limits of English idiom, and I have retained all metonyms (see p. 12) and allusive expressions; glosses make for more immediate understanding, but they detract from the poetry. I have also attempted to preserve as much as possible of Ovid's artistic repetition, alliteration and other striking sound effects; puns and *double entendres* I have aimed to reproduce too, but sometimes I admit defeat (see e.g. 1. 11, 11. 45nn.). One of my most difficult tasks has been to convey something of the varying tone and stylistic level of Ovid's language, and I urge even the Latinless reader to consult the commentary for information which may illuminate my choice of a particular word or expression.

The best modern English version of the *Amores* is Lee's; Melville is also accomplished and readable. But I know from my teaching experience that these verse translations are only fully appreciated by those who are able also to read and savour the Latin. My own is specifically intended for those who are not.[144]

---

141 See Kenney (1962) 28-9.
142 See nn. 133 and 137 above.
143 On the grounds for this see Goold (1965a) 9-11.
144 For the special difficulties of translating Ovid see p. 12. For further hints on using this edition see p. iv.

AMORES II

Text, Translation and Discussions

I

Hoc quoque composui Paelignis natus aquosis,
ille ego nequitiae Naso poeta meae.
hoc quoque iussit Amor; procul hinc, procul este, seueri:
non estis teneris apta theatra modis.
me legat in sponsi facie non frigida uirgo
et rudis ignoto tactus amore puer;
atque aliquis iuuenum, quo nunc ego, saucius arcu
agnoscat flammae conscia signa suae,
miratusque diu 'quo' dicat 'ab indice doctus
composuit casus iste poeta meos?'
ausus eram, memini, caelestia dicere bella
centimanumque Gygen (et satis oris erat),
cum male se Tellus ulta est ingestaque Olympo
ardua deuexum Pelion Ossa tulit;
in manibus nimbos et cum Ioue fulmen habebam
quod bene pro caelo mitteret ille suo:
clausit amica fores; ego cum Ioue fulmen omisi;
excidit ingenio Iuppiter ipse meo.
Iuppiter, ignoscas: nil me tua tela iuuabant;
clausa tuo maius ianua fulmen habet.
blanditias elegosque leuis, mea tela, resumpsi:
mollierunt duras lenia uerba fores.
carmina sanguineae deducunt cornua lunae
et reuocant niueos solis euntis equos;
carmine dissiliunt abruptis faucibus angues
inque suos fontes uersa recurrit aqua;
carminibus cessere fores, insertaque posti,
quamuis robur erat, carmine uicta sera est.
quid mihi profuerit uelox cantatus Achilles?
quid pro me Atrides alter et alter agent,
quique tot errando quot bello perdidit annos,
raptus et Haemoniis flebilis Hector equis?
at facie tenerae laudata saepe puellae,
ad uatem, pretium carminis, ipsa uenit.
magna datur merces! heroum clara ualete
nomina: non apta est gratia uestra mihi.
ad mea formosos uultus adhibete, puellae,
carmina, purpureus quae mihi dictat Amor.

1

I, Naso, born in the well-watered land of the Paeligni, am the author of this collection too – yes, I, the celebrated poet of my own shameless ways. This collection too was written at the command of Love; keep away, keep away from it, puritans: you are no fit audience for elegiac verse. Let my reader be the girl who thrills at the sight of her suitor's face, and the callow youth experiencing love for the first time. And let some young man, wounded by the self-same bow as I am now, recognise the tell-tale signs of his own burning passion and cry, as he marvels again and again, 'From where has this poet got the knowledge to write about *my* troubles?'

I once ventured, I remember, to tell of wars in heaven and hundred-handed Gyges (I had the verbal capacity, too – and the audacity[1]), when Earth exacted her wicked vengeance, and steep Ossa, piled on Olympus, bore the slopes of Pelion; I had storm-clouds in hand, with Jupiter and a thunderbolt which he might worthily launch in defence of his heaven: my girl-friend slammed her door; I dropped the thunderbolt and Jupiter as well – yes, Jupiter himself slipped out of my mind. Forgive me, Jupiter: your weapons were no help to me; a closed door has a bolt more powerful than yours. I took up my own weapons again – blandishments and lightweight elegiacs: gentle words weakened the door's resistance.

Magical verse draws down the horns of the blood-red moon and recalls the snow-white horses of the sun in mid-course; magical verse makes snakes split open, with jaws ripped apart, and rivers turn round and run back to their source; it was magical verse which made the door give way and overpowered the bar slotted into the doorpost, though it was of solid oak.

What good will it do me to sing of swift-footed Achilles? What will the two sons of Atreus do for me? Or the man who wasted as many years in wandering as in war? Or piteous Hector, dragged along by Thessalian steeds? On the other hand, the poet's reward for verse which praises a young girl's beauty is often the girl herself. And a grand reward it is! Farewell, you heroes and your famous names: your gratitude is no good to me. Girls, turn your pretty faces to my verses, which rosy Love dictates to me.

---

1 See n. *ad loc.*

DISCUSSION
Poem 1

In announcing theme and intent at the start of his work, Ovid is following a tradition dating back to the Homeric epics, but his aim to amuse at tradition's expense is already plain in v. 3. When he avers that his poetry was commissioned by Love and in sacerdotal tones (see 3n.) warns the puritanically-minded to steer clear of it, he is making fun of the poet's conventional claim to direct mandate from a god, Muse, or other august personage (cf. Hes. *Th.* 22-34 with West's note, Call. *Aet.* fr. 2) and of his familiar pose as a priest or prophet (cf. Pi. fr. 83. 3-4, and see further Nisbet-Hubbard I. 349). In Ovid's own time the priestly stance had been most memorably adopted by Horace (*Carm.* iii. 1. 1-4) and Propertius (iii. 1. 1-4) to lend an air of grave authority to their programmatic statements, and a certain mischievous parallelism may be detected between the whole of Ovid's opening section (1-10) and the celebrated first stanza of Hor. *Carm.* iii. 1:

> I do not want the uninitiated masses, and I exclude them; give
> me silence; I, the priest of the Muses, sing to young girls and
> boys songs unheard before.

Horace too claims to be the mouthpiece of a superior authority. He too first warns off a section of the populace with which he is not in sympathy and then specifies 'young girls and boys' as his intended readers. And his language, like Ovid's, has a distinctly religious timbre. But Horace is about to dilate on the need for moral purity, not on the ups-and-downs of sexual love.

Ovid is similarly mischievous in vv. 11-22. The Alexandrian poet Callimachus, had claimed that he was deterred from writing epic in the grand manner by the personal intervention of Apollo, who instructed him to stick to a 'slender Muse' (*Aet.* fr. 1. 24), and the Augustans subsequently weary us with accounts of how their pastoral, lyric or elegy was produced only after they had likewise been warned off epic by Apollo (Verg. *Ecl.* 6. 3-5, Prop. iii. 3. 1-24, Hor. *Carm.* iv. 15. 1-4). The motif (whose history and development are minutely examined by Wimmel) has become known as the *recusatio* (the term explains nothing in itself, meaning simply 'refusal' or 'objection'; cf. Brink's note on Hor. *Ep.* ii. 1. 259, and see p. 7). Callimachus used it as a picturesque means of showing his rejection of epic pomp and grandiloquence in favour of a refined style and miniaturist technique (see G. O. Hutchinson, *Hellenistic Poetry* (Oxford, 1988), 26-84), but Horace and Propertius turned it into an urbane excuse for not writing the national epic for which Augustus was apparently pressing (some scholars believe that the pressure was largely invented, but I doubt it; see Griffin (1984), *id.* (1985) 29). By having the deity forbid their epic enterprises on grounds of their insufficient talent, these poets enabled themselves to shelter behind a decorous show of modesty (the same charade is to be found outside the context of the strictly 'Callimachean' *recusatio*; see Nisbet-Hubbard I. 81-2). Not so Ovid, however, as the opening lines of *Am.* i. 1 clearly indicate. All the basic ingredients of the *recusatio* – intention to write epic, divine intervention and subsequent renunciation of epic – are there; but Ovid has replaced Apollo, the dignified god of poetry, with Cupid, the mischievous god of love, who, instead of warning off the aspiring epic poet in the conventional manner, allows him to write two splendid hexameters and then promptly steals a foot from the second one to leave him with an elegiac couplet. In our poem Ovid has more daringly still dispensed with the deity altogether and substituted a mere girl, who deflects him from his epic undertaking simply by slamming her door in his face. No conventional Callimachaean ideals or Augustan diffidence here (cf. *Am.* ii. 18. 5-12, and see pp. 86-7).

The fervent championship of elegy against epic on grounds of its greater usefulness in the cause of love is nothing new (Stroh (1971) makes it the subject of special study), and vv. 29ff. here are in their phraseology and use of epic examples particularly reminiscent of Prop. i. 9. 9-12. The whole of 11-36 may be seen as a comic re-working of the general sentiments of Prop. i. 9 and i. 7, which extol the utility of elegy in matters of love (see further Stahl 48-71). Propertius' own treatment of the theme is light-hearted, but Ovid introduces extra humour by 'dramatising' Propertius' arguments. While Propertius merely intimates that pretty girls are unimpressed with epic poetry, Ovid actually demonstrates it by telling how his writing of epic only resulted in his becoming a 'locked-out lover' (see 17n.), and while Propertius speaks of the usefulness of elegy only in general terms, Ovid shows that 'lightweight elegiacs' solved for him the specific, practical problem of the closed door. Indeed, elegy, we gather, acts like magic in such circumstances (see 23-8nn.). But Ovid is quick to undercut his own hyperbole. The 'magical' powers of elegy are easily explained: most pretty girls are susceptible to poetry which praises their beauty (33-4)!

So there is much in this piece which parodies the conventional programmatic poem (see p. 11), but it is nevertheless a programmatic poem in its own right, for it makes two fundamental points: (i) that Ovid's concern is less with any unique personal experience than with the universal aspects of love (see 5-10n.) – his beloved is neither named nor described, and the semi-personified *Amor* which he claims impels him to write is a far cry from the erotic poet's traditional *grande passion* (cf. especially Prop. ii. 1); and (ii) that he repudiates the Augustan convention of apology for the choice of a non-epic genre – this is made clear by his frivolous treatment of the *recusatio* motif. Neither in this nor in any other of his programmatic poems in the *Amores* does Ovid profess *inability* to write anything more elevated than elegy, but rather the opposite: both here and at *Am.* i. 1. 1-4 he claims that he had actually begun an epic, and a good one, when he was rudely interrupted (cf. *Am.* ii. 18. 5-12 and 13-18); and at no time does he rule out epic for the future.

This, then, is not just an amusing piece of nonsense; it is a spirited declaration of literary and political independence.

Further reading:

Boyd 191-4; *Buchan 77-9; L. Cahoon, 'A program for betrayal. Ovidian *nequitia* in *Amores* i. 1, ii. 1, iii. 1', *Helios* 12 (1985), 29-39; *D.J. Califf, 'Ovid, *Amores* ii. 1. 7-8: a programmatic allusion by anagram', *CQ* n.s. 47 (1997), 604-5; Cameron (1995) 54-83 (a reappraisal of the Augustan *recusatio*); *Gauly 18-24; *Giangrande 33-40; D. Korzeniewski, 'Ovids elegisches Proömium', *Hermes* 92 (1964), 182-93; Luck (1970); Morgan 12-17; Neumann 47-9; Otis; Reitzenstein; Stroh (1971) 149-54; Wimmel 303-5; *Wyke 133-4.

* * *

II

Quem penes est dominam seruandi cura, Bagoe,
dum perago tecum pauca, sed apta, uaca.
hesterna uidi spatientem luce puellam
illa quae Danai porticus agmen habet.
protinus, ut placuit, misi scriptoque rogaui:
rescripsit trepida 'non licet' illa manu.
et cur non liceat quaerenti reddita causa est
quod nimium dominae cura molesta tua est.
si sapis, o custos, odium, mihi crede, mereri
desine: quem metuit quisque, perisse cupit.
uir quoque non sapiens: quid enim seruare laboret
unde nihil, quamuis non tueare, perit?
sed gerat ille suo morem furiosus amori
et castum multis quod placet esse putet:
huic furtiua tuo libertas munere detur,
quam dederis illi reddat ut illa tibi.
conscius esse uelis? domina est obnoxia seruo –
conscius esse times? dissimulare licet.
scripta leget secum: matrem misisse putato;
uenerit ignotus: postmodo notus erit;
ibit ad affectam quae non languebit amicam:
uisat; iudiciis aegra sit illa tuis.
si faciet tarde, ne te mora longa fatiget,
imposita gremio stertere fronte potes.
nec tu linigeram fieri quid possit ad Isin
quaesieris, nec tu curua theatra time.
conscius assiduos commissi tollet honores:
quis minor est autem quam tacuisse labor?
ille placet uersatque domum neque uerbera sentit,
ille potens: alii, sordida turba, iacent.
huic, uerae ut lateant, causae finguntur inanes,
atque ambo domini, quod probat una, probant.
cum bene uir traxit uultum rugasque coegit,
quod uoluit fieri blanda puella facit.
sed tamen interdum tecum quoque iurgia nectat
et simulet lacrimas carnificemque uocet;
tu contra obicies quae tuto diluat illa;
tu ueris falso crimine deme fidem.
sic tibi semper honos, sic alta peculia crescent;
haec fac, in exiguo tempore liber eris.
aspicis indicibus nexas per colla catenas?
squalidus orba fide pectora carcer habet.

2

Bagous, you whose special responsibility it is to guard your mistress, give me your attention while I put to you just a few – but pertinent – points. Yesterday I saw a girl strolling in the portico which contains the row of Danaids. Since she took my fancy, I immediately sent a note asking her to oblige me **(5)**; she wrote back with a trembling hand 'I can't'. And when I enquire why she can't, I am told it is because your tutelage cramps your mistress' style.

You are a fool, chaperon, believe me, if you don't stop giving cause for hatred: everyone wishes dead the man he fears **(10)**. The husband[1] must be a fool too – or why would he bother to guard what has nothing to lose, even if one leaves it unguarded? But let the madman pander to his own passion and believe that a thing attractive to many can remain untouched. You should secretly make your mistress a present of her freedom **(15)**, so that she in turn may grant you yours.

You would like to be an accomplice? It puts the mistress under an obligation to her slave – You are *afraid* to be an accomplice? You can turn a blind eye! If she's reading a note to herself, assume it's from her mother; if a stranger comes along – next time you will know him **(20)**! If she goes to see a 'sick' girl-friend who is not unwell at all, let her make the visit – the woman can be sick as far as you are concerned. If she's slow about it, you can put your head down and snore away so that you don't get tired of the long wait. Don't enquire what may go on in the temple of linen-robed Isis **(25)**, and have no fear of the bent[2] theatre. An accomplice will collect a steady flow of tips for his services; really, what could be less trouble than keeping quiet? An accomplice finds favour, turns the house upside-down and does not feel the lash. He is a powerful person: the others – the common lot – are down-trodden **(30)**. For the husband's benefit, false reasons are invented to conceal the true ones, and what wins the mistress' approval wins the master's too. After the husband has pulled a long face and forced a frown, he does what his wheedling darling wanted done. But sometimes let her pick a quarrel even with you **(35)**; let her pretend to cry and call you a murderer. You, for your part, bring up against her something she can easily explain away; by trumping up a false charge, rob a true one of its credibility. In this way you will get tips, in this way your personal pile will grow high; do this, and in no time you will be free **(40)**.

Have you noticed informers wearing chains around their necks? Faithless souls are confined in mouldering dungeons. Tantalus craves water with water

---

[1] See p. 6

[2] See n. *ad loc.*

quaerit aquas in aquis et poma fugacia captat
  Tantalus: hoc illi garrula lingua dedit;
dum nimium seruat custos Iunonius Io,
  ante suos annos occidit: illa dea est.
uidi ego compedibus liuentia crura gerentem
  unde uir incestum scire coactus erat.
poena minor merito. nocuit mala lingua duobus:
  uir doluit, famae damna puella tulit.
crede mihi, nulli sunt crimina grata marito,
  nec quemquam, quamuis audiat, illa iuuant:
seu tepet, indicium securas perdis ad aures;
  siue amat, officio fit miser ille tuo.
culpa nec ex facili quamuis manifesta probatur;
  iudicis illa sui tuta fauore uenit.
uiderit ipse licet, credet tamen ille neganti
  damnabitque oculos et sibi uerba dabit.
aspiciat dominae lacrimas, plorabit et ipse
  et dicet 'poenas garrulus iste dabit!'.
quid dispar certamen inis? tibi uerbera uicto
  adsunt, in gremio iudicis illa sedet.
non scelus aggredimur, non ad miscenda coimus
  toxica, non stricto fulminat ense manus:
quaerimus ut tuto per te possimus amare:
  quid precibus nostris mollius esse potest?

III

Ei mihi quod dominam nec uir nec femina seruas,
  mutua nec Veneris gaudia nosse potes.
qui primus pueris genitalia membra recidit
  uulnera quae fecit debuit ipse pati.
mollis in obsequium, facilisque rogantibus esses,
  si tuus in quauis praetepuisset amor.
non tu natus equo, non fortibus utilis armis,
  bellica non dextrae conuenit hasta tuae.
ista mares tractent: tu spes depone uiriles;
  sunt tibi cum domina signa ferenda tua.
hanc imple meritis, huius tibi gratia prosit;
  si careas illa, quis tuus usus erit?
est etiam facies, sunt apti lusibus anni
  indigna est pigro forma perire situ.
fallere te potuit, quamuis habeare molestus:
  non caret effectu quod uoluere duo.
aptius at fuerit precibus temptasse; rogamus,
  dum bene ponendi munera tempus habes.

all around him and reaches after fruit that eludes his grasp: this was the reward of his tale-telling tongue. In keeping too close a watch on Io (**45**), the guard appointed by Juno met an untimely death: Io is now a goddess. I have myself seen fetters bruising the legs of one from whom a husband had had to learn of infidelity. The punishment was less than he deserved. His wicked tongue harmed two people: the man was grieved; the girl lost her reputation (**50**). Believe me, no husband likes to hear accusations, and no one benefits from them, even if he listens. If his feelings are cool, you are wasting your time telling tales to unimpressionable ears: if he is in love, you make him miserable by doing your 'duty'. And guilt, however plain, is not easily proven (**55**); madame is safe, thanks to the bias of her judge. He may even have seen for himself, but he will still accept her denial, condemn his eyes and deceive himself. Let him just see his lady's tears, and he will howl himself and say 'That tell-tale shall be punished!' (**60**). Why enter an uneven contest? There's a beating for you, the loser, while she sits in the judge's lap.

We are not planning a crime; we are not getting together to make a poisonous mixture; no drawn sword is flashing dangerously in our hand: we are asking you to grant us your permission to love unmolested (**65**). What can be more seductively innocuous than our request?

3

You poor thing! Neither male nor female, you're the keeper of a mistress and cannot experience the shared pleasure that is love. The man who first cut off boys' genitals should himself have suffered the wound he inflicted. You would easily be persuaded into compliance and be responsive to requests (**5**), if you had ever burned with love for any woman.

You are not cut out for riding; you are incapable of wielding powerful weapons; the spear of war is out of place in your right hand. Leave those things to Men. Put away male ambitions; your duty is to be your mistress' standard-bearer (**10**). Ply her with favours; let her gratitude be to your advantage; without her what use can you be? What is more, her looks and age are ripe for amatory adventures; it is a shame for her beauty to go to waste through being put to no active use.

We could have deceived you, although you make yourself a nuisance (**15**): what two people want, they always get. But it will be better to try to prevail upon you; by asking, we are giving you a last chance to get a good return for your favours.

DISCUSSION
Poems 2 and 3

Any study of 2 demands consideration also of 3. Both pieces are dramatic monologues (see p. 7) addressed to a eunuch who chaperons a girl Ovid fancies, and both end with his request for access to her. 3 is a uniquely brief poem for the *Amores*, and two of our MSS join it with 2. Did Ovid, therefore, as some scholars have suggested, intend these 84 lines to form a single elegy? I doubt it.

Firstly, not much weight can be given to the testimony of those MSS which do join 2 and 3, since one is *Y*, which also joins *Am.* i. 1-3, 8-11, 13-15 and ii. 1-2, 3-4, 18-19, and the other is the totally undistinguished 15th century Hauniensis. Secondly, Ovid in the *Amores* shows a predilection for the dramatic diptych, i.e. two consecutive poems presenting two consecutive stages of the same action; i. 11 and 12, ii. 7 and 8, and ii. 13 and 14 have long been recognised as pairings of this kind. An easily imagined development following the first 'scene' in each of these cases prompts a change of tone or attitude in the second poem of the pair, where some of the points made and stances adopted in the first are modified or inverted. Our two pieces appear to fit very largely into this category. Specific points of contact and contrast between them are easily detectable. *dominam ... seruas* at 3. 1 echoes *dominam seruandi* at 2. 1, and in each piece the addressee is immediately identified as a eunuch. But whereas in 2 all direct mention of the eunuch's sexual status is avoided (the reader is apprised of it only through the use of the name *Bagous*; see 2. 1n.), in 3 Ovid's adversary is bluntly described as 'neither male nor female', and his lack of manhood is emphasised throughout in cruelly emotive language and a mass of obscene *double entendre* (see 3. 1, 5-11nn.). In both pieces Ovid acknowledges that the eunuch's activities make things difficult for his mistress, but whereas at 2. 7-8 he implies that the guard's vigilance effectively rules out any amatory escapades, at 3. 15-16 he claims that it is no real deterrent. In both pieces Ovid argues that if the eunuch obliges his mistress, the benefits will be mutual, but whereas he claims at 2. 17 that the slave's goodwill is indispensable to *her*, at 3. 12 he insists that *her* goodwill is indispensable to *him*. Both pieces end with essentially the same request, but whereas the tone at 2. 65-6 is one of courteous petition, at 3. 17-18 it is one of sinister ultimatum. And the reason for Ovid's change of tack in 3 we naturally assume to be the eunuch's refusal to grant his request at the end of 2 (cf. especially Ovid's technique in *Am.* i. 11 and 12).

In some respects 2 and 3 do *not* follow the pattern of the typical Ovidian dramatic diptych. They are strikingly disparate in length, while the two poems in all the above-mentioned pairs are roughly equal (*Am.* ii. 13 may be incomplete; see 13. 17-18n.); and the shortness of the imaginary interval between them is unparalleled in the recognised diptychs, while pauses of this momentary nature *are* accommodated in *single* poems containing changes of tone (e.g. *Am.* i. 6). Yet disproportion is arguably appropriate here, garrulity being in keeping with Ovid's measured civility in 2 and brevity with his unconcealed annoyance in 3, and never within a *single* poem does Ovid resort to the parallelism so easily discernible in 2 and 3 and so typical of the recognised pairs. It is perhaps worth noting also that poem 19, which clearly recalls 2 on a number of occasions, shows no significant connections with 3; this too suggests, if anything, the independence of 3. But when all is said, the issue is one of largely academic interest (see pp. 10-11), for 2 and 3, whether conjoined or not, are obviously meant to be read consecutively, and there is no sense in judging them except together.

'Get the underdogs on your side', Ovid urges the prospective lover at *Ars* ii. 259-60, – the doorkeeper, without fail, and the one who blocks the entrance to the bedroom'. In our two pieces we see him attempting to practise what he was to preach. The scene is not entirely new in the *Amores*: i. 6 also shows him attempting to win over a slave who stands between him and his beloved, and it too is a dramatic monologue. In *Am.* i. 6 the slave is a doorkeeper and Ovid is the familiar lover on the doorstep (see 1. 17n.): here in 2 and 3 the doorstep setting is dispensed with and the doorkeeper replaced by a chaperon who has the special distinction of being a eunuch. It is this above all which makes for novelty, for the eunuch's peculiar shortcomings open up the possibility of a completely new approach for the frustrated lover in 3, when all the arguments which might be addressed to a normal slave-chaperon have been exhausted in 2.

Of course, the situation is preposterous – not because chaperons did not exist (Tac. *Ann.* xi. 35. 3 suggests that the surveillance and confinement of women to safeguard their fidelity was no mere elegiac fiction), but because it is unthinkable that anyone confronted with one of these characters would launch into such a lengthy and elaborate harangue as that in 2 or such a calculatedly provocative one as that in 3. Some critics insist that the argumentative section of 2 (i.e. vv. 17-62) is artificial in structure as well as in conception (see e.g. Jäger 26, Davis (1977) 92-4), but I think Ovid achieves some degree of dramatic realism in his choice and arrangement of material. For, provided that we suspend our disbelief in the fundamentally fanciful situation, vv. 17-62 present a reasonably convincing picture of a quick-thinking man tailoring his arguments to suit the changing reactions of his addressee: easily imagined are the look of fear which might prompt 18-28 (for the force of the direct question in 18 see 8. 23n.), the spark of interest which might give rise to the extravagant promises of 29-30, and the renewed suspicion which might demand the reassurance of 30-34. We could expect the arguments offered in such circumstances to be inconsistent and illogical, and Ovid's certainly are: having first suggested that Bagous need *never* feel obliged to speak out in accusation (17-28), Ovid later recommends that he should occasionally make false accusations to destroy the credibility of his true ones (33-8); and he warns him that he will certainly be punished for telling the truth (41-60) – as if he would not just as certainly be punished for telling lies.

When Ovid promises Bagous at 2. 29-30 power and privilege within the household, he takes his readers into the fantasy-world of Roman comedy, for it was only there that slaves regularly enjoyed the kind of advantages promised to the eunuch. Ovid seems in fact to have drawn a considerable amount of inspiration from comedy in these two poems. Terence at *Eu.* 570-80 provides a precedent for a eunuch in the role of chaperon, while Bagous' unenviable position, as Ovid sees it in 2, has much in common with that of Sceledrus, the slave allotted the task of guarding his master's concubine in Plautus' *Miles Gloriosus*. And the advice which Ovid gives to Bagous at 2. 27ff. is essentially the same as that given to Sceledrus by another slave at *Mil.* 476-7 when Sceledrus thinks he has seen his charge being unfaithful: 'If you have any sense, you will keep quiet; a slave does not have to tell all he knows'. Didactic material is not infrequently taken over from comedy by the elegists, but the pieces of advice adapted are more often those addressed to comic lovers by experienced madams (*lenae*) and prostitutes (see A. L. Wheeler, 'Erotic teaching in Roman Elegy and the Greek sources', *CPh* 5 (1910), 440-50 and *CPh* 6 (1911), 56-77, Burck 186, and for the general relationship between elegy and comedy, p. 5).

Poems 2 and 3 are certainly not devoid of humour or artistic merit. 2 has good moments of entertaining cynicism and wry comment on the curious psychology of sexual relationships (11-14, 31-4, 55-60), while 3 may amuse by its malicious mockery and sly innuendo. The adaptation of comic material is enterprising, and the change of

IV

Non ego mendosos ausim defendere mores
 falsaque pro uitiis arma mouere meis.
confiteor, si quid prodest delicta fateri;
 in mea nunc demens crimina fassus eo.
odi, nec possum, cupiens, non esse quod odi:
 heu, quam, quae studeas ponere, ferre graue est!
nam desunt uires ad me mihi iusque regendum;
 auferor ut rapida concita puppis aqua.
non est certa meos quae forma inuitet amores:
 centum sunt causae cur ego semper amem.
siue aliqua est oculos in se deiecta modestos,
 uror, et insidiae sunt pudor ille meae;
siue procax aliqua est, capior quia rustica non est
 spemque dat in molli mobilis esse toro;
aspera si uisa est rigidasque imitata Sabinas,
 uelle sed ex alto dissimulare puto;
siue es docta, places raras dotata per artes
 siue rudis, placita es simplicitate tua.
est quae Callimachi prae nostris rustica dicat
 carmina; cui placeo, protinus ipsa placet.
est etiam quae me uatem et mea carmina culpet;
 culpantis cupiam sustinuisse femur.
molliter incedit: motu capit; altera dura est:
 at poterit tacto mollior esse uiro.
huic quia dulce canit flectitque facillima uocem,
 oscula cantanti rapta dedisse uelim;
haec querulas habili percurrit pollice chordas:
 tam doctas quis non possit amare manus?
illa placet gestu numerosaque bracchia ducit
 et tenerum molli torquet ab arte latus:

tone and tactics from one poem to the other is an interesting feature. But these two pieces have rightly never been among the most highly rated of Ovid's amatory compositions.

Further reading:

*Barsby 144-6; J. Booth, 'Double entendres in Ovid, *Amores* ii. 3', *LCM* 8 (1983), 101-2; Damon 280-85; Davis (1977) 86-97; D'Elia 122-3; Gauly 203-10; Jäger 25-31; F. W. Lenz, 'Ovidio, *Amores* ii. 2 e 3, una sola poesia?', *Maia* 17 (1965), 119-24 [=*id. Opuscula Selecta* (Amsterdam, 1972), 449-54] (Damon, Davis and Lenz all regard 2 and 3 as separate poems, but their supporting arguments differ in detail from mine.)

* * *

4

I would not venture to defend my imperfect morals and use spurious weapons to fight for my faults. I confess, if it does any good to confess one's crimes; and, having confessed, in my madness, I now proceed to accuse myself. I hate what I am, and yet, in spite of my wishes, I cannot help being what I hate (**5**). Ah, how difficult it is to tolerate the characteristics one strives to shed! The fact is that I have not the strength and power to keep myself under control; I get carried away like a ship swept along by the rushing waves. It is not one particular type of beauty which invites my amorous advances; there are a hundred reasons why I am always in love (**10**).

If a girl modestly keeps her eyes directed down at herself, I am all ablaze, and that shyness is my downfall. If one is forward, I am captivated because she is not *gauche* and promises to be an agile performer in a soft bed. If a girl seems severe and just like the strait-laced Sabines (**15**), I think she is willing deep down, but does not show that she is. You, the accomplished type, take my fancy because of your exquisite artistic gifts, and you, the unsophisticated, appeal through your simplicity. Then there is the sort of girl who says Callimachus' poetry is unpolished in comparison with mine; she who admires me immediately wins my admiration (**20**). Then there is the sort who criticises my poetic profession and output; I wouldn't mind lifting that critic's thigh! One girl walks sensuously: her movement captivates me; another is stiff, but a man's touch will loosen her up. From one, because she sings sweetly and modulates her voice with the greatest of ease (**25**), I should like to snatch kisses as she sings. Another runs agile fingers over the plaintive strings – who could help falling in love with such accomplished hands? Another's dance postures are appealing; she moves her arms rhythmically and bends her slender body with

ut taceam de me, qui causa tangor ab omni,
illic Hippolytum pone, Priapus erit.
tu, quia tam longa es, ueteres heroidas aequas
et potes in toto multa iacere toro;
haec habilis breuitate sua est: corrumpor utraque;
conueniunt uoto longa breuisque meo.
non est culta: subit quid cultae accedere possit;
ornata est: dotes exhibet ipsa suas.
candida me capiet, capiet me flaua puella;
est etiam in fusco grata colore uenus.
seu pendent niuea pulli ceruice capilli,
Leda fuit nigra conspicienda coma;
seu flauent, placuit croceis Aurora capillis:
omnibus historiis se meus aptat amor.
me noua sollicitat, me tangit serior aetas:
haec melior specie, moribus illa placet.
denique quas tota quisquam probat Vrbe puellas,
noster in has omnis ambitiosus amor.

DISCUSSION
Poem 4

The lover's susceptibility to a wide range of charms is a common theme in ancient erotic poetry of all periods. The Hellenistic and later Greek epigrammatists muse on the attractions of various types of boys (e.g. Rhian. *AP* xii. 93, Mel. *AP* xii. 94, 256, Strat. *AP* xii. 244) and the Latin elegists on the competing charms of different women (cf. Prop. ii. 22. 1-10, 25. 41-6, [Tib.] iii. 8. 7-14; Tibullus alone in Latin uses the motif in the context of male homosexual love (i. 4. 9-14)). Like Propertius in ii. 22, Ovid here uses the word *uitium* of his 'weakness' (v. 2; cf. Prop. ii. 22. 17) and refers to the problem in which it results as *semper amare*, 'constantly being in love' (v. 10; cf. Prop. ii. 22. 18). In sentiment and phraseology vv. 29-30 closely recall Prop. ii. 22. 5-6. But there the likeness to Propertius' poem ends, for Ovid's piece is no attempt at self-excuse or justification to a favoured confidant but an Augustan Don Giovanni's swaggering warning to all it may concern of what can be expected from him. Even when he claims to be ashamed of himself (vv. 5-6), he does so with such conspicuous wit that he cannot be taken seriously.

The elegy is to be savoured not least for the wicked contrast it provides with *Am.* i. 3: the poet who here boasts of his chronic infidelity there professes eternal devotion to sensuous skill (**30**). Put Hippolytus in front of her – not to mention me, who am susceptible to every stimulus – and he will become a Priapus. You, because you are so tall, resemble the heroines of old, and with your ample proportions you can take up the whole of the bed; another girl's shortness makes her easy to hold. Both types are my undoing (**35**); my taste accommodates the tall and the short. One girl is not *soignée*: I imagine what she could be if she were. Another is all decked out: she makes the most of herself. By a fair-skinned girl I am captivated; captivated I am by a fair-haired one; and there is a charming attractiveness in dusky colouring too (**40**). If dark hair cascades over a snowy white neck – Leda was renowned for her black locks; if a girl's hair is fair – Aurora was attractive because of her saffron tresses. My love adapts itself to all the stories. A young woman excites me, one of maturer years impresses me (**45**): the former wins on looks, the latter has appealing ways.

To sum up, all the girls that anyone admires throughout the town, these my love aspires to embrace.

one woman and one only. But it is also an entertaining poem in its own right, its most memorable feature being the catalogue of women which illustrates the all-embracing nature of Ovid's amatory tastes. This has prompted some notable imitations; see F. H. Candelaria, 'Ovid and the indifferent lovers', *Renaissance News* 13 (1960), 294-7. There were also predecents of a kind: an imitator of Hesiod and an Alexandrian Greek, Nicaenetus of Samos, both composed a *Catalogue of Women*, but these were poems several hundred lines long and collections of stories about mythological heroines (genealogical in the case of the Hesiodic poem; see M. L. West, *The Hesiodic Catalogue of Women* (Oxford, 1985)). Ovid's catalogue, short and non-mythological, is a new departure.

Nowhere does Ovid write with more wit and ingenuity, and nowhere with more fluency and grace (see 11-46n.). Yet nowhere does he more invite Seneca the Elder's famous criticism that 'he never knew when to stop' (cf. p. 10, with n. 72). Some modern critics, however, decline to see Ovid's exhaustive treatment here as a pure *tour de force*, but rather interpret the catalogue of his supposedly promiscuous tastes as an oblique statement of *poetic* intent: 'many of the *puellae* can be read as incarnations of the aesthetic principles that inform Ovid's elegies' (Keith 33).

Further reading:

Bürger 18-23; *Gauly 27-8; *Keith 33-5; Labate 321-5; Luck (1969) 167-73; Morgan 50-54; Neumann 63-8; Sabot 410-14; Tremoli 45-6.

* * *

V

Nullus amor tanti est – abeas, pharetrate Cupido! –
  ut mihi sint totiens maxima uota mori.
uota mori mea sunt, cum te peccasse recordor,
  o mihi perpetuum nata puella malum.
non mihi deceptae nudant tua facta tabellae
  nec data furtiue munera crimen habent.
o utinam arguerem sic ut non uincere possem!
  me miserum, quare tam bona causa mea est?
felix, qui quod amat defendere fortiter audet,
  cui sua 'non feci' dicere amica potest!
ferreus est nimiumque suo fauet ille dolori,
  cui petitur uicta palma cruenta rea.
ipse miser uidi, cum me dormire putares,
  sobrius apposito crimina uestra mero.
multa supercilio uidi uibrante loquentes;
  nutibus in uestris pars bona uocis erat.
non oculi tacuere tui conscriptaque uino
  mensa, nec in digitis littera nulla fuit.
sermonem agnoui quod non uideatur agentem
  uerbaque pro certis iussa ualere notis.
iamque frequens ierat mensa conuiua relicta;
  compositi iuuenes unus et alter erant;
improba tum uero iungentes oscula uidi
  (illa mihi lingua nexa fuisse liquet),
qualia non fratri tulerit germana seuero
  sed tulerit cupido mollis amica uiro,
qualia credibile est non Phoebo ferre Dianam,
  sed Venerem Marti saepe tulisse suo.
'quid facis?' exclamo. 'quo nunc mea gaudia defers?
  iniciam dominas in mea iura manus.
haec tibi sunt mecum, mihi sunt communia tecum:
  in bona cur quisquam tertius ista uenit?'
haec ego, quaeque dolor linguae dictauit; at illi
  conscia purpureus uenit in ora pudor.
quale coloratum Tithoni coniuge caelum
  subrubet, aut sponso uisa puella nouo;
quale rosae fulgent inter sua lilia mixtae
  aut, ubi cantatis, Luna, laborat equis;
aut quod, ne longis flauescere possit ab annis,
  Maeonis Assyrium femina tinxit ebur;
his erat aut alicui color ille simillimus horum,
  et numquam casu pulchrior illa fuit.

5

No love is worth so much – begone, Cupid with your quiver! – that my constant wish should be to die. To die is my wish, when I recall that you have been unfaithful, girl born to be my everlasting torment. It is not camouflaged writing-tablets which reveal your conduct to me, nor do secretly given presents incriminate you. Oh, if only I could press charges in such a way that I could not win! Damn it, why is my case so good? Fortunate is he who bravely dares defend the object of his love – he to whom his girl-friend can say 'I am not guilty'! Iron-hearted, and over-keen to indulge his own indignation, is the man who insists on his pound of flesh[1] when the defendant is beaten.

It was my misfortune to see with my own eyes what the two of you were up to when the wine was flowing; cold sober I was, when you thought me asleep. I saw you both saying many things through the twitch of an eyebrow; your nods were almost as good as words. Your eyes spoke volumes, and the table was covered with writing in wine; your fingers, too, formed many a letter. I detected conversation with a hidden meaning and words being used in accordance with a set code. By now most of the company had left the table and gone, just one or two young men in a drunken stupor remaining; it was at this point that I saw you giving each other wanton kisses (and they obviously involved you twining your tongues together). They were not the sort of kisses a blood-sister gives to her upright brother, but the sort a compliant sweetheart gives to her lustful lover – not the kind which, we might assume, Diana gives Apollo, but which Venus often gives her darling Mars.

'What are you doing?' I cried. 'Where are you now conveying the pleasures which belong to me? I shall lay hands on what is mine by right. We hold those pleasures in common, you with me and I with you; how is it that some third party is entitled to that property?'

These words did I utter and others which anguish suggested to my tongue; and a deep blush of shame came over her guilty face. Like the upward-spreading flush of the sky, when it is tinged by Tithonus' wife, or of a young girl beheld by her bridegroom; like roses glowing amidst their lilies, or the moon in eclipse, when her horses are bewitched; or like Assyrian ivory which Lydian women tint to prevent its being yellowed by the passage of time: very like these – or one of these – was that colour of hers, and never was she fortuitously

[1] See n. *ad loc.*

spectabat terram: terram spectare decebat;
maesta erat in uultu: maesta decenter erat.
sicut erant (et erant culti) laniare capillos
et fuit in teneras impetus ire genas.
ut faciem uidi, fortes cecidere lacerti:
defensa est armis nostra puella suis.
qui modo saeuus eram, supplex ultroque rogaui
oscula ne nobis deteriora daret.
risit et ex animo dedit optima, qualia possent
excutere irato tela trisulca Ioui.
torqueor infelix, ne tam bona senserit alter,
et uolo non ex hac illa fuisse nota.
haec quoque quam docui multo meliora fuerunt,
et quiddam uisa est addidicisse noui.
quod nimium placuere malum est, quod tota labellis
lingua tua est nostris, nostra recepta tuis.
nec tamen hoc unum doleo, non oscula tantum
iuncta queror, quamuis haec quoque iuncta queror:
illa nisi in lecto nusquam potuere doceri;
nescioquis pretium grande magister habet.

DISCUSSION
Poem 5

The poet accuses his beloved of infidelity: nothing new in that (cf. Theoc. 2. 154-8, Mel. *AP* v. 175, 184, Diosc. *AP* v. 52, Posidipp. *AP* v. 186, Catul. 11, 70, 72; Lilja collects many Latin elegiac examples at 157-69). He displays ambivalent and vacillating feelings towards her: again, not particularly surprising (cf. Mel. (or Phld.) *AP* v. 24, Catul. 8, 76, 85, Tib. ii. 6, Prop. i. 1). And yet Ovid's poem is full of surprises.

For one thing, unlike most poems on the subject of infidelity, it is funny. Most obviously so, perhaps, in that all the affected distress of the opening leads (as in *Am.* ii. 4) only to a joke: Ovid is suffering from a nasty dose of his own medicine (the idea probably came from Tibullus: compare Tib. i. 2. 15-22 with Tib. i. 6. 9-14). This we realise as soon as we reach vv. 13-32, for these lines immediately bring to mind *Am.* i. 4. There Ovid, playing the illicit lover, advises his beloved how he and she may communicate and enjoy each other's company during a dinner-party at which her *uir* (see p. 6) is also to be present: here, exchanging the role of illicit lover for that of *uir*, he makes himself, trick for trick, victim of his own ruses (see 15-18, 29-32nn. and further G. B. Ford, 'An analysis of *Amores* i. 4', *Helikon* 6 (1966), 645-52; for other similarly paired poems in the *Amores* see pp. 11-12). Here also Ovid exposes the major flaw in his earlier advice: the apparently drunken or otherwise oblivious *uir* may be shamming.

more beautiful. She stared at the ground: staring at the ground became her. She wore a sorrowful expression: the sorrow was becoming. I had felt an impulse to tear her hair, looking as it did (and it looked a work of art) **(45)**, and to fly at her tender cheeks. When I saw her face, my strong arms dropped: my girl-friend was saved by weapons of her own. I, who was brutal but a moment before, became the suppliant myself and begged her to give me kisses just as good **(50)**.

She laughed and heartily gave of her best – kisses such as could knock an angry Jupiter's three-pronged thunderbolt out of his hand. And now I am tortured, hapless wretch that I am, lest the other man experienced any as good; I don't want the kisses he had to have been of this stamp. These were much better than those I taught her, too **(55)**; she had, it seemed to me, learned a certain 'something' new. It's distressing that these kisses gave me more pleasure than I bargained for – that your tongue went right inside my lips and mine inside yours. But it's not just this that troubles me – not just your *kissing* each other that I'm grieving about (though I *am* grieving about this too) **(60)**: kisses like those can have been taught nowhere but in bed; so some teacher is being handsomely paid.

Funny too is the shockingly unsentimental attitude to infidelity which gradually emerges. Ovid spends half his poem extravagantly deploring his mistress' mere kissing of a guest at a bibulous party, but is able to dismiss with just a brief parting witticism (61-2) the idea of her sharing another man's bed. And why? Because he has actually *seen* the first, but only *suspects* the second. Not for him, then, either the amatory ideal of absolute faithfulness or the generous tolerance of a few minor misdemeanours which Catullus (68. 135-7) and Propertius (ii. 23. 29ff.) claim to be willing to show (see further Luck (1974) 21-3); what matters to Ovid, apparently, is not the frequency or the gravity of the infidelity, but only whether or not he has proof of it.

In fact he says as much himself in vv. 7-12, and in the manner of his saying it there is more mischief. For, by using a series of legal metaphors to express his feelings, Ovid, the self-confessed amatory adventurer, makes his current predicament sound uncommonly like that of a married man compelled under the terms of Augustus' *lex Iulia de adulteriis coercendis* to divorce his wife because he has himself witnessed her adultery (see 2. 46-60n.). This reminiscence of the unpopular moral legislation can only be regarded as an insolent and, to all but the most committed Augustans, amusing attempt to trivilalise it.

Ovid's poem surprises not only by its lightness of tone but also by its unusual form and structure. Dramatic monologue (see p. 7) is the favoured form for poetic accusations of infidelity (see e.g. Tib. i. 8, 9, Prop. i. 15), and indeed it looks at first as if that is the form Ovid is adopting here; but when he slips (almost imperceptibly) from direct address (1-20) into straight narrative (21-56) and briefly back again (57-62), it seems that we must understand the poem as a soliloquy. This, certainly, is a popular form for the display of emotional conflict or instability (see the examples of poems on these subjects cited above), but those who use it generally present themselves as undergoing all their vacillations of mood at the time of writing, and their shifts of feeling are not linked to any particular occurrence. Here, the two changes of heart which Ovid describes – from distress and anger to love, and then from love back to distress again – are directly related to a specific sequence of events and have actually taken place

VI

Psittacus, Eois imitatrix ales ab Indis,
 occidit: exsequias ite frequenter aues.
ite piae uolucres, et plangite pectora pinnis
 et rigido teneras ungue notate genas;
horrida pro maestis lanietur pluma capillis,
 pro longa resonent carmina uestra tuba.
quod scelus Ismarii quereris, Philomela, tyranni,
 expleta est annis ista querela suis.
alitis in rarae miserum deuertere funus:
 magna sed antiqua est causa doloris Itys.
omnes quae liquido libratis in aere cursus,
 tu tamen ante alios, turtur amice, dole.
plena fuit uobis omni concordia uita
 et stetit ad finem longa tenaxque fides;
quod fuit Argolico iuuenis Phoceus Orestae,
 hoc tibi, dum licuit, psittace, turtur erat.
quid tamen ista fides, quid rari forma coloris,
 quid uox mutandis ingeniosa sonis,
quid iuuat, ut datus es, nostrae placuisse puellae?
 infelix, auium gloria, nempe iaces.
tu poteras fragiles pinnis hebetare smaragdos,
 tincta gerens rubro Punica rostra croco.
non fuit in terris uocum simulantior ales:
 reddebas blaeso tam bene uerba sono.
raptus es inuidia: non tu fera bella mouebas;
 garrulus et placidae pacis amator eras.

in the past. In the poem they are merely being re-lived, though in the case of the first, the sudden burst of direct speech (29-32) makes the reader feel as if he is witnessing a drama in the present, and in that of the second, the attitude which finally resulted is presented as being also Ovid's current attitude. Yet a shift of feeling does take place within the course of the poem itself: Ovid's recollections cheer him up.

A loosely structured piece, then, with no pretence to temporal unity (cf. ii. 11 and 16). But at the same time a sophisticated and entertaining poem.

Further Reading

Boyd 10-16; K. Büchner in *Gedenksschrift für G. Rohde* (Tübingen, 1961), 77-8 [*id.* (1970) 196-7]; *R. Dimundo, 'L'ingenuo rivale e il silenzio richiesto (Ovid., *Am.* i. 4, ii. 5)' in *Ovidio poeta della memoria. Atti del Convegno Internazionale di Studi. Sulmona, 19-21 Ottobre 1989*, ed. G. Papponetti, (Sulmona, 1991), 275-91; Fränkel 30; Jäger 128-32; Keul 181-90.

* * *

6

Parrot, the mimic-bird from the easternmost Indies, is dead: go in your multitudes, you birds, to his funeral. Go, good birds, beat your breasts with your wings, and scratch your tender cheeks with your hard claws. Let your plumage, instead of hair, be ruffled and torn in grief (**5**); instead of the long trumpet, let your song ring out. As to your lamenting, Philomela, the Thracian tyrant's crime – that lament has had its allotment of years. Turn your attention to the sad demise of a rare bird: Itys is a great, but ancient, cause of grief (**10**). Mourn, all you who steer your course through the limpid air, but you especially, turtle-dove, his friend. There was perfect harmony between you throughout his life, and a firm and long-standing loyalty existed to the end; what the young Phocian was to Orestes of Argos (**15**), such, while heaven permitted it, parrot, was turtle-dove to you.

But of what avail that loyalty, of what avail the beauty of that incomparable colouring? Of what avail the voice so clever at producing a variety of sounds? Of what avail was it to have given pleasure to my sweetheart from the moment she received you? Alas, prince among birds, you lie dead all the same (**20**). Your plumage could make fragile emeralds look dull; your beak was scarlet tinged with orange. There was no bird on earth which imitated speech more closely; you used to render words so well with your broken cries.

You were carried off by envy. You did not stir up fierce warfare (**25**); you were voluble, and a lover of peace and tranquillity too. But quails, look, live on

ecce coturnices inter sua proelia uiuunt,
  forsitan et fiant inde frequenter anus.
plenus eras minimo, nec prae sermonis amore
  in multos poterant ora uacare cibos;
nux erat esca tibi causaeque papauera somni,
  pellebatque sitim simplicis umor aquae.
uiuit edax uultur ducensque per aera gyros
  miluus et pluuiae graculus auctor aquae;
uiuit et armiferae cornix inuisa Mineruae,
  illa quidem saeclis uix moritura nouem.
occidit ille loquax humanae uocis imago
  psittacus, extremo munus ab orbe datum.
optima prima fere manibus rapiuntur auaris:
  implentur numeris deteriora suis;
tristia Phylacidae Thersites funera uidit
  iamque cinis uiuis fratribus Hector erat.
quid referam timidae pro te pia uota puellae,
  uota procelloso per mare rapta Noto?
septima lux uenit non exhibitura sequentem,
  et stabat uacuo iam tibi Parca colo,
nec tamen ignauo stupuerunt uerba palato;
  clamauit moriens lingua 'Corinna, uale'.
colle sub Elysio nigra nemus ilice frondet
  udaque perpetuo gramine terra uiret.
si qua fides dubiis, uolucrum locus ille piarum
  dicitur, obscenae quo prohibentur aues.
illic innocui late pascuntur olores,
  et uiuax phoenix, unica semper auis;
explicat ipsa suas ales Iunonia pinnas,
  oscula dat cupido blanda columba mari.
psittacus has inter nemorali sede receptus
  conuertit uolucres in sua uerba pias.
ossa tegit tumulus, tumulus pro corpore magnus,
  quo lapis exiguus par sibi carmen habet:
COLLIGOR EX IPSO DOMINAE PLACVISSE SEPVLCHRO.
  ORA FVERE MIHI PLVS AVE DOCTA LOQVI.

amidst their battles, and, thriving on them perhaps, often reach a ripe old age. You were satisfied with very little, and, because of your love of talking, your mouth was never free for much food (30). Nuts and soporific poppy seeds were your diet, and the moisture of plain water slaked your thirst. The greedy vulture lives on, the kite, wheeling in circles on high, and the jackdaw, herald of rain. The crow, enemy of armed Minerva, lives on (35) and, moreover, is destined to survive for at least nine generations. Dead is that famous parrot, a talking replica of the human voice, a gift from the ends of the earth. Greedy hands generally carry off the best things first: the numbers of inferior things are always at full strength (40). Thersites saw the sad obsequies of the hero from Phylace, and Hector was already ashes when his brothers were still alive.

What is the use of mentioning the pious vows made by an anxious girl on your account – vows carried away across the sea by the stormy south wind? The seventh day dawned, destined to be followed by no other (45), and now the Fate was in your case standing with distaff empty. But words still did not cease to issue from your throat, weak though it was; with a dying tongue you cried 'Farewell, Corinna'.

At the foot of a hill in Elysium a grove of black ilex grows, and the moist ground is ever lush with green grass (50). If there is any truth is myths,[1] that place is designated the good birds' home, and fowls of evil omen are excluded from it. There feed ranging flocks of harmless swans and the long-lived phoenix, the bird which is always unique; there the bird of Juno displays its plumage of its own accord (55), and the gentle dove gives kisses to her eager mate. Parrot has been welcomed to a shady perch among them and makes the good birds flock to hear his speeches.

His bones are enclosed in a tomb, a tomb of appropriate size for his body, and upon it a tiny stone bears an equally tiny inscription (60): 'My grave itself is evidence of the pleasure I gave my mistress. My voice had mastered a repertoire greater than a bird's'.[2]

---

1 See n. *ad loc.*

2 See n. *ad loc.*

DISCUSSION
Poem 6

Numerous ancient poets before Ovid had mourned pets – Hellenistic epigrammatists in witty and sentimental epitaphs (see e.g. *AP* vii. 198 (Leonidas of Tarentum on a singing locust), 203 (Simmias on a partridge), 207 (Meleager on a leveret), 211 (Tymnes on a dog)) and, most famously, Catullus (3) in his lament for Lesbia's sparrow (see further G. Herrlinger, *Totenklage um Tiere in der antiken Dichtung* (Stuttgart, 1930)). In treatment, however, Ovid's elegy owes nothing to these short pieces; it is a full-scale funeral dirge or (to use the pseudo-technical term popular with modern scholars; see p. 7) *epicedion*.

The lament for the dead had a long history in antiquity, and by the Augustan period it had become established as a poetic set-piece with a battery of stock motifs (for a very good brief discussion of all types of funeral literature, with many examples, see Nisbet-Hubbard I. 280-81, and for exhaustive treatment of the Latin poetic specimens, J. Esteve-Forriol, *Die Trauer- und Trostgedichte in der römischen Literatur untersucht nach ihrem Topik und ihrem Motivschatz* (Diss. Munich, 1962)). The stock motifs are displayed as clearly as anywhere in Ovid's own poem on the death of Tibullus (*Am.* iii. 9): address to the mourners (vv. 1-16); lament for the deceased, including (a) complaint of the inefficacy of virtue and achievement as insurances against death (21-34) and (b) protest (sometimes termed *schetliasmos*) at the injustice of death (17-20, 35-46); a death-bed scene (47-58); consolation for the bereaved in the form of a picture of the deceased's happy after-life in Elysium (59-66; the *consolatio* is itself a set-piece represented in both prose and verse); and allusion to the deceased's tomb (67-8). It will be obvious at once how closely the present poem follows this pattern, and the result is a superbly entertaining parody of the conventional funeral dirge, with all the main stock

VII

Ergo sufficiam reus in noua crimina semper?
 ut uincam, totiens dimicuisse piget.
siue ego marmorei respexi summa theatri,
 eligis e multis unde dolere uelis;
candida seu tacito uidit me femina uultu,
 in uultu tacitas arguis esse notas;
si quam laudaui, miseros petis ungue capillos:
 si culpo, crimen dissimulare putas;
siue bonus color est, in te quoque frigidus esse:
 seu malus, alterius dicor amore mori.

themes brilliantly adapted and every standard technique of elaboration suitably employed. Statius' imitation – a lament for the parrot of Atedius Melior (*Silv.* ii. 4) – is turgid and pretentious in comparison. A Christianized version is attempted by Alcuin in his mediaeval Latin lament for a nightingale (see M.I. Kim, 'A parrot and piety: Alcuin's nightingale and Ovid's *Amores* ii. 6', *Latomus* 51 (1992), 881-91).

Scholars' frequent censures of this elegy's frivolity perhaps tell us more about scholars than they do about Ovid, but I suppose one might reasonably ask why such a piece was included in a book of love-poems. My guess is that it was meant to tease. When Ovid's contemporary readers, well acquainted with Catullus' attempt to turn the traditional pet-epitaph into a love-poem, came upon an elegy beginning 'Parrot is dead' in a collection entitled *Amores,* they would almost certainly have been encouraged to expect something similar from Ovid (see further 1n.), and Ovid, I suspect, will have thought it an excellent joke to offer his public the *un*expected: an *epicedion* for a parrot, no more and no less. If he had known that a number of scholars centuries later would be postulating a variety of improbable allegories in the attempt to prove the poem a love-poem, or at least a poem about love-poetry, after all (see e.g. Lenz on vv. 59-60 and p. 19 of his edition, Jäkel 19, B. W. Boyd, 'The death of Corinna's parrot reconsidered: Poetry and Ovid's *Amores'*, *CJ* 82 (1987), 199-207), he might well have come to the conclusion that the joke was even better than he thought.

The determination to uncover an allegory persists in the late 1990s: U. Schmitzer ('Gallus im Elysium. Ein Versuch über Ovids Trauer-elegie auf den toten Papagei Corinnas (*Am.* ii. 6)', *Gymnasium* 104 (1997), 245-70) contends that the parrot is the dead poet Gallus (see p. 6), and Boyd revisits the issue in her 1997 book (170-79). The latest commentator, McKeown, however, appears to share my scepticism.

Further Reading
*L. Cahoon, 'The parrot and the poet: the function of Ovid's funeral elegies", *CJ* 80 (1984), 27-35; *id.*, '*Psittacus redux*: Boyd's bird and mine (or, some thoughts on aims and methods in literary studies), *CJ* 86 (1990-91), 368-76 (an attack on metaliterary readings of Latin poetry); *Davis (1989) 89-98; J. Ferguson, *AJPh* 81 (1960), 352-3; *K.S. Myers, 'Ovid's *tecta ars*: *Amores* ii. 6, "programmatics and the parrot" ', *EMC* n.s. 9 (1990), 367-74; Sabot 268-74; *V. Schmidt, 'Corinnas *psittacus* im Elysium', *Lampas* 18 (1985), 214-28; E. Thomas, 'A comparative analysis of Ovid, *Amores* ii. 6 and iii. 9', *Latomus* 24 (1965), 599-609.

* * *

7

So then, am I to be for ever the butt of new charges? Even though I win, it's irksome to have had to fight so often. Every time I look around at the highest tiers of the marble theatre, you select from the crowd one you wish to make a cause of grievance. Whenever some fair lady, without speaking, turns her face in my direction (5), you contend that there is an unspoken message in that face. If I praise a girl, you go for my poor hair with your nails: if I criticise one, you think I'm covering up a misdemeanour. If I look well, you say I've lost my ardour even for you, and if I look ill, that I'm dying of love for someone else

atque ego peccati uellem mihi conscius essem:
  aequo animo poenam, qui meruere, ferunt.
nunc temere insimulas credendoque omnia frustra
  ipsa uetas iram pondus habere tuam:
aspice, ut auritus miserandae sortis asellus
  assiduo domitus uerbere lentus eat.
ecce, nouum crimen: sollers ornare Cypassis
  obicitur dominae contemerasse torum.
di melius, quam me, si sit peccasse libido,
  sordida contemptae sortis amica iuuet!
quis Veneris famulae conubia liber inire
  tergaque complecti uerbere secta uelit?
adde quod ornandis illa est operosa capillis
  et tibi per doctas grata ministra manus;
scilicet ancillam, quae tam tibi fida, rogarem?
  quid, nisi ut indicio iuncta repulsa foret?
per Venerem iuro puerique uolatilis arcus
  me non admissi criminis esse reum.

VIII

Ponendis in mille modos perfecta capillis,
  comere sed solas digna Cypassi deas,
et mihi iucundo non rustica cognita furto,
  apta quidem dominae, sed magis apta mihi,
quis fuit inter nos sociati corporis index?
  sensit concubitus unde Corinna tuos?
num tamen erubui? num uerbo lapsus in ullo
  furtiuae Veneris conscia signa dedi?
quid quod, in ancilla si quis delinquere possit,
  illum contendi mente carere bona?
Thessalus ancillae facie Briseidos arsit,
  serua Mycenaeo Phoebas amata duci;
nec sum ego Tantalide maior nec maior Achille:
  quod decuit reges, cur mihi turpe putem?
ut tamen iratos in te defixit ocellos,
  uidi te totis erubuisse genis.
at quanto, si forte refers, praesentior ipse
  per Veneris feci numina magna fidem!
(tu, dea, tu iubeas animi periuria puri
  Carpathium tepidos per mare ferre Notos.)
pro quibus officiis pretium mihi dulce repende
  concubitus hodie, fusca Cypassi, tuos.

And would that I *were* conscious of some offence on my part: those who have deserved their punishment bear it philosophically. But as it is, you accuse at random, and, by jumping to all the wrong conclusions, you yourself ensure that your anger carries no weight. See how slowly moves the long-eared ass whose wretched lot it is to be subjected to continual beating.

And now, look, a new charge: Cypassis the hairdresser is accused of having polluted her mistress' bed. God forbid that, if I had the urge to be unfaithful, my fancy should be taken by a partner of such mean and lowly status! What free man would want to make love to a slave-sweetheart and to embrace a body cut by the lash? There is also the fact that she is a painstaking hairdresser and a favourite of yours because of her clever hands; of course, I *would* ask a maid who was so devoted to you, wouldn't I? What would be the point, unless I wanted to make sure of both rejection and exposure? I swear by Venus and the bow of her winged son that I am being accused of a crime I did not commit.

8

Cypassis, expert at arranging hair in a thousand styles, coiffeuse such as only goddesses deserve, you whom I have found, from indulging in love's clandestine pleasure, to be far from unsophisticated, you who suit my mistress, but suit me better still, who was it who told the tale about our sexual intimacy? From what source did Corinna come to hear of your sleeping with me?

But still, I didn't blush, did I? I didn't slip up in one word that I said and give away any guilty indications of our secret love? What of it, if I did maintain that anyone who can have an affair with a slave-girl is out of his mind? Achilles was fired with passion by the beauty of the slave-girl Briseis; the servile priestess of Apollo was loved by the general from Mycenae: I am no mightier than Agamemnon and no mightier than Achilles; why should I think degrading to me what was good enough for kings?

When she gave *you* an angry stare, though, I saw you blush all over your face. How much greater presence of mind *I* showed, on the other hand, in swearing, if you happen to remember, by the great divinity of Venus. (Bid, goddess, you bid the warm south winds carry away across the Carpathian Sea the perjuries of a pure heart.)

In return for these services, give me the sweet reward, dusky Cypassis, of

quid renuis fingisque nouos, ingrata, timores?
  unum est e dominis emeruisse satis.
quod si stulta negas, index ante acta fatebor
  et ueniam culpae proditor ipse meae,
quoque loco tecum fuerim quotiensque, Cypassi,
  narrabo dominae quotque quibusque modis.

DISCUSSION
Poems 7 and 8

Ovid's denial of infidelity with Corinna's hairdresser, Cypassis ('Mini-skirt'; see 7. 17n.), makes an excellent dramatic monologue (see p. 7) – apparently spontaneous, though in fact subtly contrived. A man who really was in Ovid's position would never think to structure his defence with all the orderliness of a court-room speech (introduction (1-2), statement of general charges (3-10), refutation of them (11-16), statement of a specific charge (17-18), refutation of that (19-26), and final plea of 'Not guilty' (27-8)). Nor would he be likely to express himself with such studied elegance (notice especially the sustained use of legal metaphors, the neat antitheses in vv. 7-8 and 9-10, the decorative illustration in 15-16 and the suave witticism in 26). And no woman in Corinna's position, of course, would be likely to listen to all this in silence (at no point is there indication of any reaction or interruption from her). But Ovid's counters to Corinna's accusations essentially ring true, and his rhetorical questions (1-2, 21-2, 25-6), ejaculation (17), deprecation (19-20) and 'cross my heart' type of oath (27-8) all help to give the impression of sincere indignation. A racy piece of writing, then, to admire and dismiss?

By no means. This poem is merely the first half of Ovid's most outrageous and celebrated dramatic diptych (see p. 30): in the very next piece, 8, we find him, in the wake of Corinna's departure, making up to none other than the lately scorned Cypassis and asking how Corinna can have discovered their affair.

This second piece is another dramatic monologue, as impressive as the first for its general air of spontaneity, and technically even better managed than 7 in that the addressee's reactions are conveyed as an integral part of it (see 9-10, 23nn.). But the poem is most memorable, of course, for its content. The reader, suspecting nothing (despite the ending of 7 with a 'lover's oath', which may with hindsight look to be a pointer to the disingenuousness of that piece; see 8. 17-20n., and for suggestions of further 'give-aways' in 7 see S. Mills, 'Ovid's donkey act', *CJ* 73 (1978), 343-6, C.F. Ahern, 'Ovid, *Amores* 2. 7. 27-8', *CJ* 82 (1983), 608-9) is shocked to discover (i) that all the weary self-righteousness and apparently unshakeable logic of 7 were pure humbug; (ii) that the wretched Cypassis was actually present throughout the previous 'scene' and heard Ovid's insulting remarks; (iii) that Ovid's oath to Corinna (7. 27-8) was a carefully calculated bit of perjury (cf. 8. 17-20); (iv) that the purpose of his talking to Cypassis now is not to comfort her or generally conciliate her, but to seduce her afresh; and (v) that he has no qualms about using moral blackmail to gain his ends your company in bed today. Why are you making gestures of refusal and inventing new fears, you ungrateful girl? It is enough if you oblige *one* of your masters. But if you stupidly refuse, I shall turn informer and confess what happened earlier (**25**), betraying my own guilt. And I shall tell the mistress, Cypassis, where I had you and how often, and in how many and what kinds of ways.

(some would add the revelation of Cypassis' skin-colour in 22 to the list of shocks, but I doubt if it was intended to be one; see n. *ad loc.*). This use of the second of two consecutive elegies to show up the first in an entirely new light is unique, and 7 and 8 together display with unparalleled clarity the attitude to love which is so characteristic of Ovid in the *Amores:* hard-bitten, unromantic and flippant.

The implications of erotic liaisons between the free and the servile interested both poets and prose-writers of varying kinds throughout antiquity (for examples and discussion see Nisbet-Hubbard II. 67-8). Propertius in iii. 15, like Ovid in 7 here, offers a reply to a mistress who has accused him of making love to a slave-girl (probably to be thought of as her personal maid), and this poem could have encouraged Ovid to take up the theme – as a dramatic monologue it is dull, obscure and over-literary, and Ovid doubtless knew he could do better. It seems likely, however, that both Ovid and Propertius were most directly inspired by comedy and/or mime: a triangular situation involving lover, mistress and slave and a confrontation arising from it were regular features of both these genres (see McKeown (1979) 78), and the swift, two-scene dramatic sequence presented by Ovid is particularly suggestive of mimic influence (an altogether more important one in 7 and 8, I think, than that of forensic or declamatory technique, on which some scholars lay heavy emphasis). Ovid later returns to the material he explores in this diptych: at *Ars* i. 375-98, discussing academically whether or not it is advisable for a lover to seduce his beloved's maid, he concludes that, whilst it can be very risky indeed, a man can just about get away with it, provided he goes all the way, for this will ensure that the maid cannot inform on him without exposing her own guilt. That is theory: this is practice.

Long-winded analyses do 7 and 8 no service; these poems speak for themselves through their dramatic immediacy, sparkling wit and 'sheer breath-taking impudence' (Wilkinson (1955) 67).

Further reading:
Damon 279-80; Davis (1977) 98-107; *J. Henderson, 'Wrapping up the case; reading Ovid, *Amores* 2. 7 (+ 8), I and II' *MD* 27 (1991), 37-88, 28 (1992), 27-83 (a heavily theoretical essay on reader-response to the poems); Jäger 9-14, 118-19; *S.L. James, 'Slave-rape and female silence in Ovid's love-poetry', *Helios* 24 (1997), 60-76; Lee (1962) 158; Lyne (1980) 269-71; J. R C Martyn, *ANRW* 31. 4 (1981), 2442-9; Tremoli 33-6; *P. Watson, 'Ovid, *Amores* ii. 7 and 8: the disingenuous defence', *WS* n.s. 17 (1983), 91-103.

* * *

IX A

O numquam pro re satis indignande, Cupido,
o in corde meo desidiose puer,
quid me, qui miles numquam tua signa reliqui,
laedis, et in castris uulneror ipse meis?
cur tua fax urit, figit tuus arcus amicos?
gloria pugnantes uincere maior erat.
quid? non Haemonius, quem cuspide perculit heros
confossum medica postmodo iuuit ope?
uenator sequitur fugientia, capta relinquit,
semper et inuentis ulteriora petit.
nos tua sentimus, populus tibi deditus, arma:
pigra reluctanti cessat in hoste manus.
quid iuuat in nudis hamata retundere tela
ossibus? ossa mihi nuda reliquit amor.
tot sine amore uiri, tot sunt sine amore puellae:
hinc tibi cum magna laude triumphus eat.
Roma, nisi immensum uires promosset in orbem,
stramineis esset nunc quoque tecta casis.
fessus in acceptos miles deducitur agros,
mittitur in saltus carcere liber equus,
longaque subductam celant naualia pinum,
tutaque deposito poscitur ense rudis:
me quoque, qui totiens merui sub Amore †puellae†,
defunctum placide uiuere tempus erat.

IX B (X)

'Viue' deus 'posito' si quis mihi dicat 'amore',
deprecer: usque adeo dulce puella malum est.
cum bene pertaesum est, animoque relanguit ardor,
nescioquo miserae turbine mentis agor.
ut rapit in praeceps dominum spumantia frustra
frena retentantem durior oris equus,
ut subitus prope iam prensa tellure carinam
tangentem portus uentus in alta rapit,
sic me saepe refert incerta Cupidinis aura
notaque purpureus tela resumit Amor.
fige, puer: positis nudus tibi praebeor armis;
hic tibi sunt uires, hic tua dextra facit,

9 A

O Cupid, you who can never be reviled as much as the situation warrants,[1] O boy, loitering in my heart, why do you harm me, a soldier who has never deserted your standards, and why am I wounded in my own camp? Why does your torch burn and the shaft from your bow pierce your friends? There would have been greater glory in conquering those who put up a fight. Come now, didn't the Thessalian hero in the end give healing treatment to the man he had struck and pierced through with his spear? The hunter pursues the prey which flees and leaves aside what has been captured, ever seeking the quarry not yet run to earth. It is we, your band of devotees, who feel your weapons: you do not lift a finger against the enemy who resists. What is the point of blunting your barbed weapons on bare bones? *My* bones have been left bare by love. There are so many men without experience of love, without experience of love so many girls: let these be a source of triumph with high acclaim for you. If *Rome* had not extended her power across the wide world, she would even now be a community of thatched huts.

The weary soldier is settled in land allotted to him; the horse emancipated from the starting-stall is put out to pasture; the line of the dry dock shields the vessel winched out of the water, and the safe wooden dagger is called for when the gladiator's sword is laid down. It is time that I too, who have served in so many campaigns under Love['s command (?)[2]], bowed out and lived in peace.

9 B (10)

If a god should say to me 'Live your life without love', I should say 'Please, no!'. A girl is always such a delectable torment. Whenever I have become sick and tired, and the passion in my heart has died down, I get driven on by a kind of whirlwind within my wretched mind. Just as a horse which is too hard of mouth runs away with his rider, who uselessly pulls at the foaming reins, just as a sudden gust of wind sweeps out into the open sea the vessel coming into port when it has all but reached land, so Cupid's unpredictable breeze often carries me back, and rosy Love takes up his familiar weapons again. Shoot, boy: I present myself to you unarmed, having given up all resistance. Here you can show your strength; here your right hand is effective.

---

1 The text is uncertain; see n. *ad loc.*

2 See n. *ad loc.*

huc tamquam iussae ueniunt iam sponte sagittae;
  uix illis prae me nota pharetra sua est.
infelix tota quicumque quiescere nocte
  sustinet et somnos praemia magna uocat!
stulte, quid est somnus gelidae nisi mortis imago?
  longa quiescendi tempora fata dabunt.
me modo decipiant uoces fallacis amicae
  (sperando certe gaudia magna feram),
et modo blanditias dicat, modo iurgia nectat;
  saepe fruar domina, saepe repulsus eam.
quod dubius Mars est, per te, priuigne Cupido, est,
  et mouet exemplo uitricus arma tuo;
tu leuis es multoque tuis uentosior alis
  gaudiaque ambigua dasque negasque fide.
si tamen exaudis pulchra cum matre, Cupido,
  indeserta meo pectore regna gere;
accedant regno, nimium uaga turba, puellae;
  ambobus populis sic uenerandus eris.

DISCUSSION
Poems 9A and 9B (10)

Poem 9 in all our MSS has 54 lines, but should vv. 1-24 and 25-54, as first proposed by L. Müller (*Philologus* 11 (1856), 89-91), be regarded as separate poems? The question arises not because of the mid-way *volte-face* in itself (Ovid would not be the first to declare himself ready to renounce love and then change his mind within one and the same poem; cf. Mel. *AP* v. 178, Hor. *Carm.* iii. 26), but because of the abrupt and awkward manner of its introduction in vv. 25-6. (i) The possibility of a release from love being granted by an unspecified god follows most uneasily straight on a protest against the tyranny of Cupid and Cupid alone, and (ii) we miss badly the 'but', 'still' or 'however' which normally prefaces sudden turnabouts within single Ovidian elegies (cf. *Am.* ii. 10. 15, 11. 33). Advocates of unity find (rightly) in the 54 lines taken together an example of 'ring-composition' (for which see Nisbet-Hubbard I. 263): the end (51-4) seems intended to recall the beginning (though we cannot be sure of the exact wording of 1-2; see n. *ad loc.*), and the beginning of the second 'half' (25-6) recalls the end of the first (23-4), *uiue* in 25 picking up *uiuere* in 24. In addition, 35-8 recall 5-6 and 13-14, *fige* in 35 echoing *figit* in 5 and *nudus* in 35 echoing *nudis* and *nuda* (though the sense is different) in 13-14; in both 'halves' Ovid uses illustrations from racing (20 and 29-30) and sea-faring (21 and 31-2); and in both there is oblique mockery of the military might of Augustus (15-18 and 47-8). But there is no reason at all why Ovid should not have used this technique over a *pair* of poems, and in any case (ii) above remains a stumbling-block to unity. This, moreover, cannot be removed by the assumption of a pause after v. 24. For how long is a pause before it becomes a break?

Your arrows now make their own way in this direction, just as if they had been bidden to come; they hardly know their own quiver better than they know me.

A poor fool is every man who can bear to spend the whole night at rest and who counts sleep as a great blessing (**40**). What is sleep, you idiot, but a replica of chill death? Fate will grant plenty of time for sleeping. As for me, now let the words of an unfaithful sweetheart deceive me (from hoping, at any rate, I shall derive great pleasure), now let her murmur endearments, now let her pick a quarrel (**45**); let me often enjoy my mistress and often go away rebuffed. Mars gets his unpredictability from you, Cupid, his stepson, and he, your stepfather, wields his weapons after your example. You are fickle and much more flighty than your wings, and you are unreliable in your granting and denying of pleasure (**50**). But if you, along with your beautiful mother, Cupid, will hear my prayer, come and hold eternal sway in my heart. Let girls, those all too inconstant creatures, be included in your kingdom; and then both sexes will have to pay you homage.

On balance I favour division and for convenience refer to vv. 1-24 as 9A and vv. 25-54 as 9B. But there can be no certainty on this issue, nor does it matter for the purpose of interpretation any more than in the case of *Am.* ii. 2 and 3 (see pp. 30-31); for whether 9A and 9B appear as one poem or two, they will be judged not least on the impact they make together.

That impact is one of considerable originality. For while many an earlier erotic poet has protested at the relentless attack of the mischievous, winged boy with arrows and torch (cf. especially Prop. ii. 12, from which Ovid may have drawn some direct inspiration, Mel. *AP* v. 176-80), none has ever attempted to portray the lover's ambivalent feelings in terms of his relationship with this individual rather than with a particular beloved. Thus Cupid here brings a new detachment to what is normally a highly emotional theme; contrast e.g. Catul. 8, 76, Prop. i. 1, ii. 5 (Ovid deals directly with Cupid to similar effect in *Am.* i. 2; for his specially close and personal relationship with this god throughout his love-poetry see Donnet 277-9).

Both 9A and 9B are skilful mosaics of erotic themes, some familiar from Hellenistic epigram (see 5, 6, 9-10, 15-16, 19-24, 35, 38nn.), some originating in much earlier erotic poetry (see 26, 27-34nn.), and some perennial favourites of Ovid's own (see 39-40, 43-6nn.). But neither piece is a mere synthesis of traditional material; in particular both derive a piquancy from the novel way in which a traditional idea – the likeness of love to war – is handled within them (Spies provides a vast collection of references for amatory uses of military imagery in Greek and Latin verse). The concept of the lover as a soldier is already adumbrated in Hellenistic poetry (see P. Murgatroyd, '*Militia amoris* and the Roman Elegists', *Latomus* 34 (1975), 59-79), but it was most fully exploited by the Latin elegists, who were disinclined to the life of military service encouraged by the Augustan régime. For Tibullus and Propertius the presentation of their own life of love as itself a form of soldiering was a useful and picturesque means of asserting their independence (see R. J. Baker, '*Miles annosus*: the military motif in Propertius', *Latomus* 27 (1968), 322-49, Lyne (1980) 71-8). Ovid differs from them in using the 'warfare of love' motif not so much to make a statement of distaste for Augustan militarism as to make jokes at its expense (see especially *Am.* i. 2. and 9, ii. 12, and further Thomas (1964)). In 9A he presents Cupid as a commanding officer who assaults one of his own most loyal men; this seems an innocuous enough variation on a familiar theme (cf. Tib. ii. 6. 5-6) – until the position of the supreme commander of the forces of love begins to sound remarkably like that of the supreme commander of the Roman army: Augustus. In vv. 15-16 it is suggested that Cupid can win a 'triumph', if only he ventures to conquer further afield: Augustus was particularly proud of the number of formal triumphs accorded *him* for his military victories (see pp. 64-5), and *his* empire, as Ovid subtly reminds us in vv. 17-18 (see n.), was won by conquest abroad. In vv. 23-4 Cupid is faced with a long-serving soldier clamouring for demobilisation: Augustus throughout *his* reign had to contend with the disgruntlement of legionaries who had been kept under arms far longer than they were entitled to expect

X (XI)

Tu mihi, tu certe, memini, Graecine, negabas
  uno posse aliquem tempore amare duas.
per te ego decipior, per te deprensus inermis
  ecce duas uno tempore turpis amo.
utraque formosa est, operosae cultibus ambae,
  artibus in dubio est haec sit an illa prior;
pulchrior hac illa est, haec est quoque pulchrior illa,
  et magis haec nobis et magis illa placet.
erro uelut uentis discordibus acta phaselos,
  diuiduumque tenent alter et alter amor.
quid geminas, Erycina, meos sine fine dolores?
  non erat in curas una puella satis?
quid folia arboribus, quid pleno sidera caelo,
  in freta collectas alta quid addis aquas?
sed tamen hoc melius quam si sine amore iacerem:
  hostibus eueniat uita seuera meis;
hostibus eueniat uiduo dormire cubili
  et medio laxe ponere membra toro.
at mihi saeuus amor somnos abrumpat inertes
  simque mei lecti non ego solus onus;
me mea disperdat nullo prohibente puella
  si satis una potest, si minus una, duae.

(their discontent culminated in the mutiny of A.D. 14; see Tac. *Ann.* i. 17. 2 with Goodyear's note, Brunt 333ff.). The *Princeps* would hardly have welcomed the idea of himself as a model for the god of love (cf. *Am.* i. 2. 51-2); nor, in view of his special veneration of Mars (in 2 B.C. he was to dedicate to Mars Ultor a new temple on the Capitoline to house the Roman standards recovered from the Parthians; see further Zanker 195-201), would he have been amused by Ovid's preposterous suggestion in 47-8 that the god of war imitates the behaviour of his stepson, Cupid (a naughty *double entendre* in 48 makes the idea all the more outrageous).

This is archetypal Ovidian writing in its artistic symmetry, emotional detachment and irreverent humour.

Further reading:

*F. Cairns, 'Self-imitation within a generic framework: Ovid *Amores* ii. 9 and iii. 11 and the *renuntiatio amoris*', in *Creative Imitation and Latin Literature*, edd. A. J. Woodman and D. A. West (Cambridge, 1979), 121-41; Damon 274-6, 285-8; *Giangrande 41-51; *Jäger 148-53 (with a substantial bibliography of support for division at 148-9, though he himself opposes it); Keul 195-211; *Lörcher 14-25; Morgan 30-31, 37-8, 82-3; Neumann 34-7.

* * *

10 (11)

It was you, Graecinus, yes, you, I remember, who used to tell me that it was impossible for anyone to be in love with two women at one time. Through you I have been misled, through you I have been caught off guard, for look, here I am, to my shame in love at one time with two women. Both of them are beautiful, attentive to grooming both; it's a moot point whether this one or that is the more artistically accomplished. That one is prettier than this, and yet this one is prettier than that; this one appeals to me more, and yet more appeals the other. I go to and fro like a little boat buffeted by battling winds, and I am torn in two by a twin passion. Lady of Eryx, why do you double my endless anguish? Would not one girl have brought cares enough? Why do you add leaves to the trees, why stars to the crowded sky, why masses of water to the open sea?

But still, this is better than lying without love; may the life of chastity befall my enemies. May it befall my enemies to sleep in a companionless bed and lie with limbs relaxed in the middle of the couch. But in my case, let savage love put an end to indolent slumbers, and let me not be the only burden to my bed; let no one stop my girl-friend from being the ruin of me – one girl-friend, if one is enough, and if not one, then two.

sufficiam: graciles, non sunt sine uiribus artus;
  pondere, non neruis, corpora nostra carent.
et lateri dabit in uires alimenta uoluptas:
  decepta est opera nulla puella mea.
saepe ego lasciue consumpsi tempora noctis,
  utilis et forti corpore mane fui.
felix quem Veneris certamina mutua perdunt;
  di faciant leti causa sit ista mei!
induat aduersis contraria pectora telis
  miles et aeternum sanguine nomen emat;
quaerat auarus opes, et quae lassarit arando,
  aequora periuro naufragus ore bibat;
at mihi contingat Veneris languescere motu,
  cum moriar, medium soluar et inter opus;
atque aliquis nostro lacrimans in funere dicat
  'conueniens uitae mors fuit ista tuae.'

DISCUSSION
Poem 10 (11)

Ovid plays Proteus here, frustrating our expectations not once but several times. His opening couplet, with its personal addressee and theme of simultaneous love for two different women, most obviously recalls Prop. ii. 22. But before anyone can cry '*déjà vu*', he establishes a contrast with that poem: whereas Propertius presents attraction to two women at once as an acceptable, even desirable, state of affairs (ii. 22. 35-42), Ovid presents it as a catastrophe (3-10). He makes no attempt, however, at emotional realism, discussing his supposed dilemma with the verbal acrobatics so typical of him and with the easy detachment of the Hellenistic epigrammatists who also handle the theme (e.g. Polystr. *AP* xii. 91, Phld. *AP* xii. 173, Anon. *AP* xii. 88, 89 – the motif reappears in later Greek literature; see e.g. Aristaenet. ii. 11). This encourages the reader to expect a continuing dilation on the initial statement (cf. *Am*. i. 9). But it only leads to an airing of the ancient erotic commonplace that the life of love is preferable to any other (see 15-22n.), and this in turn leads to a favourable reassessment of amatory involvement with two women at once (22). Contact again, then, with Prop. ii. 22, and when Ovid goes on to boast of his physical fitness for love (23-4), we might imagine that it is after all his intention to assemble to left-overs of that Propertian poem, when

I shall be up to it. My limbs may be slender, but they are not without strength. My body lacks weight, not muscle. Pleasure is a food which will strengthen my loins (**25**); no girl has ever been disappointed by my performance. Often I have spent the hours of night in wanton fashion and been fit and in fine fettle the morning after. Blessed is he whose death results from Venus' contests for two; you gods, let that be the cause of *my* demise (**30**)! Let the soldier run his breast on to the enemy's weapons and buy eternal fame with blood; let the miser seek wealth, and the shipwrecked sailor drink with perfidious lips the water of the deep which he has tired out with his ploughing back and forth. But let it be *my* good fortune to fade away in the activity of Venus (**5**), and when I die, let me be taken in mid-performance. And let someone weeping at my funeral say 'That death of yours was in keeping with your life'.

material for *Am.* ii. 4 has already been extracted (see p. 34). But once more Ovid deftly proceeds to establish a contrast: whereas Propertius merely maintains that a hectic sex-life does not impair his virility (ii. 22. 21-34), Ovid boldly claims that it positively increases his (25-8; the impotence he grieves over in *Am.* iii. 7 looks rather like nemesis for the cockiness of v. 26). Now at last, however, the series of unexpected modulations has ended, and the poem has reached its home key. The rest is characterised by an unrestrained delight in the mischievous and the *risqué*, displayed in an accumulation of erotic euphemisms and *double entendres* (see 24, 25, 26, 28, 29, 35, 36nn.) and in Ovid's final wish to die making love rather than making war or making money (29-38).

Those who look for romance in love-poetry will find nothing here – no real anguish, no real affection and no believable beloved. What they will find instead is something arguably more modern: a witty and entertaining celebration of the joy of sex.

Further reading:

J. Booth and A. C. F. Verity, *G & R* n.s. 25 (1978), 125-40; Boyd 38-40; Jäger 154-6; *Keith 36-7; Kennedy 60; Labate 315-21; Morgan 50-51, 54-6; Neumann 79-85; Sabot 414-17; Tremoli 46-8.

* * *

XI (XII)

Prima malas docuit mirantibus aequoris undis
  Peliaco pinus uertice caesa uias,
quae concurrentis inter temeraria cautes
  conspicuam fuluo uellere uexit ouem.
o utinam, ne quis remo freta longa moueret,
  Argo funestas pressa bibisset aquas!
ecce, fugit notumque torum sociosque Penates
  fallacisque uias ire Corinna parat.
quam tibi, me miserum, Zephyros Eurosque timebo
  et gelidum Borean egelidumque Notum!
non illic urbes, non tu mirabere siluas:
  una est iniusti caerula forma maris;
nec medius tenuis conchas pictosque lapillos
  pontus habet: bibuli litoris illa mora est.
litora marmoreis pedibus signate, puellae
  (hactenus est tutum, cetera caeca uia est),
et uobis alii uentorum proelia narrent,
  quas Scylla infestet quasue Charybdis aquas,
et quibus emineant uiolenta Ceraunia saxis,
  quo lateant Syrtes magna minorque sinu.
haec alii referant; at uos, quod quisque loquetur,
  credite: credenti nulla procella nocet.
sero respicitur tellus, ubi fune soluto
  currit in immensum panda carina salum,
nauita sollicitus cum uentos horret iniquos
  et prope tam letum quam prope cernit aquam.
quod si concussas Triton exasperet undas,
  quam tibi sit toto nullus in ore color!
tum generosa uoces fecundae sidera Ledae
  et 'felix' dicas 'quem sua terra tenet!'.
tutius est fouisse torum, legisse libellos,
  Threiciam digitis increpuisse lyram.
at si uana ferunt uolucres mea dicta procellae,
  aequa tamen puppi sit Galatea tuae.
uestrum crimen erit talis iactura puellae,
  Nereidesque deae Nereidumque pater.
uade memor nostri uento reditura secundo;
  impleat illa tuos fortior aura sinus.
tum mare in haec magnus proclinet litora Nereus,
  huc uenti spectent, huc agat aestus aquas.
ipsa roges Zephyri ueniant in lintea soli,
  ipsa tua moueas turgida uela manu.

11 (12)

A pine tree felled on the summit of Pelion pioneered wicked voyaging, to the wonder of ocean's waves, when it recklessly carried between the Clashing Rocks the sheep famous for its golden fleece. Would that, to deter anyone from disturbing the expanse of the deep with an oar **(5)**, the Argo had been crushed and drunk in the deadly waters! Now, look, Corinna is shunning the bed she knows and the hearth she shares and preparing to go on a treacherous voyage.

How I, poor wretch, shall dread on your account westerlies and easterlies, chilly northerlies and unchilly southerlies **(10)**! Out there you will have no cities, no woods to admire; the cruel sea has a single, dark blue face. And mid-ocean does not offer delicate shells and coloured pebbles; those distractions belong to the thirsty beach.

On the beach, girls, leave the imprint of your marble-bright feet **(15)** (so far it is safe; beyond lies a journey into the unknown). Let others describe to you the battles of the winds, what the waters blighted by Scylla and Charybdis are like, and the rocks with which the stormy Ceraunians jut forth, and the bay in which the Great and Lesser Syrtes lurk **(20)**. Let others tell you about these things; *you* just believe what they all say: one who believes is safe from every storm. It is too late to look back at the shore when the mooring-rope has been cast off and the curved hull is running towards the measureless deep, when the anxious sailor trembles at the unfavourable winds **(25)**, and sees death as close as the water.

So, if Triton should toss and ruffle the waves, how all the colour would drain from your face! Then you would invoke fertile Leda's noble stars and say 'Fortunate is he who sticks to his native earth!' **(30)**. It is safer to keep a couch warm, read little books and strum the Thracian lyre with your fingers.

But if my words are carried away by the flying breezes to be of no avail, may Galatea favour your vessel all the same. The loss of such a girl will be your fault **(35)**, Nereid goddesses and father of the Nereids. Go, remembering me, to return with a favouring wind; when that breeze fills your sails, let it be a stronger one. Let mighty Nereus at that time tilt the sea towards these shores; let the winds turn their faces in this direction; let the swell drive the waves this way **(40)**.

You yourself must pray for westerlies alone to strike your canvas; you yourself must trim the billowing sails with your own hand. I shall be the first to

primus ego aspiciam notam de litore puppim
  et dicam 'nostros aduehit illa deos!',
excipiamque umeris et multa sine ordine carpam
  oscula; pro reditu uictima uota cadet,
inque tori formam molles sternentur harenae
  et cumulus mensae quilibet esse potest.
illic apposito narrabis multa Lyaeo,
  paene sit ut mediis obruta nauis aquis,
dumque ad me properas, neque iniquae tempora noctis
  nec te praecipites extimuisse Notos.
omnia pro ueris credam, sint ficta licebit:
  cur ego non uotis blandiar ipse meis?
haec mihi quam primum caelo nitidissimus alto
  Lucifer admisso tempora portet equo.

DISCUSSION
Poem 11 (12)

11 forms with 16 a pair of related elegies about travel separating the lover from his mistress (see p. 81) and is a variation of the 'send-off poem' or *propempticon*, as modern scholars like to call it (there is some doubt whether Ovid and his contemporaries would have recognised the term). This was a popular set-piece (possibly influenced by rhetorical technique, but see p. 7), which expressed concern for a departing traveller through a range of stock motifs, e.g. condemnation of sea-faring and 'protest' (*schetliasmos*) against the traveller's journey, with reminders of its dangers and the anxiety caused to those at home, expressions of affection for the traveller and prayers for his safety (some of these motifs are inverted in Horace's maledictory 'send-off' poem, *Epod.* 10); see further 1-6, 9, 11, 19, 29, 34nn., and for the history and development of the 'send-off' piece (with further bibliography), Nisbet-Hubbard I. 40-43. At *Ecl.* 10. 46-9 Virgil has Cornelius Gallus (see p. 6) express his fears for his mistress, Lycoris, who is travelling overseas without him, and the ancient commentator Servius (on v. 46) claims that lines of Gallus himself are being used; this suggests that Gallus may have written one of the earliest love-*propemptica*. Horace's 'send-off' poem for Galatea (*Carm.* iii. 27) also constitutes a specimen of sorts, but it is not explicitly amatory, and it is largely taken up with what initially seems to be a tangential mythological narrative. Ovid's poem is most obviously reminiscent of Prop. i. 8A, i.e. i. 8. 1-26 (27-46 I regard as a separate poem (8B), which Ovid recalls more loosely in *Am.* ii. 12; see further Fedeli's introduction to Prop. i. 8).

spy the familiar vessel from the shore, and I shall say 'The gods she is carrying are mine'.[1] And I shall take you on my shoulders and snatch many a random kiss (45); the victim pledged for your return shall fall. Soft sand shall be spread out to make a couch, and any heap can serve as a table. There, over the wine, you shall tell many a tale of how your ship was all but overturned on the open sea (50) and say that you feared neither the hostile hours of darkness nor the rushing south winds, whilst ever you were hurrying home to me. I shall believe it all to be true, invented though it may be: why should I not delude myself with wishful thinking? May Lucifer, the brightest star in the lofty heavens (55), give his horse his head and bring me this day as early as he can.

Like Propertius, Ovid begins with a protest against his mistress' proposed sea-voyage and then, just over half-way through the poem, abruptly switches to prayers for her safety; this turnabout is introduced in v. 34 with words which closely echo Propertius' announcement of a similar turnabout at i. 8A. 18 (*sit Galatea tuae non aliena uiae*, 'May Galatea not be ill-disposed to your journey').

Yet Ovid's piece is full of contrasts with Propertius'. Propertius tells us (i. 8A. 1-4) where his mistress is going and why (to Illyria to be with a rival admirer): Ovid tells us neither. Propertius thinks throughout only of Cynthia going away: Ovid envisages Corinna coming back, concentrating his sudden goodwill on her *homeward* journey (37-42) and indulging in a fantasy about her return (43-52). This includes some of the stock motifs of another well-established set-piece, the 'welcome home' poem, e.g. the special status of the welcomer, a show of affection for the returning traveller, sacrifice in fulfilment of vows, a celebratory feast, and traveller's tales (see further 43, 45, 46, 47-9, 49-52nn., Cairns 21-3, Nisbet-Hubbard II. 107). Propertius' poem is a simple dramatic monologue which leaves his change of mood – from indignation to resignation – unaccounted for: Ovid's is a complex soliloquy (it accommodates a long direct address to Corinna (9-52) and, within that, an aside to 'girls' in general (15-26)) which allows *his* change of mood – from indignation to cheerfulness – to result, apparently naturally, from his own musings (cf. *Am.* ii. 5). Arguably, then, even though Ovid sacrifices the realism of Propertius' precise setting, he marries content and structure more successfully. But Propertius all the time is serious, and Ovid is not.

---

[1] See n. *ad loc.*

There are early indications of the tongue-in-cheek approach: vv. 1-7, with their grandiloquent diction and tragic/epic associations (see nn. *ad loc.*), make a ludicrously pompous prelude to the announcement that an elegiac girl-friend is planning to go on a journey (8; the postponement of the proper name intensifies the bathos), and in v. 10 a flash of precious wit undermines any suggestion of real emotional involvement. Then, so fatuous and patronising are Ovid's arguments against girls venturing upon the sea (11-14, 21-2, 31-2) that they beg to be recognised as teasing disparagement of the tastes and intellect of women (for a different view see Quinn 269, Lee (1962) 168). In the second half of the poem we could well at first believe Ovid to have abandoned teasing for genuine romantic tenderness; but more flamboyant wit (36), together with faint, incongruous reminiscences of scenes in Virgil's *Aeneid* (see 45, 47-9nn.), begin to sabotage that impression, and Ovid's subsequent declaration that he will still enjoy hearing Corinna claim to have been sustained by her love for him, even though he knows she may well be lying (53-4), finally destroys it (we notice, too, that Ovid,

XII (XIII)

Ite triumphales circum mea tempora laurus!
  uicimus: in nostro est ecce Corinna sinu,
quam uir, quam custos, quam ianua firma (tot hostes!)
  seruabant, ne qua posset ab arte capi.
haec est praecipuo uictoria digna triumpho
  in qua, quaecumque est, sanguine praeda caret.
non humiles muri, non paruis oppida fossis
  cincta, sed est ductu capta puella meo.
Pergama cum caderent bello superata bilustri,
  ex tot in Atridis pars quota laudis erat?
at mea seposita est et ab omni milite dissors
  gloria, nec titulum muneris alter habet:
me duce ad hanc uoti finem, me milite ueni;
  ipse eques, ipse pedes, signifer ipse fui.
nec casum fortuna meis immiscuit actis:
  huc ades, o cura parte triumphe mea.
nec belli est noua causa mei: nisi rapta fuisset
  Tyndaris, Europae pax Asiaeque foret;
femina siluestris Lapithas populumque biformem
  turpiter apposito uertit in arma mero;
femina Troianos iterum noua bella mouere
  impulit in regno, iuste Latine, tuo;

unlike Propertius at i. 8A. 21-6, at no point promises absolute faithfulness on *his* part during his mistress' absence). After this, the prayer for swift reunion, which impudently echoes the sentimental Tibullus, is a hollow formality (see 55-6n. and p. 9).

This is a burlesque *propempticon*, playfully inconstant in tone and marked by Ovid's usual pragmatic attitude to infidelity (cf. p. 9) instead of the extremes of jealousy and devotion which characterise the Propertian counterpart.

Further reading:

A. Bobrowski, 'The *propemptikon* in the Augustan poetry (Horace, *Od.* iii. 27, Prop. i. 8, Ovid, *Am.* ii. 11): a comparative study', *Eos* 97 (1991), 203-15; Boyd 20-30; Bürger 12-14; *Cairns 37-8; Davis (1981) 2496-8; W. Görler, 'Ovid's Propemptikon (*Am.* ii. 11)', *Hermes* 93 (1965). 338-47; *Greene 95-9; Jäger 120-24; *W Kühn, 'Die Meerfahrt der Corinna (*Am.* ii. 11)' in *Festschr. für K. Büchner* II, ed. W. Wimmel (Wiesbaden, 1970), 151-7; Labate 32-33; Lee (1962) 164-8; Morgan 75-7; Quinn 266-73; Neumann 93-100; Stirrup; Wilkinson (1955) 21-3.

* * *

12 (13)

Encircle my temples, triumphal laurel! I have won a victory: look now, Corinna is in my arms – Corinna, who was guarded by her husband,[1] by a chaperon and by a stout door (so many enemies!) to make sure that she could not be captured by any ruse. Worthy of a special triumph is this victory (**5**) in which, no matter what else, the booty is unsullied by blood. My generalship has resulted in the capture not of paltry walls, not of fortifications surrounded by little ditches, but of a girl! When Pergamum fell, overcome by ten years of war, how much of the credit belonged to the sons of Atreus among so many campaigners (**10**)? *My* glory, on the other hand, is exclusive to me and unshared by any ranker; no one else is entitled to the reward. Playing officer myself and playing ranker too, I have now reached my goal; I was my own cavalry, my own infantry and my own standard-bearer. And Fortune did not make luck play a part in my achievements either (**15**): come hither, triumph won by my own efforts. Nor is the cause of my war a new one: if the daughter of Tyndareus had not been carried off, Europe and Asia would have stayed at peace. A woman drove the forest-dwelling Lapiths and the twin-bodied race to an unseemly brawl when the wine had been served (**20**); a woman it was, again, who caused the Trojans to wage war anew in your kingdom, just Latinus; women, when our city was still

---

[1] See p. 6.

femina Romanis etiamnunc Vrbe recenti
  immisit soceros armaque saeua dedit.
uidi ego pro niuea pugnantes coniuge tauros:
  spectatrix animos ipsa iuuenca dabat.
me quoque, qui multos, sed me sine caede, Cupido
  iussit militiae signa mouere suae.

DISCUSSION
Poem 12 (13)

Like Propertius (i. 8B), Ovid follows his love-*propempticon* (see pp. 60-63) with a piece celebrating his success with his mistress, and the exuberant *uicimus* ('I've won a victory!') in v. 2 echoes Propertius exactly (i. 8B. 27). But despite the obvious influence of the Propertian sequence, it is clear from v. 3 (see n. *ad loc.*) that Ovid's poem celebrates a successful assignation, and not, like Prop. i. 8B, the beloved's decision to forego the voyage deprecated in the preceding piece.

The theme of successful love-making finds substantial earlier treatment only in *Am.* i. 5 and Prop. ii. 14 and 15. *Am.* i. 5. depicts Corinna willingly seduced in a siesta-time assignation, and Propertius in both his poems celebrates a single night's sexual conquest of his beloved, luxuriating in the memory of bliss, while fearing the impermanence of his ascendancy. Ovid here, however, regards his victory as one over his mistress' 'protectors' (v. 3) rather than his mistress herself; Corinna has been removed from the front line and with her all trace of passion, romance and pathos. Nor is Ovid interested even in celebrating purely physical satisfaction (cf. *Am.* ii. 10). His preoccupation throughout is with the contemporary shock-value of claiming military status for his amatory activity.

All the military imagery so beloved of the Augustan elegists was politically sensitive (see pp. 53-4), but perhaps no single aspect of it more so than the triumph metaphor, which Ovid has already wickedly exploited at *Am.* i. 2. 23ff., and to which he resorts again in vv. 1-16 here, apparently taking up cues in Prop. ii. 14 and 15. A 'triumph' was the public honour traditionally bestowed on a spectacularly successful Roman general; he was driven through the streets of Rome to the temple of Jupiter Capitolinus in a four-horse chariot, with a procession including state officials, senators, members of his victorious army, and prestigious captives and spoils (see further C. Barini, *Triumphalia* (Turin, 1952), 13-47). Augustus himself was particularly proud of having been awarded this highest and most coveted of Roman honours three times in 29 B.C. following the victories of Dalmatia, Illyria and Actium (Aug. *Anc.* 4, Suet. *Aug.* 22; cf. Verg. *A.* viii. 714ff.). Subsequently he declined further triumphs offered by the senate (*Anc.* 4), thus making it difficult for anyone else to accept one, and eventually the young, set their fathers against their Roman husbands, arming them with cruel weapons. I have seen with my own eyes bulls fighting over a snow-white mate (25), while the heifer herself looked on and encouraged them.

Me too, like many others, Cupid has ordered to carry the standards of his warfare, but he has had me do it without shedding any blood.

distinction became offered only to members of the imperial family (the last private citizen to receive a triumph was L. Cornelius Balbus in 19 B.C.; see further Eck 138ff.). Propertius had already boldly ventured to say that the only sort of triumph he wanted was triumph in love: 'This (amatory) victory means more to me than the conquest of the Parthians; this can be my booty, my kings and my chariot' (ii. 14. 23-4); and he had claimed the life of love to be free of the slaughter concomitant with war (ii. 15. 41-6). But Ovid here outdoes him with the claim that *his* amatory victory, specifically because of its bloodlessness, actually deserves a triumph (5-6) – the very honour now no longer available even to generals. And equally impudent are his further claims (which owe nothing to Propertius) that he has won that victory single-handed (9-14) and unassisted by fortune (15-16): Augustus invariably claimed personally all the credit for the martial victories of his reign (see e.g. Aug. *Anc.* 1-3, 25-30), even though, as many doubtless knew, his military career was in fact undistinguished and much of his success was owed to luck and to M. Agrippa (see further Syme (1939) 227ff., 296ff.).

In vv. 17-26 Ovid turns, as often, to citing epic precedent for his own behaviour. Here again he takes a cue from Propertius, using the same examples of battles fought over women as Propertius uses at ii. 6. 15-22; but while Propertius sees these conflicts as resulting from male lust, Ovid attributes them (with the exception of the Trojan War in 17-18) to female provocation (see 19-26n.). Moreover, in phraseology with a distinct Virgilian ring (see 21nn.), he mischievously adds the contest for Lavinia to his list (21-2), thus reducing even Aeneas' war with the Italians, so carefully dignified by Virgil in *A.* vii-xii, to the status of an unseemly amatory squabble encouraged by the woman concerned (see further G. K. Galinsky, *Ovid's Metamorphoses. An Introduction to the Basic Aspects* (Oxford, 1975), 26-31). And Ovid's ending, though somewhat shakily engineered (see 27-8n.), is at once both bathetic and exultant: the great tradition of Menelaus, Aeneas, Romulus and the amorous bulls of exalted literary pedigree (see 25-6n.) is now being continued by Ovidius Naso – with one important difference: *there is no blood on his hands*. The implication is clear: the behaviour of soldiers of love, unlike that of soldiers proper, is in keeping with the supposedly more civilised standards of Ovid's own time. The Augustan Establishment might not have been amused.

Further reading:

Boyd 81-9; Cahoon 298; Galinsky (1969) 94-5; Neumann 102-6; E. Pianezzola, 'Il canto di trionfo nell' elegia latina. Trasposizione di un topos' in *Filologia e Forme litterarie. Studi offerti a F. Della Corte III* (Urbino, 1987), 131-42; E, Reitzenstein, *Philologus Suppl.* 29. 2 (1936), 91ff.; Thomas (1964) 161-2.

XIII (XIV)

Dum labefactat onus grauidi temeraria uentris,
  in dubio uitae lassa Corinna iacet.
illa quidem clam me tantum molita pericli
  ira digna mea, sed cadit ira metu.
sed tamen aut ex me conceperat aut ego credo:
  est mihi pro facto saepe quod esse potest.
Isi, Paraetonium genialiaque arua Canopi
  quae colis et Memphin palmiferamque Pharon
quaque celer Nilus lato delapsus in alueo
  per septem portus in maris exit aquas,
per tua sistra precor, per Anubidis ora uerendi
  (sic tua sacra pius semper Osiris amet
pigraque labatur circa donaria serpens
  et comes in pompa corniger Apis eat),
huc adhibe uultus et in una parce duobus:
  nam uitam dominae tu dabis, illa mihi.
saepe tibi sedit certis operata diebus,
  qua tingit laurus Gallica turma tuas.
tuque, laborantes utero miserata puellas
  quarum tarda latens corpora tendit onus,
lenis ades precibusque meis faue, Ilithyia:
  digna est quam iubeas muneris esse tui.
ipse ego tura dabo fumosis candidus aris,
  ipse feram ante tuos munera uota pedes;
adiciam titulum SERVATA NASO CORINNA:
  tu modo fac titulo muneribusque locum.
si tamen in tanto fas est monuisse timore,
  hac tibi sit pugna dimicuisse satis.

XIV (XV)

Quid iuuat immunes belli cessare puellas
  nec fera peltatas agmina uelle sequi,
si sine Marte suis patiuntur uulnera telis
  et caecas armant in sua fata manus?
quae prima instituit teneros conuellere fetus
  militia fuerat digna perire sua.

13 (14)

Through recklessly loosening the burden of her pregnant womb, Corinna lies exhausted, her life in the balance. For contriving such great danger without telling me, moreover, she deserves my anger, but my anger collapses through fear. All the same, she had conceived by me, or so I believe – possibility for me is often as good as fact.

Isis, you who dwell at Paraetonium and in the genial country of Canopus, at Memphis and palm-growing Pharos, and where the swift Nile, after flowing down in a broad bed, runs out through seven mouths into the waters of the sea, by your *sistra*,[1] by the head of worshipful Anubis, I beseech you (so may pious Osiris always be devoted to your rites, the serpent slide slowly round your altar, and horned Apis participate in your procession), turn your face this way, and by sparing one, spare two: for you will grant life to my mistress, and she to me. Often, in your service, she has sat on the appointed days where [the Gallic troop wets your laurel].[2]

And you, Ilithyia, who pity girls in labour when their bodies are sluggish and distended by their hidden burden, give your kindly attention, and answer my prayers: she deserves that you bid her live, by your grace. I, for my part, in shining white, shall offer incense at your smoking altars, and I shall personally lay at your feet the gifts I vowed. I shall add the inscription 'From Naso for Corinna's recovery': just make sure that you provide the occasion for the inscription and the gifts.

But if it is right to issue a warning amidst such great fear, let it be enough for you to have engaged in this battle once.

14 (15)

What is the good of girls living an easy life exempt from war and refusing to join the fierce battle-lines armed with Amazonian shields, if, without Mars, they suffer wounds from their own weapons and blindly equip their hands for self-destruction? She who first started the practice of tearing out the tender foetus should have perished as a result of her own bout of action. It will be to prevent

---

[1] See n. *ad loc.*

[2] The text is probably corrupt, and a section may have been lost after v. 18. See n. *ad loc.*

scilicet ut careat rugarum crimine uenter,
sternetur pugnae tristis harena tuae?
si mos antiquis placuisset matribus idem,
gens hominum uitio deperitura fuit,
quique iterum iaceret, generis primordia nostri,
in uacuo, lapides, orbe parandus erat.
quis Priami fregisset opes, si numen aquarum
iusta recusasset pondera ferre Thetis?
Ilia si tumido geminos in uentre necasset,
casurus dominae conditor Vrbis erat;
si Venus Aenean grauida temerasset in aluo,
Caesaribus tellus orba futura fuit.
tu quoque, cum posses nasci formosa, perisses,
temptasset, quod tu, si tua mater opus;
ipse ego, cum fuerim melius periturus amando,
uidissem nullos matre necante dies.
quid plenam fraudas uitem crescentibus uuis
pomaque crudeli uellis acerba manu?
sponte fluant matura sua; sine crescere nata:
est pretium paruae non leue uita morae.
uestra quid effoditis subiectis uiscera telis
et nondum natis dira uenena datis?
Colchida respersam puerorum sanguine culpant,
aque sua caesum matre queruntur Ityn:
utraque saeua parens, sed tristibus utraque causis
iactura socii sanguinis ulta uirum.
dicite, quis Tereus, quis uos irritet Iason
figere sollicita corpora uestra manu?
hoc neque in Armeniis tigres fecere latebris,
perdere nec fetus ausa leaena suos.
at tenerae faciunt, sed non impune, puellae:
saepe, suos utero quae necat, ipsa perit.
ipsa perit ferturque rogo resoluta capillos,
et clamant 'merito' qui modo cumque uident.
ista sed aetherias uanescant dicta per auras,
et sint ominibus pondera nulla meis.
di, faciles peccasse semel concedite tuto;
et satis est: poenam culpa secunda ferat.

your stomach from becoming disfigured by wrinkles, I suppose, that the grim sand is strewn for your personal battle? If the mothers of ancient times had seen fit to behave in the same way, the human race would have died out altogether through their wrong-doing, and someone would have had to be found to throw stones again –the seeds of our species – in an empty world.

Who would have crushed the might of Priam, if Thetis, divinity of the waters, had refused to bear her rightful burden? If Ilia had killed the twins in her swollen belly, the founder of our mistress-city would have died. If Venus had violated Aeneas in her pregnant womb, the world would have been bereft of Caesars. You too would have perished, when you could have been born a beauty, if your own mother had attempted the deed that you have. I myself, when it may be my destiny to die more agreeably of love, would never have seen the light of day, if my mother had killed me.

Why rob a laden vine of its grapes when they are swelling and with a cruel hand pick fruit when it is sour? Let things come forth of their own accord when they are ready; allow things which have germinated to grow: no small reward for a little patience is life. Why do you women gouge out your flesh and blood with weapons introduced from below and administer deadly poisons to your unborn children? People condemn the Colchian, spattered with the blood of her sons, and they lament for Itys, butchered by his own mother: each of those parents was cruel, but each had grievous cause to wreak vengeance on her husband by the sacrifice of their common blood. Tell me, what Tereus, what Jason provokes you to pierce your own bodies with a distressed hand? Tigresses in their Armenian lairs do not do this, nor does a lioness dare to do away with her own cubs. And yet 'gentle' girls do it – but not with impunity: often she who kills her own children in the womb dies herself. She dies herself and is carried out to the pyre with her hair undone, and all who see her cry 'It serves her right'.

But let these words of mine melt away into the airy breezes, and let my ominous utterances carry no weight. Gods, be lenient and allow her to have sinned once safely. And that is enough: let a second offence bring punishment.

DISCUSSION
Poems 13 (14) and 14 (15)

In 13 Corinna is at death's door after an attempt at abortion and Ovid, who assumes the child was his, desperately prays for her survival – too afraid, he says (13. 3-4), to be angry, as she deserves. Though the specific situation is startlingly new to personal love-poetry, the broader theme of the lover's concern for a sick mistress is common (cf. *Ep.* 19 (20). 129-42, 20 (21). 183-206, Tib. i. 5. 9-16, Prop. ii. 9. 25-8, [Tib.] iii. 10); it reappears in later Greek literature and may be of Hellenistic origin (see Yardley (1977) 401). 13 particularly invites comparison with Prop. ii. 28 (probably one poem, despite its abrupt transitions and changes of addressee; see M. Hubbard, *Propertius* (London, 1974), 48-58), where Propertius charts Cynthia's progress through a severe illness of unestablished cause, praying for her survival (1-4, 47-50), making vows in return for it (44-6), and identifying with her fate (41-2) in language very similar to Ovid's (see 13. 15-16n.); by the end of the poem she has recovered completely, enabling Propertius to close with a hint of humour (59-62). By contrast, Ovid's Corinna is still ill at the end of 13, and Ovid himself accordingly still fearful and subdued. But in 14 he delivers a broadside condemning her action: obviously the immediate danger, at least, is supposed to be over.

The two-scene sequence is typical of an Ovidian dramatic diptych (see p. 30), and the characteristic presence in the second poem of points of contact and contrast with the first confirms that this is how 13 and 14 are to be understood: the military imagery with which 14 begins (1-6) recalls the metaphor which which 13 ends (28); the phraseology of 14. 17 echoes that of 13. 1; the brutal expressions for abortion at 14. 5 and 27-8 contrast with the relatively euphemistic one at 13. 1; the implication that aborting mothers deserve to die at 14. 40 contrasts with the assertion that Corinna deserves to live at 13. 22; and the warning at the end of 14 reiterates more menacingly that at the end of 13 ('enough' at 14. 44 echoing 'enough' at 13. 28). In addition, the constituent elements of the two poems are nicely counterbalanced: a long prayer and two-line admonition (27-8) in 13; a long admonition and two-line prayer (43-4) in 14 (see further Jäger 25-6). The diptych is structurally slightly unusual in that its constituent pieces differ in form and length. 13 is part narrative, part prayer and part direct address to Corinna, and is best understood as Ovid's 'thinking aloud' during a bedside vigil (see 13. 5n. *conceperat)*, while 14 is a straightforward, if unrealistic, dramatic monologue (see p. 7). The very passing of the crisis might reasonably account for Ovid's looser tongue in 14 (cf. p. 30), but there is a possibility that a section of 13 has been lost; see 13. 17-18n.

Ovid obviously saw the potential of the diptych form for exploring a dimension of the 'sickness' theme untouched by Propertius (or anyone): the question of how the lover himself will behave, when his beloved is out of danger. In view of the clearly self-inflicted nature of Corinna's illness, an outburst of anger in Ovid's case seems not unreasonable, but that anger in 14 is not related to his love for Corinna: rather, he condemns abortion in general as unfeminine (14. 1-8), unpublic-spirited (in its diminution of population; 9-22), unnatural (23-36) and unsafe (37-40). Such attitudes are in themselves unlikely to have disconcerted a contemporary reader. Child-bearing was primarily what Roman *wives*, at least, were thought to be for (see Pomeroy 166), and abortion was openly condemned by conservative men as dereliction of duty to the family, by jeopardizing its survival, and to the state, by depriving it of future citizens (Cic. *Clu.* 32, Sen. *Dial.* xii. 16. 3); this attitude is reflected in the first known law on abortion, dating from the reign of Septimius Severus, which penalised not the act itself, but the infringement of the potential father's rights to legitimate heirs (*dig.* xlvii. 11. 4). Terminating anything but a very early pregnancy had long been regarded by some philosophers as an offence against Nature (see e.g. Arist. *Pol.* vii. 1335b and see further 14. 29-34n.), and the pregnant woman's death from haemorrhage, infection or poisoning by abortifacients (see further 14. 27-8n.) must indeed have been the norm. What *is* disconcerting is to find Ovid, whose far from husbandly relations with Corinna supposedly resulted in her conceiving his illegitimate child, castigating her for something tantamount to an *unwifely* attitude towards her pregnancy. Furthermore, his strongest point – the mortal danger to the woman herself – is made with more wit than emotional realism, and the others seem generally over-embellished or otherwise misjudged. In particular, one would hardly think this the time for a throw-away gibe at Augustus: note in 13-22 the cheekily climactic sequence 'no Achilles, no Romulus, no Caesars, no you and no ME', and see also 17-18n.

But I doubt if 14 is to be dismissed as an aberration or, at best, an untimely display of rhetorical virtuosity for its own sake (so e.g. Lenz, in his commentary, Jäger 23-4, Watts 100-101). Rather, I think it is intended, like the second piece of another dramatic diptych, *Am.* ii. 8, to show Ovid attempting to recover his position after a setback. Here the position can, and probably should, be understood as that in ii. 12, where Ovid boasts of his sexual victory over Corinna, achieved, unlike victories on the battlefield, without death or bloodshed. 13 subsequently reveals three blows to his ego: (i) that celebrated 'victory' has led to the shedding of blood after all – Corinna's own; (ii) 'conquest' of Corinna may not be exclusive to him (his determination in vv. 5-6 to *believe* that the child was his betrays his suspicion); and (iii) the once 'conquered' mistress did not even consult him about what she intended to do (v. 3). But 14 seems calculated to demonstrate that the Ovid we know is back in business. When he attacks the unfeminine violence of the abortionist, he boldly returns to the military imagery he used of his own masculine prowess in poem 12, implying that *his* form of 'soldiering' is harmless, but women's is lethal (see further 14. 1-6nn.): the double standard is typical of him (contrast his complaint in *Am.* ii. 5 with his 'confession' in ii. 4); typical too are his resort to moral preaching when it is strategically expedient (cf. *Am.* i. 10), and his adoption of the Augustan husband's view-point without any of his authority (cf. *Am.* ii. 5. 7-12, and see also 14. 33-4n.). Entirely in character is his taunting of his mistress with the folly of her own actions until she breaks down (as she surely must after vv. 37-40), and only then patronisingly relenting (cf. *Am.* i. 14, where almost identical treatment is meted out to a Corinna who has lost all her hair through using a dye on it). Also characteristic are the facile logic of vv. 9-22 (cf. the arguments against women travelling overseas at *Am.* ii. 11. 11-14 and 31-2, with nn. *ad loca*) and the jokes at the expense of Augustan self-aggrandizement (cf. the flippant designation of the defeated Sygambri as convenient providers of blonde wigs for victims of cosmetic disasters at *Am.* i. 14. 45-50). And wholly true to form is the chauvinistic inclusion of not just Corinna but all of womankind in Ovid's finger-wagging lecture (notice the generalising 'girls' of the opening outcry and the plural 'you' in vv. 27-34, and cf. *Am.* ii. 11. 15-22). 14 is his amusing and subtly self-mocking answer to the question of how the lover will behave when the crisis is over: just like Delia (see Tib. i. 5. 17-18) and Cynthia (see Prop. ii. 9. 23-8), he will immediately revert to normal.

If one of the the diptych's main aims is to show male superiority threatened and reasserted (and this does not exclude the possibility of standard rhetoric providing some of the material in 14; see 14. 29-30n.), it is unreliable evidence of Ovid's real view of abortion. There is no reason to credit him with moral indignation prompted by instinctive revulsion (so Due), a retreat into conservatism through shock and fear (Cahoon 301), or an anachronistically 'humanitarian' attitude (Courtney on Juv. 6. 595-7). He does not argue that the foetus itself has a sacred right to life (a later Christian concept; see Watts 98-9), and his development of the idea of abortion as killing springs from the traditional view of it as an offence against Nature (see 14. 29-34n., and cf. 14. 15n. *necasset*). But is either his choice or his treatment of the subject 'singularly tasteless' (Balsdon 192)? We may be reasonably sure that nothing at the time would have called for him to avoid it altogether out of mere delicacy, if he thought it could serve a literary purpose (he touches on it also at *Ep.* 11. 39-42 and *Fast.* i. 619-24).

XV (XVI)

Anule, formosae digitum uincture puellae,
 in quo censendum nil nisi dantis amor,
munus eas gratum; te laeta mente receptum
 protinus articulis induat illa suis;
tam bene conuenias quam mecum conuenit illi
 et digitum iusto commodus orbe teras.
felix, a domina tractaberis, anule, nostra:
 inuideo donis iam miser ipse meis.
o utinam fieri subito mea munera possem
 artibus Aeaeae Carpathiiue senis!
tunc ego, cum libeat dominae tetigisse papillas
 et laeuam tunicis inseruisse manum,
elabar digito quamuis angustus et haerens
 inque sinum mira laxus ab arte cadam.
idem ego, ut arcanas possim signare tabellas
 neue tenax ceram siccaque gemma trahat,
umida formosae tangam prius ora puellae –
 tantum ne signem scripta dolenda mihi!
si dabor ut condar loculis, exire negabo
 astringens digitos orbe minore tuos.

And the absence from the *Ars* of any advice on it or on contraception (with which it was frequently confused) does not necessarily indicate that our poems had proved offensive to Ovid's contemporary public; the reason could well be that these matters had already received exhaustive didactic treatment (see *Tr.* ii. 415 with Luck's note). Today, when abortion is no longer the taboo subject it used to be, fewer readers, perhaps, than in the past are likely to be repelled by its very presence in a collection of love-poems; but 14 at least, because of its facetious and chauvinistic treatment of what is still an emotive moral issue, remains hard to take.

Further reading:
(On the two poems) *Cahoon 299-300; *Cairns 128-9, 157; Connor 34-6; Damon 380; Davis (1977) 108-17; *id.* (1981) 2498-9; *Due; M-K. Gamel, '*Non sine caede*: abortion politics and poetics in Ovid's *Amores*', *Helios* 16 (1989), 183-206; *Gauly 41-120; Jäger 19-24; Lilja 245-7; Morgan 80-82; Neumann 54-9; Pokrowskij 396-9; *H. Walther, Zur Gedichtgrenze zwischen Ovid *Am.* ii. 13 und 14', *RhM* 129 (1986), 306-21 (an unconvincing attempt to show that 13. 27-8 belong at the beginning of 14): *Watts

(On abortion in antiquity) A. Keller, *Die Abortiva in der romische Kaiserzeit* (Stuttgart, 1988); Krenkel; E. Nardi, *Procurato Aborto nel Mondo Greco-Romano* (Milan, 1971) with S. K. Dickison's perceptive review in *Arethusa* 6 (1973), 159-66; Pomeroy 168-9; J.M. Riddle, *Contraception and Abortion from the Ancient World to the Renaissance* (Cambridge, Mass., 1992).

* * *

15 (16)

Ring, destined to encircle the finger of a beautiful girl, ring, to be valued only in terms of the giver's love, may you be a welcome gift. May she receive you with joy in her heart and immediately run you over her knuckles. May you fit her as well as she fits me (**5**) and comfortably rub her finger with your made-to-measure band. Lucky ring, you will be handled by my mistress: I, poor fellow, am now jealous of my own gift !

Oh, if only I could suddenly be turned into my present by the Aeaean witch's or the Carpathian ancient's skills (**10**)! Then, when my mistress felt the urge[1] to touch her breasts and slip her left hand inside her dress, I should slide off her finger, in spite of being a tight, close fit, and, miraculously loosened, fall into her bosom. I, that same ring, to make sure of being able to seal her secret communications (**15**) without my stone sticking, because dry, and pulling away the wax, should first touch the moist lips of my beautiful girl – only don't let me seal letters bound to grieve me! If I am going to be handed over to be put away in your jewel case, I shall refuse to come off, gripping your finger with a tighter

non ego dedecori tibi sum, mea uita, futurus,
  quodue tener digitus ferre recuset onus.
me gere, cum calidis perfundes imbribus artus,
  damnaque sub gemmam perfer euntis aquae.
sed, puto, te nuda mea membra libidine surgent,
  et peragam partes anulus ille uiri.
irrita quid uoueo? paruum, proficiscere, munus.
  illa datam tecum sentiat esse fidem.

DISCUSSION
Poem 15 (16)

Rings, often affectionately inscribed (e.g *CIL* XIII. 10024. 65 *pignus amantis*, 'a lover's token'), were popular Roman love-gifts (see *RE*, 2nd series, I. 824, Nisbet-Hubbard I. 125), and Ovid's poem, apparently intended to accompany such a gift, has the same function as the conventional inscription, beginning with the claim that the ring is a symbol of the giver's devotion (v. 2) and, fittingly, coming 'full circle' to end likewise (v. 28). The essential elements of the traditional gift-poem are all there: despatch-formula, identification of gift, giver and recipient, profession of affection for the recipient, and direct address to her (cf. *AP* v. 90, 91, 301, vi. 227, 229, 249, 250, Catul. 1; for further examples see Murgatroyd (1984) 51). But there is something else: Ovid's longing to be metamorphosed into his present. The wish for transformation into some object or entity in physical contact with a beloved is a recurrent motif in Greek epigram from Hellenistic to Hadrianic times; see e.g. Anon. *AP* v. 84 (a rose), Mel. *AP* v. 174 (sleep), Anon. *AP* v. 83 (the wind) and Strat. *AP*. xii. 208 (a book). But no Greek precedent survives for Ovid's longing to become a signet-ring. The only parallels are to be found in an Egyptian love-song of c.1300-1100 B.C. (see W. K. Simpson (ed.), *The Literature of the Ancient Egyptians* (New Haven-London, 1973), 311) and graffiti from Pompeii featuring a Latin elegiac distich of uncertain date, in which the author wishes he could be transformed into a (ring-)stone for just an hour so as to be able to 'kiss' his addressee engaged in sealing (she would lick the seal-stone first; see 17n.). There is no reason to suppose that the Pompeian distich influenced our piece (see 15-18n.), but the Egyptian poem Ovid may have known (see M. L. West, *HSPh* 73 (1969), 132).

The Greeks develop the transformation-wish motif by ever widening the range of things into which metamorphosis is desired: e.g., in addition to those mentioned above, the sky ([Pl.] *AP* vii. 669); a dolphin (Mel. *AP* xii. 52. 5-6), a thrush or a blackbird (Rhian. *AP* xii. 142. 5-6), and a bee (Theoc. *Id*. 23. 12-14), all touched by the beloved; a mirror, a cloak, water, perfume, a brassière, a pearl necklace and a sandal (all at *Anacreont*. 22. 5ff. West); and – the *pièce de résistance* – two different varieties of woodworm burrowing into a wooden picture of the beloved (Strat. *AP* xii. 190); see also *Carmina Conuiuialia* 17 and 18 Page (= *Poetae Melici Graeci* 900-901), Longus ii. 2, band (**20**). I shall never disgrace you, my darling, or become a burden which your delicate finger would refuse to bear. Wear me when you trickle warm showers over your limbs, and don't mind the damage caused by water getting under my stone. But, I think, when you are naked, my member will rise with desire (**25**), and I, the ring, will play out the part of a man.

Why do I dream of the impossible? Go, little gift; let her recognise you as a token of fidelity.

iv. 16, Nonn. *D*. 258-62, Theoph. *AP* xv. 35. Ovid, by contrast, subjects a single, unremarkable object to a uniquely detailed and imaginative treatment, expanding the simple transformation wish into a lengthy fantasy about his behaviour as a ring, which reaches a climax (spoiled by some of the proposed emendations in v. 11; see n. *ad loc.*) in his imagining his mistress' naked beauty, as she bathes, stimulating him, the ring on her finger, to a penile erection (25-6). This is more explicitly erotic than anything in the Greek treatments of the transformation-wish theme and infinitely more fantastic too: not only has the inanimate ring, in Ovid's imagination, developed a penis, but, if it is right to credit him with earlier envy of the ring's vagina-like function (see 5, 6, 7nn.), it has also, in his mind, changed sex! Timely and typical (see p. 9) is the subsequent self-deflating ending to the fantasy and the poem.

But for all its sensuality, there is an unromantic detachment about Ovid's elegy in that the beloved is unnamed and unappreciated for any personal qualities other than her sex-appeal, and Ovid offers her little but his lust in return, his professions of 'love' (v. 2) and 'fidelity' (v. 28) seeming largely formulaic (contrast Tennyson's hints of comfort and support for his beloved in *his* transformation-wish poem, *The Miller's Daughter*). Many subsequent poetic treatments of the age-old basic conceit, including the mediaeval, pseudo-Ovidian *De Pulice* ('The Flea'; see F. W. Lenz, *Maia*, n.s. 14 (1962), 299-333), show the influence of Ovid's ring-poem, though most of its English successors work through a series of desired metamorphoses in the Anacreontic fashion. One, however, outdoes even Ovid in the *risqué* ingenuity of its ending: 'Or [would I were but chang'd to] that sweet wine, which downe her throate doth trickle, / To kisse her lippes, and lye next at her hart, / Runne through her vaynes, and passe by pleasure's part' (Barnabe Barnes, Sonnet 63 from *Parthenophil and Parthenophe* (1593), ed. M. Evans (London, 1977)).[1]

Further reading:

Davis (1989) 89-98; Hiltbrunner (1970), especially 290ff.; Murgatroyd (1984); Oliver (1958); Scivoletto 34-7

[1] Mr G. A. Pursglove kindly brought this poem to my attention.

XVI (XVII)

Pars me Sulmo tenet Paeligni tertia ruris,
parua, sed irriguis ora salubris aquis.
sol licet admoto tellurem sidere findat
et micet Icarii stella proterua canis,
arua pererrantur Paeligna liquentibus undis,
et uiret in tenero fertilis herba solo.
terra ferax Cereris multoque feracior uuis,
dat quoque baciferam Pallada rarus ager,
perque resurgentes riuis labentibus herbas
gramineus madidam caespes obumbrat humum.
at meus ignis abest – uerbo peccauimus uno:
quae mouet ardores est procul; ardor adest.
non ego, si medius Polluce et Castore ponar,
in caeli sine te parte fuisse uelim.
solliciti iaceant terraque premantur iniqua
in longas orbem qui secuere uias;
aut iuuenum comites iussissent ire puellas,
si fuit in longas terra secanda uias.
tum mihi, si premerem uentosas horridus Alpes,
dummodo cum domina, molle fuisset iter.
cum domina Libycas ausim perrumpere Syrtes
et dare non aequis uela ferenda Notis;
non quae uirgineo portenta sub inguine latrant
nec timeam uestros, curua Malea, sinus
nec quae summersis ratibus saturata Charybdis
fundit et effusas ore receptat aquas.
quod si Neptuni uentosa potentia uincat
et subuenturos auferat unda deos,
tu nostris niueos umeris impone lacertos:
corpore nos facili dulce feremus onus.
saepe petens Hero iuuenis tranauerat undas;
tum quoque tranasset, sed uia caeca fuit.
at sine te, quamuis operosi uitibus agri
me teneant, quamuis amnibus arua natent
et uocet in riuos currentem rusticus undam,
frigidaque arboreas mulceat aura comas,
non ego Paelignos uideor celebrare salubres,
non ego natalem, rura paterna, locum,

16 (17)

I am detained at Sulmo, a riding[1] of the Paelignian country, a small but healthy region because of its refreshing waters. Though the sun may crack the earth, when its beam is at close range, and the savage star of the Icarian dog may blaze, the Paelignian fields are traversed by limpid streams, and there is lush green growth on the soft earth. The land is productive of Ceres[2] and much more productive still of grapes, and the odd field supports Pallas the fruit-bearer[3] too. And throughout the meadows, springing anew because of their rippling brooks, tussocky grass covers the moist ground. But my flame is absent – I have one word wrong: she who makes me burn is far away; the burning is present.

Even if I were to be put between Castor and Pollux, I should not want a share in heaven without you. Uneasily may they lie and pressed by an extra-heavy weight of earth, those who opened up the world for long journeys. Or they should have bidden girls to accompany young men on their travels, if the earth *had* to be opened up for long journeys. Then, even if I had been destined to plod over the windy Alps all a-shiver, as long as I had had my mistress at my side, the journey would have been a comfortable one for me. With my mistress at my side, I should venture to force my way through the Libyan Syrtes and expose my sails to be whipped along by unfavouring south winds; I should not fear the monsters which bark around the virgin's groin,[4] nor your gulfs, crooked Malea, nor Charybdis, who, glutted with sunken vessels, spews out water and keeps on swallowing again what she has spewed out. But if Neptune's windy power should prevail and the waves carry off the gods[5] who would help us, you put your snowy white arms over my shoulders: with agile body I shall carry the sweet burden. Often, to get to Hero, the youth had swum across the waves; and he would have swum across on *that* occasion too, but his way was unlit.[6]

Without you, however, even though I am detained amidst fields of labour-intensive vines, even though the land is bathed by rivers and the peasant directs the running water into channels, and a cool breeze fondles the trees' tresses, I seem to be residing not in the healthy Paelignian climes, not in my birthplace,

---

[1] I.e. one of three territorial divisions, as traditionally of the English county of Yorkshire.

[2] I.e. grain; see n. *ad loc.*

[3] The fruit is the olive; see n. *ad loc.*

[4] See n. *ad loc.*

[5] See n. *ad loc.*

[6] Ovid means the occasion when Leander ('the youth') was drowned because Hero's guiding lamp blew out. There may be a hidden pun here; see n. *ad loc.*

sed Scythiam Cilicasque feros uiridesque Britannos
  quaeque Prometheo saxa cruore rubent.
ulmus amat uitem, uitis non deserit ulmum:
  separor a domina cur ego saepe mea?
at mihi te comitem iuraras usque futuram
  per me perque oculos, sidera nostra, tuos.
uerba puellarum, foliis leuiora caducis,
  irrita, qua uisum est, uentus et unda ferunt.
si qua mei tamen est in te pia cura relicti,
  incipe pollicitis addere facta tuis,
paruaque quam primum rapientibus esseda mannis
  ipsa per admissas concute lora iubas.
at uos, qua ueniet, tumidi, subsidite, montes,
  et faciles curuis uallibus este, uiae.

DISCUSSION
Poem 16 (17)

'I am staying at Sulmo', says Ovid (v. 1): 'My girl-friend is staying in the country', said Tibullus (ii. 3. 1). The Tibullan echo hints at what is eventually to emerge as the main theme of Ovid's poem: his reaction to being separated from his mistress. But in Ovid's case it is he, and not she, who has decamped (for the woman's leaving cf. also Prop. i. 11, ii. 19, Verg. *Ecl.* 10. 21-3, 45-9). This situation is more reminiscent of Tibullus i. 3 and, especially, Propertius i. 17 and 18, where these poets bewail, from distant shores or on board ship, their self-imposed separation from their respective beloveds. But Ovid, far from being in danger or in any inhospitable, unfamiliar spot, is surrounded by the smiling landscape of his provincial homeland, which only *seems* inhospitable because of his mistress' absence. Moreover, he blames her for their continuing separation (for the relationship with Prop. i. 17 in particular see further Davis (1981) 2499-502). His distress in home surroundings recalls Catullus' at 68. 1-40, but Catullus' grief is the result of his brother's death, and his separation from his mistress is incidental. The qualities of Sulmo recall those of Tibur at Hor. *Carm.* i. 7. 11-21 and Tarentum at *Carm.* ii. 6. 5-24 (see further Pöschl 24-5); but while Horace extols the soothing effects of these places, Ovid complains that his mistress' absence robs Sulmo of all its attractions. Tib. ii. 3 is recalled again when Ovid professes his willingness to face various hardships in his mistress' company; but in Tibullus' case they are the hardships of farm-labour (cf. also Gallus' outlook at Verg. *Ecl.* 10. 35-6; for Gallus see p. 6) and in Ovid's the hardships of travel. Not that his readiness to face even these is unique: it is shared by Propertius at ii. 26. 29-42; see 19-20n.). Tibullus (in i. 1 and i. 5) offers precedents for oscillation between fantasy and reality, and so perhaps did Gallus (to judge from Verg. *Ecl.* 10. 35-69). In a sense, then, we have heard it all before – but never all together. The rich fabric of familiar themes, inverted, varied and interwoven my ancestral country domain, but in Scythia, or with the wild Cilicians or the green-hued Britons, or the rocks reddened with Prometheus' blood.

The elm loves the vine, the vine does not leave the elm: why am I separated from my mistress often? To think that you had sworn to me by my own person and by your eyes, my stars, that you would always be at my side! Girls' words, lighter than falling leaves, wind and wave carry away null and void, just as it suits them. But if you feel any dutiful concern for me, forsaken as I am, begin to back up your promises with action and as soon as possible, with your ponies hurtling your little carriage along, personally shake the reins about their free-flying manes. You, though, bulky mountains, sink down wherever she approaches, and in the winding valleys you be obliging, roads.

is something new. Ovid reuses some of his ideas in *Ep.* 17 (18) (Leander to Hero; see 11-12, 13-14, 31-2, 32, 47nn.), and the general situation and some motifs recur in one of Alciphron's erotic letters (iv. 18; but on this see p. 5).

In structure as well as content our poem is characterised by inversion, variation, correlation and cross-reference (the following analysis, with key elements underlined, is a modification of Pöschl's at 22-3). Ovid begins with a dilation on the pleasantness of his real surroundings (1-10); I will call it theme A. Next (11-12) comes a single, witty couplet stating his problem: his mistress' absence (B). Then (13-14) he declares by way of a mythological allusion that her absence would make pleasant, imaginary surroundings seem undesirable (C). A link-passage in 15-18, leads to a fantasy (19-32) in which his mistress' presence makes unpleasant, imaginary surroundings seem tolerable and even desirable (D); a mythological allusion closes this section (31-2). This is followed (33-40) by the assertion that the mistress' absence makes even pleasant, real surroundings seem like undesirable, imaginary ones (C varied); a mythological allusion closes this section. Then comes a single, witty couplet (41-2) restating the basic problem: the mistress' absence (B). This leads to reflection on the unpleasantness of the real situation (A varied). And finally we have a coda in which the foregoing conflict between imagination and reality, physical surroundings and emotional situation, and absence and presence – all punctuated by mythological allusion – is resolved by a simple expedient which would give Ovid the best of all worlds: his beloved must come (47-52). The poem is much more tightly structured than most of Ovid's reveries (see p. 7) and even has something of 'Chinese boxes' about it (ABCDC^{2}BA^2+ coda), with the section dealing with the mistress' magical effect on Ovid's mood and surroundings (19-32, i.e. D) centrally placed. But there is little to support the theory that *arithmetical* patterning is the *raison d'être* of the poem's structure. Lenz (1959 and 1962) has difficulty in accommodating some lines into his mathematical schema at all, and his perception of blocks of 8 or 6 lines is easily challenged.

Some would have it that the poem is distinguished by its (for Ovid) unusual intensity of feeling (see e.g. Wilhelm 139, n. 5, Lenz (1959)). But apart from those passages which celebrate the Paelignian landscape, the earnestness of the poem is questionable. It is difficult to take seriously a man who claims to be willing to face all kinds of far-flung terrors in his beloved's company, when he makes no attempt to travel even from Sulmo to (presumably) Rome to join her, but must get *her* to face a hazardous journey to join *him* in his comfortable retreat. And his silence on what they will do when she gets there – no mention of the healthy outdoor pursuits envisaged by Tibullus (ii. 3. 5-10) and Propertius (ii. 19. 17-26) – suggests that Propertius' obvious doubt about the chastity of life in the country (see ii. 19. 1-16 and 27-8) is well-founded. Even his day-dreaming has a humorous touch of expediency: rather than wallowing passively, like Propertius at ii. 26. 43-4 and 57-8, in the prospect of being shipwrecked – and even drowning – with his mistress, Ovid envisages taking smart action to save them both!

XVII (XVIII)

Si quis erit qui turpe putet seruire puellae,
  illo conuincar iudice turpis ego.
sim licet infamis, dum me moderatius urat
  quae Paphon et fluctu pulsa Cythera tenet.
atque utinam dominae miti quoque praeda fuissem,
  formosae quoniam praeda futurus eram.
dat facies animos: facie uiolenta Corinna est.
  me miserum, cur est tam bene nota sibi?
scilicet a speculi sumuntur imagine fastus,
  nec nisi compositam se prius illa uidet.
non, tibi si facies nimium dat in omnia regni –
  o facies oculos nata tenere meos! –
collatum idcirco tibi me contemnere debes:
  aptari magnis inferiora licet.
traditur et nymphe mortalis amore Calypso
  capta recusantem detinuisse uirum;
creditur aequoream Pthio Nereida regi,
  Egeriam iusto concubuisse Numae;
Volcani Venus est, quamuis incude relicta
  turpiter obliquo claudicet ille pede;
carminis hoc ipsum genus impar, sed tamen apte
  iungitur herous cum breuiore modo.

It is this poem's echoes of *Am.* ii. 11, however, which most obviously give the lie to the seriousness of its general intent. The essential situation of 11 is, of course, here reversed. Almost exactly the same hazards as Ovid mentioned to dissuade his mistress from her proposed voyage at 11. 17-20 he here (21-6) relishes the prospect of facing when he is travelling with her. At 11. 27-32 he tried to frighten her with the thought of shipwreck, while here (27-32) he sees it as an opportunity for carrying her ashore on his back – something he imagined doing only on her safe return to him at 11. 43-6. So in our poem he has evidently written himself into the part he deliberately wrote out in 11: that of the accompanying lover who would save a travelling mistress from all imaginable horrors – and enjoy it (see also 11-12, 51-2nn.).

Altogether a splendid poem in its intricate craftsmanship and subtle irony.

Further reading:

Boyd 53-66; Connor 30-31; *F. Della Corte, 'L'elegia della lontananza', *AFLNice* 50 (1985), 367-71 (an unconvincing argument that the 'mistress' in this poem is Ovid's first wife); *Lenz (1959), (1962); Pöschl; *Scivoletto 25-7; Stirrup.

* * *

17 (18)

If there is anyone who thinks it disgraceful to be a slave to a girl, I shall go down in his judgement as a disgrace. I would not mind being notorious, if only she who rules Paphos and wave-lashed Cythera burned me less fiercely. And would that I had fallen prey to a mistress who was gentle too, seeing that I was destined to fall prey to a beautiful one. Beauty engenders haughtiness: because of her beauty Corinna is cruel. Damn it, why does she know herself so well? It's from the mirror's reflection, of course, that she gets her pride, and she only looks at herself after she's been brushed and combed.

Even if beauty gives you too much power over everything – O beauty destined to hold fast my eyes! – you should not for that reason disdain me, when I am compared with you: the more lowly can be coupled with the great. The nymph Calypso, even, is reputed to have been captivated by love of a mortal and to have detained a man against his will; a Nereid of the sea, it's believed, slept with the king of Pthia, and Egeria with Numa the just; Venus belongs to Vulcan, even though, when he leaves his anvil, he limps horribly because of his twisted foot; this very type of poetry[1] displays imbalance, but nevertheless the heroic measure goes nicely with the shorter one.

[1] I.e. elegy; see n. *ad loc.*

tu quoque me, mea lux, in quaslibet accipe leges;
  te deceat medio iura dedisse foro.
non tibi crimen ero nec quo laetere remoto;
  non erit hic nobis infitiandus amor.
sunt mihi pro magno felicia carmina censu,
  et multae per me nomen habere uolunt.
noui aliquam quae se circumferat esse Corinnam:
  ut fiat, quid non illa dedisse uelit?
sed neque diuersi ripa labuntur eadem
  frigidus Eurotas populiferque Padus,
nec nisi tu nostris cantabitur ulla libellis:
  ingenio causas tu dabis una meo.

DISCUSSION
Poem 17 (18)

A familiar elegiac figure is on parade: the poet who claims to be his beloved's 'slave' (see F. O. Copley, '*Seruitium amoris* in the Roman Elegists', *TAPhA* 78 (1947), 285-300, Lilja 76-89, Lyne (1979), P. Murgatroyd, '*Seruitium amoris* and the Roman elegists', *Latomus* 40 (1981), 589-606, and, for further bibliography, Davis (1981) 2467-8, n. 15). But this is an unusually cheerful individual, who eschews the masochism of Tibullus (ii. 4. 1-6) and Propertius (ii. 13. 35-6; see further Lyne (1979) 126-9) in favour of a flippant acknowledgement of his status and a pragmatic request for easier terms of servitude (vv. 1-6). His complaint of his beloved's haughtiness because of her beauty strikes a familiar note too (see 7-9nn.), but his intimation that her selective use of the mirror makes her over-estimate herself (v. 10) suggests that he is less than conventionally cowed. And this wry humour undercuts the compliment, when he implicitly puts her on a par with four goddesses who all condescended to accept an inferior partner (15-20).

The final example supposed to justify the pairing of unequals is the conceit which characterises the elegiac couplet as a pair of unmatched lines (see 21-2n.), and this heralds the poem's metamorphosis from a dilation on the lover's servitude into a celebration of the poet's power. Mischievously Ovid begins with an apparent withdrawal of even his modest initial request for reasonable treatment, pleading for Corinna to accept him in language replete with servile imagery (see 23-4n.) which strongly recalls one of Propertius' most vivid depictions of his own subjugation (iv. 8. 71-8). He then seems to promise irreproachable behaviour (vv. 25-6), and only when he goes on to announce that his special asset is 'a wealth of poetry' (27), do we begin to suspect that the promised irreproachability could well relate not to his behaviour but only to his elegies – polished in composition and complimentary in content (see further 25-6n.); now, too, the 'public' place where Ovid conceded that Corinna could 'dictate the conditions' of his servitude (23-4) looks to be no more than the poetry he may publish

You too, my darling, take me – on whatever terms you like; it can be your privilege to lay down the conditions in the middle of the forum.[1] I will not be a discredit to you nor be someone you will be glad to be without (**25**); this will not be a love we need disown. Instead of a large fortune I have a wealth of poetry, and many women want to win a name[2] through me. I know someone who is putting it about that she is Corinna: what wouldn't she be willing to give to become her (**30**)? But neither do those separate streams the cold Eurotas and the poplar-clad Po flow in the same bed nor will any girl but you be celebrated in my little books; you alone will give my talent inspiration.

about her. And, what is more, he says menacingly, there are plenty of women eager for his services in that area (28). The 'slave' has suddenly acquired the whip-hand!

But the biggest surprise is still to come: nobody knows who 'Corinna' really is – or so it would seem, for a 'pretender' can even claim to be her (v. 29). And this, Ovid implies, is entirely to his liking (30). Whether Corinna is entirely fictitious he does not say (see further pp. 8-9), but, by promising never to celebrate anyone but this elusive figure (31-4), he as good as tells any real girl that she will never be identifiable in his poetry. This is all the more outrageous in the light of *Am.* i. 3, which we must be intended to recall here, as (a) it is the only other poem in the *Amores* pervaded by the 'slavery of love' motif; (b) its form is the same as our poem's, i.e. initial soliloquy (1-3; cf. 1-10 here) followed by a longer direct address to the beloved; and (c) the linguistic and more detailed thematic similarities between the two are too numerous to be coincidental (see 1, 3-6, 5, 14, 23, 25, 27, 28, 34nn.). In *Am.* i. 3 Ovid promises the girl who has 'made him her prey' (v. 1) exclusive love (15-16) and the celebration of her name in poetry (25-6), but, pointedly, he does not at this stage actually name her; the implication is that he will, when she has given him what he wants. Here he both hints more plainly at the seduction-value of this tactic (see 30n.) and exposes the promise of being named in his poetry for the sham that it is in view of the impossibility of identifying 'Corinna'; exclusive love is not even on offer. There, then, the romantic illusion: here, the chauvinistic reality. I am tempted to think that these two elegies could have been at some stage the opening and closing poems of a cycle; see further p. 11.

At all events, 17 must be recognised as a programmatic piece of some significance.

Further reading:
*Cahoon 301-2; Morgan 72-5; Neumann 29-30; Stroh (1971) 156ff.

[1] I.e. 'in public'; see n. *ad loc.*
[2] See n. *ad loc.*

XVIII (XIX)

Carmen ad iratum dum tu perducis Achillem
  primaque iuratis induis arma uiris,
nos, Macer, ignaua Veneris cessamus in umbra,
  et tener ausuros grandia frangit Amor.
saepe meae 'tandem' dixi 'discede' puellae:
  in gremio sedit protinus illa meo;
saepe 'pudet' dixi: lacrimis uix illa retentis
  'me miseram, iam te' dixit 'amare pudet?'
implicuitque suos circum mea colla lacertos
  et, quae me perdunt, oscula mille dedit.
uincor, et ingenium sumptis reuocatur ab armis,
  resque domi gestas et mea bella cano.
sceptra tamen sumpsi curaque tragoedia nostra
  creuit; et huic operi quamlibet aptus eram.
risit Amor pallamque meam pictosque cothurnos
  sceptraque priuata tam cito sumpta manu;
hinc quoque me dominae numen deduxit iniquae,
  deque cothurnato uate triumphat Amor.
quod licet, aut artes teneri profitemur Amoris
  (ei mihi, praeceptis urgeor ipse meis!),
aut quod Penelopes uerbis reddatur Vlixi
  scribimus et lacrimas, Phylli relicta, tuas;
quod Paris et Macareus et quod male gratus Iason
  Hippolytique parens Hippolytusque legant,
quodque tenens strictum Dido miserabilis ensem
  dicat et Aoniam Lesbis †amata† lyram.
quam cito de toto rediit meus orbe Sabinus
  scriptaque diuersis rettulit ipse locis!
candida Penelope signum cognouit Vlixis,
  legit ab Hippolyto scripta nouerca suo;
iam pius Aeneas miserae rescripsit Elissae,
  quodque legat Phyllis, si modo uiuit, adest;
tristis ad Hypsipyle ab Iasone littera uenit,
  dat uotam Phoebo Lesbis amata lyram.
nec tibi, qua tutum uati, Macer, arma canenti
  aureus in medio Marte tacetur Amor:
et Paris est illic et adultera, nobile crimen,
  et comes extincto Laodamia uiro.
si bene te noui, non bella libentius istis
  dicis, et a uestris in mea castra uenis.

18 (19)

While you take your poem down to the wrath of Achilles and invest the oath-bound men with their earliest arms,[1] I dally, Macer, in the indolent shade of Venus, and tender Love shatters my grand intentions. Often I have said to my girl-friend 'For goodness' sake, go away' (**5**): immediately she has sat in my lap. Often I have said 'I am ashamed': barely holding back her tears, she has said 'Oh poor me, ashamed of loving now, are you?' And she has twined her arms around my neck and given me a thousand kisses, which are the ruin of me (**10**). I am beaten, and my talent is recalled from the arms it took up, and I sing of exploits on the home-front and of my personal wars.

Nevertheless, I did take up the sceptre, and a tragedy grew under my nurturing care; and I was as suited as anything to this genre. Love laughed at my cloak, painted buskins (**15**) and the sceptre so easily taken up by a commoner's hand; from here too the divine power of a unsympathetic mistress has drawn me away, and Love is triumphant over the buskined bard.

Doing what is left open, I either teach the arts of tender Love (and, horrors, I am harassed by my own precepts!) (**20**), or I write what might be conveyed to Ulysses in Penelope's words and of your tears, forsaken Phyllis; what Paris and Macareus, and what ungrateful Jason, Hippolytus' father and Hippolytus might read, and what pitiable Dido, holding the unsheathed sword (**25**), might say, and what the Lesbian [? rejected (in love)], holding her Aonian lyre.[2]

How quickly my friend Sabinus has returned from his tour all round the world and himself brought back letters from scattered places! Spotless Penelope has recognised the seal of Ulysses, and the stepmother has read a letter from her Hippolytus (**30**); now dutiful Aeneas has written back to poor Elissa, and there is something for Phyllis to read, provided she is alive; a grim letter from Jason has reached Hypsipyle, and the Lesbian, accepted in love, is dedicating to Phoebus the lyre she vowed.

Nor with you, Macer, wherever you can risk it, as a bard of war (**35**), is golden Love silently passed over in the midst of Mars: both Paris and his adulteress – a famous scandal – are there, and Laodamia, companion to her husband in death. If I judge you rightly, you do not tell of wars more gladly than of these, and you are moving over from your camp into mine (**40**).

---

[1] See n. *ad loc.*

[2] The text is uncertain; see n. *ad loc.*

DISCUSSION
Poem 18 (19)

An interim report on Ovid's poetic career, addressed to his friend, the epic poet Macer. After professed attempts at both epic (5-12) and tragedy (13-18), Ovid has returned to love-elegy in the form of (probably) the *Ars Amatoria* (19-20; some have taken this couplet to refer to the *Amores* but see n. *ad loc.)* and the 'single' *Heroides,* i.e. the imaginary letters from deserted mythological heroines to their absent lovers or husbands which constitute *Ep.* 1-14. Vv. 21-6 refer to 8 of these. The surviving *Epistula Sapphus* is almost certainly not the letter from Sappho to Phaon mentioned in v. 26 (see n. *ad loc.*; to the bibliography there cited add, for further arguments against Ovidian authorship, P.E. Knox, *Ovid, Heroides. Select Epistles* (Cambridge, 1995), 12-14 and, for arguments in support of it, G. Rosati, 'Sabinus, the *Heroides* and the poet-nightingale. Some observations on the authenticity of the *Epistula Sapphus*', *CQ* n.s. 46 (1996), 207-16). Another poet-friend, Sabinus, we hear, has composed 'replies' to six epistles, including the letter from Sappho (these have been lost; the extant elegiac epistles under the name Sabinus are by an Italian humanist). Ovid was clearly tickled by the challenge (though some critics think he should not have been; see e.g. Green's note on vv. 27-34, but cf. the plausible explanation of Ovid's reaction by K. Heldmann, 'Ovids Sabinus-Gedicht (*Am.* ii. 18) und die *Epistulae Heroidum*', *Hermes* 122 (1994), 188-219), and it may well have prompted him to write his own 'replies' in future in the form of the 'double' letters, *Ep.* 15 (16) - 20 (21) (their authenticity has sometimes been doubted, as e.g. by E. Courtney, *BICS* 12 (1965), 63-6, but is now generally accepted; see V. A. Tracy, CJ 66 (1970-71), 328-30, E.J. Kenney, *Ovid, Heroides XVI–XXI* (Cambridge, 1996), 20-26). Here, within his catalogues of both his own and Sabinus' epistles, we are given a small taste of the ingenious variety Ovid brings to his actual collection: two contrasting writers are coupled in 21-2 – Penelope, who had her patience rewarded, and Phyllis, who did not; in 23-4 five recipients are listed who had their culpability in common; in 25-6 two potential suicides are linked; and in the list of Sabinus' replies, the two writers in each couplet are contrasted with each other – Penelope, Phyllis and Sappho evidently would have read something to their advantage, while Phaedra, Dido and Hypsipyle would not (see further nn. *ad loca).* The lists, however, are no reliable evidence of either the number of original letters Ovid had written by this stage or of the full complement of Sabinus' replies.

All this advertising of 'work in progress' and poems recently circulated is grafted on to a conventional programmatic (see p. 11) motif. For in vv. 5-12 Ovid reaffirms his allegiance to elegy rather than epic by way of the most frivolous of all his versions of the *recusatio* (the scenario does not quite follow the classic pattern here, but all the essential elements are present; see p. 24). These lines especially recall *Am.* ii. 1. 11-18 in that here again it is Ovid's unnamed girl-friend, and not a god, who has aborted his attempts at epic, but instead of doing so by slamming her door on him at the crucial moment, she has coquettishly sat on his knee. And his recounting of his venture into tragedy also has enough of 'the *recusatio* according to Ovid' about it – Love laughing, as at *Am.* i. 1. 3-4, the boast of the work's quality, as at *Am.* i. 1. 1-2 and ii. 1. 12, and the mistress again calling the tune – to arouse suspicion that the play had no more existence than the aborted martial epics of *Am.* i. 1. 1-2, ii. 1. 11-16 and vv. 5-12 here. But, while the claims to have attempted epic are suspect not least because no one but Ovid himself in these very stylised passages mentions any such work by him, finished or otherwise (see 1.

11-16n.), we know that he did at some stage write a tragedy, the *Medea* (now lost), which was highly regarded in antiquity (see 14n., and for Ovid's general interest in Medea see S.E. Hinds, 'Medea in Ovid: scenes from the life of an intertextual heroine', *MD* 30 (1993), 9-47); this play, substantially advanced, but temporarily interrupted, may be what he is referring to here (see 13-14n.). The unwritten rules of the *recusatio* did not demand that the grand poetry abandoned must be fictitious, but only that it must be abandoned, and then not necessarily for good.

The 'epic versus elegy' theme is used to frame the entire poem. At the beginning, closely echoing Propertius' address to the epic poet Ponticus at i. 7. 1-6 (see 1-4n.), Ovid contrasts Macer's commitment to epic, the poetry of action, with his own commitment to love-elegy, the poetry of *in*action (see 3nn.), and at the end, recalling Propertius' prediction that Ponticus will want to abandon epic for elegy when he falls in love (i. 7. 15-20; in i. 9 the prediction has come true), Ovid predicts Macer's defection to the elegiac 'camp' (military metaphors underline the opposition of love-poetry and war-poetry at both extremities of the 'frame'). But, unlike Propertius, who claims that he finds elegy indispensable for winning his difficult mistress' attention (i. 7. 4), Ovid complains that the delicious, ever-willing presence of *his* mistress is what prevents him from getting down to anything more serious. And Macer, he intimates, will turn from epic to elegy, not because of its greater usefulness, but because of its greater attractiveness (39-40). So here not only does Ovid, as always, make it clear that his continued resistance to writing in the 'higher' genres is a matter of inclination, not want of talent (cf. p. 25), but he also suggests that elegy's much-vaunted ability to perform amatory miracles is in his case redundant (see further Du Quesnay 25-7, Stroh (1971) 141-3). And if by any chance Macer had already written some elegy, but had abandoned it for epic on becoming something of an 'establishment figure' (see 3n.), Ovid's addressing to him in particular his own renewed commitment to love-poetry is nicely pointed (the other two friend-addressees in the *Amores*, Atticus in i. 9 and Graecinus in ii. 10, have a purely mechanical function).

Of all the poems in the collection, this is the only one which shows any clear indication of having been written specially for the second edition (see 19-20n.). Its penultimate rather than final placing in its book, however, is puzzling; see pp. 10-11.

Further reading:

Boyd 194-5; Davis (1981) 2477-8. n. 42; *Holzberg (1997a) 42-4, *id.*, (1997b) 12-15 (a contention that Ovid's *Medea* never existed); Morgan 14-15; Neumann 85-9; C. Neumeister, '*Mimesis* und *Imitatio* in Ovids Elegie *Am. ii.* 18', *A & A* 28 (1982), 94-102; *A. Primmer, 'Datierungs- und Entwicklungsfragen bei Vergil und Ovid', *WS* n.s. 16 (1982), 245-59; Sabot 70-79 (largely concerned with the problems of dating raised by this poem); Wimmel 305-6; *Wyke 132-3.

* * *

XIX (XX)

Si tibi non opus est seruata, stulte, puella,
  at mihi fac serues, quo magis ipse uelim.
quod licet, ingratum est; quod non licet acrius urit:
  ferreus est, si quis quod sinit alter amat.
speremus pariter, pariter metuamus amantes,
  et faciat uoto rara repulsa locum.
quo mihi fortunam, quae numquam fallere curet?
  nil ego quod nullo tempore laedat amo.
uiderat hoc in me uitium uersuta Corinna,
  quaque capi possem callida norat opem.
a, quotiens sani capitis mentita dolores
  cunctantem tardo iussit abire pede!
a, quotiens finxit culpam, quantumque licebat
  insonti, speciem praebuit esse nocens!
sic ubi uexarat tepidosque refouerat ignis,
  rursus erat uotis comis et apta meis.
quas mihi blanditias, quam dulcia uerba parabat!
  oscula, di magni, qualia quotque dabat!
tu quoque, quae nostros rapuisti nuper ocellos,
  saepe time insidias, saepe rogata nega,
et sine me ante tuos proiectum in limine postis
  longa pruinosa frigora nocte pati.
sic mihi durat amor longosque adolescit in annos;
  hoc iuuat, haec animi sunt alimenta mei.
pinguis amor nimiumque patens in taedia nobis
  uertitur et, stomacho dulcis ut esca, nocet.
si numquam Danaen habuisset aenea turris,
  non esset Danae de Ioue facta parens;
dum seruat Iuno mutatam cornibus Io
  facta est quam fuerat gratior illa Ioui.
quod licet et facile est quisquis cupit, arbore frondes
  carpat et e magno flumine potet aquam;
si qua uolet regnare diu, deludat amantem
  (ei mihi, ne monitis torquear ipse meis!)
quidlibet eueniat, nocet indulgentia nobis:
  quod sequitur fugio; quod fugit ipse sequor.
at tu, formosae nimium secure puellae,
  incipe iam prima claudere nocte forem;
incipe, quis totiens furtim tua limina pulset,
  quaerere, quid latrent nocte silente canes,
quas ferat et referat sollers ancilla tabellas,
  cur totiens uacuo secubet ipsa toro:

19 (20)

If you do not need your girl under guard for your own sake, idiot, at least see that you guard her for mine, so that I may want her the more. What is allowed is unattractive; what is not allowed burns more fiercely: made of iron is any man who loves what another man permits. Let us lovers hope and fear, fear and hope simultaneously **(5)**, and let the odd rebuff leave room for longing. What use to me would be good fortune which never bothered to deceive me? I love nothing which never gives pain.

Clever Corinna had seen this weakness in me and cunningly found out the means by which I could be ensnared **(10)**. Ah, how often she feigned an ache in a healthy head and told me to go away when I showed reluctance, dragging my feet! Ah, how often she invented a misdemeanour and put on as good an appearance of being guilty as one who was innocent could! Whenever she had tormented me in this way and rekindled my cooling flames **(15)**, she resumed being agreeable and accommodating to my desires. What blandishments, what sweet words she bestowed on me! Great gods, what quality and quantity of kisses she gave me!

You too, who have recently ravished my eyes, often be fearful of traps, often refuse my requests **(20)**, and let me, stretched out on the threshold in front of your door, suffer long spells of cold on a frosty night. Through this my love lasts and becomes established for a long span of years. This gives me pleasure, these things are food for my emotions. Love which is full of goodies and too easily accessible becomes boring to me **(25)** and is bad, like sweet food for the stomach.

If a tower of bronze had never confined Danae, Danae would not have been made a mother by Jupiter. Whilst ever Juno guarded Io, transformed by horns, the girl was rendered more attractive to Jupiter than she had been before **(30)**. Let anyone who wants what is permitted and easy pick leaves from a tree and drink water from a great river; if a woman wants her reign to last, let her trick her lover (horrors, let me not be tortured by my own advice!). At all events, indulgence is counter-productive **(35)**: what pursues I flee; what flees I myself pursue.

You, though, all too careless of a beautiful girl, now begin to lock the door at nightfall. Begin to enquire who secretly knocks at your gate so often, why the dogs bark at dead of night **(40)**, what sort of tablets they are that the resourceful maid carries to and fro, why madame so often sleeps apart in an empty

mordeat ista tuas aliquando cura medullas,
  daque locum nostris materiamque dolis.
ille potest uacuo furari litore harenas,
  uxorem stulti si quis amare potest.
iamque ego praemoneo: nisi tu seruare puellam
  incipis, incipiet desinere esse mea.
multa diuque tuli; speraui saepe futurum,
  cum bene seruasses, ut bene uerba darem.
lentus es et pateris nulli patienda marito;
  at mihi concessi finis amoris erit.
scilicet infelix numquam prohibebor adire?
  nox mihi sub nullo uindice semper erit?
nil metuam? per nulla traham suspiria somnos?
  nil facies cur te iure perisse uelim?
quid mihi cum facili, quid cum lenone marito?
  corrumpit uitio gaudia nostra suo.
quin alium, quem tanta iuuet patientia, quaeris?
  me tibi riualem si iuuat esse, ueta.

DISCUSSION
Poem 19 (20)

The lament of an *un*excluded lover (see 1. 17n.)! Here Ovid turns elegiac convention upside-down by begging the partner of a desirable girl to keep her under guard (contrast e.g. *Am.* i. 6, ii. 2 and 3, iii. 4, Tib. i. 2. 5ff., ii. 1. 75-8, and for the possible realism of this situation see p. 31) and the girl herself to lead him a dance (contrast e.g. *Am.* ii. 5, 17, iii. 2, 8, 11, Tib. i. 6. 5-10, ii. 6. 43-52, Prop. i. 1, 15), while appropriating the instructive role of the elegiac lover's usual arch-enemy, the madam (see *Am.* i. 8, Prop. iv. 5 and also pp. 6, 31-2; Ovid offers much the same advice in his 'professional' capacity at *Ars* iii. 590ff.). Admittedly, Tibullus at i. 6. 15-22 and 33-6 recommends Delia's partner to exercise surveillance, and Propertius in iii. 8 wants his mistress to make him suffer; but while Tibullus just wishes life to be made difficult for any rival, and Propertius takes his mistress' cruelty as a sign of her true love, Ovid wants trouble *because he enjoys it* – in moderation, anyway; note that he asks for only 'the odd' repulse (v. 6) and experiences a momentary pang of fear that his beloved might misinterpret his advice to 'trick' him (34; see n. *ad loc.*)! Love for him is a game; he expects to be allowed to win in the end, but here the other participants are unsportingly depriving him of the thrill of a challenge by not playing according to the rules.

bed: let that sort of worry at last gnaw your marrow, and give me opportunity and reason for intrigue. Capable of stealing sand from a deserted beach (**45**) is any man who is capable of loving the wife of a fool. I'm warning you now: unless you start to guard your girl, she will start to stop being mine. I've put up with a lot and for a long time; I've often hoped that I would be able to make a good job of deception, when you had made a good job of guarding (**50**). You show no reaction and tolerate things no husband should; but I shall call a halt to making love with permission. What? Is it to be my misfortune, never to be prevented from coming? Shall I always have my night without the prospect of anyone exacting retribution? Shall I have nothing to fear? Shall I heave no sighs in my sleep (**55**)? Will you do nothing to give me good cause to wish you dead? What do I want with an easy-going, with a pimping, husband? He ruins my pleasure with his remissness. Why don't you look for someone else who would appreciate such great tolerance? If you enjoy having *me* as your rival, ban me (**60**).

The shameless cynicism of all this is amusing enough in itself, but Ovid's demand that the girl's partner should be more vigilant gains an extra edge of humour from its contemporary setting. There is just enough ambiguity in the terms *maritus* and *uxor*, used of the man and the girl, to cover Ovid, should he so wish, against the charge of posing as an adulterer (see 46n.), but at the same time there is much to suggest that that is exactly how he wants to be seen (according to Propertius in ii. 23 and Horace at *S.* i. 2. 125-34, it is specifically affairs with *married women* which bring the dangers and difficulties Ovid delights in). Climactically he accuses the man of 'connivance' or 'pimping', a punishable offence in a husband under the *lex Iulia* of 18 B.C. (see 51, 54, 57, 2. 47-60nn.). Though this clause of the law was indeed intended to force husbands to make it harder for their wives to have lovers, it was not, needless to say, designed to protect the interests of a rake whose sex-life was being made boring by their inertia (see further Stroh (1979) 337-9).

The poem takes the form of a couple of imaginary lectures (we need not suppose either of the addressees to be present). The advice to the man (1-2, 36-60) frames that to the girl (19-22), and these two dramatic elements are linked by a pair of epigrammatic *leitmotive*: (i) the assertion that 'forbidden fruit' is more appealing (3, 31-2, 36; this is illustrated by mythological examples in 27-30), and (ii) the claim that rejection (or delusion) is the spice of love (5-8, 33; this is illustrated from personal experience in 9-18 and by a sustained metaphor in 27-30). (ii) is, as I have already intimated, a fundamentally Ovidian conception, but (i) is a traditional illustration of the lover's perversity (see 9A. 9-10n.) and offers ample scope for Ovid's sententious wit. It is also the *leitmotiv* of *Am.* iii. 4. There Ovid argues *against* keeping the girl in custody on basically the same principle as he argues for it here: i.e. if men can have her, they will not want her. But he is not being inconsistent: for in *Am.* iii. 4, with the 'husband' playing the game, he can happily revert to the lover's conventional line of attack (for related poems within the *Amores* see pp. 11-12).

As the epilogue to Book ii, our poem surprises in having no obvious programmatic (see p. 11) significance. It has, however, been thought to be a programmatic poem in disguise – a declaration of Ovid's preference for the challenging in poetry as well as in love, through echoes of some of Callimachus' most famous utterances (so D. Lateiner, 'Ovid's homage to Callimachus and Alexandrian poetic theory (*Am.* ii. 19)', *Hermes* 106 (1978), 188-96). But this is very questionable. Here I take up just two of Lateiner's main points (cf. 32n.). (i) Ovid's version of the 'forbidden fruit' theme in v. 36 would certainly have reminded his contemporary readers of Callimachus' in *Epigr.* 31 (cited at 9A. 9-10n.); but this theme is not exclusive to Callimachus, and even he uses it with reference *only* to his behaviour as a lover, and never to his literary creed. (ii) Ovid in v. 25 rejects 'rich' love, and Apollo in *Aet.* fr. 1. 23-4 instructs Callimachus to offer him 'rich' or 'fat' sacrifices, but only 'slim' poetry (cf. Verg. *Ecl.* 6. 3-5): Ovid's taste in love, then, evidently has affinities with Callimachus' in poetry, but does that necessarily indicate that when Ovid *says* 'love' he *means* 'poetry'? Some scholars insist that the Augustans were so wrapped up in Callimachus and his poetic values that any vocabulary they use which has even remote associations with him must, *regardless of context*, have some literary polemical significance (see e.g. Hinds 22-3); but I have yet to see proof of it.

In any case, more obvious reasons for Ovid's decision to end Book ii with this poem are not far to seek. Corinna has to all intents and purposes disappeared in Book iii; all mentions of her there relate to her *past* role in Ovid's life and poetry. Thus it is appropriate that the closing poem of the preceding book should 'phase her out' (the girl in it is a new one, and she is apparently not like Corinna, who is retrospectively appreciated in vv. 9-18). Secondly, the last poem of the book is linked with the first via the 'locked-out lover' theme, which featured there briefly in its conventional form (1. 17-20). And finally it may be noted that *leitmotiv* (ii) echoes the statement of Ovid's amatory outlook at *Am.* ii. 9B. 43-6, which stands almost exactly in the middle of the book.

Still, it is not certain that ii. 19 was originally intended for its present position (see p. 11).

Further reading:

Boyd 195-6; Davis (1989) 45-6; *Greene 99-108; W. G. Hardy, 'On *Amores* ii. 19 and iii. 4', *CPh* 18 (1923), 263-4; Labate 301-5; *Lee (1962) 159-60; Lyne (1980) 274-80; Morgan 35-6; Neumann 18ff.; Pokrowskij 364; Tremoli 51-3.

SIGLA

Codices in uno quoque loco laudantur:

P = Parisinus Latinus 8242 (Puteaneus), saec. ix/x
p = eiusdem manus secunda (saec. xi) uel tertia (saec. xii/xiii)
S = Sangallensis 864, saec. xi
Y = Berolinensis Hamiltonensis 471, saec. xi
y = eiusdem manus secunda (saec xi/xii) uel tertia (saec. xiii/xiv)
*Y*⁴ = G. Pontani in eodem marginalia (saec. xv)

Hic illic aduocantur:

Ab = Londiniensis Lib. Brit. Add. 21169, saec. xiii
Ac = Londiniensis Lib. Brit. Add. 11975, saec. xiii
B = Bernensis 478, saec xii/xiii
D = Diuionensis 497, saec. xiii. ex.
Ea = Coll. Etonensis 91 (Bk. 6. 18), saec. xiii
F = Francofurtanus Barth. 110, saec. xii/xiii
H = Londiniensis Lib. Brit. Add. 49368 (olim Holkhamicus 322), saec. xiii
M = Edinburg. Bibl. Nat. 18. 2. 9 (Heinsii Arondelianus), saec. xv
N = Neapolitanus Bibl. Nat. IV. F. 13 (Borb. 261), saec. xii/xiii
Ob = Oxoniensis Bibl. Bodl. Canon. class. Lat. 1, saec. xiii
Pa = Parisinus Latinus 7993, saec. xiii
Pb = Parisinus Latinus 7994, saec. xiii
Pc = Parisinus Latinus 7997, saec. xv
Pf = Parisinus Latinus 8430, saec. xiii
Ph = Parisinus Latinus 8245, saec. xiii
Q = Antuerpiensis Plant. Lat. 68, saec. xii/xiii
T = Turonensis 879, saec xiii in.
Va = Vaticanus Barb. Lat. 26, saec. xiii
Vb = Vaticanus Palat. Lat. 1655, saec. xiii
W = Perpinianensis 19, saec. xiii
X = Lipsiensis Rep. I, fol. 7, saec. xiii ex.
Z = Lentiensis 329, saec. xii/xiii

ω = codices praeter *PpSYyY*⁴ omnes uel plures
ς = eorundem aliquot uel pauci

Florilegia et excerpta

e = Escorialensis Q. I. 14, saec. xiv in.
p_1 = Parisinus Latinus 7647, saec. xii ex.
p_3 = Parisinus Latinus 17903, saec. xiii
ϕ = horum consensus

exc. Put. = excerpta Puteani } ab Heinsio laudata
exc. Scal. = excerpta Scaligeri

APPARATUS CRITICUS

INCIPIT LIBER SECVNDVS (.II. *S*) *PSY* **I 3** seueri *PSy* (*om. Y*) ω: seuerae ς **12** gygen (gi- *Y*ω) *PSY*ω: gigem ς gigan *HPa:* gigam ς: giam *Heinsii Palatinus; id cum* Gyan *exaequauisse uidetur D. Heinsius*: Gyen *Scaliger* **15** in manibus nimbos et ς: in manibus et *PY*: iuppiter in manibus et *Sy*ω: in manibusque iouem *B* **17** fulmen omisi yς: fulmen amisi *PYDN*^{2}: fulmina misi (-sit *N*) *pS*ω: fulmen abiuit *Ea* **19** tela *T*, *Itali*: uerba *PSY*ς: bella *y*ς **30** quid pro me atrides ς: quid uero atrides ς: quidue romethides (*uel* quidue rome thides *ut censet Munari) P*: quid uero methides *Y*: et quid tytides *S*: quid pro me aiaces ς: quid uero aiaces ς: quidue (-que ς) mihi aiaces *Y*^{4} ς **33** at facie (*corr. ex* -ies) *cod. Romanus Casanatensis* 3227 *teste Munari, Heinsius*: at (et *H*^{1}) facies *codd. cett.* laudata *PS*^{1} (-a *eras.*): laudate *Y*ς: ut laudata est ς: laudata est ς: laudataque *Y*^{4} ς saepe puellae *PSY*ω: semper amicae *Y*^{4} at facie tenerae laudata *edd. plerique, Heinsium secuti*: ut facies tenerae laudatast *Ehwald*

II *praecedenti continuat Y (separauit y)* SVASORIVM AD SE *P* **1** dominam seruandi *PSY*ω: dominae seruandae ς bagoe *PS*ω: bagoge *Y* (-oge *in ras. y*) ς: Bagoa *Kenney, fortasse recte* **5** misi scriptoque (missis *Y*, *corr. y*) *PSY*ς: misso scriptoque ς: misi noctemque ς **10** perisse *PSY*ς: perire ς **11** laboret *PS*ς: laborat *Y*ς: labores ς: laboras *pTZ* **18-27** *om. PSY; add. in marg. p, in ima pag. Y*^{4} **19** misisse *pTZ*: scripsisse *Y*^{4}ω **20** erit *pY*^{4}ς: eat ω **21** affectam ω: afflictam *pY*^{3}ς: effetam (-ectam *Vb*) *NVb* **22** uisat iudiciis ς: uisaque iudiciis *PaPc*: uisa et iudiciis *X*: uisat et indiciis *pY*^{4}ω: uisere; iudiciis *Heinsius* **23-4** *uix satis explicati; seclusit Kenney, nescio an recte* **25** linigeram *ed. Ald.* 1502, *exc. Put., Heinsii unus Moreti*: lanigeram *pY*^{4} *ω* niligenam *Q* Isin *Heinsius*: isim *codd.* **30** potens alii *PY*ς: potens dominae *S*ω: placet dominae ς: sordida turba iacent *PSY*ς: sordida turba iacet ς: cetera turba iacet ω: **31** finguntur *P*ς: fingentur *SyAcT*: fingantur ς: fingunt *Y* inanes *pSy*ω: honores *PYD* **37** obicies (ab- *Y*, *corr. y*) *PSY*ω: obiciens *Itali* **38** tu ueris falso *Kenney, eleganter, sed res non omnino certa est*: et ueri falso *Pc*: et ueri in falso *T*: in ueri falso *AcB*: in uerum falso (inuerum *Y*) *PY*ς: in uero falso *pS*ω: in falso uero ς: in falso ueri *EaVb*: in falso uerum *W*: i ueris falso *Heinsius*: et ueris falso *Ehwald*: in ueris falso *Magnus* **39** alta *PSY*ω: orta *D* peculia *PY*ς: pecunia *Sy*ω crescent (-ant *y*) *PSYDF*: crescet ω: crescit ς **40** fac in *PY*: face in *Va*: facis *S*ς: face, fac, face et, fac et ω **45** io ω: ion *PSY*ς **53** perdis *PSY*ω: prodis *cod. Oxon. Bodl. Auct. F.* I. 17, *teste Munari* **54** officio *PSY*ς: indicio ς **59** aspiciat *PSY*: aspiciet *py*ω

III *cum praecedenti continuat Y* (*separauit y*) *cod. Hauniensis Bibl. Reg. Ny Kgl. Saml.* 219b; *coniungendam censuerunt Scaliger, Bentleius, edd. nonnulli recc.* ad eunuchum custodem dominae *P (litt. grand.) S* **6** quauis *PYς*: quamuis *Sς* **9** tractent *PSYς*: tractant *ς* **17** aptius at fuerit *Heinsius*: aptius ut fuerit (fuerat *N*, fieret Y^4 *H*) *PSω*: aptus erait fuerit *Y* temptasse *PSYω*: temptare Y^4 *Ob* rogamus *PSYω*: rogabo Y^4

IV *praecedenti continuat Y*, separauit *y* ad se quod multas amet *P (litt. grand.) VaF* (de se) *Z* (ad se *om.*): ad se quod multas amicas <habeat> *S* **5** non esse Y^4 *ςφ*: non nosse *PSYς*: odisse *ς*: non odisse *AcVa* **9** inuitet *PSYω*: irritet *y uel* Y^4 *in marg.*, *Ea* **11** in se *ς*: in me *PSYω*: in humum *Timpanaro, olim Heinsius dubitanter* **17** es places (-ges *PY*, *corr. py*) *PSYς*: est ... placet ω **18** placita (-da *H*) es *AbH*: placita est *PaVb*: places (*eras. Y*) *PY*: placeas *pSPh*¹ (*ut Kenney uid.*): placeat *X*: capior *y* (*in ras.*) ω tua *PSYς*: sua ω: mea *D* **23** incedit ω: incessit *PSYς* **23-4** dura est ... mollior esse *codd.*: dure ... mollius isse *Heinsius* (ire *Bentleius*) **24** at *PYω*: ac *N*: sed *SObX*: et *BH* **25** huic *Heinsius*: haec *codd.* **27** habili *PSYω*: agili Y^4 **33** longa es (*non dist. Y*, *corr. y*) *PYω*: longas *S* **39** capiet *semel tantum PY* (*add. y*) **46** moribus *VbW*: corporis *PSYω* placet (*eras. Y*) *PSYω*: sapit *y* (*in ras.*) **47** probat *PSYω*: probet *ς*

V ad amicam corruptam *S* **3** pecasse *pSYω*: peccare *P* **4** o *Q*, *Itali*: ei *PSYω*: in *Ker* **5** mihi deceptae *PSYω*: mihi decepto *ς*: mihi delatae *H*: mihi deletae *Heinsii optimus Palatinus* (*Vat. Pal. Lat.* 910): male deletae *uel* interceptae *uel* mi interceptae *Heinsius; alii alia* **27** Phoebo ... Dianam *Bentleius*: phoebum ... dianae *codd.* **29** defers *ς*, *exc. Scal.*: differs *PSYω* **34** pudor *PSYω*: rubor Y^4 **41** his *PSYω*: is *ς*: hic *ς* alicui *FPbPc*² (*in ras.*): aliqui *PYAc*: aliquis *Syω* **42** casu *codd.*: uisu *Housman* **51** optima *PYς*: oscula *Sω* **53** senserit *PSyω*: senserat *Y*: sumpserit *Pc*, *exc. Put.*, *Scal.* **61** nusquam *PSYς*: numquam ω

VI psitaci alitis epitaphium *P* (*ut Kenney uid.; litt. grand.*) *SD* (e. p. a.) **1** imitatrix ales *PSς*: ales mihi missus ω: ales transmissus *y* (*in ras., de Y incert.*) *ς* ab indis *PSYς*: ab undis *N*² (*ex* oris) *Ob*: ab oris *ς* **2** ite *PSY*: ferte Y^4ω **6** uestra *PSYω*: nostra *M*, *Heinsii unus Mediceus* **7** quod *PSNW*¹ (*ut Kenney uid.*): quid *Yω* **8** annis *yω*: animis *PSYς*: numeris *Bentleius* suis *ς*: tuis *PSYς* **9** deuertere *Heinsius*: deuertite (-ice *Y*) *PYς*: diuertite *Sς* **11** libratis *P* (*ut Kenney uid.*) *SYς*: uibratis *ς* cursus *PSω*: pennas (-is *Y*, -as *y*) *Yς* **12** alios *PSYς*: alias *ς* **15** orestae *PYN*: oresti *Sω* **21** fragiles *PSYω*: uirides *N* **25-32** *uersuum ordo uarie temptatus, sed frustra* **27** sua *PSYω*: fera *ς* **28** fiant *PY*: fiunt ω: fient *Sς* **30** poterant *Syς*: poteras *PYς* **33** ducensque *DF*, *Itali*: ducitque *PSYω* **34** miluus (miluius *yς*) et *PYς*: miluus et est (et in *H*) *SAcHNVa* graculus (grag- *PY*, *corr. y*) *PYς*: garrulus *Sς* **37** ille *ς*: illa *PSYω* **39** manibus *om. S*, *habent PYω*: Parcis *Müller*: auaris *PSYω*: amaris *cod. Vat. Lat.* 1602, *teste Munari*: Auernis *Heinsius*: ab atris *Baehrens* **46** uacuo *PSYς*: uacua ω **55** ipsa suas ales (ales *om. S*) *PSyς*: uasales ipsas *Y*: atque suas ales *ς*

VII AD AMOREM ANCILLE PELICES *P*: ad amorem ancile pelicis uel excusatio ancille *Z* **1** ergo *PSYς*: ergo ego *yω* **7** miseros *yω*: misero *PSY* **8** culpo *yω*: cui pro *PY*: cui do *Sς* **11** essem *PSYς*: esse ω **17** nouum crimen sollers ornare *PSYς*: tuum sollers caput exornare *ς* **19** si sit *Itali, Naugerius*: sic sit *PSYω* peccasse *PSYω*: peccare *ς* **23** ornandis ω: ornatis *PSYς* operosa ω: operata *PSYN* **24** per doctas ω: perdocta est *PSY*, *unde* perdocta ... manu *Heinsius; alii alia* **25** quae tam ω: quae sit *BEa*: quierat (qui erat *Y*) *PY*, *unde* quod erat *y*, *Kenney*, quia erat *Palmer*: quae erat *Sς*

VIII ad ancillam cuius stuprum sensit amica *P (litt. grand.) Y* (*in marg. dextro*) *PhVa* (domina *pro* amica) **7** num *S*: nam *Pf*: nunc *P*: nec *D*: non *Yω* num *PSY*: num(ero collapsus in ullo) *H*:

nec ω: non ς **9** ancilla *PSYς*: ancillam ω **13** nec sum ego *PSYς*: non sum ego ς: non sum ω: non ego ς **19** puri *PYM*: nostri *S*ω **24** emeruisse (domini semeruisse *Y*, *corr. y*) *PSYς*: promeruisse ς: demeruisse *W*

IX ad amorem *P (litt. grand.) Y (-re in marg. dextro) SZ* **1** pro re ... indignande *Madvig*: pro me ... indignate *PSY*ω: per me ... indignate ς: pro re ... indignate *Burmannus. alii alia; nil omnino placet* **4** meis *PSYς*: tuis ω **8** confossum (conp- *P*) *PSYς*: confessum ς: cum petiit ς **14** reliquit *Y*ω: relinquit *PSVb* **17-18** *seclusit Bentleius* **17** promosset *Yςφ*: promouisset *PB*: mouisset *S*ω: misisset *Q* **21** pinum *PSςp*¹*p*³: puppim *ςe*: *de Y incert.* **22** cum **20** commutant *ςφ* **23-4** amore puellae defunctum *codd.*, puellae *probabiliter ex u.* **15** *oriundum*: Amore, periclo (periclis *iam Bentleius*) defunctum *Goold*: Amore, puella defunctum *Burmannus*, puella *uel ablatiuo uel uocatiuo casu intellegens*: Amore, duello defunctum *Markland. locus sine dubio corruptus, ut opinor; coniecturarum tamen nulla satis placet* **25** *nouam elegiam incipere censuit L. Müller, quem secuti sunt edd. plerique* **27** animoque *PSYVb*: animique *y*ω relanguit *M*, *Itali*: resa/nuit (resannuit *Y*, n *pr. exp. y*) *PY*: reuanuit *Sy*ω: euanuit ς **31** prensa *PSY*ω: pressa ς **36** hic ... hic *codd.*: hic ... huc *Heinsius*: hic ... hac *Luck* facit (*eras. Y*) *PSYς*: ualet *y* (*in ras.*) ς **37** huc *Y*ω: hic *PSAb*(*N*)*Ea* **38** sua *PSYς*: tua ς **44** *parenthesi inclusit Francius* **45** nectat *PSY*ω: quaerat *p* (*u.l.*) ς **51** cupido *PSY*ω: rogantem *p* (*u.l.*) **52** gere *PY*ω: geret *S*: geras *T*: geris *FVb*: gerem *Ob* rege *P* (*u.l.*) *Pc* (*u.l.*) *Q*: tene *Itali*

X quod duae (dne *S*) simul amentur *P* (*litt. grand.) SZ* **3** ego *om. Sς*: *habent PY*ω: **4** turpis (*eras. Y*) *PSYς*: solus *y* (*in ras.*) ω **7** hac ... haec ς: haec ... haec *PSY*ω: haec ... hac ς **9** erro uelut *Camps*: erramus *Führer audacter*: auferor ut *Bentleius* **17** uiduo (b- *P*) *PYς*: uacuo *pSy*ω **18** laxe (-xo *S*) *PSYς*: late *p*ω **23** sufficiam *PY*: sufficiant *S*ω: sufficiunt ς: sufficient *H* **27** lasciue *P*ω: lasciuae *SYPcZ* consumpsi tempora *PSYς*: consumpto tempore ς **29** perdunt *PY*ω: rumpunt *pSς* **33** lassarit *PY*ω: lassarat *Sς*: lassauit *pHφ* arando *Y*, *Heinsius ex* arundo *P*: eundo *pS*ωφ

XI ad amicam nauigantem *P (litt. grand.) SY* (*in marg. sin.)* **1** undis *Sς*: undas *PYς* **9** quam *Markland*: quid *codd.* **10** egelidumque *Seneca* (*Con.* ii. 2. 12): et gelidumque (*eras. Y*) *PSY*: non gelidumque ς: praecipitemque (pre- *y in ras.*) *y*ω: praetrepidumque ς **11** mirabere *SY*ω: miserabere *P* **13** pictosque *PYς*: pictosue *H*: uiridesque *Sς*: uariosque *F* **15** signate *F*, *cod. Vat. Chis. H.* VI. 205, *teste Munari*, *Naugerius*: signata *PSYς*: signanda *y*ω **18** quasue *PYς*: quasque *Sς* **21** at *Y*ω: ad *PS edd. nonnulli distinctione mutata* loquetur *PYς*: loquatur *S*ω **22** credenti *Sy*ω: quaerenti *PY* **25** cum ς: tum *T*: quia *PYMς*: qui *Ab*: iam *Sς*: quoque *yς* **27** quod *PSYς*: quid ς exasperet (et a- *P*) *PYς*: exasperat *Sς* **28** quam tibi *PSYς*: quam si *Ob*: qui tibi ς: quid tibi *T*: tunc tibi *Pc* sit *PSY*ω: si *Pf*: nunc ς **30** quem *PSς*: quam *Yς* **40** huc *PS*²*Y*ω: haec *S*¹: hac *DF* uenti ς: uentis *PYW*: uentus *SY*⁴ς spectent *Pς*: spectet *SY*⁴ ς: *om. Y*: spirent *Heinsius ex exc. Dousae, quem secuti sunt edd. plerique, sed iniuria, ut opinor* aestus ω: eurus *PSYς* **41** soli *PYς*: pleni *SY*⁴ω: **45** umeris (h- *Y*) *PSYς*: ulnis ς, *exc. Put.* carpam *PSY*ω: sumam ς: iungam *AcW*¹ **48** et cumulus mensae *PSYς*: et cumulus mensa ς: pro mensa cumulus ς: et tumulus mensae *Pc*: et tumulus mensa *PbBf*: pro mensa tumulus *D* (*ut Kenney uid.*) esse potest *PSY*ω: instar erit ς

XII ad custoditam et (aet *P*) a se stupratam *P* (*litt. grand.) S* (*ut Kenney uid.*) *Y* (*in marg. dextro*) *Ph* (*add.* amicam) *Va* **1** laurus *PY*: lauri *S*ω **3** firma tot hostes ω: firmat ut hostis *PSY*: firmus ut hostis ς: fortis ut hostis *Y*⁴: firmaque sera *H*: *de ceteris sileo* **10** atridis *PY*ω: atrida *DN*: atride *PaPf*: atridas *Sς*: atrides *H* **11** dissors (s *alt. eras. Y*) *PY*: discors (c *in ras. y*) *Sy*ω **13** hanc PSY*Ob*: hunc ω **17** est *PSYς*: *om.* ς causa *Y*⁴ς: cura *PSYς* **21** noua *PSY*ω: fera ς **27** qui multos *PSYς*: cum multis ς sed me *PY*ω: sed nunc *SHVa*

XIII *praecedenti continuat S. titulus in PSY nullus*: ad amicam grauidam *DFZ* **3** clam me ς: clamat *PSY*ω **4** mea *PSY*ς: mea est ς **7** genialiaque *y uel Y*[4] *in marg.* ς: gentiliaque *PSY*ς: genitaliaque ς **9** delapsus *PSY*ω: dilapsus ς in alueo *PSY*ω: ab alueo *Ac*: ab aruo *Pf* delapsus in alueo *edd. plerique*: dilapsus ab alueo *Burmannus* **10** portus *PSY*ω: portas *FPa* **11** sistra *PSY*ω: sacra ς **13** circa *PSY*ς: circum ω **17** sedit *Z, Heinsius*: dedit *PYPf*[1]: meruit *SY*[4] (*in marg.*) ω: seruit *ObPh* (*u.l.*) **18** qua *PSY*ω: quis ς: quam *D*: quas *Pf* tingit *PYF*[1]*Vb*: tangit *SF*[2] (*ut Kenney uid.*): cingit *y*ω turma *PSY*ς: turba *y*ς. *locus obscurissimus; post u.* 18 *lacunam suspicor.* **21** meis faue ilithyia (*eras. Y*) *PSY*: faue lucina puellae *y* (*in ras.*) ω: meis lucina faueto *PcX*

XIV ad amicam quae fecit abortum (abortiuum *Va*[2]: abruptum *H*) *P* (*litt. grand.*) *SHVa*[2] **10** fuit *PY*ςφ: foret *S*ω **18** fuit *PSY*ς: foret ω **25** fluant *PSY*ς: fluent *y*ςφ: fluunt ς s. f. m. s. *PSY*ω: s. s. m. f. ςφ **29** puerorum *PSY*ω: natorum ς culpant *PY*ω: matrem *SFH* **30** aque *QX*: atque *PSY*ω **32** uirum *PSY*ς: uirum est ς **33** iason *SY* (-son *ex corr. y*) ω: iaso *P* **35** hoc *PSY*ω: haec ς

XV *praeter codd. pp.* 93-4 *nominatos separatim tradit cod. Bernensis* 505, *saec.* xiii ad anulum quem miserat (misit *S*) amicae *P* (*litt. grand.*) S: ad anulum ς **1** uincture ς: iuncture ς (*sed sunt nonnulli diiudicatu difficiles, ut affirmat Kenney*): iuncturae *Y*: uinc&ire *P*: uincire *SH* **5** illi *PSY*ς: illa ς **9** fieri subito *PSY*ς: subito fieri ς **10** aeaeae *PSY*ς: eoe ς: ethee *FQ*: eolie *Pf*: aonii *D*: emoniis *B*: et circes *X*: aut circes *AcVb* carpathiiue *PYObPh*: carpathiique *S*ω **11** tunc ego cum libeat dominae *ego* (t. e. si dominae libeat *iam Bentleius*): tunc ego si cupiam dominae *F*: tunc ego te cupiam dominae *PSY*ω: tunc (nunc *Ph*) ego me (met *cod. Bern.* 505) cupiam dominae *A, cod. Bern.* 505, *Ph*: tunc per te cupiam dominae *Pc* (*u.l.*) *T*: tunc ego cum cupiat domina et *Rappold*: tunc ego te cupiam, domina, et *Madvig*: tunc ego cum cupiam dominae *Oliver* **14** sinum *PSY*ω: sinus ς: sinu ς laxus *PSY*: lapsus *y*ω **19** si dabor *codd.*: sit labor *Ehwald*: si trahar *Némethy* **21** sum ω: sim *PSYOb* **23** perfundes *Sy*ς: perfundis *PY*: perfundens ς: *de ceteris sileo* **24** gemmam *Ab*: gemma *PSY*ω perfer euntis *codd.*: fer pereuntis *Dousa* **25** nuda *PSDPf*: uisa *y* (*in ras., de Y incert.*) ω **26** peragam *PSY*ς: peraget *y*ω ille *PSY*ς: ipse *Y*[4] ς: iste *T* **27** uoueo *PY*ω: foueo *S*: moueo *PPf*: moneo *cod. Bern.* 505, *Vb*

XVI AD RVS SVVM ET AMICAM *P* **1** pars me *PSY*ω: me pars ς **7** cereris *PY*ω: ciceris ς multoque ... uuis *codd.*: Cereris ... multoque ... uuae *Heinsius in textu*, (multaeque ... uuae *in notis*): Cereri ... multoque uuis *Lee, dubitanter.* **11-12, 23-26** *totos*, **13, 16-18, 21-22** *partim restituit p sine mutatione, ut Kenney uid., cum P paene euanuisset* **17** aut *pSY*ς: at ω **19** premerem *Sy*ω: premerent *PY*: premerer ς uentosas horridus alpes (-is *PY*) *PY*ω: uentoso (-os *S*) turbine ponti *S*ς **23** non *pY*ς: nec *S*ς **25** nec *SY*ω: non *p*ς quae *pSY*ς: quas ω **26** effusas ore receptat *py*ω: effusa sorore (*incert.*) captat *Y*: effusas ore repotat *T*: effusas ore reportat (-et *Vb*) *SVbX* **27** uincat ς: uincet ω: uincit *PSY*ς **28** auferat ς: auferet *PSY*ς **31** Hero *Heinsius*: heron *codd.* **32** tum *y, Itali*: tu *PYB* (transnasses): tunc ω: nunc *SOb* **35** currentem *codd.*: parentem *Heinsius ex exc. Put. et Scal.* **40** saxa cruore *PSY*ω: sanguine saxa ς rubent *PSY*ς: madent ω uitem *PY* (m *ex corr. y*) ω: uites *S*ς **43** iuraras *PSY*: iurabas ω **44** sidera nostra tuos *PSY*ω: qui rapuere meos ς, *ex* III xi 48 **46** inrita qua *PY*: irritaque ut *S*ω unda *PSY*ς: aura ω **51** qua *P* (*ut Kenney uid.*) *Y*ς: cum *S*ς

XVII ad corinnam *P* (*ut uid.; litt. grand.*) *S* **1-14** *in P uix legi possunt* **4** et fluctu *S*[2] (*corr. ex* -u) ω: ex fluctu *X*: in fluctu Z: et fluctus (-s *eras. Y sed dispicitur*) *PY*ς pulsa *PSY*ς: nata ς: culta ς **5** miti *SY*ς: *om. P* **7** facie *S*[2]ς: facies *PS*[1]*Y*ω corinna *S*ω: corinnae *PY*ς est *PSy*ω: *om. Y*ς **11** nimium dat in omnia ω: animum dat in omnia (inomnia *Y*) *YNVa*: animum dat nomina *P* (*ut Kenney uid.*) *SObZ* regni *PSVaZ*: regna *Y*: regnum ω **15** traditur (tard- *P*) *PSYς*: creditur ω **16** recusantem *PSYς*: reluctantem ς **17** creditur *PSYς*: credimus ω Pthio *Knoche*: Phthio *Itali*: phtio *Pc*: pithio *Sς*: phitio uel phicio *uel sim.* ω: pythio *y* (*de Y non liquet*): io *P*: peleo *H²Ph²* **19** uolcani uenus est *PSYPc* (*u.l.*) *X*: uulcano uenerem ω **24** deceat *PSYς*: decet e *DF*: decet in ω foro *PYς*: toro ς: modo *S* **25** nec *Syω*: ne *PYPh*: non ς **27** sunt *PYω*: sint *Sς* mihi *PSYω*: tibi ς **32** eurotas *PYω*: eurotes *Sς*: europas *Vb*: euphrates ς: orontes *H*

XVIII ad macrum poetam *DZ*: ad macrum *AcF* **3** ignaua *T*, *Itali*: ignaue *P* (*ut Kenney uid.*) *SYωφ* **5-6** *om. P*, *add. in. marg. P an p incert.* **5** tandem dixi *PYς*: dixi tandem *Sς* **13** curaque ... nostra *PYς*: uersuque ... nostro *Sς* **16** cito *PSYω*: bene ς **19** aut artes *PYς*: aut partes *SFN²*: ad partes ω: et partes *VaVb*: in partes *Ac* profitemur *PSYω*: proficiscor ς **20** urgeor *PSYς*: torqueor ς **21** Penelopes *PSYω*: penelope (*i.e.* -ae) ω uerbis reddatur *PYς*: uerboso reddat *Sς* **22** scribimus *PSYς*: scripsimus ς **23** iason *Sω*: iaso *PY* **26** dicat *pς*: dictat *PSYς* Aoniam ... amata lyram *Bornecque*: aoniae (aoniare *P*) ... amata (-e *S*) lyrae (-is *Y* (*incert.*), -ae *y*) *PSYObT*: aoniae ... amica lyrae ς: aonio ... amata uiro ω: aonio ... amica uiro *Y⁴ς*: Aoniam ... amica lyram *Goold. alii alia;* amata *ex u.* 34 *oriundum et sine dubio corruptum censeo* **27** meus *PYς*: celer *Sς* **28** ipse *pς*: ille *PSYω* **31** iam pius *PYς*: impius ς: si pius *S* **32** uiuit *PYς*: uiuat *Sς* adest (*eras Y.*) *PY*: habet *pSy* (*in ras.*) ω **34** uotam *yω*: uotum *Yς*: uoto *S*: notam *pς*: notum *P*: nomen *N* amata *PSYς*: amica ς lyram *PYω*: lyrae *Sς* **35** qua *PSY*: quam *yω* tutum *pSyω*: tuto *PYς* **38** laodamia *PY*: laodomia ω: lauodamia *S*: lauodomia *H*: laudomia *VaX* **40** uenis *PSYς*: redis ς

XIX *praecedenti continuant PSY*, *separauit y. titulus in PSY nullus*: ad stultum de uxore custodienda *Va*: ad uirum puellae non custodientem eam *H* **7** quo *PSY*: quid ω: mihi *PYω*: modo *S*: cum ς fortunam *pSWX¹*: fortuna (-no *P*, *quod in* -na *mutauit m¹*, *ut Kenney uid.*, *a sscr.*) *PYω*: formosam *Lee* curet *PY*: curat ς: possit *pSY⁴* ω **8** laedat *PYω*: laedit ς: laesit *pSς* **11** dolores *PSYς*: dolorem ω **14** insonti *PY*: insontis *Sω* esse *PSYς*: illa ς: ipsa *Y⁴ω* **15** refouerat *PSYQ* (*u.l.*): remouerat ω: resoluerat ς **20** time insidias *PSYς*: fac insidias *W* (*u.l.*) *X*: face insimulas *Y⁴ω*: time simulans *Goold; alii alia* **25** patens *p* (*ex* lat- *P*) *SYς*: potens ω **29** io *PSYω*: ion *X* **32** magno *PSYς*: medio *ςφ* potet *PSY* (-t *ex corr. y; quid eras. sit incert.*) *ςφ*: portet *ObVa*: sumat ς aquam *PSYφς*: aquas ς **34** ne *PSYω*: quod *EaH*: nunc *NPf* torquear *pSyω*: torqueor *PYς*: urgeor *H* **35** quidlibet *PSς*: quodlibet (-uet *Y*) *yς*: quod licet ς **37** *nouam elegiam inc. Sς* ad amicam *S* **38** forem *PSYς*: fores ς: domum ς **41** quas *PYω*: quo *Sς*: quid ς **42** ipsa *PSYς*: illa ω **44** daque *PYς*: datque *SVb*: detque S (*ex corr. m¹*) ς **52** concessi *Sω*: concessa *PYH* **58** corrumpit ... suo *PSYς*: corrumpis ... tuo ω **59** quaeris *PY*: quaeres *pSVb* (*ut Kenney uid.*): quaeras ω: quaere ς EXPLICIT LIBER SECVNDVS *P*: P. OVIDI NASONIS AMORV(M) EXPLIC(IT) LIBER SECVNDVS *Y*

Commentary

Poem 1

1-3. **hoc quoque ... hoc quoque:** an indication that Ovid expected his readers to be familiar with some earlier amatory work, and apparently a simple reference to the first book of the *Amores* as we know it, but see pp. 2-3.

1. **Paelignis natus aquosis:** Ovid is always keen to record his birthplace (cf. *Am.* iii. 15. 3, *Fast.* iv. 685, *Tr.* iv. 10. 3, *Pont.* iv. 14. 49); here (and at *Am.* ii. 16. 37) the name of the people stands for their territory (cf. *Indi* = *India* at *Am.* ii. 6. 1). For the area and its 'watery' character see *Am.* ii. 16. 1-10, with notes on vv. 1 and 2.

2. **Ille ego:** a favourite identificatory formula of Ovid's, used with exuberant confidence here, mock-solemnity at *Am.* iii. 8. 23 and unmistakable poignancy at *Tr.* iv. 10. 1.

The end of a book of poetry, or a series of books, is the usual place to find an ancient author identifying himself, if he chooses to do so at all (see e.g. Hor. *Carm.* ii. 20 with Nisbet-Hubbard's introduction), but Martial, like Ovid here, reverses the standard procedure and introduces himself at the beginning of *Epigr.* i.

nequitiae: the term is not seriously censorious in Ovid but denotes the carefree immorality which is the staple of his love-elegy.

Naso: Ovid's usual form of reference to his own name. *Ouidius* is intractable in dactylic verse except in the vocative and contracted genitive, and Ovid chose not to use these forms at all. Like other Latin poets, he uses his own name readily enough for formal purposes, i.e. in 'signatures', as here (cf. *Am. Epigr.* 1), dedications (e.g. *Am.* i. 11. 27), epitaph (e.g. *Tr.* iii. 3. 74, 76) and letters (e.g. *Tr.* v. 13. 1 and *passim* in the exile poems). But, unlike his more emotional fellow love-poets, he never uses it in his amatory works in pathetic self-address or pathetic reference to himself in the third person (see further Donnet 261).

3. **Amor:** modern convention demands the capital letter to show that Ovid has Love the god in mind here (his words are clearly intended to recall Cupid's action at *Am.* i. 1. 23-4). But he is no doubt thinking of love the emotion too, and the capital tends to 'obscure this trick' (Kenney (1958a) 61). Cf. 18. 15n.

procul hinc ...: the phraseology mischievously recalls the ritual warning-off of the impure or uninitiated at religious ceremonies and sacrifices; cf. especially Call. *Ap.* 2 ἑκὰς ἑκὰς ὅστις ἀλιτρός ('Keep away, keep away, any who is sinful'), Verg. *A.* vi. 258 *procul, o procul este, profani*, and see p. 24. With similar ironic gravity Ovid styles himself *Musarum purus Phoebique sacerdos* at *Am.* iii. 8. 23.

seueri: the derogatory sense 'puritanical' is very much a usage of the erotic poets; cf. *Am.* ii. 10. 16, Catul. 5. 2, Prop. ii. 34. 23. The generalising masculine is appropriate here, since vv. 5-6 show that, despite his call to *puellae* alone in vv. 37-8, Ovid envisages his poetry being read by both sexes.

4. **teneris ... modis:** i.e. love-elegy. *tener* is a favourite, and often purely ornamental, elegiac epithet, but when used of poets and poetry, it is virtually a technical term for 'erotic' or 'elegiac'; cf. *Rem.* 757, Catul. 35. 1.

theatra: 'audience'; works of literature were normally first offered to the Romans not in written form but *viva voce*. *legat* in v. 5, however, suggests that *theatra* here is intended to cover readers as well as listeners (cf. *Pont.* i. 5. 69, and see Luck (1970) 469, n. 7).

5-10. Cf. Prop. i. 7. 13-14 (with Fedeli's note), 23-4, ii. 14. 81-2. Like Propertius, Ovid suggests that young lovers will find something to identify with in his poetry, but, unlike Propertius, he makes it clear that the experiences and emotions he describes are meant to be *primarily* typical rather than personal.

5. **in sponsi facie:** I follow Némethy and Goold ((1965a) 30) in taking *in* + ablative to denote the object of emotion after *non frigida* (see 3. 6n., and cf. *Am.* ii. 7. 9). *facie*, however, I understand simply as 'face', and not 'gaze' (Goold), a meaning for which there is no evidence, or *pulchritudine* (Némethy), one for which there is no need. Alternatively *in sponsi facie* may be understood as = *coram sponso* and the whole line construed 'Let my reader be the girl who thrills *in the presence of* her suitor', i.e. when she knows *he* is looking at *her* rather than when *she* looks at *him*; cf. *Am.* ii. 5. 35-6.

sponsi: not necessarily 'fiancé', but probably just 'boy-friend' or 'suitor'; cf. Catul. 65. 19, Hor. *Ep.* i. 2. 28.

non frigida: litotes (see p. 13). *frigidus* of a sexually unresponsive human being first appears in Ovid (Virgil uses it of an ageing stallion at *G.* iii. 97).

6. **rudis:** a regular elegiac epithet for the newcomer to love; cf. *Ars* iii. 559, Prop. i. 9. 8 with Fedeli's note.

7. **arcu:** the bow is, of course, Cupid's; cf. *Am.* i. 1. 21-6, and see 9A. 5n.

8. Cf. Verg. *A.* iv. 23 *agnosco ueteris uestigia flammae*. For the very extensive use of heat and fire imagery in amatory contexts see Pease on Verg. *A.* iv. 2, Fantham 86-8.

conscia signa: not 'secret signs' (so most editors), but 'signs which reveal what is hidden, private, or obscure'; cf. *Am.* ii. 8. 8, [Quint.] *Decl.* 4. 16 *futuras tempestates ... conscium nemorum murmur enuntiat*, Tib. i. 8. 3 *conscia fibra deorum*.

9. **indice:** see 8. 5n.

doctus: modern punctuation correctly attaches this to *ab indice*, but it also resonates with *poeta*, cleverly suggesting that this poet of passion is also a poet of erudition and sophisticated technique (*doctrina*); see Nisbet-Hubbard I. 13. Cf. 18. 7-8n. *me miseram*.

11-16. Almost certainly we need not mourn a lost Ovidian *Gigantomachia* (that title may loosely describe the *mêlée* here envisaged, which involves not only the Giants and the gods but also the Hecatoncheires, the Titans and the Aloidae (see 12, 13, 14nn.); confusion of the myths concerning two or more of these is very common (see Bömer on *Met.* v. 35)). There is no ancient testimony to the existence of such a work by Ovid, unfinished or otherwise, and his claim to have embarked on one here is immediately suspect because it appears within a passage which is but a variation of familiar humbug (see pp. 24-5). What is more, the battle of the Giants and the gods is a stock example of the epic subject-matter which lyric and elegiac poets traditionally reject (cf. Hor. *Carm.* ii. 12. 5-12, Prop. ii. 1. 17-20, 39-40, D. C. Innes, 'Gigantomachy and natural philosophy', *CQ* n.s. 29 (1979), 165-71), and the parenthetical *memini* (v. 11) is a device regularly used by Ovid to lend an air of authenticity to a questionable assertion (cf. *Am.* i. 6. 43, ii. 10. 1, *Tr.* ii. 89). It may be argued that Ovid's unequivocal claim (*ausus eram*) to have actually begun a *Gigantomachia* rather than to have been about to begin one, or contemplating beginning one, when he was deterred from his undertaking by outside interference, suggests that his essay at epic was indeed genuine, but he could easily have stretched the traditional fiction to this length in order to emphasise his rejection of the Augustan poet's standard excuse of inadequacy of talent for his failure to write epic. All this is not to say, of course, that Ovid never toyed with epic themes in his youth, but only that his claim to have made substantial progress with a particular epic need not be taken seriously (so F. Pfister, 'Hat Ovid eine Gigantomachie geschrieben?', *RhM* 70 (1915), 472-7, Reitzenstein 87-8; *contra*, H. de la Ville de Mirmont, 'La Gigantomachie d'Ovide', *RPh* 28 (1904), 103-21, S. G. Owen, *Ouidius, Tristium Liber II* (Oxford, 1924), 63-81, F. Della Corte, 'La Gigantomachia di Ovidio', *Studi in onore di V. Falco* (Naples, 1971), 435-45).

11. **ausus eram:** 'I once ventured'. The idiomatic use of pluperfect for perfect (or imperfect) is particularly common in elegy, where it is often metrically convenient; cf. *Am. Epigr.* 1, Prop. iii. 3. 1, and see further Fordyce on Catul. 10. 28, 64. 158, Kühner-Stegmann II. i. 139-41.

12. **centimanumque Gygen:** one of the hundred-handed giants (Hecatoncheires) imprisoned in the depths of the earth by their father Uranus on account of their frightening power; for the story see Hes. *Th.* 714ff.

Gygen, the reading of the vast majority of our MSS, must be reinstated in place of Scaliger's widely accepted conjecture *Gyen*. Forms of *Gyes* and Γυής, with first syllable short, do appear as MS variants for the name of the hundred-handed giant at *Tr.* iv. 7. 18, Hes. *Th.* 149, 618, 714 and Apollod. i. 1. 1, whereas *Gyges*, with first syllable long, is most familiar as the name of the celebrated king of Lydia (see especially Hdt. i. 8-12, and for the quantity, Bentley on Hor. *Carm.* ii. 17. 14). But a remark of Herodian (ii. 678. 27 Lentz) cited by West on Hes. *Th.* 149 reveals that the ancients recognised *Gyges* as the name of *both* the Lydian king *and* the mythical giant, and also recognised a prosodical distinction between the two, the first syllable of *Gyges* the king's name being counted long and the first syllable of *Gyges* the giant's name short.

et satis oris erat: an untranslatable pun on *os*: both 'grandiloquence' (cf. *Ars* i. 206 with Hollis' note), and 'cheek' (cf. *Ep.* 16 (17). 102).

13. **cum male se Tellus ...:** Earth avenged herself on her husband Uranus, when he imprisoned their sons, the Hecatoncheires (see 12n.), by inciting the Titans to castrate him.

male: with *ulcisci* something of a stock adverb. Cf. *Met.* vii. 397, Hor. *Carm.* iv. 12. 7-8; also *Am.* i. 7. 9 *malus ultor, Orestes.*

ingestaque Olympo: the Aloidae (Otus and Ephialtes) attempted to reach the sky by piling the mountains Pelion, Ossa and Olympus on top of each other (Hom. *Od.* xi. 305ff.) and were struck down by Zeus with a thunderbolt (Lib. *Narr.* 37 Foerster). The mountains are generally said to have been piled up in the order given here, but at *Met.* i. 154-5 Ovid gives Olympus on Pelion on Ossa, and Virgil at *G.* i. 281-2 gives Olympus on Ossa on Pelion (cf. *Aetna* 49).

14. **deuexum:** 'sloping downwards'; a redundant epithet as far as sense is concerned, but obviously included to balance *ardua* in this highly artistic line (see p. 15).

15. The text printed (= ς) is the most satisfactory of the alternatives offered by the MSS to the unmetrical reading of *PY*. *nimbos* may be no more than a scribal guess, but it complements *fulmen* well (cf. *Pont.* iv. 8. 59-60, Verg. *G.* i. 328-9) and recalls the Homeric νεφεληγερέτα Ζεύς ('cloud-gathering Zeus'). It is easy to see, too, how the juxtaposition *-nibus nimbos* could have resulted in the omission of *nimbos* by haplography.

I assume *nimbos et cum Ioue fulmen* = *et nimbos et Iouem et fulmen*. This line prepares the ground for v. 17, where *cum Ioue* so interpreted is essential to the pun on *omisi*. Kenney ((1962) 28, n. 1) prefers to take *cum Ioue* 'apo koinou' (i.e. *cum Ioue in manibus nimbos et cum Ioue fulmen habebam*), but this does not cohere very well with v. 16 ('Along with Jupiter, *I* held in my hands storm-clouds and a thunderbolt which *he* might launch ...').

16. **quod bene mitteret:** Kenney ((1962) 28, n. 1), dismissing the 'conventional renderings of *bene* (e.g. 'si à propos' (Bornecque), 'opportunamente' (Munari), 'wohlgezielt' (Lenz)) as 'feeble', persuasively suggests that Ovid really meant a thunderbolt which Jupiter might *worthily* launch in defence of his realm, i.e. a thunderbolt of truly epic calibre.

17. **clausit amica fores:** for the bathos see p. 25. The 'locked-out lover' is a familiar figure in ancient love-poetry (see especially *Am.* i. 6, Tib. i. 2, Prop. i. 16, Hor. *Carm.* i. 25, iii. 10, Asclep. *AP* v. 189, Posidipp. *AP* v 213), and the plea or lament he traditionally utters before his beloved's house-door (modern scholars call the motif the *paraclausithyron*; for

such labels see p. 7) has been the subject of many special studies; still the fullest is F. O. Copley's *Exclusus Amator: a Study in Latin Love Poetry*, *Am. Phil. Ass. Monogr.* 17 (Baltimore, 1956), but see also Cairns 76, 123, 152, 230-31, J. C. Yardley, 'The elegiac paraclausithyron', *Eranos* 76 (1978), 19-34, and Fedeli's introduction to Prop. i. 16.

Ovid's experience here seems to have something in common with Tibullus' at ii. 6. 9-12:

castra peto, ualeatque Venus ualeantque puellae:
   et mihi sunt uires et mihi laeta tuba est.
magna loquor, sed magnifice mihi magna locuto
   excutiunt clausae fortia uerba fores.

Tibullus, like Ovid, would have us believe that his grandiose plans (ostensibly for enlisting in the army, though plans for writing war-poetry, i.e. epic, may be what he means) were shatttered by the *clausae fores*. Tibullus' version, however, is characterised by a pathos completely absent from Ovid's.

amica: like *puella* and *domina*, a regular elegiac word for 'mistress' or 'girl-friend'; Ovid uses all three more or less interchangeably (see further Booth (1981) 2688-90).

fulmen omisi: 'I dropped the thunderbolt', i.e. both 'I let it fall from my hands' and 'I abandoned my poetic treatment of it'; cf. 15n. For *omisi* (= ς) see Kenney (1962) 28, n. 1.

19. **Iuppiter, ignoscas:** a touch of mockery of other poets' over-deferential attitude towards that 'Jupiter on earth', Augustus?

20. **tuo maius ... fulmen:** the ablative of comparison enjoyed a vogue in Augustan poetry; see Löfstedt I. 314ff.

fulmen: did Ovid intend, as first proposed by J. van Wageningen ('*Fulmen*', *Mnemosyne* n.s. 45 (1917), 135-9), that *fulmen* here and at *Am.* i. 6. 16 (*tu, me quo possis perdere, fulmen habes*) should suggest *fulmentum* and hence 'bolt of a door' as well as 'bolt' = 'deadly weapon'? Certainly the dropping of noun-endings in *-tum* was a well-established practice in Latin poetry (see Leumann 130, O. Skutsch, *SIFC* 27-8 (1956), 537 [= *id.*, *Studia Enniana* (London, 1968), 146]); but *fulmentum* normally means 'prop' or 'support' (see e.g. Vitr. v. 1. 9 *contra capitula ex fulmentis dispositae pilae sunt conlocatae*, Cels. ii. 15. 4 *uni pedi subiciendum fulmentum est*), and examples of it meaning 'bolt' or 'bar' are to seek. The use of *fulcire* at *Am.* i. 6. 28 *roboribus duris ianua fulta riget* and *Ars* ii. 244 *opposita ianua fulta sera*, however, suggests that such a meaning for *fulmentum*, and hence *fulmen*, is not impossible. It is difficult to imagine, too, why Ovid at *Am.* i. 6. 16 should have chosen to use *fulmen* at all, unless it had been to create a pun of the kind postulated, and in our passage the presence of puns and word-play in the immediate vicinity (see 12, 15, 17, 23-8nn.) would seem to make another pun at this point all the more likely. For further discussion and bibliography see J. Perrot, *Les dérivées latins en -men et -mentum* (Paris, 1961), 60-63, and for arguments against assuming a pun here, G. Dittmann and H. Rubenbauer, '*Fulmen* = Stütze', *Philologus* 76 (1920), 351ff.

21. **blanditias:** the lover's wooing words and the endearments and caresses of love-making. *Blanditiae* take their place in the front rank alongside *Error* and *Furor* in the triumph of Cupid at *Am.* i. 2. 35 and are part of the stock-in-trade of the *exclusus amator* (cf. *Rem.* 35-6, Prop. i. 16. 16). Sometimes, as here, the word may virtually stand for 'love-poetry'; cf. *Am.* iii. 1. 46, Tib. i. 4. 71.

elegosque leuis: as *grauis* conventionally describes the 'higher' poetic genres of epic and tragedy (e.g. *Am.* i. 1. 1, Hor. *Ars* 14 with Brink's note), so *leuis* regularly indicates the 'lower' ones of elegy and lyric; cf. *Am.* i. 1. 19, Prop. ii. 12. 22, Hor. *Carm.* ii. 1. 40.

22. **duras:** both 'strong' and 'obdurate'; the epithet frequently used of the door's owner or guardian is here transferred to the door itself (cf. *Am.* i. 6. 62, 74).

lenia uerba: i.e. *uersus elegiaci*; cf. Prop. i. 9. 12 *carmina mansuetus lenia* (some MSS give *leuia*) *quaerit Amor*, and see Stroh (1971) 18-20. Doubtless Ovid has in mind the familiar pleading of the *exclusus amator*.

23-8. Knowing that lovers in ancient poetry often resort to the use of charms and philtres (see especially Theoc. 2 with Gow's notes, Verg. *Ecl.* 8. 64ff., Hor. *Epod.* 5, 17), Ovid's reader may well expect the celebration of the power of magic in vv. 23-6 to lead to a confirmation of its efficacy as an aid to amatory success, but these lines in fact only prepare the way for a mischievous exploitation of the double-meaning of *carmina* ('verses' as well as 'spells') in vv. 27-8. The striking anaphora and polyptoton (*carmina* ... *carmine* ... *carminibus* ... *carmine;* see pp. 14, 16), which are common in passages of Latin poetry dealing with magic (cf. *Am.* i. 8. 9-10, Tib. i. 2. 47ff., 8. 19-21), may be intended not only to stress the power of *carmina* but also to recall real magical formulae and incantations, since an element of verbal repetition of the 'abracadabra' variety seems to have been a standard feature of them; see e.g. *P. Osl.* I. 70-71 ιωερβηθ / ιωπακερβηθ / ιωβαλχοσηθ' / ιωαπομψ / ιωεσευρω / ιωβιματ, Cato, *Agr.* 160 *mota uaeta daries*, *dardares astataries dissunapiter*, and cf. Stroh (1971) 151, nn. 37, 38, Tupet 166ff.

23-6. The *locus classicus* for all forms of ancient magic is Luc. vi. 483ff.

23. Ancient writers frequently tell of the moon's being drawn down to earth by spells (see Smith on Tib. i. 2. 43, Bömer on *Met.* vii. 207-8), and Ovid speaks once elsewhere (*Am.* i. 8. 12) of its being turned bloody by witches. The first of these notions was probably developed to explain the darkening of the moon by an eclipse (see Smith on Tib. i. 8. 21-2, and for an alternative theory, Tupet 93-103), and the second to account for the reddish tinge sometimes taken on by the moon in eclipse owing to a little sunlight being refracted by the atmosphere under certain meteorological conditions (cf. 5. 38n.); here Ovid, obviously intent only on picturesque effect, has conflated the two.

24. Ovid is thinking of the darkness caused by a total eclipse of the sun; cf. *Ep.* 6. 86, and see further Tupet 387, Bömer on *Met.* vii. 209.

niueos ... equos: for the horses of the sun see 5. 38n. *niueus* is a favourite poetic epithet of horses and is regularly applied to the team of the sun and moon (see *Rem.* 258, *Fast.* iv. 374, and cf. Theoc. 13. 11 λεύκιππος 'Αώς ('white-horsed Dawn'), and cf. 12. 25n.). No doubt the adjective is used here, hard on the heels of *sanguineae* in 23, to produce a suggestion of the red/white colour contrast so beloved of the Latin poets (see 5. 35-42n.).

solis euntis: for *ire* of the sun cf. *Met.* iv. 264-5, Man. i. 186, and similarly of the moon, Luc. i. 77-8.

25. **carmine dissiliunt ... angues:** for the power of spells to split open snakes cf. *Met.* vii. 203 with Bömer's note, Tib. i. 8. 20 with Murgatroyd's note. The bones and entrails of snakes were frequently used in magical ritual (see Tupet 363-4, and cf. Shakespeare, *Macbeth* 4. 1 'Fillet of a fenny snake / in the cauldron boil and bake'), but whether witches were thought to split them open to obtain ingredients for their potions, or simply to amuse themselves, is not clear.

26. A popular poetic *adynaton* ('impossibility'), used not only as an example of the effects of magic (cf. *Met.* vii. 199-200 with Bömer's n., Tib. i. 2. 46 (44) with Murgatroyd's n.) but also in all manner of other contexts (see Nisbet-Hubbard I. 341-2, with bibliography on *adynata* in general).

27-8. **carminibus ... carmine:** with a pun on *carmina* Ovid puts his own *leues elegi* on a par with conventional love-magic. Possibly he also wished to suggest that his own brand of 'magical verse' was just as effective as the well-known 'Open sesame' type of door-charm (see e.g. *P. Osl.* I. 412ff., Pl. *Cur.* 147-54).

29-36. The 'usefulness motif (see p. 25). Propertius at i. 7. 9 and 9. 9-12 was the first to use it; cf. also Prop. ii. 34. 43ff., Tib. ii. 4. 15-20. Of course, Ovid and Propertius *do* find a role for famous epic heroes in their poetry: their actions are used as *exempla* in various love-situations (e.g. *Am.* i. 9.33-8, ii.8. 11-14,12. 19-24, *Ars* ii.709-14, Prop.ii. 8.29-38, 22.29-34).

29. **uelox:** = ποδώκης ('swift-footed'), one of the formulaic epithets of Achilles in Homer.

30. **alter et alter:** i.e. *duo* (Agamemnon and Menelaus). The usage is confined to Ovid: cf. *Am.* ii. 10. 10, *Fast.* v. 226.

31. **quique:** *-que* = 'or', not 'and', here. The distinction between *-que* and *-ue* was already beginning to disappear by Ovid's time; see A. Ernout, 'Les enclitiques *-que* et *-ue', RPh* 32 (1958), 89-97, Kenney on Lucr. iii. 150.

errando: the reference is, of course, to Odysseus. For the popularity of the ablative of the gerund with Augustan writers see Tränkle 14.

32. For the story see Hom. *Il.* xxii. 395ff., xxiv. 14ff.

et: for the position see p. 13, with n. 107.

Haemoniis ... equis: cf. Prop. ii. 8. 38 *fortem illum Haemoniis Hectora traxit equis. Haemonius* (from *Haemonia*, an area of Thessaly) is a favourite poetic epithet of Thessalian heroes and their attributes; it relates especially frequently to Achilles (cf. *Am.* ii. 9A. 7, *Met.* xii. 81, *Fast.* v. 400, *Tr.* iii. 11. 28).

33. **at facie ... laudata:** Heinsius' conjecture (see apparatus on p. 94) convinces by its very simplicity. For *facies* see 3. 13n.

34. **uatem:** this is a quasi-religious word originally meaning 'seer' but adopted by Virgil and other Augustans as a special term for an inspired poet of serious and high-flown themes (see Nisbet-Hubbard I. 15, Hardie 16-17). Sometimes Ovid exploits the specialised Augustan meaning of *uates* to create a subtle self-mockery (e.g. *Am.* i. 1. 6, 24), and sometimes he makes the word serve as a generally honorific term for 'poet' (e.g. *Am.* iii. 9. 17), but I think he uses it here, as at *Am.* ii. 4. 21, iii. 15. 1, *Ars* ii. 739 and *Rem.* 3, without any perceptible distinction from the basically more mundane *poeta* (*contra*, J. K. Newman, *Augustus and the New Poetry, Coll. Latomus* 88 (Brussels, 1967), 183).

35. **heroum clara ualete ...:** Ovid's words are strongly reminiscent of *Anacreont.* 23. 10-12 West χαίροιτε λοιπόν ἡμῖν / ἥρωες· ἡ λύρη γὰρ / μόνους ἔρωτας ᾄδει ('It's goodbye to you, heroes, from now on for me; for the lyre only sings of love'). But the *Anacreontea* are of varied and uncertain date, and though the group to which 23 belongs may contain poems from as early as the 2nd century B.C. (so J. M. Edmonds, *Anacreontea* (with *Elegy and Iambus* II) (Cambridge Mass.-London, 1931), 1ff.), it has also been assigned to the Christian period (O. Crusius, *RE* I. 2047; see now also D. A. Campbell, *Greek Lyric* I (Cambridge Mass.-London, 1988), 10-18). Cf. also Prop. iii. 1. 7 with Fedeli's note.

37. **uultus adhibete:** cf. 13. 15n.

38. **carmina ... dictat Amor:** a direct link with v. 3. For the expression cf. *CLE* 937. 1 *scribenti mihi dictat Amor*, Prop. iv. 1. 133.

purpureus: not 'dressed in purple clothes' (thus Harder-Marg and Lenz), for *Amor* is traditionally naked, but 'rosy'; cf. *Am.* ii. 9B. 34, *Rem.* 701, Apul. *Met.* v. 22. The adjective has a wide range of meanings (see André 93ff.), but when used of Cupid/*Amor*, it seems to indicate his youthful, healthy glow (cf. Verg. *A.* i. 590-91 *nato* (i.e. *Cupidini*) *genetrix lumen ... iuuentae / purpureum ... adflarat*) – perhaps in contrast to the usual sickly pallor of his victims.

Poem 2

1. **quem penes:** the placing of *penes* after its accusative is common; see Brink on Hor. *Ars* 72.

dominam seruandi: see 3. 1n. The gerund with object accusative replaces the originally preferred gerundive construction, particularly in the genitive case, with increasing frequency from Sallust onwards (see Hofmann-Szantyr 373, Kühner-Stegmann II. i. 735). For the implications of *seruare* see 19. 1n.

Bagoe: *Bagous* or *Bagoas* was the name of several notorious Persian eunuchs and eventually became synonymous with *eunuchus* itself (Plin. *Nat.* xiii. 41; see also L. Alfonsi, 'Ovid, *Amores* ii. 2. 1', *Latomus* 23 (1964), 348-9, *id.*, *Latomus* 28 (1969), 207-8). Eunuch-slaves were common throughout antiquity and into the Byzantine period. Castration was apparently first practised in the East (Amm. Marc. xiv. 6. 17, Claud. *Eutr.* i. 339-45, Don. Ter. *Eu.* 168); in Rome it was declared a serious crime under Domitian, Nerva and Hadrian, but Romans generally felt greater distaste for the victims of the mutilation than for the perpetrators of it (see *RE* III. 1772-3, *ibid. Suppl.* III. 449ff.). Eunuchs were despised for their supposed lack of physical strength, and historical as well as poetic sources suggest that they were often degraded by being made to act as ladies' maids (see Ter. *Eu.* 167-9, 583ff., Claud. *Eutr.* i. 106-9, Amm. Marc. xviii. 4. 4, *Hist. Aug. Alex. Sev.* 23. 7).

Kenney (1958a) 59-60) maintains that Ovid will have written *Bagoa*, and not *Bagoe*. Admittedly, *Bagoas* and Βαγώας are very well attested forms of the name (see *RE* II. 2771-2), while the putative *Bagous* is paralleled only by Βαγῶος at Strabo xv. 3. 23. But some variation in the Hellenised, and subsequently Latinised, form of an originally Persian proper name seems not at all unlikely (other Persian names have at least Greek parallel forms in -ας and -ος; see e.g. 'Αρκαθίας /'Αρκαθίος and Γουνδαβοῦνας / Γουνδαφοῦνδος *ap*. F. Justi, *Iranisches Namenbuch* (Marburg, 1895), 26, 120). Βαγώας / *Bagoas* was obviously standard by the lst century A.D., but Βαγῶος / *Bagous* may well have been known and used at an earlier time. The two attestations of the name in Ovid and Strabo are among the earliest we possess, and though the MSS of Strabo are indeed of 'notorious badness' (Kenney), those of Ovid's *Amores* are relatively good and are nowhere else guilty, in almost complete consensus, of false declension of a proper name.

3-4. The colonnades of Rome feature prominently in Ovid's guides in the *Ars* to the best hunting-grounds for lovers on the look-out for a congenial partner; see i. 67-74, 491-6, iii. 387-8, and cf. *Rem.* 627-8, Catul. 55. 6-7, Prop. ii. 23. 5-6, 32. 11-12, iv. 8. 75, Juv. 6. 60). The portico to which he refers here adjoined the temple of Palatine Apollo vowed by Octavian in return for his victory over S. Pompey in 36 B.C. and dedicated in 28 B.C. (Aug. *Anc.* 19, Suet. *Aug.* 29. 3); a row of statues between the columns represented the fifty daughters of Danaus (scholiast on Pers. 2. 56). The temple and portico were among the most splendid buildings of Augustan Rome (see Hor. *Carm.* i. 31 with Nisbet-Hubbard's introduction, and cf. Prop. ii. 31, iv. 6. 11-12).

4. **illa quae ... porticus ... habet:** i.e. *illā porticu quae habet* ...; part of the antecedent has been attracted into the case of the relative pronoun (cf. 16. 25n.).

5. **placuit:** see 4. 17-18n.

misi: for the absolute use = 'send a letter' cf. Cic. *Att.* xii. 12. 2 *institui cotidie mittere*. For the use of letters in courtship cf. *Am.* i. 11 and 12, *Ars* i. 437-86, iii. 469-98.

rogaui: see 3. 5n.

8. **molesta:** cf. *Am.* ii. 3. 15. *molestus* is largely confined to prose and the 'lower' poetic genres of comedy, satire and epigram (see Axelson 60).

9-10. This couplet is characterised by a note of controlled menace, which contrasts with Ovid's blandness throughout most of the poem. The enjambement (see p. 15), the impassioned *o* with the vocative (see 9A. 1-2n.), and the basically colloquial expressions *si sapis* and *mihi crede*, to which the poets often resort where a ring of extra intensity is required (see Hofmann 126, 134, 199-200, Tränkle 9-10, 165), all contribute to the sinister tone.

10. **quem metuit quisque ...:** proverbial; cf. Enn. *trag*. 348 Jocelyn, *Am*. ii. 19. 56, and see further Otto 252. *perisse* has full perfect force: 'to have died', i.e. 'to be dead' (cf. 4. 22n.).

11. **uir quoque non sapiens:** understand *esse potest*. For the elegiac *uir* and his role see p. 6. **enim:** an idiomatic use of the conjunction (particularly common in rhetorical questions) to introduce an explanation for the previous statement. Here a conditional clause is suppressed: 'The *uir* can have no sense either, for (if he had) why would he bother...?'; cf. Petr. 97. 9 *scio te ... ad occidendum me uenisse. quo enim secures attulisti?*, and see further *OLD* s.v. 3b.

12. **unde nihil ... perit:** doubtless a veiled reference to the sexual parts of a woman's body; cf. *Ars* iii. 90, *Priap*. 3. 1-2 Bücheler.

13. **furiosus:** the description of love as *furor*, 'madness', is a favourite poetic cliché, but I have found no parallels for the related use of *furiosus*, and it probably means 'mad' in a general sense here.

14. The implication is that 'fair means fickle'; cf. *Ep*. 15 (16). 285-8, Juv. 10. 293ff. The word-order displays mild hyperbaton (see p. 16).

castum: not 'chaste', but, as often in elegy, with reference to both wives and mistresses, 'faithful'; cf. *Am*. iii. 4. 3, Tib. i. 3. 83, Prop. iii. 12. 15, and see Luck (1974) 20ff.

quod: Ovid is fond of the neuter relative pronoun where the feminine might be expected (cf. *Am*. ii. 5. 9, 19. 36, *Ars* i. 35, 175, 263, 741, and see also Courtney on Juv. 6. 62). He often uses the idiom to give amatory observations a ring of hard-boiled objectivity (it reminds me of once hearing an old man say to a young one, on the subject of choosing a wife, 'I'd get myself something to look at').

15-16. *libertas* is neatly ambiguous here: the slave should grant his mistress freedom to indulge in amatory adventures (15) so that she may grant him freedom proper (16).

huic ... illi ... illa: *huic* = the *puella* in contrast with *ille* = the *uir* in 13, and the change of pronoun cuts short the digression on the man's foolishness. *illi* and *illa* in 16, however, also refer to the *puella* (cf. *Am*. ii. 3. 11-12). *hic* and *ille*, when used in close proximity, do not generally designate the same person (see Hofmann-Szantyr 181-2), but the poets use all demonstrative pronouns with considerable flexibility (see E. Wölfflin, 'Zur Geschichte der Pronomina demonstratiua', *ALL* 12 (1902), 239-46).

15. **furtiua:** see 8. 8n.

16. Though a Roman woman *sui iuris* (i.e. one with some legal rights of her own) might herself manumit a slave with the consent of her *tutor* (see W. W. Buckland, *A Textbook of Roman Law from Augustus to Justinian* (Cambridge, 1921), 166-9), the most likely method of obtaining freedom for her favourite would be by interceding with the *dominus* on his behalf (cf. 31-2).

17. **conscius esse uelis?:** the sudden direct question bids for the continued attention of the addressee. The 'accomplice' or 'confidant' in elegy is normally a woman; cf. *Ars* i. 351ff., iii. 619ff.

18-27. This is one of three passages in the *Amores* (the others are i. 13. 11-14 and 33-4) which are present in the *recc*. but not in the original text of any of our oldest MSS. A question-mark remains over 23-4 (see n. *ad loc*.), but the authenticity of 18-22 and 25-7 is clear.

In both sense and Latinity these lines are quite unexceptionable. They make essentially the same point as the undisputed 28, namely that the eunuch can render very useful service to his mistress by remaining entirely passive; he can simply pretend not to notice (*dissimulare*, 18) any suspicious behaviour and keep quiet (*tacuisse*, 28). Characteristically Ovidian stylistic features include (i) anaphora (see p. 14) to point a contrast (17-18; cf. *Met*. i. 470-71); (ii) paratactical sentence-structure (see p. 16); (iii) *dissimulare* beginning the second half of a pentameter (18; 14 occurrences of this altogether in Ovid); and (iv) the so-called future imperative in *-to* (*putato*, 19) within a didactic passage (see n. *ad loc*.). Totally in Ovid's manner, too, is the invitation to the reader in v. 18 to picture from the poet's own words the reaction of his addressee (see 8. 23n.).

Moreover, *PY*'s curious *honores* for *inanes* in v. 31 (see apparatus on p. 94) 'can have come from nowhere but the *honores* of 27' (Kenney ((1955) 14), and v. 27 at least must therefore have been present in a MS from which our oldest witnesses are descended, probably the exemplar of **α** (see p. 17). It does not, of course, necessarily follow that the rest of the disputed lines also stood in *PY*'s ancestor, but there must be a strong probability that they did. And the omission of all those lines from the descendants of the MS in question may easily be explained as the result of the copyist's eye wandering from *conscius* in 17 to *conscius* in 27.

18. **dissimulare:** sc. *dissimulare te aliquid uidisse*; cf. Cic. *Planc*. 48 *quid taces, quid dissimulas, quid tergiuersaris?*, Sen. *Dial*. ii. 33. 1.

19-20. For letters as a source of incriminating evidence against an unfaithful *puella* cf. *Am*. ii. 5. 5, *Ars* ii. 543, iii. 483ff.

19. **putato:** the archaic 'future' imperative in *-to* occurs most frequently in legal Latin. It appears to have had an authoritative tone which Ovid in didactic vein found useful (cf. *Am*. i. 4. 29, 35, 8. 85, 95, *Ars* i. 139, 353, and see Zingerle I. 13). *putare* is one of the verbs which most regularly exhibit this form of the imperative, but *puta* is also found (see Kühner-Stegmann II. i. 196, 199).

21-2. The claim to be visiting a sick friend or relative is a frequently cited feminine ruse; cf. *Ars* iii. 641-2, Mart. xi. 7. 7-10, Juv. 6. 235-8.

21. **affectam:** 'ill'; cf. Prop. ii. 28. 1.

22. The general sense of this line is clear enough – the *custos* is to go along with the 'sick friend' story – but the precise wording is open to dispute (see apparatus on p. 94).

I reject *indiciis* ('*according to your evidence*, let her (the *amica*) be sick'; i.e. 'you can say that she is sick') because it is doubtful whether testimony favourable to the 'defendant' could be described as *indicium* (the word is normally used of *incriminating* evidence; cf. v. 53, and see *ThLL* VII. 1146. 2ff.). The alternative *iudiciis*, 'in your eyes', 'as far as you are concerned', is unobjectionable in itself (for the plural cf. *Ep*. 3. 104, *Ars* ii. 416), and it allows this couplet, like the rest of 19-26, to advise the *custos* to assume that there is an innocent explanation for any suspicious behaviour.

If *iudiciis* is right, the rest of the line is easily settled. The unmetrical *uisat et* must be ruled out, and, since a paratactical presentation of hypothesis (21) and reply (22) seems desirable (cf. vv. 19 and 20), so must *uisaque* and *uisa et*. That leaves the simple and perfectly tolerable *uisat*.

23-4. A couplet widely condemned as spurious, even by those who believe 18-22 and 25-7 to be authentic (see 18-27n.).

Although objections to *facere* + adverb may be withdrawn (it is not, as was once supposed, unclassical; see E. J. Kenney, 'Palinode', *CR* n.s. 7 (1957), 16), two points remain: (i) 'the rest of this passage consists of variants on *dissimulare*, while this couplet is a recipe against boredom' (Kenney (1955) 13), and (ii) *stertere* is generally avoided in all but the 'lowest' genres of Latin poetry, satire and comedy (it appears once elsewhere in the MSS of Ovid (*Ep*. 8. 21), but again in a line widely thought to be spurious). I am still not convinced. Is a 'recipe against boredom' – or perhaps better 'impatience' (see *ThLL* VI.

349. 73ff.) – so very inappropriate here, given that, if the *custos*, pursuing a policy of 'turning a blind eye', *should* become impatient, he might well go to investigate the delay and so discover something he could not conceivably ignore without exposing his complicity? And can we be completely sure that Ovid would never have admitted *stertere*? Latin poets writing in the more elevated genres do admit the occasional 'vulgarism' (see Axelson 25-45, and cf. 59n.); here Ovid could perhaps have introduced *stertere* to create a bluff, light-hearted tone, for some of the contexts in which it is used elsewhere (e.g. Hor. *S.* i. 5. 19, Mart. xi. 104. 15-16) suggest that the word was capable of a jocular nuance. Or, if Roman comedy was the direct model for this poem (see pp. 31-2), he could have deliberately chosen a word whose stylistic level connoted that genre (see Yardley (1987)). Furthermore, some positive support for Ovidian authorship may perhaps be drawn from the presence of *imponere* + dative in v. 24, since the use of the dative, rather than a prepositional phrase, after compound verbs is a notable Ovidian trait (see Hau 37-51).

In the end, then, in spite of my misgivings, I let the couplet stand.

25-6. **nec tu ... nec tu:** for the admonitory use of the personal pronoun cf. Hor. *Carm.* i. 11. 1 with Nisbet-Hubbard's note.

25. **fieri quid possit ad Isin:** the cult of Isis (see further 13. 7n.) required her devotees to attend twice-daily rituals and twice-yearly festivals, for which they prepared with a period of retreat in her temple and a ten-day abstinence from sexual relations (see Witt 191). The elegiac poets would have us believe that one of the cult's major attractions for contemporary women was the cover it could provide for one who wanted to avoid obliging her regular lover (*Am.* i. 8. 74, Prop. iv. 5. 33-4) or, as here, be sure of a chaperon-proof place for an assignation with his rival (cf. *Ars* iii. 635-6; also i. 77-8, iii. 393). But they were not short of imagination.

linigeram: Isis in ancient art and sculpture sometimes wears a linen robe (see Heyob 100). Her priests and devotees also traditionally wore linen. *liniger* is first attested in Ovid (also at *Met.* i. 747); for the formation see p. 13.

ad Isin: i.e *ad templum Isidis* (cf. Catul. 10. 26 *ad Serapim*). The Roman temple of Isis stood on the Campus Martius adjoining that of Serapis. For the spelling *Isin* see Kenney (1958a) 60.

26. **nec tu curua theatra time:** cf. *Ars* iii. 633. Serious misdemeanour at the theatre was in fact unlikely, for men and women were not even allowed to sit together there in Augustan times (see 7. 3n.), but a chaperoned woman could certainly be spotted, and perhaps signalled to, by a would-be lover (cf. *Ars* i. 89, 99, 133-4). *curua*, 'bent', neatly evokes both the theatre's semi-circular shape and the sort of behaviour it allegedly encouraged.

27. **honores:** 'tips'; cf. Cic. *Fam.* xvi. 9. 3 *Curio misi, ut medico honos haberetur.*

28. **autem:** Ovid is fond of this in interrogative sentences (see Axelson 85-6).

tacuisse: for the tense see 4. 22n.

29-30. Cf. the remarks of the ill-used slave Sceledrus about a more fortunate colleague at Pl. *Mil.* 349-51: *sed hic illi subparasitatur semper, hic eae proxumust, / primus ad cibum uocatur, primo pulmentum datur; / nam illic noster est fortasse circiter triennium / neque quoiquam quam illic in nostra meliust famulo familia.* See also p. 31.

29. Cf. *CLE* 1276. 5 (of a freed slave) *officiis uicit* [*dom*]*inum nec uerbera sens* [*it.* Clearly the writer knew Ovid.

uersat ... domum: 'turns the house upside-down'; cf. Verg. *A.* vii. 336 *odiis uersare domos.*

30. **alii:** = *ceteri*; see A. Ernout, *Aspects du vocabulaire* (Paris, 1954), 15.

sordida: 'lowly', 'common'; *sordere alicui* = 'to be beneath someone' (see e.g. Catul. 61. 129).

turba: 'bunch'; sc. 'of household slaves'? R.P. Winnington-Ingram (*CR* n.s. 5 (1955), 140-41) suggests that *turba* used colloquially with this meaning may have prompted the subsequent use of it for 'family' = 'children' (cf. *Met.* vi. 200 *Latonae turbam*). Ovid is fond of the word, which does not necessarily imply large numbers and is not always derogatory; cf. *Am.* ii. 9B. 53, *Ars* ii. 281.

iacent: 'are of no consequence'; cf. *Fast.* i. 218 *pauper ubique iacet.*

31. **huic ... causae finguntur inanes:** *huic* refers not to the last mentioned, i.e. the *custos*, but to the *uir* (cf. 15-16n.). Ovid's argument is that the eunuch need not fear that the *uir* will be suspicious when the mistress claims that he (the eunuch) deserves special treatment, since she can invent, for the benefit of the *uir* (*huic* I take to be an ironical dative of advantage), 'false reasons' for favouring the slave, and the *uir* will go along with what she wants (32-4).

32. **ambo domini:** i.e. *dominus et domina*; cf. *Am.* ii. 8. 24.

35. **iurgia nectat:** cf. *Am.* ii. 9B. 45.

36. **simulet lacrimas:** for the method see *Ars* i. 661-2.

carnificem: a common term of abuse, especially for slaves in Roman comedy. Like others of the same nature (*crux, furcifer* etc.), it was probably originally so used because the task of carrying out barbaric punishments normally fell to slaves, but eventually all these words came to serve as conventional insults (see Hofmann 85-9, Opelt 59-61, S. Lilja, *Terms of Abuse in Roman Comedy* (Helsinki, 1965) 56).

37-8. Ovid seems to be suggesting that the *custos* should make the odd false accusation so as to destroy his credibility whenever he makes a true one.

Our MSS are corrupt at the beginning of 38 (see apparatus on p. 94). Most editors adopt Ehwald's *et ueris falso*, but the indicative *obicies* (37) and the imperative *deme* (38) are most unhappily joined by *et*. I find Kenney's tentative *tu ueris falso* a much more attractive suggestion: it produces a neat and thoroughly Ovidian rhetorical balance with the hexameter, and palaeographically it is not implausible. *in ueris falso* (H. Magnus, *BPhW* 19 (1899), 1019), 'in making true accusations, use a false one (to destroy credibility)', makes no sense, for true accusations and false ones cannot be made simultaneously, and Heinsius' *i, ueris falso* (which necessitates reading *obiciens* in 37) succeeds only in introducing a tone quite unsuitable to the context (see *OLD* s.v. *eo* 10b).

37. **obicies:** the future indicative in commands has a more insistent tone than either the imperative or the perfect subjunctive; see Tränkle 154.

39-40. A return to the point of departure in vv. 15-16.

39. **sic alta peculia crescent:** *alta* must be taken proleptically: 'thus will your pile (of money) grow high'. A slave's *peculium* was his personal nest-egg and the nearest thing he ever had to private property (strictly speaking, even this belonged to his master). The *peculium* could ultimately be used to purchase freedom; normally only part of it need be surrendered to this end, and a master often made a slave a present of his *peculium* on manumission (see R. H. Barrow, *Slavery in the Roman Empire* (London, 1928), 53, 100-104). Metrical necessity will account for the plural here (see Löfstedt I. 44ff.).

41. **aspicis?:** a formula regularly used in didactic contexts to draw attention to some supposedly vital truth or to introduce an illustration of a proverbial nature; cf. *Am.* ii. 7. 15 (*aspice*), *Rem.* 235-6, and see further Kenney (1958b) 203.

indicibus: possessive dative, 'informers' (see 8. 5n.).

42. **orba fide pectora:** i.e. *eos quorum pectora orba fide sunt*. For *pectus* as the seat of moral qualities cf. Quint. *Decl.* 377 (p. 419, l. 9) *non sunt eiusdem pectoris uitia et uirtutes*.

43-4. Ovid mentions two of the three fabled and supposedly eternal (note the present tenses) punishments of Tantalus (see Smith on Tib. i. 3. 77-8), who divulged the secrets of the gods; cf. *Am.* iii. 7. 51, *Ars* ii. 605-6. Ovid's expression seems to owe something to Hor.

S. i. 1. 68-9 *Tantalus a labris sitiens fugientia captat / flumina,* but the witty *aquas in aquis* makes it his own. Note also the 'tantalising' postponement of the proper name.

45. **dum nimium seruat ...:** Argus, the hundred-eyed guard set by Juno to watch over Io, whom Jupiter loved and turned into a cow to protect her from his wife's wrath, was killed by Mercury after his hundred eyes had been lulled to sleep (see also 6. 55n.). The *exemplum* really illustrates the penalties of over-conscientious vigilance rather than those of tale-telling. Cf. *Am.* ii. 19. 29-30.

Io: Goold ((1965a) 12-14) establishes that the spelling *Io* (= Greek accusative 'Ἰώ), and not *Ion*, should be adopted here and at *Am.* ii. 19. 29, and similarly *Hero* (= Greek accusative Ἡρώ), not *Heron,* at *Am.* ii. 16. 31, but that *Iason* (= Greek nominative Ἰάσων), and not *Iaso*, should be read at *Am.* ii. 14. 33.

46. **suos annos:** see 6. 8n.

illa dea est: with Argus dead, Io escaped and after many wanderings eventually reached Egypt, where she regained her human form and became identified with the goddess Isis.

47-60. Ovid now relates his arguments against tale-bearing directly to the situation of the *custos* and the *uir*. A slave can expect to suffer, he says, for forcing knowledge of a woman's infidelity on her partner; it will upset him, and he will ignore it anyway.

If this poem was in circulation in or around 18 B.C., as it may well have been (see pp. 3-4), Ovid's words here will have had special significance. For 18 B.C. is the year in which Augustus' controversial *lex Iulia de adulteriis coercendis* is thought to have been passed (for ample bibliography see Stroh (1979) 324, nn. 3, 4, and now add Stahl 139ff., E. Badian, 'A Phantom Marriage Law', *Philologus* 129 (1985), 82-98, Galinsky (1996) 128-40). The law contained a clause which stated that a husband in possession of clear evidence of his wife's adultery must divorce her immediately or run the risk of being prosecuted himself for *lenocinium* ('connivance'); if he had witnessed the offence personally and still failed to institute divorce proceedings, he would suffer severe penalties (*dig*. xlviii. 5. 30; see further P. E. Corbett, *The Roman Law of Marriage* (Oxford, 1930), 142-3, H. Last, *Cambridge Ancient History* X (Cambridge, 1934), 446). Whether or not the relationship of the *puella* and the *uir* is to be understood as that of man and wife in the strictest legal sense (see p. 6), it seems very likely that Ovid's remarks were intended to recall the unpopular legislation and draw attention to the strong psychological disincentives to comply with it (notice especially vv. 57-8). Two things lend weight to this idea: (i) the use of the conveniently ambiguous word *maritus* in v. 51, which *can* refer to the male partner in any stable relationship, but most often (and far more often than *uir*) means 'husband' (see the discussion of Stroh (1979), especially 333ff.); and (ii) the sustained legal metaphor in vv. 51-61 (see nn. *ad loc.* and p. 12, with n. 91). See also pp. 39 and 91.

47. **uidi ego:** a common way of introducing an admonitory illustration, especially in a didactic context (see Kenney (1958b) 202). The formula is intended to give a ring of truth to the observation which follows (see Tränkle 24).

48. **unde:** = *ex quo* or *a quo* (see Kühner-Stegmann II. ii. 284-5).

incestum: 'infidelity'. This is the only occurrence of *incestum* in poetry. The technical quality of the word (it is used most often of the unchastity of Vestal Virgins; see *ThLL* VII. 895. 23ff.) suits the legalistic context.

51. **crede mihi:** see 9-10n.

marito: see 47-60n.

53-4. **seu ... siue:** see 4. 11-18n.

53. **tepet:** here 'cool in his love' (cf. *Am.* ii. 19. 54) and the opposite of *amat* (54), but *tepere* and *tepescere* and their compounds may also indicate a growing passion; see e.g. *Am.* ii. 3. 6, Hor. *Carm.* i. 4. 20. See also 1. 8n.

indicium ... perdis ad aures: we should perhaps assume some sort of ellipse, e.g. *operam perdis, securas ad aures indicium ferens*. For *indicium* see 8. 5n.

54. **officio ... tuo:** a nice touch of irony: 'by you doing your "duty" '.

55. **ex facili:** 'easily'; cf. *Ars* i. 356.
quamuis manifesta probatur: a legalism: 'however conclusively proven' (see Berger s.v. *probationes manifestissimae*; also 47-60n.).

56. **iudicis ... fauore:** again juristic: 'the judge giving (her) the benefit of the doubt' (see Berger s.v. *fauor*).
uenit: in the legalistic context one is tempted to understand *uenit in iudicium* (see Berger s.v. *uenire*), but Ovid may not have intended *uenit* to be any more than a synonym for *est* or *fit*; cf. *Am.* i. 10. 33 *quae Venus ex aequo uentura est grata duobus*, Prop. i. 4. 9-10 with Fedeli's note.

59. **plorabit:** this verb appears to have had a 'vulgar' tone – 'howl' or 'blubber' rather than 'weep'. It is generally avoided by the writers of literary prose and is excluded altogether from epic and tragedy, but in elegy and lyric, where the idea of noisy, undignified crying is perhaps less unacceptable, it is admitted occasionally (Axelson collects examples at 28-9). Here Ovid may well have used *plorare* to emphasise the indecorum of the behaviour he envisages. It is much more difficult to account for his choice of this verb in the first line of his funeral elegy for Tibullus (*Am.* iii. 9).

61. **certamen:** 'contest' in a legal sense. Cf. 7. 2n.

62. **in gremio ... sedet:** for Ovid, an especially disarming female ploy; see *Am.* ii. 18. 5-12.

63-6. **aggredimur ... coimus ... quaerimus ... possimus:** true plurals, indicating that Ovid is making the request on behalf of the *puella* as well as himself.

63-4. **non ... non ... non:** anaphora (see p. 14) emphasises the non-violent and non-criminal nature of Ovid's request.
non ad miscenda coimus / toxica: Ovid ends his harangue with a splendid joke: both *miscere* and *coire* may mean 'to have sexual intercourse' (see e.g. *Fast.* iii. 193, Verg. *A.* vii. 661 and further Adams (1982) 178-9, 180-81), and the *custos* is encouraged to think, when he hears *non ad miscenda coimus*, that his fears of sexual misdemeanour may after all have been unfounded – only to have his hopes dashed utterly when *toxica* follows at the beginning of the pentameter. Cf. 5. 49-50n.

66. **mollius:** a parting shot, perhaps: *mollis* can mean 'seductive' (see 4. 23-4n.) as well as 'mild and inoffensive'.

Poem 3

The immediate sequel to 2; see pp. 30-33.

1. **ei mihi:** a strong cry of anguish or dismay (see Hofmann 13). Here the tone is ironic (cf. *Am.* ii. 18. 20, 19. 34), but Ovid often uses the expression for genuinely pathetic effect (e.g. *Met.* vi. 227, *Ep.* 3. 14).
dominam ... seruas: an echo of 2. 1 (see n.), but the general tenor of 3 suggests that a sarcastic *double entendre* is intended here: both 'You guard the lady of your house' and 'You keep a mistress'. For *domina* see 1. 17n.
nec uir nec femina: for the expression cf. *Ib.* 453 *de ... uiro fias nec femina nec uir*, V. Max. vii. 7. 6, *CLE* 129. 5-6, Eur. *Or.* 1528.

2. **mutua ... Veneris gaudia:** i.e. the pleasures experienced by both the male and the female partner in sexual intercourse (cf. *Am.* iii. 6. 87-8, Lucr. iv. 1192ff., v. 853-4). It would appear from v. 3 that Ovid conceives of his addressee as one who has been castrated in

boyhood. This is consistent with the idea that he can never know what it is to copulate, or want to copulate, with a woman; neither the urge nor the capacity necessarily deserted those castrated only after reaching full manhood (see Juv. 6. 366-78 with Courtney's note on 366).

nec: for the position see p. 13, with n. 107.

3-4. Abuse of the inventor or discoverer of an implement, skill or practice is a literary commonplace dating back to Euripides (*Hipp.* 407-9), and one which became especially popular with the Roman elegists; cf. *Am.* ii. 14. 5-6, Tib. i. 10. 1-2, Prop. ii. 6. 31-2 (for useful bibliography see Nisbet-Hubbard I. 49-50).

3. **genitalia membra recidit:** horribly explicit. *genitalia membra* probably means 'testicles' alone, not 'testicles and penis' (see Adams (1982) 69).

5. Here Ovid mischievously suggests prurient jokes which never materialise. First *mollis* leads the reader to expect a standard gibe, for it was a regular derogatory epithet of effeminates of all kinds (see e.g. *Ib.* 454, Pl. *Aul.* 422), but when it is followed by *in* + accusative (an apparently unique alternative to *ad* + accusative with *mollis*; see *ThLL* VIII. 1380. 56ff.), he realises it can only mean 'easily persuaded into'. Then the next words suggest that Ovid is going to accuse the eunuch of being all too ready to indulge in intercourse of a perverted kind, for *obsequium* may indicate specifically *sexual* compliance (see e.g. Liv. xxxix. 42. 9, Curt. x. 1. 25), *facilis* willingness to oblige with *sexual* favours (see e.g. *Ars* iii. 475) and *rogantibus* those who request them (cf. *Am.* ii. 2. 5, 7. 25, 19. 20, and see Tränkle 163ff.). But all we are left with in the end is the relatively innocuous claim that the eunuch would be more sympathetic to lovers requesting access to his mistress, if he had ever been in love himself (v. 6).

6. **in quauis praetepuisset:** *in* + ablative regularly denotes the object of passion with expressions of 'burning' and 'growing warm' (for the metaphor see 1. 8n.); cf. *Am.* i. 9. 33, and see also 1. 5, 8. 11nn.). This is the only recorded instance of *praetepescere*; see further p.13, with n. 97.

7-8. At first it would seem that Ovid simply means to imply that the eunuch is debarred from a military career because he *is* a eunuch and *ipso facto* a weakling; but slaves were not normally eligible for military service anyway (though they could be enlisted as a last resort; see Brunt 64, 418-20, 474, 499-500, 648-51), and it soon becomes clear that all Ovid is really concerned with here is accommodating a series of sexual *double entendres* (see nn. below) and paving the way for a variation on the standard military metaphor of the elegists in v. 10.

7. **non tu natus equo:** not just 'You are not made for the cavalry', but doubtless also 'You are not made for sex'. The equestrian metaphor is fairly common in Greek and Roman descriptions of sexual intercourse; it normally describes the *schema* in which the woman is positioned astride the man, but there is evidence to suggest that it was also used when the positions of male and female were reversed (see Adams (1982) 165-6).

non fortibus utilis armis: not only 'useless with heroic weapons', but also 'powerless to wield the weapon of manhood', i.e. the penis. For other exploitations of the double meaning of *arma* cf. *Am.* i. 9. 25-6, ii. 9B. 48, Petr. 130, and see also Spies 69ff., Adams (1982) 21. *fortibus* and *utilis* reinforce the *double entendre*, for *fortis* can mean 'virile' (cf. *Am.* ii. 10. 28, *Ars* ii. 709, Juv. 6. 0 25) and *utilis* 'potent' (cf. *Am.* ii. 10. 28, *Ars* ii. 710, and see further Adams (1982) 46) in the sexual sense.

8. Like words for other pointed weapons, *hasta* sometimes = 'penis' (see e.g. *Priap.* 43. 1 Bücheler, Aus. *Cent. Nupt.* 117 Peiper, and further Adams (1982) 19-20). Thus *bellica ... hasta* here will suggest not only the 'spear' of *bellum* proper but also the 'spear' of *bellum amoris*, and when Ovid claims that this is 'out of place' in the eunuch's right hand, I think he intends to imply that his penis will not even respond to manual stimulation – a climactic

insult with which to end the couplet. The *left* hand is the one most frequently associated with self-stimulation (see Adams (1982) 209), but *laeua* will not accommodate the double meaning as well as *dextra* here.

9. **ista:** this relates back to *equo*, *arma* (7) and *hasta* (8) and so will include both war and sex.

mares: *mas* is a semi-technical term meaning 'a fully potent male'; cf. Catul. 16. 13.

tu: see 2. 25-6n.

spes ... uiriles: i.e. both military and sexual ambitions.

10. Active participants in the 'war of love' (see pp. 53-4) are frequently depicted as 'carriers of standards' (cf. *Am.* ii. 9A. 3, 12. 14, 28); but the most that the non-combatant eunuch can hope for is to do some standard-carrying on an active participant's behalf – and a woman's at that.

11-12. **hanc imple meritis ... quis tuus usus erit?:** *prima facie* this means '*She* is the one you must load with favours ... without *her* what use can you be?'. But again there is the possibility of indecent innuendo: *implere* can mean 'make pregnant' (see e.g. *Met.* vi. 111) or 'inseminate'; it is especially often used of a male animal 'serving' the female (see Adams (1982) 207). And it seems reasonable to suppose that *usus* could, like *utilis* (see 7n.), indicate specifically sexual 'usefulness'.

hanc ... huic ... illa: see 2. 15-16n.

12. **si careas ... erit:** the combination of present subjunctive and future indicative in remote conditions is common in poetry (see Kenney (1958a) 63); Ovid's choice of it here allows one of his favourite types of pentameter-ending – a disyllabic part of *esse* in *e-* (see further B. Axelson, 'Der Mechanismus des ovidischen Pentameterschlusses', *Ovidiana* 121-35); cf. the paratactic construction at *Am.* ii. 9B. 53-4.

13. For the expression cf. [Ov.] *Ep. Sapph.* 21. *facies* = 'good looks' (cf. *Am.* ii. 1. 33, 17. 7, 11, 12); *lusibus* = 'love-making' (cf. Prop. i. 10. 9 with Fedeli's note).

14. The idea of sexual abstinence leading to the decline of physical attractiveness (cf. *Am.* i. 8. 53, *Ars* iii. 79-80) is a variation on the ancient and proverbial notion that beauty is ephemeral; see Otto 141.

forma: see 4. 9n.

15. **quamuis habeare molestus:** literally 'although you are found to be a nuisance'; the active voice of *habere* is more frequently used in this manner (cf. *Met.* v. 559, Prop. iv. 11. 13).

16. **uoluere:** probably a gnomic perfect.

17. **aptius at fuerit...:** Heinsius' *at* for *ut* (full apparatus on p. 95) must be right: an adversative particle is desirable after the remarks in vv. 15-16, and *fuerit* needs no subordinating conjunction. For the position of *at* see p. 13 with n. 107.

rogamus: see 2. 63-5n.

18. **bene ponendi munera:** 'get a good return for your services'. A metaphor from business language: *pecuniam ponere* or *collocare* means 'to invest money' (see e.g. Hor. *Epod.* 2. 69-70, *Ars* 421).

Poem 4

1. **ausim:** the archaic perfect subjunctive, which is regularly used in so-called 'modest assertions'.

2-3. **uitiis ... delicta:** 'faults' and 'wrongdoings' in a general sense, but both words are used often enough of amatory misdemeanours (see e.g. *Am.* iii. 4. 11, 6. 49) to give the reader an inkling of what is to come.

4. **in mea crimina ... eo:** literally 'I proceed to (make) my own charges'.

5. *cupiens* must be taken concessively; cf. *Am.* iii. 7. 5 *nec potui cupiens, pariter cupiente puella*. Ovid is making fun of Catullus' celebrated *odi et amo* (85. 1) here. Catullus was torn between hatred and love of a woman: Ovid claims to be torn between hatred and love of himself.

7. **iusque:** *ius* with the sense 'power', 'control' is most commonly found in the phrases *sui iuris* and *suo iure*, but cf. Pers. 5. 176-7 *ius habet ille sui, palpo quem ducit ... / ... ambitio?*. For the postponement of *-que* see p. 13 with n. 107.

8. **auferor:** both 'I am swept away' (cf. *Rem.* 264), in anticipation of the image of the buffeted ship, and, more generally, 'I am robbed of my reason' (cf. *Rem.* 343, Verg. *Ecl.* 8. 41).
ut rapida ...: for the simile cf. *Am.* ii. 10. 9, and see also 9B. 29-32n. *rapidus* is a conventional epithet of wind and water.

9. **certa:** a 'particular' type, i.e. one and one only. The usage is found mainly in late Latin (*ThLL* III. 903. 78ff.), but cf. Lucr. iii. 98 *sensum animi certa non esse in parte locatum*.
forma: the word embraces three meanings here: (i) 'appearance' (cf. *Ars* i. 509), (ii) 'beauty' (cf. *Am.* ii. 3. 14, 6. 17) and (iii) 'a beautiful woman' (cf. Prop. ii. 28. 53).
meos ... amores: the plural is idiomatic; see Smith on Tib. ii. 2. 11, La Penna 199-201.

10. Cf. *Am.* i. 3. 1-2, 15.

11-46. A masterpiece of systematic exposition and artistic *uariatio*. Ovid divides female attractions into three categories – traits of character (11-16), accomplishments (17-32) and physical appearance (33-46) – and, for the most part, arranges the different types within these categories in antithetical pairs. He relieves simple statement with apostrophe (17-18, 33-4) and rhetorical question (27-8) and variously points contrasts with (a) *siue ... si ... seu* (11-18, 41-4), (b) *est quae ... est quae* (19-21) and (c) emphatic demonstrative or personal pronouns (25-30, 33-6, 46). Sentence-length and sentence-structure are also skilfully varied throughout. Cf. *Am.* i. 15. 9-30.

11-18. **siue ... siue ... si ... siue:** Ovid shows a marked liking for *siue ... siue* or *siue ... seu* rather than *seu ... seu*, but metrical necessity forces him to set aside his preference at 41-4 below.

11. **in se:** this (= ς; full apparatus on p. 95) gives good sense; cf. (*pace* Goold (1965a) 31) *Am.* i. 8. 37 *cum bene deiectis gremium spectabis ocellis*, *Ep.* 11. 35 *gremio ... pudor deiecit ocellos*, *Ep.* 20 (21). 113 *lumina ... in gremio ueluti defixa tenebam*. Some prefer *in me* (= *PSY*ω), but 'in my case' is pointless here; others favour the conjecture *in humum*, but it is difficult to see how this could ever have become corrupted to *in me* or *in se*.

12. **uror:** see 1. 8n.
insidiae ... meae: 'what entraps me'; the possessive adjective replaces an objective genitive.

13. **procax:** generally very derogatory when used of a woman; see e.g. Cic. *Cael.* 49, Liv. xxxix. 43. 4.
capior: 'I am hooked' (cf. *Ars* iii. 425-6), a continuation of the metaphor introduced by *insidiae* in v. 12.
rustica: see 8. 3n.

14. **molli ... toro:** i.e. a couch used for love-making; *mollis* is virtually a technical term; cf. *Ars* ii. 712, Tib. i. 2. 56.
mobilis: 'sexually athletic'. *mobilis* as an erotic euphemism first appears in Ovid; the similar use of *motus* and *mouere* is well attested in earlier writing (see Booth (1981) 2692-3).

15. **rigidas ... Sabinas:** Sabine chastity was proverbial; cf. Juv. 6. 163-4, Mart. ix. 40. 4-5, and see further Otto 304. It is often cited with approval (see e.g. Hor. *Carm.* iii. 6. 37-41),

but Ovid's references to it are generally mocking; cf. *Am.* i. 8. 39-40, iii. 8. 61 and especially *Ars* i. 100-32.

16. The syntax is puzzling. It seems best to assume a combination of hyperbaton (see p. 16) and ellipse and understand *puto eam uelle ex alto, sed dissimulare*. For *ex alto* = 'deep down' cf. Lucr. iv. 73 *non solum ex alto penitusque*. Some take *ex alto* with *dissimulare* rather than *uelle* (e.g. Munari, 'dissimula profondamente'), but 'dissimulation', by its very nature, takes place 'on the surface', not 'deep down'. For the ellipse of the subject accusative see R. C. Manning, 'On the omission of the subject of the infinitive in Ovid', *HSPh* 4 (1893), 117-41, Löfstedt II. 262-3.

17-26. For the polyptoton see p. 16

17-18. **places ... placita es:** a regular amatory usage: 'you appeal', 'take my fancy'. Passive *placitus* = 'pleasing' is well attested; cf. *Ars* i. 37, Verg. *G.* ii. 425.

17. **dotata:** 'richly endowed', 'gifted'. A rare usage of a rare word; in classical Latin cf. only *Met.* xi. 301 (*Chione*) *dotatissima formā.*

18. **rudis:** i.e. not accomplished in any *artes*.

simplicitate: here 'simplicity' in a complimentary sense; cf. the pejorative tone at *Ars* iii. 113.

19. **Callimachi prae nostris ...:** *rustica* indicates that the point of comparison is style, not subject-matter (cf. Catul. 36. 19-20 *pleni ruris et inficetiarum / annales Volusi*). Stylistic refinement was one of the qualities by which Callimachus set greatest store (*Aet.* fr. 1. 17-18, *Ap.* 105-12), and Ovid evidently admired him for it (see *Am.* i. 15. 13-14).

prae: here and at *Am.* ii. 9B. 38 = 'in comparison with'.

21. **uatem:** see 1. 34n.

22. **cupiam sustinuisse:** here, as often (cf. v. 26 below, *Am.* ii. 11. 31-2, iii. 2. 30), perfect infinitive for present is metrically convenient, but the usage is also frequently found where there is no metrical necessity for it (e.g. *Am.* ii. 7. 19, *Ars* i. 406, 496); it even appears in the prose of Livy and Tacitus. For its development see Kühner-Stegmann II. i. 133 (with bibliography), Bömer on *Fast.* ii. 322.

femur: this occurs in several of the elegists' euphemistic expressions for sexual intercourse; cf. *femur femori committere* (*Am.* i. 4. 43), *femur femori conserere* (Tib. i. 8. 26), and see further Adams (1982) 180.

23-4. For the importance of a graceful and seductive gait cf. *Ars* iii. 298-306, Petr. 126. *mollis* = both 'supple' and 'sensuous' or 'sexy'. Cf. 2. 66n.

24. **tacto ... uiro:** another euphemism for sexual intercourse; cf. *Ars* ii. 633-4, and see Adams (1982) 185-6.

25-6. Singing and playing the lyre were the branches of music in which the women most attractive to the elegists were supposed to excel; cf. *Ars* iii. 311-28, Prop. i. 2. 27-30, ii. 1. 9-10, 3. 19-20.

25. **huic:** the transmitted *haec* (see apparatus on p. 95) is perfectly intelligible, but it 'unnecessarily deprives the sentence of smoothness by raising and then frustrating the anticipation of a third person singular verb' (Goold (1965a) 32-3).

dulce: adverbial accusative; cf. *Am.* iii. 1. 4. Only neuter accusatives such as *multum*, *plus* and *tantum* are used adverbially in republican and Augustan prose, but the poets extend the usage to many other adjectives, and even prose-writers adopt it later; see Kühner-Stegmann II. i. 280-81.

flectit ... uocem: for the expression cf. Tib. i. 7. 37, Lucr. v. 1406.

facillima: a common and idiomatic adverbial use of the adjective; see Löfstedt II. 368ff., Kühner-Stegmann II. i. 234ff., and cf. *numerosa* in v. 29.

26. **oscula ... rapta dedisse:** 'to steal kisses' (for the perfect infinitive see 22n.). *oscula rapere* alone will convey this meaning (see e.g. Hor. *Carm.* ii. 12. 25-8), but Ovid has conflated the phrase with the simpler *oscula dare*. Here the person who takes the initiative gives the kisses; contrast Tib. i. 4. 55 (with Smith's note).

27. **querulas ... chordas:** sc. *lyrae*. *querulus* is used by the poets not only of stringed instruments but also of the pipes (*tibiae*, e.g. Hor. *Carm*. iii. 7. 30) and the trumpet (*tuba*, e.g. Prop. iv. 3. 20). Doubtless its function is largely ornamental.

percurrit pollice chordas: alliterative *p* and *c* perhaps suggest the sound of plucking.

27-8. **pollice ... manus:** the technique of playing the lyre is obscure in some details, but it is clear enough that both hands were actively involved in plucking, stopping or damping the strings (*RE* XIII. 2. 2480, Daremberg and Saglio III. 1447, E. Borthwick, 'Κατάληψις a neglected technical term in Greek music', *CQ* n.s. 9 (1959), 23-9). Ovid's frequent use of *pollex* in the context of lyre-playing does not necessarily indicate that the thumb had an important technical role, for *pollex* is sometimes used simply as a convenient metrical alternative to *digiti* or *manus*; see e.g. *Am*. iii. 6. 71, *Met*. ix. 395, xiii. 746.

29-30. The sensual quality of the ancient dance (see especially Autom. *AP* v. 129), with its supple movements of the arms and body rather than of the feet, suggests that it was akin to oriental dancing.

29. **numerosa:** see 25n. *facillima.*

30. **torquet ... latus:** cf. *artifices lateris* for 'dancers' at *Ars* iii. 351.

ab arte: 'with skill'. *ab* with the instrumental ablative in this phrase seems to be idiomatic, and not merely a matter of metrical convenience (cf. p. 13), for it is used not only by poets, Ovid in particular (see Bömer on *Fast*. ii. 764), but also occasionally by prose-writers; see e.g. Cic. *de Orat*. ii. 220, Var. *R*. i. 59. 2, Vitr. v. 4. 3.

31. **ut taceam:** 'to say nothing of'. An idiomatic use of the final *ut*; see further Lewis and Short's *Latin Dictionary*, s.v. II. 5c.

ab: see p. 13, with n. 106.

32. **Hippolytum ... Priapus:** the former the supreme example of chastity (cf. 18. 24n.), the latter of lechery; cf. *Priap*. 19. 5-6 Bücheler *haec si non modo te, Priape, posset / priuignum quoque sed mouere Phaedrae.*

33-6. The ancient poets' ideally beautiful woman was tall and broad (see Catul. 86. 1-4 with Fordyce's notes, Lilja 127; cf., however, *Ars* ii. 645-6), and attraction to a small woman apparently required some explanation (see v. 35, and cf. Phld. *AP* v. 121. 1-2). Women's own ideas on the perfect figure were possibly somewhat different: see Ter. *Eu*. 313ff.

34. **multa:** = *magna*; cf. *Am*. i. 15. 42, Hor. *Carm* iii. 30. 6.

35. **habilis:** literally 'easily holdable'; cf. *Ars* ii. 661 *dic 'habilem' quaecumque breuis*, *Am*. i. 4. 37 *habiles ... papillae.*

utraque: ablative of agent; see p. 13, with n. 106.

37. Cf. *Met*. i. 497-8 *spectat inornatos collo pendere capillos / et 'quid, si comantur?' ait.*

culta: 'smart' in dress, coiffure and make-up; cf. Prop. i. 2. 5, Tib. i. 8. 15.

38. **ornata:** *ornare* is most often used of hair-styling (see e.g. *Am*. ii. 7. 17, 23, *Ars* iii. 244, and cf. *ornatrix* at *Am*. i. 14. 16, *Ars* iii. 239) and at least once of making up the face (Tib. i. 8. 11), but *ornata* here, contrasting with *non culta* in 37, will mean 'got up' generally.

dotes exhibit ipsa suas: 'she brings out her good points'. For *dotes* in this sense cf. *Rem*. 325. For *ipsa suas* see 6. 55n.

39-44. Ovid would appear to be distinguishing three types of appearance here: a fair-haired type (*flaua* – this word always refers to hair-colour and never to skin-colour; see E. Laughton, '*Flauus Pudor*', *CR* 62 (1948), 109-11, *id*., '*Flauus* again', *CR* 64 (1950), 88-9) and two dark-haired types, one fair-skinned (*candida*) and the other dark-skinned (*fusco ...colore*). The first of the two mythological *exempla* in 41-4 makes it clear that the fair-skinned beauty in Ovid's mind here will have dark hair, while no indication of hair-colour is needed in the case of the dark-skinned beauty, for we should naturally assume such a girl also to be dark-haired. Cf. *Am.* iii. 7. 23-4, where *Libas* in 24 suggests *Libys*, 'African', and hence *fusca*. For the general elegiac preoccupation with hair and complexion see Lilja 119-32.

39-40. Cf. Prop. ii. 25. 41-2.

39. **candida:** 'whiteness' and 'brightness' are the basic notions conveyed by this adjective, and it accordingly describes a fair complexion, not dead white, but tinged with rosiness (see e.g. *Am.* iii. 3. 5-6, Prop. ii. 3. 9-12, iii. 24. 7-8); it is also an adjective of commendation, as our 'fair' used to be. See further André 325, and cf. 7. 5n.

flaua: = ξανθή: hair (see 39-44n.) of a light, reddish-gold shade is indicated (Nisbet-Hubbard I. 75). Blondes, being comparatively rare in southern Europe, were (and still are) particularly appreciated there, and Greek and Roman women evidently resorted to the use of wigs and dyes to achieve the desired effect; see *Am.* i. 14. 45, Juv. 6. 120 with Courtney's note, [Lucian] *Am.* 40.

40. **fusco ... colore:** Ovid may have a swarthy south-European or near-eastern girl in mind or perhaps a negress (cf. *Moretum* 33 *Afra genus ... fusca colore*). *fuscus* obviously denoted a lighter colour than *niger* and could serve as a euphemism for it (see e.g. *Ars* 657-8 *'fusca' uocetur, / nigrior Illyrica cui pice sanguis erit, Rem.* 327), and the fact that need for a euphemism was felt, together with writers' frequent defensiveness on the subject of attraction to a dark-skinned love (see e.g. Verg. *Ecl.* 10. 38-9 and further Nisbet-Hubbard II. 70), seems to suggest that dark-skinned peoples were considered inferior at least in appearance, but it is not necessarily indicative of colour-prejudice of a more general kind. For attitudes to negroes see F. M. Snowden, *Blacks in Antiquity* (Cambridge Mass., 1970) and *Before Color Prejudice* (Cambridge Mass., 1983); both books are somewhat tendentious (and the later one does not add much to the earlier), but they nevertheless contain a useful collection of material. Cf. 8. 22n.

41. **ceruice:** local ablative; for the absence of preposition see p. 13.

41-2. **capilli ... coma:** these words are synonymous, and clearly Ovid varies his terms only for aesthetic effect.

42. **Leda ... nigra conspicienda coma:** nowhere else is Leda renowned for having black hair (for her chief claim to fame see *Am.* i. 10. 3-4); indeed she is on at least one occasion called ξανθή, 'blonde' (Anon. *AP* v. 65. 2). For the scansion of *nigra* with first syllable long cf. Hor. *Carm.* i. 32. 11 with Nisbet-Hubbard's note.

43. **flauent:** one of only two recorded instances of the finite verb *flauere* (the other is at Col. x. 311).

placuit croceis Aurora capillis: deities in classical literature are conventionally blond, but the description of Aurora's hair as *croceus*, 'saffron', i.e. yellow tinged with red, is specifically meant to evoke the colour of the dawn sky. The epithet is transferred to other features and accoutrements of Aurora, e.g. *genae* (*Fast.* iii. 403), *amictus* (*Ars* iii. 179), *rotae* (*Met.* iii. 150), *cubile* (Verg. *G.* i. 447).

44. An ideal motto for the non-individualistic love-poetry of the *Amores* (cf. 1. 5-10n.). For *historiis* = 'myths', 'legends', cf. Prop. i. 15. 24 (to Cynthia) *uti fieres nobilis historia.*

45. For *serior aetas,* 'one of riper years', cf. *Ars* i. 65, ii. 667; *noua aetas* for 'a young one' seems to be a unique expression.

46. The text is in doubt (full apparatus on p. 95). Most editors read with Heinsius and Burman *haec melior specie corporis, illa sapit*, 'the one (i.e. the young woman') has better physical appearance, the other (i.e. the older woman) has the "know how" '. This reading gives excellent sense (cf. *Ars* ii. 675ff.), but produces (in contrast with 45) an oddly unbalanced line. The alternative is to read *haec melior specie, moribus illa placet.* Sponsoring this reading, Kenney ((1958a) 60), collects examples to show that *mores* can mean simply 'character' or 'behaviour'; this disposes of Burman's objection to *moribus* on the grounds that *mores* = *pudicitia* and so is inappropriate here (*CIL* IV. 4592, which Kenney cites as a postscript ((1959) 240), does reinforce his point, but it is extravagant to claim that 'the case for *moribus* is clinched' by it). Lenz objects to *moribus* on the grounds that, while 'appearance' and 'character' may be an effective antithesis in itself, it does not make much sense in contrasting a young woman with an older one, since the better-looking younger woman could also have an agreeable character. And yet not even this objection really disables *moribus*, for Ovid may in fact be saying: 'Both young women and older women attract me (because I do not insist on good *species* and good *mores* at the same time); a young woman has better looks (and so her character is immaterial), but an older woman can win me over by her character alone (in which case her looks are immaterial)'.

On balance, then – and for the sake of it – I elect to follow Kenney.

haec ... illa: 'the former' ... 'the latter' rather than *vice versa*, as would be more normal; see 2. 15-16n.

48. **ambitiosus:** this often means 'eager for' (cf. *Tr.* v. 7. 28), but its literal sense is 'embracing' (see e.g. Hor. *Carm.* i. 36. 20), and thus we have a neat *double entendre*. But this is not all; *ambitiosus* is also used of a candidate for political office who 'goes around' canvassing for votes (see Gel. xi. 12. 1). So there is a cheeky suggestion that Ovid the rakish lover sets about making conquests as purposefully as the committed politician sets about winning votes.

Poem 5

1-2. Ovid's apparent renunciation of love is perhaps too bland (notice especially the glib dismissal of Cupid, which is no more than a line-filler here) to be taken altogether seriously even at this stage of the poem; contrast Catul. 8. 1.

1. **pharetrate:** see 9A. 5n.

3. **peccasse:** see 7. 11n.

4. **o:** the vulgate *ei* (full apparatus on p. 95) is not contemptible, given (a) that *ei mihi* is an expression Ovid uses a lot (46 times in all) and almost always in the first foot, and (b) that *mihi* could perhaps both be taken with *ei* (the exclamatory *ei* standing alone is largely a pre-classical usage; see Camps on Prop. i. 7. 16) and serve as dative of disadvantage with *nata ... malum* (cf. 18. 7-8n. *me miseram*). But I favour the variant *o*, because this regularly introduces extended vocatives and parenthetical exclamations and is particularly common in Ovid with those of a reproachful nature (cf. *Am.* i. 6. 62, ii. 9A. 1-2, 17. 12, iii. 1. 16, *Ep.* 1. 41, 11. 121; see further Goold (1965a) 31-2). The conjecture *in* (A. Ker, *Ovidiana* 226) is unnecessary; if we understand *esse* with *nata*, *perpetuum malum* is, as Goold points out, perfectly acceptable as a predicative nominative.

5. **deceptae ... tabellae:** for *deceptae* = 'camouflaged' cf. Liv. xxii. 4. 4 *ab tergo ac super caput deceptae insidiae*, Sen. *HF* 155-6 (of a fisherman) *deceptos / instruat hamos*, and see further Booth (1982) 156-7. Wax tablets traditionally carried elegiac love-letters (see e.g. *Am.* i. 11. 7ff., i. 12, *Ars* i. 437ff., Tib. ii. 6. 45-6, Prop. iii. 23); for the type of camouflage Ovid probably has in mind see *Ars* iii. 483ff.

6. **munera:** presents, much to the poets' vexation, were *de rigueur* in courtship of the conventional elegiac mistress; see e.g. *Am.* i. 8. 93ff., i. 10, *Ars* i. 417ff., ii. 261ff., Prop. ii. 16. 15ff., 23. 8, iii. 13.

crimen habent: 'give grounds for accusation, complaint'. Ovid is fond of the expression; cf. *Ars* ii. 272, *Rem.* 328, *Tr.* ii. 265.

7-12. See p. 39.

7. **o utinam:** hiatus after the interjections *o, heu* and *a* is regular in elegy (see Platnauer 57).

9-10. A slight 'hysteron proteron' (see p. 13). What Ovid means is 'Fortunate is he to whom his mistress can deny her infidelity (since he has not himself witnessed it), because *then* he can venture to defend her'.

9. **felix, qui:** this formula, so common in heroic and solemn contexts (cf. especially Verg. *G.* ii. 490 and see further Nisbet-Hubbard I. 177), is humorously incongruous here (cf. *Am.* ii. 10. 29, 11. 30).
quod: see 2. 14n.

10. **'non feci':** 'Not guilty'; cf. Juv. 6. 638 with Courtney's note.
amica: see 1. 17n.

11. **dolori:** not 'pain', but, as often in the context of sexual infidelity, 'indignation' (cf. v. 33 below, *Met.* i. 736 with Bömer's note, Juv. 10. 315). Ovid is accusing the man who insists on proving his mistress' infidelity of being vindictive. His phraseology seems to owe something to Tib. ii. 5. 110.

12. **cui:** = *a quo*; see p. 13, with n. 100.
palma cruenta: literally 'a blood-stained palm'. A palm branch was the emblem of victory in sporting contests, and Ovid uses the expression *palma cruenta* here as a vivid metaphor for a victory unconscionably extracted at undue cost to the loser.

13-32. The banquet is a favourite elegiac setting for flirtation and seduction (cf. *Ars* i. 229ff., 565ff., iii. 749ff., and see 15-20nn.). Such behaviour was possibly not uncommon at real Augustan dinner-parties (see Hor. *Carm.* iii. 6. 25-6, and cf. Griffin (1985) 22), but it seems likely that Ovid drew some inspiration for the present scene from the Adultery Mime. This popular form of entertainment featured the eternal triangle, with a saucy wife attempting to cuckold a credulous husband and being surprised *in flagrante delicto* with her paramour (cf. 33n.). See further R. W. Reynolds, 'The Adultery Mime', *CQ* 40 (1946), 77-84, McKeown (1979).

13. **ipse uidi:** contrast vv. 5-6, and note the continued emphasis on personal observation with *uidi* again in 15 and 23.
cum me dormire putares ...: cf. *Am.* i. 4. 51-4. The *uir* who can be induced to doze off in his cups is often presented as an easy and/or willing dupe; cf. *Ars* ii. 545-6, Tib. i. 6. 27-8, Juv. 1. 55-7.

15-18. The methods of secret communication described are standard in love-poetry, but here they remind us especially of Ovid's own instructions to his *puella* in *Am.* i. 4. For the eloquently twitching eyebrows (15) cf. *Am.* i. 4. 19, *Ars* i. 500, *Ep.* 16 (17). 82, Prop. iii. 8. 25; for the significant nods (16) cf. *Am.* i. 4. 17, iii. 11. 23, *Ars* i. 138, *Tr.* ii. 453, Tib. i. 2. 21; for the talking eyes (17) cf. *Ars* i. 573, *Ep.* 16 (17). 77, 89, Paul. Sil. *AP* v. 262. 2; for the vinous writing on the table (17-18) cf. *Am.* i. 4. 20, *Ep.* 16 (17). 88, *Ars* i. 571, *Tr.* ii. 454, Tib. i. 6. 19-20; and for the finger-language (18 – the idea must be one of spelling out words by displaying the fingers in the shape of their individual letters) cf. *Am.* i. 4. 20, *Ep.* 16 (17). 81-2, *Tr.* ii. 453, Prop. iii. 8. 26 with Fedeli's note. See further Sittl 213-14.

16. **pars bona:** i.e. *pars magna*; cf. Hor. *S.* i. 1. 61 *bona pars hominum.*

17. **conscripta:** *conscribere* is generally rare and used in the Augustan period only by Ovid (cf. *Pont.* ii. 9. 73) and Livy; see further p. 13, with n. 97.

19-20. A verbal as well as a visual code has evidently been agreed upon; for a good idea of how it might work see *Ep.* 15 (16). 241-4, *Ars* i. 569-70 and Hollis' note on *Ars* i. 601.

19. **sermonem ... quod non uideatur agentem:** 'conversation dealing with something it does not appear to be dealing with' (understand *aliquid* with *agentem*); for *uideri* of things audible rather than visible cf. Verg. *A.* vi. 257 *uisaeque canes ululare*, with Norden's note, and see Nisbet-Hubbard I. 183.

20. Literally 'words made to carry meaning in accordance with a pre-arranged code'; cf. *Am.* iii. 11. 24 *uerbaque compositis dissimulata notis*, Tib. i. 2. 22 *blandaque compositis abdere uerba notis*, *Ars* i. 489-90, and note also *per notas scribere* = 'to write in cipher' at Suet. *Aug*. 88.

21. **iamque:** the particle signals the beginning of a new phase of the narrative (see Hand III. 151-2).

frequens ... conuiua: collective singular, 'the guests in large numbers' (cf. *Ars* i. 50, 93, 603, and for this usage in general, Nisbet-Hubbard I. 241); here Ovid must mean 'the majority of the guests'. His habitual way of describing the breaking up of social gatherings (cf. *Am.* i. 4. 55-6, *Ars* i. 603-5) makes one think of something more on the scale of a disco-dance than a private dinner-party. In fact the usual number present at a Roman banquet was nine, three reclining on each of three couches placed around the table (Daremberg and Saglio I. 1278-9), but, if those departing could still be described as *frequens conuiua* when at least five (Ovid, his mistress, her new admirer and *iuuenes unus et alter* (22)) remained, obviously more than that were involved in the poet's imagination here.

22. **compositi:** i.e. stupefied with drink; cf. *Am.* i. 4. 53 *bene compositus somno uinoque.*

23. **improba:** placed at the beginning of the line to convey maximum outrage.

iungentes oscula: a favourite Ovidian expression; cf. v. 60 below, *Ep.* 2. 94, *Met.* ix. 458 with Bömer's note.

24. **lingua nexa fuisse:** for kissing with the tongue – always, of course, the most sensual variety – cf. v. 57 below, *Am.* iii. 7. 9, Tib. i. 8. 37.

25-8. For all their impressive artistry, these similes only keep the reader waiting for the *dénouement*; I suspect that this effect is deliberate. Cf. 35-42n.

25-7. **qualia ... qualia:** the commonest comparative particle for introducing purely decorative catalogues of similes and those intended to carry the reader into the realms of romantic fancy; cf. 35-40 below, *Am.* i. 10. 1-6, Prop. i. 3. 1-6 with Fedeli's note, and see Morgan 70-72.

25. **germana:** usually 'full' (as opposed to 'half') 'sister', and so particularly appropriate with respect to the relationship of Diana and Phoebus (v. 27; both were the children of Zeus and Leto). *germanus* and *germana* can, however, be used of siblings without both parents in common; see e.g. *Met.* ix. 382 and further Skutsch on Enn. *Ann.* 40.

seuero: see 1. 3n.

26. **cupido ... uiro:** cf. [Tib.] iii. 3. 52. *uir* clearly = 'lover' and not 'husband' here (cf. p. 6).

27. **Dianam:** a particularly good choice of *germana* to reinforce the point made in 25, since Diana was the divine paragon of chastity.

28. **Venerem Marti:** according to some accounts Mars was the husband of Venus, but he was equally well known as her paramour (see e.g. *Ars* ii. 561ff., Hom. *Od.* viii. 266.). Cf. 9B. 47-8n.

suo: for the affectionate use of the possessive adjective with a proper name cf. *Ep.* 8. 78 *orabat superos Leda suumque Iouem.*

29-32. The sudden switch to direct speech coupled with the use of the historic present (a rare phenomenon in the *Amores*; see 18. 11-12n.) recharges the atmosphere with tension after the lull brought about by the artistic digression in 25-8. But Ovid's high indignation is really just a joke, for here, in the role of *uir*, he does exactly what he threatens to do in the role of *amator* at *Am.* i. 4. 39-40 if his mistress kisses her official escort instead of him.

The whole of Ovid's outburst has a strongly juristic flavour. Scholars of Roman law have detected in Ovid's *iniciam ... manus* in v. 30 (and also in *iniciamque manum* at *Am.* i. 4. 40 and *iniceremque manus* at *Ep.* 12. 158) an echo of the formula used by the plaintiff in *manus iniectio*, an archaic legal enactment *apud praetorem* associated with the ancient process of *uindicatio*, by which one man might reclaim his rightful property from another (see especially D. Daube, 'No kissing or else ...' in *The Classical Tradition: Literary and Historical Studies in Honor of H. Caplan*, ed. L. Wallach (New York, 1966), 222-31). Daube (230-31) further sees in vv. 31-2 a reflection of the indictment for a type of theft in cases of co-ownership where one party has taken it upon himself to dispose of what is not entirely his or, alternatively, has admitted a third person to the partnership without the consent of the original partner (I suspect Ovid is already thinking of this when he uses *defers* in 29; see n. *ad loc.*). See further p. 12, with n. 91.

29. **gaudia:** i.e. the kisses and the pleasure Ovid gets from them. *gaudium* is a blanket term for amatory gratification of all kinds.

defers: a semi-technical term often used in legal contexts of 'awarding' or 'conferring' benefits etc. (see Berger s.v. *deferre hereditatem)* and, as such, obviously preferable to the alternative reading *differs* (see apparatus p. 95), which gives the inappropriate sense 'postpone'.

30. **dominas:** for the adjectival use of *dominus* cf. *Am.* ii. 14. 16, Prop. iii. 9. 23 with Fedeli's note, Juv. 3. 33.

mea iura: Ovid, I think, means the kisses and not his mistress' person. There is a humorous absurdity in treating something as evanescent as a kiss as if it were a piece of stolen property which could be recovered by invoking the solemn and ponderous processes of the law.

32. **in bona ... uenit:** more juristic language: *uenire in* + accusative = 'to become legally entitled to the possession of' (*OLD* s.v. 10, Berger s.v.) and *bona* here = 'property'.

33. **quaeque dolor linguae dictauit:** 'and such things as indignation' (for *dolor* see 11n.) 'dictated to my tongue' (for the expression cf. *CLE* 521. 3 *inscripsi uersus dictante dolore*). These words seem to me to prove Ovid not guilty, as some have supposed (e.g. Fränkel 187, n. 2, Jäger 128), of presenting the 'banquet' scene and the 'conciliatory kiss' scene unrealistically as a single continuous sequence which does not even allow for the departure of the embarrassed paramour, for they indicate that the poet's tirade lasted for some time, during which the unfortunate *amator* might easily be imagined making his escape (in the Adultery Mime (see 13-32n.) he would have leapt through the window).

34. **purpureus ... pudor:** here, obviously, a blush of shame, but at *Am.* i. 3. 14, apparently, a blush of modesty. Cf. also *Tr.* iv. 3. 70.

35-42. Ovid imitates Virgil and is in turn (I think) imitated by 'Lygdamus' (see 36-8n.). The Virgilian model is *A.* xii. 64-9:

accepit uocem lacrimis Lauinia matris
flagrantis perfusa genas, cui plurimus ignem
subiecit rubor et calefacta per ora cucurrit.
Indum sanguineo ueluti uiolauerit ostro
si quis ebur, aut mixta rubent ubi lilia multa
alba rosa, talis uirgo dabat ore colores.

Like Virgil, Ovid describes the blush's gradual creeping over the girl's face, and he uses the same two similes to convey the colour of her complexion (a third simile in Ovid (36) could also have been suggested by the Virgilian passage, since Lavinia's fiancé *was* watching as she blushed (*A.* xii. 70)). Ovid's word-order, like Virgil's, is distorted in the 'tinted ivory' simile, and, like Virgil, Ovid includes a final summarising comment.

The effect of the two blushes described is exactly the same: both men who observe them are filled with desire. But while it is fitting enough for Virgil to elaborate on Lavinia's blush of virginal modesty, it is quite inappropriate for Ovid to wax lyrical on his flirtatious mistress' blush of guilt. And this is no doubt precisely why he does it: he found the humour of incongruity irresistible (cf. *Am.* i. 7. 51-8, and see also 25-8n.).

For the ancient preoccupation with the red/white colour contrast see Kroll 277, André 345-7, 351, Bömer on *Met.* vi. 46.

35-7. **quale ... quale:** adverbial accusative; for the choice of particle see 25-7n.

35. **Tithoni coniuge:** i.e. Aurora, the dawn (for her unusual marriage see *Am.* i. 13. 35-8, Prop. ii. 18, *h. Hom. Ven.* 218-38); see further H. Bardon, 'L'aurore et le crépuscule', *REL* 24 (1946), 82-115, Bömer on *Met.* ii. 112, and cf. especially *Met.* vi. 46-9, where the 'dawn' simile also describes a blush of guilt.

For the plain ablative of agent with metonyms (see p. 12) cf. Stat. *Silv.* iv. 4. 27, *Theb.* x. 927, but see also p. 13

36. **subrubet:** literally 'reddens from below'; an extremely felicitous Ovidian coinage (see p. 13, with n. 96) to evoke both the flush of dawn starting at the horizon and a human blush starting at the neck.

36-8. Cf. [Tib.] iii. 4. 29-34, where Apollo is described thus:

candor erat qualem praefert Latonia Luna,
  et color in niueo corpore purpureus,
ut iuueni primum uirgo deducta marito
  inficitur teneras ore rubente genas,
et cum contexunt amarantis alba puellae
  lilia et autumno candida mala rubent.

This is one of a number of passages of 'Lygdamus' which show a marked similarity to passages of Ovid (cf. 14. 23-6n.). As the clumsier of the two (contrast the silly likening of the colour of Apollo's body to the face of a blushing bride in vv. 31-2 with Ovid's much more apposite, if mischievous, use of the same simile), it suggests that 'Lygdamus', and not Ovid, was the imitator. The date and identity of 'Lygdamus', however, are vexed questions; his own claim ([Tib.] iii. 5. 17-18) makes him an exact contemporary of Ovid, and some scholars have thought that he *was* the young Ovid, while others, with some justification, would assign him to the Flavian period (see A. G. Lee, 'The date of Lygdamus and his relationship to Ovid', *PCPhS* n.s. 5 (1958-9), 15-23, K. Büchner, 'Die Elegien des Lygdamus', *Hermes* 93 (1965) [= *id.* (1970) 116-77] 65-112 with copious bibliography at 89, n. 1, and for more recent work see H. Dettmer, 'The Corpus Tibullianum (1974-80)', *ANRW* II. 30. 3 (1983), 1962-75.

36. **sponso uisa puella nouo:** a particularly cheeky simile, given the difference between Ovid's mistress and a shy, newly-wed (*sponso ... nouo* = 'bridegroom'), and presumably chaste, girl.

37. **quale rosae fulgent ...:** Virgil's 'like white lilies reddening when mixed with roses' (*A.* xii. 68-9), i.e. looking pink because of the reflection of the roses, better evokes the effect of a blush on white skin than Ovid's 'like roses glowing amidst lilies', which is a more apt description of a normally rosy-cheeked, 'peaches and cream' complexion. Variations of the motif are common; cf. Prop. ii. 3. 10-12, and for many more examples see H. Blümner, *Philologus* 48 (1899), 157-8.

sua is not just a metrical stop-gap: the Romans thought lilies and roses 'went' together; see Plin. *Nat.* xxi. 22 *et interpositum* (*lilium*) *etiam maxime rosas decet*.

38. Cf. *Met.* iv. 332-3. I have adopted Kenney's punctuation to clarify the complex construction of this line, i.e. *quale Luna* (*fulget*) *ubi laborat cantatis equis*; this is one of the most violent instances of hyperbaton (see p. 16) in the *Amores*.

cantatis ... equis: the moon, sun and personified celestial phenomena such as Night and Dawn are conventionally endowed with horses and chariot in Greek and Roman art and literature (see Daremberg and Saglio III. 1388-92, Bömer on *Fast.* ii. 314). The moon's horses are here said to be 'bewitched' when she is in eclipse (see next n.) because any irregularity in the course or appearance of a heavenly body in antiquity was commonly believed to be the result of black magic.

laborat: *laborare* and *labor* are frequently used of the moon's activity in eclipse; cf. Prop. ii. 34. 52, Verg. *G.* ii. 478 (more examples at *ThLL* VII. 793. 15ff.), and see W. Richter, 'Lunae labores', *WS* n.s. 11 (1977), 96-105. For the redness of the moon in eclipse see 1. 23n.

39-40. I.e. *aut quale (fulget) Assyrium ebur quod tinxit Maeonis femina, ne longis* ...; mild hyperbaton (see p. 16). Cf. Hom. *Il.* iv. 141-7, Verg. *A.* xii. 67-8 (cited at 35-42n.). The Homeric simile suggests that ivory was dyed for the sake of decoration, not preservation. *tinxit* is gnomic perfect and *femina* collective singular.

39. **ab:** causal; cf. Prop. i. 16. 14 *supplicis a longis tristior excubiis* (with Fedeli's note), Liv. ii. 14. 3 *inopi tum urbe ab longinqua obsidione*. See also p. 13.

40. **Maeonis:** 'Lydian', a transliteration of the Homeric Μηονίς (*Il.* iv. 142).

Assyrium: probably Ovid means 'Indian'; the Latin poets, notorious for their geographical (and scientific) imprecision (see Kroll 280ff.), often use this adjective of anything vaguely oriental (see Kroll on Catul. 6. 8, Smith on Tib. i. 3. 7). Cf. 6. 1, 21nn.

41. A line with a very prosaic ring due to the conglomeration of pronouns; for some interesting statistics and observations on pronouns, and particularly on the comparative rarity in poetry of demonstratives in the genitive plural, see Axelson 70-74. *his*, despite its vagueness, is surely right, *hic* almost certainly being only a false correction of the variant *is* (full apparatus on p. 95).

44. **maesta erat in uultu:** i.e. *maestum uultum gerebat*. For *in* see p. 13.

decenter: Ovid and Horace (in his hexameter works) are exceptional among poets in the extent to which they admit adverbs formed on participial stems.

45-50. Physical ill-treatment of the beloved, or the contemplation of it, is common in elegiac love-affairs (Smith collects examples in his note on Tib. i. 6. 73-4; see also Lilja 164-5, Davis (1981) 2494, n. 84). Ovid handles the theme in some detail at *Ars* iii. 568ff. and in *Am.* i. 7 (for discussion of affinities between the latter piece and ours see H. A. Kahn, 'Ouidius Furens', *Latomus* 25 (1966), 880-94).

45-6. For tearing the hair cf. *Am.* i. 7. 11, 49, ii. 7. 7, and for scratching the face, *Am.* i. 7. 50, *Ars* iii. 568, 570.

46. **fuit:** to be taken 'apo koinou' with both *laniare* (45) and *ire* (46). *fuit* has virtually pluperfect force: Ovid *had* felt an impulse to attack his mistress, but when he saw her face, that impulse died. This use of the perfect is most common in historical writing (see Kühner-Stegmann II. i. 129-30).

47. **fortes cecidere lacerti:** cf. *Am.* i. 7. 23, Tib. i. 6. 73, 10. 56. *fortes* is, of course, ironic; cf. *Am.* i. 7. 38.

49. **saeuus:** 'physically violent'; cf. Tib. i. 10. 65-6.

49-50. **supplex ... rogaui / oscula:** an effective use of enjambement (see p. 15): *supplex* suggests that Ovid will be asking for forgiveness, not kisses. Cf. 2. 63-4, 6. 2nn.

52. **tela trisulca:** Jupiter's three-pronged thunderbolt is frequently depicted in ancient art; see Bömer on *Met.* ii. 848-9.

53-4. **torqueor ... uolo:** historic presents; see 29-32n. For the scansion *u ŏlŏ* see Goold (1965a) 21. Self-torture is a regular pastime of the poetic lover; cf. *Am.* ii. 19. 34, Catul. 85. 2, and see Fantham 89.

53. **senserit:** for *oscula sentire* cf. *Met.* x. 292-3.

54. **ex hac ... nota:** the *nota* was properly the equivalent of the label on a modern bottle of wine, i.e. an indication of its type, age and quality (see e.g. Hor. *Carm.* ii. 3. 8), but the word soon came to be used of the 'stamp' or 'mark' of quality of all sorts of other things too; see e.g. Catul. 68. 28 *quisquis de meliore nota*, V. Max. vii. 3. 10 *'oderint dum metuant' et alia huius notae*. Bertini *ad loc.* collects further examples.

55-62. Ovid views the fresh cause for alarm through the eyes of a teacher who finds himself surpassed by his favourite pupil: notice *docui* (55), *addidicisse* (56), *doceri* (61), *magister* (62).

55. **multo meliora:** a rueful reminder of *ne ... deteriora daret* in v. 50.
addidicisse: 'to have learned in addition'; an uncommon compound, here admitted for the extra meaning conveyed by the prefix (see further p. 13, with n. 97).

59-60. For the innuendo cf. *Am.* i. 4. 63, *Ars* i. 669-70. For *oscula iungere* see 23n.

62. **nescioquis:** see p. 39.
magister: one of Ovid's regular terms for a 'teacher of love'; cf. *Ars* ii. 744, iii. 812.

Poem 6

1. **psittacus ... imitatrix ales:** cf. Stat. *Silv.* ii. 4. 2 *humanae sollers imitator psittace linguae.* Ovid's phrase refers primarily to the parrot's general talent for mimicry, well known in antiquity, (see Plin. *Nat.* x. 117, and further d'Arcy Thompson 336-8); then, as now, talking birds were popular pets (see G. Jennison, *Animals for Show and Pleasure in Ancient Rome* (Manchester, 1937), 116-21, J. P. V. D. Balsdon, *Life and Leisure in Ancient Rome* (London, 1969), 151-2). But this particular *psittacus* is also an *imitatrix ales* in that it recalls the sparrow mourned in Catul. 3; see Hinds (1987) 7, *id.* (1998) 4-5.

Masculines are used with reference to the parrot in the rest of the poem, but here the common gender of *ales* (a more grandiose word than *auis* or *uolucer*, and fitting enough in a mock-solemn context) allows Ovid to qualify with the metrically convenient feminine *imitatrix*. The attributive use of nouns in *-trix* is not uncommon; for *imitatrix* cf. Plin. *Nat.* x. 68, and see further Neue and Wagener II. 36ff.

Eois ... ab Indis: for this use of *ab* indicating the place of ultimate origin cf. Verg. *G.* iii. 2 *pastor ab Amphryso,* Prop. iv. 6. 37 *o Longa mundi seruator ab Alba.* For the form *Indis* see 1. 1n.

Parrots, and especially green ones (see v. 21) are, as it happens, common on the Indian sub-continent, but the name *India* could signify anywhere loosely 'eastern' from Arabia to the borders of China (cf. 5. 40n.). The addition of the poetic epithet *Eous* (literally 'of the dawn') produces an expression with the romantic quality of our 'land of the rising sun' (cf. *Ars* iii. 537, Verg. *G.* ii. 115).

2. **exsequias ite ... aues:** for the expression cf. Ter. *Ph.* 1026, Sil. xv. 394-5. Ovid's bidding savours strongly of parody, but the idea of formal obsequies for a bird may not have been as fantastic as we imagine: Pliny tells us that a talking raven was given a public funeral in A.D. 36 (*Nat.* x. 122-3). As far as we know, however, there were no feathered mourners present on that occasion.
frequenter: here 'in great numbers', but at 28 below 'often'.

3. **piae uolucres:** *pietas,* 'devotion', is a human quality, which Ovid here boldly transfers to the animal world (cf. *Am.* iii. 9. 37).

3-5. Beating the breast, scratching the face and tearing the hair were conventional signs of mourning or other profound grief in antiquity. Here Ovid adapts all these to the bird-world: beating wings replace beating hands (cf. especially *Am.* iii. 9. 10; also *CLE* 398. 8); claws replace nails (because *unguis* = both 'nail' and 'claw' Ovid is able to retain the stereotyped expression *ungue notare genas*; cf. *Am.* iii. 6. 48, and see further Zingerle I. 96); and feathers replace hair (cf. *Am.* iii. 9. 52).

3. **plangite pectora pinnis:** one of the few really convincing examples of onomatopoeic alliteration in Latin poetry: the insistent *p* sounds suggest blows (cf. Hor. *Carm.* i. 4. 13 *pallida Mors aequo pulsat pede pauperum tabernas,* and see Pease on Verg. *A.* iv. 589-90).

5. **maestis ... capillis:** for the transferred epithet cf. *Fast.* iv. 584 *maestas ... comas, Am.* i. 6. 67 *non laetis ... capillis.*

6. For birdsong replacing conventional funeral music cf. Stat. *Silv.* ii. 4. 23, *CLE* 1549. 22-3. **longa ... tuba:** a trumpet type of instrument which was regularly used at funerals; cf. Prop. ii. 7. 12, 13. 20, Verg. *A.* xii. 192. *longa* probably refers primarily to its shape, but perhaps also hints at the long-drawn note it produced.

7-10. Philomela, according to Greek myth, was raped by her sister Procne's husband Tereus, who cut out her tongue to prevent her telling of the outrage. Procne, however, finding out what had happened from pictures woven into a tapestry by Philomela, killed Itys, the son of Tereus and herself, served up his flesh for his father to eat, and then fled with her sister. Tereus, in pursuit, was foiled as Procne was changed into a nightingale and Philomela into a swallow (see J. R. T. Pollard, *Birds in Greek Life and Myth* (London, 1977), 164-5). Ovid's attribution of the lament to Philomela, however, shows that he is thinking of her, and not Procne, as the mother of the butchered child (so also Verg. *Ecl.* 6. 81, *G.* iv. 511-15), and that, like the Latin poets generally, he identifies her with the nightingale, and not the swallow (cf. *Fast.* ii. 853ff. with Bömer's note, Verg. *G.* iv. 15), for it was the song of the nightingale which had for centuries been associated with lamentation (see e.g. Hom. *Od.* xix. 518ff., and further d'Arcy Thompson 16-22). Of course, it is particularly appropriate that Philomela, herself a bird, should abandon her accustomed dirge in favour of a lament for a fellow-bird.

7. **quod:** 'as to'. The usage is fundamentally colloquial and found mainly in comedy and Cicero's letters; Ovid is the only one of the elegists to admit it (cf. *Am.* ii. 9B. 47, *Rem.* 783-4). As often with this construction, a demonstrative in the main clause (*ista querela*) loosely refers back to the *quod* clause (see further Kühner-Stegmann II. ii. 277-8).
Ismarii ... tyranni: i.e. Tereus (see 7-10n.). *Ismarius*, from *Ismarus* (or *Ismara*), a mountain in Thrace, is a favourite poetic epithet for 'Thracian'; cf. *Am.* iii. 9. 21, Prop. ii. 13. 6, Stat. *Silv.* v. 3. 6.

8. Though the general sense of this line is clear enough – Philomela's lament for Itys has 'had its time' – the text is uncertain (see apparatus on p. 95).

It seems best to read *annis ... suis* (= ω) and construe 'That complaint has been satisfied with its proper number of years', i.e. it has been given as much expression as is due to it. For *anni sui* with this sense cf. *Ars* iii. 18 *fertur et ante annos occubuisse suos, Am.* ii. 2. 46, and for *explere, Tr.* iv. 3. 38 *expletur lacrimis ... dolor. explere querelam annis* (as opposed to *dictis, lacrimis*) is admittedly bold, but it is perfectly intelligible. A few editors adopt *annis ... tuis*, but this could only mean either 'with *your* proper number of years' (i.e. the time you would normally expect to live) or 'with your age' (cf. Luc. viii. 496), and neither makes sense here.

9. **alitis ... rarae:** obviously the literal sense 'a rare bird' is fitting here, but we are probably also intended to think of the proverbial *rara auis*, 'a marvel'; cf. Pers. 1. 46, Juv. 1. 165.
in ... miserum ... funus: for the word-order see p. 13, with n. 109.
deuertere: for the intransitive use of the passive after the manner of the Greek middle cf. *Pont.* iv. 14. 21 *ad ueteres scopulos iterum deuertar?*

11. **omnes quae liquido ...:** an elaborate periphrasis for *aues*. Its grandiloquent ring, amusingly incongruous in the context, stems from the choice of (a) *librare*, which is regularly used in descriptions of flight in the 'higher' genres of Latin poetry (e.g. *Met.* viii.

201, Sil. xv. 426) and (b) *liquidus*, a stock epithet of 'air' (*uel. sim.*) also in the 'higher' genres (e.g. Lucr. v. 500, Verg. *A.* vii. 65).

12. **alios:** understand *amicos* from the subsequent *amice*.

turtur amice: for the turtle dove's 'friendship' with the parrot cf. [Ov.] *Ep. Sapph.* 38, Plin. *Nat.* x. 207. The two birds are pictured together in a Roman mosaic (Naples 9992 in O. Keller, *Die antike Tierwelt* (Leipzig, 1909), II. 46) and were kept together in aviaries (see d'Arcy Thompson 292).

13-16. Praise of the deceased's capacity for friendship is a common feature of Latin sepulchral inscriptions (e.g. *CLE* 477. 8). Cf. Stat. *Silv.* ii. 4. 30.

14. **fides:** a technical term in the language of *amicitia*; it denotes the reciprocal loyalty between two people which was an essential ingredient in any Roman friendship (see further R. Reitzenstein, *SHA Phil-Hist.* Kl. 3 (1912) 12 Abh., 18-19, L. Alfonsi, *Aevum* 19 (1945), 374-5).

15. **iuuenis Phoceus:** i.e. Pylades, son of the king of Phocis, whose friendship with Orestes became proverbial for mutual attachment of the deepest kind; cf. *Tr.* iv. 4. 71, Cic. *Fin.* ii. 26. 84, and see further Otto 258.

Orestae: the spelling is authenticated by Heinsius (on *Ep.* 8. 9) and Housman (*JPh* 31 (1910), 251-3 [= *Classical Papers* 827-9]).

16. **dum licuit:** cf. Tib. i. 1. 69, and for many examples from Latin sepulchral inscriptions see Lattimore 156-8.

psittace: for the pathetic address to the deceased cf. *Am.* iii. 9. 41, 66, Stat. *Silv.* ii. 1. 37, *CLE* 606. 1.

17-42. *lamentatio/laudatio funebris* with *schetliasmos* at 25-42; cf. Sen. *Dial.* vi. 1. 24, Stat. *Silv.* ii. 1. 41-55, 106-36, and see p. 44. Ovid's praise of the parrot's virtues covers (i) moral qualities (loyalty, 17, gentleness, 25-6, and frugality, 29-32), (ii) physical beauty (17, 21-2), and (iii) special talent (18, 23-4). (i) and (ii) are frequently praised in sepulchral inscriptions; e.g. *CLE* 81. 1-2, 158. 2, 237, 843, 1302. 1-2 and *Laudatio Turiae* (*Inscr. Dessau* 8393) *passim*.

17-19. **quid ... quid ... quid ... quid iuuat:** a conventional cry of outrage in diverse situations (cf. *Am.* ii. 9A. 13, 14. 1), but especially in protest against death (cf. *Am.* iii. 9. 21-2, Prop. iii. 18. 11-12, iv. 11. 11-12).

17. **forma:** see 4. 9n.

18. **mutandis ingeniosa sonis:** *mutare* with plural object means 'to change constantly from one thing to another' (cf. Sil. vii. 673 *mutantem saltu ramos*), and it is thus the *range* of the parrot's voice which is in point here. Ovid's use of *ingeniosus* with the dative (rather than with *ad* or *in*) is peculiar to him (cf. *Am.* i. 11. 4 *dandis ingeniosa sonis*).

19. **ut:** temporal: 'as soon as'.

20. **infelix ... iaces:** the wording echoes that of many epitaphs; e.g. *CLE* 1205. 5 [*hi*]*c iaceo infelix cinis*, *CIL* VI. 35773 *hic iacet infelix Mamertinus* (more examples at *ThLL* VII. 1362. 33ff.).

auium gloria: an amusingly pompous phrase; cf. the sober use of similar expressions at *Am.* iii. 15. 8, Verg. *A.* vi. 767. Statius imitates Ovid closely at *Silv.* ii. 4. 24 *occidit aeriae celeberrima gloria gentis*.

21. **fragiles ... smaragdos:** true emeralds are not 'fragile'. Ovid may have been thinking of other green gems (the term *smaragdi* covered various types, and some of them were indeed brittle; see Plin. *Nat.* xxxvii. 72), but more probably he simply thought 'fragile emeralds' an aesthetically effective description (cf. 5. 40n.). At any rate, G. W. Most's emendation of *fragiles* to *fragilis*, agreeing with *tu*, (*Studies in Latin Literature and Roman History* I, ed. C. Deroux, *Collection Latomus* 164 (Brussels, 1979), 362-6), is unnecessary. Goold (1965a) 11) persuades me that *smaragdus* is more likely to be the correct spelling than *zmaragdus*, but for the opposite view see Lachmann on Lucr. ii. 805. For the shortening of the preceding *e* see Platnauer 62.

22. **tincta gerens rubro ...:** cf. Prop. iii. 3. 31-2 *columbae / tingunt Gorgoneo Punica rostra lacu*. *Punicus*, properly 'Carthaginian', came to denote 'scarlet' or 'crimson' after the famous red dye which was made from sea-shells found in the Carthage area (see André 88-90).

23. **uocum simulantior:** 'more imitative of voices'; an apparently unique use of the genitive with *simulans*. It seems analogous to that regular with *similis* and *dissimilis*.

24. **blaeso:** 'stumbling'; fondly used of the parrot's articulations, but uncomplimentary in description of adult human speech (see e.g. *Ars* iii. 294, Mart. v. 34. 8).

25-32. Markland's suggestion (in his note on Stat. *Silv*. ii. 4. 35) that 27-8 should properly be placed after 32 is attractive, for 27-8 + 33-6 seem to create a neat and logical sequence which balances 25-6 + 29-32. But the transposition spoils the contrasts within the passage of the parrot's peaceable nature with the quails' aggressiveness (25-8) and the parrot's abstemious vegetarianism with the carnivores' greed (33-6). Goold's objections to the traditional order ((1965a) 34) on the grounds that it renders *ecce* (27) 'totally devoid of its usual function of marking a break from the preceding' and allows two consecutive pentameter-endings in *-or aquae* (32, 34) are invalid: the functions of *ecce* are many and various (see Hand II. 344 and cf. 10. 4n.), and Ovid did not, any more than other Latin poets, avoid the type of repetition in question (cf. *Am*. ii. 2. 58 and 60, and see further Shackleton Bailey 9, 73).

25. **inuidia:** 'envy' or 'malice' is regularly blamed for the loved one's death in ancient funeral literature of all kinds – formal *epicedia* and *consolationes* (e.g. Stat. *Silv*. ii. 1. 121-2, Sen. *Dial*. vi. 12. 6), commemorative epigrams (e.g. Diod. *AP* vii. 74. 3-4) and sepulchral inscriptions (e.g. *CLE* 647. 2). Lattimore collects more examples at 148-9 and 153-4.

26. **garrulus ... placidae pacis amator:** in the parrot's case noisiness does not go hand in hand with aggression; cf. 27n.

27. **ecce:** see 25-32n.

proelia: quails were notorious for their noisy aggression (see Arist. *HA* iv. 9. 563A, Plin. *Nat*. xi. 268). M. G. Morgan (*CQ* n. s. 25 (1975), 118-19) points out that Ovid is here more likely to be thinking of quails' squabbles at mating-time than of their fighting to provide spectator sport, since this, far from prolonging their lives (v. 28), would result in premature death for many.

28. **forsitan ... fiant:** *forsitan* qualifies *inde*, not the verb – the possibility is that quails thrive on their aggression: that they live to a ripe old age is a fact. Some would therefore read *fiunt* (= ω; full apparatus on p. 95), apparently supposing that the indicative will have been used wherever *forsitan* does not modify the verb, and the subjunctive wherever it does (see e.g. Goold (1965a) 34). But in Ovid's case, at least, the supposition is false: note e.g. *Am*. i. 6. 45 *forsitan et tecum tua nunc requiescit amica* and *Ep*. 7. 133 *forsitan et grauidam Dido, scelerate, relinquas*. Obviously either reading could be right here, and it therefore seems proper to retain that of the generally more reliable *PY*.

anus: an adjectival usage; for its application to animals cf. *Ars* i. 766 *cerua ... anus* (more examples at *ThLL* II. 200. 24ff.).

29-32. By human standards the parrot is an extreme ascetic; but by parrot standards he is unexceptional. Ovid's commendation of his feeding-habits is thus a nice touch of whimsy and a good joke at the expense of the diet-conscious moralists (see Nisbet-Hubbard I. 355-6), who would hardly want a gaudy bird to set them an example.

29. **nec prae sermonis amore:** for the word-order see p. 13, with n. 109. *prae* = 'because of' is most frequently used with nouns expressing some kind of emotion to give the reason 'why not'; cf. Ter. *Hau*. 308, and see further Kühner-Stegmann II. i. 513, Hofmann-

Szantyr 268-9. The causal *prae*, like other causal prepositions, is for some reason generally avoided by the writers of elegy and the more elevated types of poetry; only Ovid (here) and Lucretius (iv. 1167) admit it (see Axelson 81).

30. **poterant ora uacare:** most editors read *poteras* (= PYς) and take *ora* as accusative of respect; 'eleganti Graecismo', says Heinsius, but I am not convinced. For although the 'Greek' accusative of respect was widely and variously used by Roman writers, there are to my knowledge no telling parallels for *ora uacare*, and I suspect that *poteras* is an error prompted by *eras* in 29.

31. **causaeque papauera somni:** I take this to be a purely ornamental reference to the soporific qualities of poppies; *contra*, Lee: 'Nuts were his diet, poppyseed his sleeping pills'.

32. **simplicis umor aquae:** a splendidly pompous periphrasis with an incongruous Lucretian ring; cf. Lucr. i. 307, iii. 427.

33-6. Of the birds contrasted with the abstemious and vegetarian parrot, only the vulture is characterised by explicit reference to its eating-habits; all the others too, however, are to some extent predators, the kite and the crow sharing the vulture's appetite for carrion.

33. **edax uultur:** cf. *Tr.* i. 6. 11, Hom. *Il.* iv. 237, *Od.* xxii. 30, and see further d'Arcy Thompson 82.

ducensque per aera gyros: the kite circles while waiting for an opportunity to swoop; cf. *Met.* ii. 716-19. The bird was disliked in antiquity for its predatory and thieving tendencies; see d'Arcy Thompson 119-20, Otto 222-3.

34. **miluus:** the trisyllabic scansion is normal in Ovid and earlier poets (see J. André, *Les noms d'oiseaux en latin* (Paris, 1967), 105).

pluuiae graculus auctor aquae: *auctor* = *nuntius*; cf. *Met.* xi. 666-7, Prop. iv. 3. 32. The raven and the crow are more often thought of as heralds of rain, but for the jackdaw in this capacity cf. Arat. 963-6, and see further d'Arcy Thompson 156.

35. **armiferae:** first attested in Ovid and a stock epithet of Minerva in his work; cf. *Met.* xiv. 475, *Fast.* iii. 681, vi. 421, *Tr.* iv. 10. 13, and for the formation see p. 13.

cornix inuisa Mineruae: the crow was once specially beloved of Athene/Minerva but fell from favour and was replaced in her affections by the owl; see *Met.* ii. 544ff., Call. *Hec.* fr. 260.

36. **saeclis uix moritura nouem:** cf. Hes. fr. 304 Merkelbach-West ἐννέα τοι ζώει γενεὰς λακέρυζα κορώνη ('the cawing crow lives through nine generations'); for the bird's fabled longevity see also d'Arcy Thompson 169, Otto 93. *uix* acts as a weak negative here; the usage is colloquial (see Hofmann-Szantyr 454-5).

moritura: for the attributive use of the future participle in poetry see Nisbet-Hubbard II. 56.

38. **ab:** see 1n.

39-40. A vexed couplet (see apparatus on p. 95), which I have discussed fully elsewhere ((1982) 157-8). Here I simply repeat the only positive suggestion I have for its interpretation: *numeris* in 40 might be understood as 'numbers' in the sense of 'numerical strength' (cf. *Am.* iii. 9. 66 *auxisti numeros ... pios*, and for the singular with this meaning see *OLD* s.v. 5) and *implentur* as 'are fully equipped with' or 'possessed of' (see Kenney (1959) 241). The line could then be construed 'Inferior things have their full complement of numbers', i.e. their numbers are never depleted. This provides a reasonable contrast with 39, which implies that the numbers of the 'best things' are never at full strength because they are generally the first to be carried off by Death (it is perverse to understand the 'greedy hands' in 39 as other than those of Death; cf. especially *Am.* iii. 9. 20, Tib. i. 3. 4), and it allows the whole couplet to find a place in the sequence 25-38 and 41-2, which also deal with the tendency of Death to take the good first and spare the bad for longer.

41. **Phylacidae:** i.e. Protesilaus, called *Phylacides* after his ancestor Phylacus and his Thessalian home-town Phylace. He was the first Greek to set foot on Trojan soil and was killed immediately (see Hom. *Il.* 11. 695-710, and cf. 18. 38n.).

Thersites: the notorious rabble-rouser and αἴσχιστος ('ugliest') of all the Greeks at Troy (Hom. *Il.* ii. 216).

42. **cinis:** cf. *Am.* iii. 9. 40, Prop. ii. 11. 6, Verg. *A.* x. 828, and see further Lattimore 172-3, 176.

uiuis fratribus: for Hector's surviving brothers and their faults see Hom. *Il.* xxiv. 247-64.

43-8. A return to direct address heightens the pathos of the death-bed scene.

43. **timidae:** Corinna is justifiably 'fearful' here, but Ovid is ready to apply the epithet to women in general; see e.g. *Am.* iii. 13. 23, *Rem.* 33.

uota: for prayers at the sick-bed cf. *Am.* ii. 13. 7ff., Tib. i. 1. 59-60.

44. Vain prayers, invalid oaths and unwanted advice are conventionally carried away by wind and/or water; cf. *Am.* i. 4. 12, ii. 8. 20, *Ars* i. 633-4, Catul. 30. 10 with Fordyce's note, Tib. i. 4. 21-2 with Smith's note. *Notus,* the south wind, which brought rain and gales from November to March, is often mentioned in this context (Bömer on *Fast.* v. 686 collects examples); the specification is a form of Alexandrian ornament popular with the Augustans.

45. **septima lux:** the ancient medical writers regarded the seventh day as a critical one in illness; see e.g. Hippoc. *Iudic.* 58 Littré, H. E. Sigerist, *A History of Medicine* (Oxford, 1961) II. 279-80.

exhibitura: see 36n.

46. The notion of the spinning of the Fates deciding an individual's destiny and life-span is a highly popular motif in classical literature (see B. C. Dietrich, *Death, Fate and the Gods* (London, 1965), 79-82). Most often the Fates spin at birth, but Catullus has them spinning at marriage (64. 311ff.), and Ovid here clearly imagines them continuing to spin throughout a person's life (cf. Theoc. 1. 139, Verg. *A.* x. 814-15, Mart. iv. 73. 3). *Parca* may be collective singular, for the Fates after Homer were normally a threesome, but Ovid could be thinking just of the one who holds the distaff.

uacuo ... colo: *colus* has both second and fourth declension forms, the second declension forms being mostly treated as masculine and the fourth declension forms as feminine (see *ThLL* III. 1743. 69ff.). Ovid confines himself to second declension forms, but at *Fast.* iii. 818 all the MSS agree on a feminine adjective with *colus,* while here and at *Ars* i. 702 and *Ep.* 3. 76 they are divided between masculine and feminine (see apparatus on p. 95). Since certainty is thus impossible, I follow the generally more reliable *PSY*. Cf. 12. 1n. *laurus.*

tibi: dative of person involved: 'in your case', 'as far as you were concerned'.

47-8. Paragons on the point of death conventionally find the strength to address a parting word to their loved ones; cf. Simm. *AP* vii. 647. 3-4, Stat. *Silv.* ii. 1. 149-53.

47. **ignauo:** probably concessive: 'though weak'. For the sense 'enervated' cf. Sen. *Oed.* 181-2 *piger ignauos / alligat artus languor.*

palato: here the organ of speech (cf. Hor. *S.* ii. 3. 274), but more frequently that of taste (e.g. Hor. *S.* ii. 8. 38, Juv. 10. 203).

48. **'Corinna, uale':** salutations seem to have formed the basic repertoire of talking birds in antiquity; see e.g. Pers. *Prol.* 8, Mart. xiv. 73, 74, 76, Stat. *Silv.* ii. 4. 29-30, Plin. *Nat.* x. 117, Macr. ii. 4. 29-30.

49-58. In his *consolatio* (see p. 44) Ovid pictures the parrot in a birds' paradise instead of the conventional Elysium.

Elysium in Homer was the blissful land at the ends of the earth where the heroes whom the gods chose to exempt from death dwelled eternally (*Od.* iv. 561-9), but gradually it came to be thought of as that part of the Underworld in which those who had lived righteously on earth enjoyed a pleasant existence after death (see *RE* V. 2470-76, Smith on Tib. i. 3. 68-72). Literary depictions of Elysium conventionally contain a description of the landscape, some reference to the activities of its inhabitants, and a catalogue of the most famous of them (see especially Pi. *O*. 2. 68-83, Verg. *A*. vi. 637ff.), and Ovid includes all these elements here.

49-50. Ovid's Elysian landscape has three of the standard features of any 'pleasant place' – a shady grove of trees, well-watered terrain and lush vegetation. For the literary *locus amoenus* see Nisbet-Hubbard II. 52-3.

49. **colle sub Elysio:** the poetic Elysium, though supposedly underground, has the topographic features of the upper world. The lowlands of this paradise would seem to be especially idyllic: Anchises at Verg. *A*. vi. 679 and Tibullus at *Am*. iii. 9. 60 are both pictured 'in a valley' and the parrot here, similarly, 'at the foot of a hill'.

nigra nemus ilice frondet: notice the alliteration; linguistic embellishments of this kind are common in the poetic *locus amoenus* (see Norden on Verg. *A*. vi. 638ff.). The ilex, or holm-oak, is a stock feature of the ancient poets' idyllic landscape; *nigra* describes its dark foliage and also suggests the deep shade it provides. Trees in this particular Elysium are not, of course, merely decorative, but, given the nature of its inhabitants, essential (see v. 57).

51. **si qua fides dubiis:** 'myths' for *dubiis* is my attempt to render a *double entendre* I see in the Latin. *si qua fides* is a favourite Ovidian formula, used sometimes with a following dative as an 'escape clause' to cover the eventuality of the *fides* in question being misplaced (e.g. *Fast*. vi. 715 *si qua fides uentis*, *Met*. ix. 371 *si qua fides miseris*) and sometimes alone as an acknowledgement that the claim being made strains credulity (e.g. *Met*. ix. 55 with Bömer's note, T. C. W. Stinton, *PCPhS* n.s. 22 (1976), 60ff.). Here there seems to be something of both: not only the mock-pious 'if one can believe in what is not susceptible of proof', but also the mischievous 'if one can believe in what is counterfeit'. Notice too the witty juxtaposition of the opposites *fides and dubiis* (cf. p. 16).

piarum: the adjective conventionally describes the inhabitants of Elysium; cf. *Am*. iii. 9. 66, Stat. *Silv*. v. 3. 284, *CLE* 1165. 1.

52. **obscenae:** 'of ill omen'; cf. Verg. *A*. xii. 876. For the exclusion of the unrighteous from Elysium cf. Pi. *O*. 2. 78ff.

53-6. With the exception of the peacock (see 55n.), Ovid's dead birds, like Virgil's dead Trojans at *A*. vi. 648-55, retain in Elysium the characteristics they had, or were thought to have, on earth.

53. **innocui ... olores:** swans could be said to be in the birds' paradise under false pretences, for though their appearance is aesthetically pleasing, they are in fact aggressive birds, and the sweet song just before death with which ancient writers frequently credit them is the merest fantasy (see Nisbet-Hubbard II. 333-4, 342-3).

54. **uiuax phoenix:** a fabulous bird of Greek and Egyptian mythology (the cacophonous jingle seems in keeping with its outlandishness). It was famed for its longevity, most writers crediting it with a 500-year life-span and some with an even longer one (see Lloyd on Hdt. ii. 73). Only one phoenix was supposed to exist at any one time (*unica semper*), the bird reputedly being always re-born from its own remains after death; see *Met*. xv. 395-402. The phoenix had one notable claim to *pietas*: it was said always to carry the nest in which its father died to the temple of the Sun. For further discussion and copious bibliography see d'Arcy Thompson 306ff., Lloyd *loc. cit*., and for Ovid's special interest in the phoenix, R. Crahay and J. Hubaux, *Ovidiana* 289-90.

55. **ipsa suas:** despite the often purely formulaic nature of this phrase (see Bömer on *Met*. xi. 118), *ipsa* here has real meaning: 'of its own accord'. The peacock (see next n.) is normally said to display its magnificent tail only when showered with praise (see e.g. *Ars* i. 627, Plin. *Nat.* x. 43), but it is a suitably reformed character in Elysium.

ales Iunonia: the peacock. The 'eyes' in the peacock's tail were allegedly once those of Juno's minion Argus (see 2. 45n.) and put there by her after his death; the bird was consequently sacred to Juno. Such a proud and temperamental creature (see previous n. and d'Arcy Thompson 277ff.) would seem an unlikely candidate for the birds' paradise, and no doubt Ovid admits it only because, like the swan (see 53n.), it is ornamental.

56. **blanda:** see 1. 21n.

columba: the dove was proverbial not only for the conjugal affection mentioned here, but also for gentleness and innocence (see d'Arcy Thompson 241, Otto 88-9).

mari: for *mas* of a male animal cf. Lucr. iv. 1198, Verg. *G.* iii. 64.

57-8. Ovid's *consolatio* reaches its climax with a picture of the *piae uolucres* flocking to the parrot and hanging on his words (cf. *Am.* ii. 9. 61-4, where Calvus, Gallus and Catullus are envisaged welcoming Tibullus to Elysium).

57. **has inter:** anastrophe (see p. 13, with n. 108).

59-60. Many sepulchral inscriptions testify to the ancient belief that the size and splendour of a tomb should be in keeping with the character and achievements of the deceased (Lattimore collects examples at 227-30). The length of the epitaph was obviously of importance too: in one inscription the writer apologises for its shortness (*CLE* 1172). Here Ovid burlesques all these ideas, describing a made-to-measure tomb for a tiny corpse and a brief inscription for a miniature gravestone. There may also be a joke at the expense of the Callimachean ideal of brevity in composition, to which Callimachus himself seems to allude cryptically in a sepulchral epigram playing on the idea of length to suit its recipient (*AP* vii. 447; see M.S. Celentano, 'L'elogio della brevità tra retorica e letteratura; Callimaco, *ep.* 11 Pf. = *AP* vii. 447', *QUCC* n.s. 49 (1995), 67-79). This in turn is echoed by Propertius at ii. 1. 72, where, in envisaging, with apparent pathos, his own memorial consisting of *breue in exiguo marmore nomen*, he is in fact expressing an ambition to be remembered as a Callimachean poet.

61. **COLLIGOR PLACVISSE:** literally 'I am deduced to have pleased'; for the construction cf. Plin. *Nat.* ii. 58 *quo argumento amplior errantium stellarum quam lunae magnitudo colligitur.*

DOMINAE: for the recording of an owner's affection for a pet in an epitaph cf. *AP* vii. 190, 198. 7-8, 207. 3-4.

62. **PLVS AVE:** there is no true pun here: whether or not the salutation *auē* could suffer iambic shortening, *plus aue*, 'more than a bird', is not the same as *plus quam 'aue'*, 'more than "Hail" ', but Lee is justified in suggesting that, in the context (cf. 48n.), the second might at least come to mind.

Poem 7

1-2. The legal metaphors establish the quasi-juridical atmosphere which is maintained throughout the poem. See also p. 12, with n. 91.

1. **ergo:** a particle which frequently introduces an indignant rhetorical question; cf. *Am.* i. 4. 3, Prop. ii. 16. 15. See further Nisbet-Hubbard I. 283, Tränkle 159.

sufficiam ... in: literally 'Am I to provide sufficient material for ....?'; for the construction cf. *Met.* vii. 613 *nec locus in tumulos nec sufficit arbor in ignes*, with Bömer's note.

semper: note the emphatic position.

2. **ut:** concessive.

uincam ... dimicuisse: both basically military terms, but, like many others from the same sphere, readily adapted to a legal context (cf. *Am.* ii. 4. 1-2). *dimicare* is one of Ovid's more adventurous items of vocabulary. A choice word even in prose (see *ThLL* V. i. 1197. 38ff.), it is avoided altogether by poets before Ovid, but he admits it three times (cf. *Am.* ii. 13. 28, *Rem.* 27). The perfect form in *-uisse* may have been coined by Ovid as a metrically convenient alternative to the usual form in *-auisse* (see E. Bednara, *ALL* 14 (1906), 352).

piget: this word sets the tone of weary exasperation which characterises vv. 1-16.

3-10. **siue ... seu ... si ... si ... siue ... seu:** see 4. 11-18n.

3. **marmorei ... theatri:** Ovid must be thinking of the theatre of Pompey, the inner walls of which were covered with stucco and marble; cf. *Ars* i. 103, *Pont.* i. 8. 35, and see further S. B. Platner and P. Ashby, *A Topographical Dictionary of Ancient Rome* (Oxford, 1929), 515-17, E. Nash, *A Pictorial Dictionary of Ancient Rome* Vol. II (London, 1962), figs. 1216-23.

respexi: frequentative perfect: 'every time I look round'.

summa: 'the topmost parts', i.e. the highest rows of seats (for the neuter plural with partitive genitive cf. *Fast.* ii. 465 *riparum summa*, *Met.* v. 421 *gurgitis ima*). Men and women were segregated in the Augustan theatre, the women being allocated the seats high up at the back of the auditorium (Suet. *Aug.* 44; S. Lilja, *Arctos* 19 (1985), 67-71 fails to prove that some sat with their menfolk); the men would thus have to turn round to look at them (cf. *Ars* i. 109-10, Prop. iv. 8. 77). Presumably Corinna, from her own seat up above, thought she could detect Ovid's eye roving elsewhere – as well she might, given the theatre's reputation as a showplace for attractive women (see *Ars* i. 99).

4. **eligis ... uelis:** the framing of the line with the two verbs of choice emphasises that Corinna's *dolor* is of her own making.

unde dolere: = *qua dolere*; cf. *Tr.* ii. 292 *paelicibus multis hanc doluisse deam.* Cf. also 2. 48n.

5. **candida:** here 'pretty'; see 4. 39n.

5-6. **tacito ... tacitas:** gratuitous word-play.

7. **laudaui:** see 3n.

miseros petis ungue capillos: for the sentiment see 5. 45-6n. *miseros* (= ω) is much better than *PSY*'s *misero*, which would naturally be taken with *ungue*. Kenney ((1958a) 60) cites *Ep.* 6. 92 *miserum ... iecur* and Verg. *A.* ii. 215 *miseros ... artus* as parallels for *miser* of suffering parts of the body.

8. **crimen dissimulare putas:** understand *me* with *dissimulare* (cf. 4. 16n.). The metaphorical use of *crimen* is especially fitting in the legalistic context, but the word is a generally popular elegiac term for infidelity.

9-10. The idea of pallor being symptomatic of true love goes back to Sappho (fr. 31. 14-15 Lobel-Page); see further Hollis' note on *Ars* i. 729 *palleat omnis amans: hic est color aptus amanti.*

9. **in te ... frigidus:** for the construction see 3. 6n., and for *frigidus*, 1. 5n.

10. **dicor amore mori:** 'dying' of love is, of course, common hyperbole (see Griffin (1985) 142-3). The thrice-repeated *-or* sound and the collocation *-more mori* produce the kind of jingle of which ancient writers on style disapproved (e.g. Gel. xiii. 21. 12; see further Wilkinson (1963) 24-31, J. A. Richmond, *Philologus* 112 (1968), 136, n. 1). The early Latin poets often used repetition of this type to create a solemn and grandiose tone (see Jocelyn on Enn. *trag.* 93), and I suppose Ovid could have introduced it here for melodramatic effect, but more probably it is fortuitous.

11. **peccati:** this and its cognates are regularly used of sexual misdemeanours; cf. *Am.* ii. 5. 3, Hor. *Carm.* iii. 7. 19. Sometimes *peccare* means little more than *amare*; see e.g. [Tib.] iii. 13. 9.

peccati ... mihi conscius: cf. Verg. *A.* i. 604 *mens conscia sibi recti.*

uellem ... essem: *uellem* = *utinam*: 'Would that I were (guilty) ...'; the phraseology strongly implies that he is not (see Kühner-Stegmann II. i. 180, Hofmann-Szantyr 332).

12. I.e. *qui meruere poenam, aequo animo eam ferunt*; mild hyperbaton (see p. 16).

13. **nunc:** here used with adversative force like νῦν δέ (*OLD* s.v. 11).
insimulas: 'make allegations'; a legalistic word common in comedy and prose but admitted by Ovid alone of post-republican poets; cf. *Ep.* 6. 21-2, and see further p. 12, with n. 91.

14. **pondus habere:** did this lead Ovid unconsciously to the next image?

15-16. In comparing himself here, by implication, with an ass, which, when subjected to cruel beating to make it go faster, moves with deliberate slowness, Ovid seems to be suggesting that Corinna's constant accusations will be counter-productive: they will result in his being less rather than more inclined to oblige her with satisfying denials. The ass was proverbial for its refusal to co-operate, even in the face of ill-treatment; cf. Pl. *Ps.* 136-7 (of slaves) *neque ego homines magis asinos numquam uidi, ita plagis costae callent: / quos quom ferias, tibi plus noceas.*

15. **aspice:** see 2. 41n.
auritus: a conventional epithet of long-eared animals such as asses (cf. *Ars* i. 547, *Fast.* vi. 469) and hares (cf. Verg. *G.* i. 308, Germ. *Arat.* 341). Here it may be purely ornamental, or perhaps an indication that Ovid was thinking subconsciously of the ass' proverbial dropping of its ears when it considers itself ill-used; cf. Hor. *S.* i. 9. 20-21 *demitto auriculas, ut iniquae mentis asellus / cum grauius dorso subiit onus.*
miserandae sortis: for the expression cf. Verg. *A.* vi. 332 *sortem ... miseratus iniquam*, *CLE* 541. 2 *sorte miserandus iniqua.* See also 20n.
asellus: an example of a diminutive which is much more common than the root word in poetry (see Axelson 44).

17. **ecce:** see 10. 4n.
nouum crimen: this picks up *noua crimina* in v. 1.
sollers ornare: for the construction cf. Hor. *Carm.* iv. 8. 8 *sollers nunc hominem ponere, nunc deum*, Sil. i. 79. The use of the 'epexegetic' infinitive, i.e. one which defines the scope of nouns and adjectives to which it is attached, is a notable feature of Augustan poetry, particularly that of Horace (see Wickham's edition I. 406-9). For *ornare* cf. 4. 38n.
Cypassis: a good name for a fetching slave-girl. It is a transliteration of a Greek word denoting a kind of short frock (see A. S. F. Gow, *CR* n.s. 5 (1955), 238-9); the wearing of short, leg-revealing garments was one of the things which distinguished *ancillae* from freeborn Roman women (see L. Wilson, *The Clothing of the Ancient Romans* (Baltimore, 1938), 156).

18. **obicitur:** a legalism (cf. 1-2n.) and an apparently unique classical use of the passive of *obicere* with a personal subject; the most common construction is *obicere aliquid alicui.*
contemerasse: a very strong word ('pollute', 'defile') obviously intended to stress the enormity of Cypassis' alleged crime and *ipso facto* the unlikelihood of its ever having been committed. The verb is attested elsewhere only at Mart. *Sp.* 10. 2 and Rufin. *Hist.* v. 28. 15 and may well be an Ovidian coinage. See further p. 13 with n. 96.

19. **di melius:** an abbreviated version of various deprecatory formulae found in old and colloquial Latin (see Hofmann 31-2); *di melius* is itself confined to poetry and stylistically elevated prose (see Tränkle 151).
si sit ... libido: = *si libeat.* The periphrasis is common in the Augustan period (see *ThLL* IX. 1330. 57ff.), but the frequent amatory significance of *libido* makes it particularly appropriate in this context.
peccasse: see 11n., and for the tense, 4. 22n.

20. **sortis:** a slightly different sense ('rank', 'station'; cf. Hor. *Carm.* iv. 11. 22) from that in v. 15. The phraseological echo of that line is striking, but probably not significant; see 6. 25-32n.

21. **Veneris famulae conubia:** 'intercourse with a servile sweetheart'. *conubia* = *concubitus* (cf. Lucr. iii. 776), which is regularly construed with the genitive; cf. Sen. *Con.* ii. 5. 14 *in concubitu suae uxoris*, Tac. *Ann.* xiv. 12 *in concubitu mariti.* For *Venus* = 'sweetheart' cf. Hor. *Carm.* i. 33. 13 with Nisbet-Hubbard's note, and for the adjectival use of *famulus*, Luc. iv. 207 *famulas ... ad proelia dextras excitat*, Stat. *Theb.* xi. 292.

23. **operosa:** 'meticulously attentive to (at all times)'; cf. *Am.* ii. 10. 5. The vulgate *operata* (see apparatus p. 95) would, I think, imply that Cypassis was actually doing Corinna's hair as Ovid was speaking, for *operatus* means 'engaged in (at a particular time)'; see e.g. *Ep.* 9. 35-6 *uotis operata pudicis / torqueor*, *Met.* viii. 865 *studioque operatus inhaesi.*

24. **per doctas grata ... manus:** the oldest MSS are corrupt here (full apparatus on p. 95). Heinsius' *perdocta ... manu* is seductive in view of Ovid's general liking for compounds with the intensifying *per-* prefix, but ω's text is probably sound, for *doctae manus* is paralleled at *Am.* ii. 4. 28 (cf. also *Ars* iii. 134) and *gratus per* + accusative, though apparently unique, is perfectly intelligible. For the intricacies of Roman hairdressing see 8. 1n.

ministra: metrically more tractable here than the most common word for a slave-girl in elegy, *ancilla.* *ministra* and *famula* are the favoured words in epic and tragedy, where *ancilla* is never used (see Axelson 58, Watson 434-6); cf. 8. 12n.

25. **quae tam tibi fida:** this (= ω; full apparatus on p. 95) is linguistically unobjectionable – the verb 'to be' is easily understood – and produces a rhetorical question with what seems to me to be a suitable degree of sarcasm; some, however, will prefer *y*'s *quod erat tibi fida* (see Kenney (1958a) 61, *id.* (1966) 268), which I feel makes the sarcasm unduly heavy. Goold ((1965a) 35) suggests a plausible sequence of error to account for the corrupt readings of *PSY.*

rogarem: see 3. 5n.

26. Ovid's expression is very compressed: 'Why (would I have done it), unless I had been wanting to make sure of both rejection (by her) and exposure (to you)?'.

indicio: a legalism; see 8. 5n.

repulsa: elsewhere Ovid counts the risks of this as one of the most exciting features of the life of love; see e.g. *Am.* ii. 9B. 46.

27-8. Cf. *Am.* ii. 8. 17-20.

27. **per ... pueri ... uolatilis arcus:** *pueri uolatilis* = Cupid; for his wings see 9B. 49n., and for his bow, 9A. 5n. Swearing by the attributes of deities rather than by deities themselves is common; cf. Tib. i. 4. 25-6 with Murgatroyd's note.

28. **criminis ... reum:** a clear link with v. 1.

Poem 8

The immediate sequel to 7; see pp. 48-9.

1-4. Cf. especially *Am.* ii. 7. 17-22.

1. **ponendis ... perfecta capillis:** for *perfectus* = *peritissimus* with simple ablative cf. Suet. *Gram.* 4 (p. 127 Reifferscheid) *litteratorem ... non perfectum litteris, sed imbutum.*

in mille modos: complicated hairstyles became increasingly fashionable with Roman women from the late republic onwards (cf. Mart. ii. 66, Juv. 6. 495-504, and see Daremberg and Saglio I. 1367ff., figs. 1855ff., Balsdon 255-60). Ladies' hairdressing evidently had its hierarchy even at this time: Cypassis was clearly a 'top stylist', while some had the status of 'juniors' only allowed to hold the mirror (*CIL* VI. 7297). Ovid himself advises on different styles to suit different faces with the professional air of a master coiffeur at *Ars* iii. 135-60.

2. **comere:** synonymous with *ornare* (see 4. 38n.), 'to "do" hair'.
sed: for the position see p. 13, with n. 107.

3. **non rustica:** litotes (see p. 13). Ovid gave a new signification to *rusticus* and its cognates. Properly 'of the country', and often 'clownish' or 'uncouth' (see e.g. Verg. *Ecl.* 2. 56, Hor. *Ep.* i. 2. 42), *rusticus* for Ovid often means 'sexually unsophisticated'; cf. *Am.* i. 8. 44, ii. 4. 13.
furto: literally 'theft', but first used in Catullus (68. 136) and then often in Augustan elegy of illicit or surreptitious sexual relations; cf. *Ars* i. 33, Tib. i. 2. 34, Prop. ii. 2. 4. See also 8n.

4. Cf. *Ars* iii. 665-6. The play on *apta* (first with general and then with sexual reference) is typical Ovidian wit (cf. p. 17).

5. **inter nos sociati corporis:** a crudely factual and apparently unique expression for sexual intercourse; the closest parallel is the more delicate *cubilia sociare* at *Ep.* 3. 109.
index: 'informer'; a juristic word (see Berger 498-9) imported into elegy by Ovid (cf. v. 25 below, *Am.* ii. 1. 9, 2. 41, iii. 13. 21). He similarly adopts the cognate noun *indicium* (almost as rare as *index* in poetry; see Booth (1981) 2695) to denote the amatory informer's special brand of tale-telling (e.g. *Am.* ii. 2. 53, 7. 26, iii. 13. 19). See further p. 12, with n. 91.

6. **concubitus ... tuos:** notice '*your*', and not '*my*' or even '*our*, having sexual relations'; it sounds as if Cypassis is the only one in trouble – as indeed she is! *concubitus* is one of the most common elegiac euphemisms for sexual intercourse (see Adams (1982) 177).
unde: = *ex quo*; see 2. 48n.

7. **num ...? num ...?:** the particle must be intended either to convey some self-doubt on Ovid's part ('Could it be that I blushed ...?') or to defy his addressee to challenge the truth of what he says ('You can't deny it, I didn't blush, did I ...?'). In view of Ovid's generally self-congratulatory attitude in the poem, I incline to the latter (*pace* D. R. Shackleton Bailey in a discussion of *num* in direct questions at *CQ* n.s. 3 (1953), 120-25).
tamen: here this serves to set aside what has gone before: '*Never mind* all that (i.e. who told Corinna about us (5-6)), *I* didn't blush ...'. Cf. Prop. ii. 5. 5, and see also 15n.

8. **furtiuae:** a favourite epithet of *amor* and its adjuncts (e.g. *munus* (Catul. 65. 19), *preces* (Prop. i. 16. 20), *lectus* (Tib. i. 5. 7)); cf. 3n.
conscia signa: see 1. 8n.

9-10. The rhetorical question invites us to imagine Ovid's rave review of his own performance unceremoniously interrupted by Cypassis, less interested in admiring his histrionic abilites than in finding out what he meant by suggesting that no one in his right mind would have an affair with an *ancilla* (*Am.* ii. 7. 19-22).

9. **in ancilla delinquere:** *in* + ablative regularly indicates the sphere in which an offence is committed; cf. Ter. *Ad.* 124, Sen. *H. Oet.* 1029. For *delinquere* = *peccare* in its erotic sense (see 7. 11n.) cf. *Tr.* ii. 256, and see also 4. 2-3n.

10. **mente ... bona:** 'sanity'; cf. *Am.* i. 2. 31, Petr. 61. 1.

11-14. Pointing to precedent was a traditional way of defending slave-love (see Nisbet-Hubbard II. 67-8), but here, as often, the precedents cited are hardly valid, for Briseis and Cassandra were not domestic slaves of lowly origin but high-born captives.

These lines are not a soliloquising aside, as some editors suppose: Ovid needs not to convince *himself* that it is not shameful to love a slave-girl, but to convince Cypassis that he did not mean it when he implied that it was.

11. **Thessalus:** Achilles; see 1. 32n.

facie ... arsit: for the simple ablative denoting the object of passion with *ardere* cf. Hor. *Epod*. 14. 9-10 *dicunt arsisse Bathyllo / Anacreonta Teium*; Cf. 3. 6n., and see also p. 13. For *facie* see 3. 13n.

12. **serua:** the most realistic word for a female slave, but not, like the masculine *seruus*, an 'unpoetical' word, for it is rare even in prose and at the same time not meticulously avoided in very elevated poetry (see e.g. Verg. *A*. v. 284, ix. 546, Sen. *Phaed*. 622, Sil. xvi. 568); cf. 7. 24n. Ovid's use of the word in the present context suggests direct reminiscence of Hor. *Carm*. ii. 4. 1-4.

Mycenaeo ... duci: Agamemnon. For the dative of agent cf. *Tr*. i. 6. 2 *nec tantum Coo Bittis amata suo est*, and see p. 13.

Phoebas: Cassandra. *Phoebas* is an uncommon term for 'priestess of Apollo'; cf. *Tr*. ii. 400, Luc. v. 128, 167, Sen. *Ag*. 588.

13. **Tantalide:** Agamemnon, great-grandson of Tantalus. (see 2. 43-4n.)

15. **tamen:** the particle's function here is partly that in v. 7 above and partly that of pointing the contrast between Ovid's own behaviour, already reviewed in vv. 7-10, and Cypassis', about to be appraised in vv. 15-16.

16. **totis erubuisse genis:** for the expression cf. *Ep*. 20 (21). 112.

17-20. Ovid calls into service the traditional notion of lovers being able to perjure themselves with impunity (for examples and discussion of the theme's development see Nisbet-Hubbard II. 122-3); here the dramatic setting and a touch of wit (see 20n.) enliven the trite motif.

17. **at:** this marks the return to the consideration of Ovid's own behaviour as opposed to Cypassis'.

si forte refers: a reminder (of *Am*. ii. 7. 27-8) more for the reader than Cypassis.

praesentior: for *praesens* of mental quickness cf. Plin. *Nat*. xvii. 1. 4 *Crassus, praesens ingenio semper*.

18-19. According to legend (Hes. fr. 124 Merkelbach-West, *Ars* i. 635-6), it was Jupiter who, after swearing a false oath to Juno, originally exempted perjured lovers from punishment (see Smith on Tib. i. 4. 21, 23), but Venus is often cited as the obliging deity (cf. *Am*. i. 8. 85-6, Hor. *Carm*. ii. 8. 13). Presumably Ovid saw extra security in a false oath in Venus' name (7. 27-8); cf. [Tib.] iii. 6. 48, Paul. Sil. *AP* v. 279. 5.

19. **dea:** *dea* and *diua* are frequently used to address female deities, while male gods are generally addressed by their proper names; see Nisbet-Hubbard I. 388.

animi periuria puri: a superbly impudent oxymoron. Moral purity was conventionally claimed to afford supreme security to those who possessed it; see e.g. Hor. *Carm*. i. 22 with Nisbet-Hubbard's introduction.

Carpathium ... mare: see 15. 10n.

20. **tepidos ... Notos:** probably = *Zephyros*, as Housman (on Luc. vii. 871) suggests (cf. *Am*. i. 7. 55-6, *Ep*. 11. 75-6). Proverbially benevolent winds (see 11. 41n.) would be suitable nullifiers of an oath (cf. 6. 44n.) now regretted by the speaker.

22. **concubitus ... tuos:** here = *tecum concubitum*; cf. 6n.

fusca: was Cypassis a negress? Perhaps: *fuscus* is one of the words regularly used to describe the skin-colour of negroes (see 4. 40n.); there was apparently something of a vogue for black slaves in Rome (see e.g. Ter. *Eu*. 165-7); and miscegenation was not unknown (see Snowden 193-5). Nor does the fact that Cypassis is said to have blushed (v. 16) preclude her being a black girl: the ancients recognised varying degrees of blackness in negroid skin (see Snowden 3-5), and some were obviously light enough for a blush to show (see e.g Philostr. *VA* vi. 12, Hld. x. 24). But whether Ovid conceived of Cypassis as a 'black' or as a swarthy 'white', it seems unlikely that he chose to mention her skin-colour at this point in the hope of scandalising his readers afresh with the idea of his copulating with a 'dark' girl. For if the idea *had* been shocking, Ovid would surely have cited Cypassis' skin-colour in *Am.* ii. 7 as one of the reasons why it was preposterous for Corinna to imagine that he could ever have been in bed with her. In fact it was Cypassis' servile status which he depicted as objectionable (*Am.* ii. 7. 21-2), and I think it is probably to reinforce his repudiation of that stance that Ovid pointedly calls her *fusca* here, for slaves were conventionally thought of as dusky-complexioned (cf. Cic. *Pis.* 1 *color iste seruilis* with Nisbet's note).

23. The question neatly conveys Cypassis' reaction (cf. *Am.* ii. 2. 18, iii. 2. 21-4); for the elegists' use of various forms of direct address for this purpose see W. Abel, *Die Anredeformen bei den römischen Elegikern* (Diss. Berlin, 1930).
renuis: throwing back the head (*renuere*) was, and is, an emphatic gesture of refusal or dissent in Italy and Greece; see Sittl 82-3.
fingis ... nouos ... timores: not '*imagine*' but '*invent* new things to be afraid of', i.e. 'pretend to be afraid'.
ingrata: a common term of abuse (see Opelt 31) and outrageous here in that it implies Cypassis is refusing out of cussedness, not genuine anxiety.

24. **unum ... e dominis:** i.e. Ovid, here playing the role of *dominus* (or *uir*; see p. 6) in Corinna's household; for *domini* covering both masculine and feminine see 2. 32n.
emeruisse: a nice *double entendre*: *emerere* can mean 'oblige sexually' (see e.g. Tib. i. 9. 59-60) as well as 'oblige' in a general sense. Cf. *Am.* iii. 11. 14.

25-8. Ovid plays his trump card: because of her previous compliance, Cypassis can be blackmailed. A faint resemblance between these lines and Petr. 87, where another temporarily thwarted lover similarly threatens his unobliging partner, has prompted some speculation on the possibility of a common source for both in the 'Milesian Tales' of Aristides translated into Latin by L. Cornelius Sisenna early in the 1st century B.C. (see L. Pepe, 'Un motivo novellistico negli Amores di Ovidio' in *Studi Cataudella* 3 (1972), 339-43). Certainly Ovid seems to have known Sisenna's work (*Tr.* ii. 443), but there is no need to posit a literary source for the present passage.

25-6. **index ante acta ...:** the legalistic ring so pervasive in *Am.* ii. 7 returns here, as Ovid threatens to 'turn Queen's evidence' (there was also in antiquity some hope of reduced penalties for the offender who offered his services to the prosecution; see Berger 498).

25. **negas:** see 9B. 50n.

26. **ueniam:** perhaps understand *ueniam in iudicium*, but see 2. 56n.
ipse meae: formulaic; see 6. 55n.

27-8. Ovid's climactic wit was clearly inspired by Tib. ii. 6. 51-2 (*tunc mens mihi perdita fingit / quisue meam teneat, quot teneatue modis*) and is imitated by Juvenal at 6. 405-6 (*dicet quis uiduam praegnatem fecerit et quo / mense, quibus uerbis concumbat quaeque, modis quot*).

27. **tecum fuerim:** an erotic euphemism; cf. *Ars* iii. 664, and see further Adams (1982) 177.

28. **dominae:** i.e. 'your mistress and mine'.
modis: *schemata Veneris*; cf. Tib. ii. 6. 52.

Poem 9A

1. It does not make much sense for one about to protest at having had more than his fair share of love because of Cupid's activities to begin by complaining that Cupid has never helped him enough in love's cause. Yet that only can be the meaning of the vulgate *numquam pro me satis indignate*, literally 'never angry enough on my behalf' (some have suggested that *indignate* could have passive significance, but there is no evidence for it). The most tolerable of the alternatives offered (full apparatus on p. 96) seems to be *numquam pro re satis indignande*, 'you whom no words could ever adequately revile to do justice to the facts' (so Goold (1965a) 36). *indignande* gives good sense and neatly balances *uenerandus* (v. 54) in that section of 9B which seems intended to be the antithesis of 9A. 1-2 (see also 2n. *desidiose*); moreover, MS confusion between -*atus* and -*andus* is common (see apparatus for 7. 23, 11. 15 and Brink on Hor. *Ars* 190). *pro re* may be right, but its vagueness troubles me.

1-2. **o ... o:** like other Latin poets, Ovid uses *o* with the vocative to produce a variety of impassioned tones according to context. Here the tone is one of reproach and indignation (cf. 5. 4n.), at *Am.* ii. 2. 9 one of menace, at *Am.* ii. 12. 16 one of prayerful entreaty (see Bömer on *Met.* iii. 613), and at *Ars* ii. 91 one of pathos. See also Fordyce on Catul. 46. 9. For the hiatus after *o* see 5. 7n.

2. **desidiose:** everywhere else this means 'lazy', but the sense here seems to be closer to that of the root verb *desidere*: 'hanging about', 'loitering (with intent)'. Cf. Propertius' complaint about Cupid at ii. 12. 15 (*euolat heu nostro ... de pectore nusquam*), and notice Ovid's contrasting welcoming of Cupid's permanent occupation of his heart at 9B. 52.
puer: a standard form of address to Cupid; see Bömer *Met.* i. 456. The portrayal of Love as a small child is a development of Hellenistic literature and art; see Ap. Rhod. iii. 111ff., Mel. *AP* v. 176, P. E. Easterling, 'Literary tradition and the transformation of Cupid', *Didaskalos* 5 (1977), 318-37, W. Strobel, *Eros* (Diss. Erlangen, 1952), and for iconographical representations, Daremberg and Saglio II. 1600-1601, figs. 2160-62, 1604, fig. 2174. See also 5n.

3. **miles ... signa:** for the soldiery of love see pp. 53-4, and cf. 3. 10n.

4. **castris ... meis:** i.e. the camp in which Ovid serves under Cupid's command; cf. *Am.* i. 9. 1 *militat omnis amans et habet sua castra Cupido*, i. 2. 32, *Ars* iii. 559.
ipse meis: formulaic; see 6. 55n.

5. **fax ... arcus:** Love's conventional weapons in Latin elegy; cf. *Am.* iii. 9. 7-8, *Ars* i. 23, Tib. ii. 6. 15-16, Prop. iii. 16. 16 with Fedeli's note. It is in Hellenistic poetry that Eros is first regularly equipped with bow, arrows and quiver (though Euripides refers to his bow at *IA* 549); see Ap. Rhod. iii. 278-9, Mel. *AP* v. 177. 4, 179. 2. Moschus' poem *Eros the Runaway* (a witty Hellenistic profile of the Eros Western culture has come to know so well) contains the earliest mention of the torch as part of Love's armoury (see further Bömer on *Met.* i. 461).

6. Here and at *Am.* i. 2. 22 Ovid varies an old poetic commonplace; cf. Alc. Mess. *AP* v. 10. 3-4 τί πλέον, εἰ θεὸς ἄνδρα καταφλέγει; ἢ τί τὸ σεμνὸν / δῃώσας ἀπ' ἐμῆς ἆθλον ἔχει κεφαλῆς; ('What does it profit a god to burn up a man? And what will be the grand prize he will win from *my* head by cutting me down?'), Posidipp. *AP* xii. 45, Tib. i. 6. 3-4.
erat: 'would have been'. *gloria ... maior* virtually = *melius*, and the indicative is regularly used with this and other words expressing fitness or fairness (e.g. *idoneum, aequum*) in what amounts to the apodosis of an unreal condition (here *uincere* = *si uicisses*); see further Kühner-Stegmann II. i. 171.

7. **quid?:** this, followed by a further question, always negatively phrased and often involving a mythological *exemplum*, is favourite Ovidian shorthand for 'What is wrong with what I have said? It will not seem so outrageous, if you consider ...'. Cf. *Am.* i. 7. 7, iii. 6. 29, *Met.* xiii. 852 with Bömer's note, Prop. ii. 8. 21.

7-8. **non Haemonius ...:** Achilles (see 1. 32n.) healed Telephus, after striking him down in battle, by applying to his wound the rust of the spear with which he had inflicted it. Reference to this is very frequently used to suggest that the person who has done some damage or other should be the one to undo it, and the *exemplum* is particularly apt in an amatory context, where the lover's sufferings are so often described as 'wounds'. Cf. *Rem.* 43-6, and for a large collection of further examples see Nisbet-Hubbard I. 171. The word-order displays mild hyperbaton (see p. 16).

8. **confossum:** 'pierced through'. A rare compound; see further p. 13, with n. 97.

9-10. Here Ovid reproduces the essence of a Callimachean epigram (31 = *AP* xii. 102):

> ᾽Ωγρευτής,᾽Επίκυδες, ἐν οὔρεσι πάντα λαγωὸν
> διφᾷ καὶ πάσης ἴχνια δορκαλίδος,
> στίβῃ καὶ νιφετῷ κεχρημένος· ἢν δέ τις εἴπῃ,
> 'τῆ, τόδε βέβληται θηρίον', οὐκ ἔλαβεν.
> χοὐμὸς ἔρως τοιόσδε· τὰ μέν φεύγοντα διώκειν
> οἶδε, τὰ δ' ἐν μέσσῳ κείμενα παραπέταται.

> The hunter in the mountains, Epicydes, seeks out every hare and the tracks of every antelope through frost and snow. But if anyone says to him, 'Look, here is an animal which has been wounded', he never takes that. And my love is just like this; it tends to pursue what flees and passes by what lies to hand.

Horace offers a closer version at *S.* i. 2. 105-8, and Ovid turns the idea more sententiously at *Am.* ii. 19. 36. Cf. also *Ars* i. 717, Phld. *AP* xii. 173. 5-6 with Gow-Page's note, and see further Otto 81.

10. **et:** for the position see p. 13, with n. 107.
inuentis: for the ablative see 1. 20n.

11. **populus:** 'a group of people'; this sense first appears in Ovid (see also *Ars* iii. 518, *Met.* xi. 633, xii. 499). Cf. 9B. 53-4n.

12. **pigra ... manus:** a proleptic use of the adjective: 'your hand is slow'.
cessat in: 'fails to take the necessary action in the case of ...'. A legalism; cf. Scaev. *dig.* xl. 7. 40. 8 *si in exactione nominum cessauerint*, and see further Berger s.v. For Ovid's legalisms see p. 12, with n. 91.

13-14. Cf. Prop. ii. 12. 17 *quid tibi iucundum est siccis habitare medullis?*. The poetic lover is conventionally emaciated; cf. *Am.* i. 6. 5, *Ars* i. 733, Theoc. 2. 89-90, Call. *Epigr.* 30 (= *AP* xii. 71). 3. For *quid iuuat* see 6. 17-19n.

15-16. Basically a very well-worn sentiment (cf. Mel. *AP* v. 179. 9-10 ἀλλ' ἴθι, δυσνίκητε, λαβὼν δ' ἔπι κοῦφα πέδιλα / ἐκπέτασον ταχινὰς εἰς ἑτέρους πτέρυγας ('But be off with you, recalcitrant creature; take your light sandals with you; spread your swift wings and visit others.'), Prop. ii. 12. 18-19 *si pudor, alio traice tela, puer, / intactos isto satius temptare ueneno*, Arch. *AP* v. 98, Maced. *AP* v. 224). There is an audacious new twist in the idea of a *triumphus* rewarding a Cupid who ventures into fresh territory (see p. 54), but Ovid surprisingly misses the opportunity of pointing out that, as a 'relative' of Augustus (cf. *Am.* i. 2. 51), Cupid is more eligible than most for the honour which after 19 B.C. became restricted to members of the imperial family (see pp. 64-5).

16. **hinc ... eat:** for the expression cf. Prop. i. 7. 10 *hinc cupio nomen carminis ire mei* with Fedeli's note.

17-18. This couplet obliquely confirms the suspicion that Ovid meant to suggest that Cupid's military standing could equal Augustus'. Cupid is simply reminded of *Rome*'s splendour as a result of her overseas conquests, but since Augustus took the credit for most of them at the time (see Aug. *Anc.* 3. 26-33), it is obviously he whom the god of love is really being invited to emulate.

With the reference to 'thatched huts' Ovid slyly mocks a piece of Augustan humbug. As pervasive in Roman society as in many others was the idea that ancient, rustic simplicity represented the most decent, pious and traditional way of life (see E. J. Kenney, *Moretum: a poem ascribed to Virgil* (Bristol, 1984), xxxviii-xl, R. O. A. M. Lyne in *Quality and Pleasure in Latin Poetry*, edd. A. J. Woodman and D. A. West (Cambridge, 1974), 47). This idea is reflected in much Augustan literature (e.g. throughout Virgil's *Georgics* and at *A.* viii. 359ff., Hor. *Carm.* iii. 1. 45-8, 6. 33-44) and was in tune with Augustus' policies of moral, religious and patriotic revival. Moreover, in this city of grand and sophisticated buildings (see Griffin (1985) 6-7) two 'thatched huts', one on the Capitoline, said to be the house of Romulus, and another, apparently a replica of it, on the Palatine, were objects of great veneration as symbols of what committed Augustans would doubtless have professed to regard as the ideal way of life (see D. Hal. i. 79, Plu. *Rom.* 20). And Ovid uses 'thatched huts' here as symbols of what he obviously considered a most inferior type of existence! Of course, everyone will have known that, whatever the official Augustan line might be, a life of rustic simplicity was impossible in a wealthy imperial capital; Ovid's impudence lay in his readiness to imply here (and say openly at *Ars* iii. 113-28) that he, for one, was glad of it. He may have been inspired to the present couplet by Prop. ii. 16. 18-19, where Propertius' wish to have Augustus himself living in a *straminea casa* seems to me to be not without irony.

17. **promosset:** cf. *Pont.* ii. 7. 70, and for the syncopated form see Kenney (1958a) 60.

19-24. The lover's retirement at an appropriate time is a well-established erotic theme; see e.g. Asclep. (or Posidipp.) *AP* v. 202, 203, Hor. *Carm.* iii. 26. Here Ovid introduces his own longing for it by way of three of the same *exempla* as Propertius uses at ii. 25. 5-8 to preface *his* repudiation of the idea. The Propertian parallel would seem to confirm the order of Ovid's lines as transmitted by the majority of the MSS (see apparatus on p. 96).

19. **fessus:** at all other times in the *Amores* Ovid opts for the more colloquial *lassus* (see Axelson 29-30, Watson 443).

in acceptos ... deducitur agros: the distribution of land to discharged soldiers was an old-established practice (see Brunt 294ff.), and in official language *deducere* is the technical term for 'settling' these veterans; see e.g. *CIL* IX. 4682 and further *ThLL* V. i. 273. 54ff. Ovid's use of it here mocks the much-vaunted imperial munificence in this area (see Aug. *Anc.* 16).

20. The comparison of the tired lover with the worn-out horse dates from early Greek lyric (Ibyc. fr. 6 Page), and the *exemplum* is in general very popular; cf. *Tr.* iv. 8. 19-20 with Luck's note, Enn. *Ann.* 522-3 Skutsch, Hor. *Ep.* i. 1. 8.

21. **subductam:** *subducere* is the technical term for 'winching' ships on to dry land; cf. Verg. *A.* iii. 135.

pinum: both more euphonious than *nauis* here (cf. *Tr.* iv. 8. 17), and, as a highly poetical metonym (see Bömer on *Met.* ii. 185; cf. Watson 443), more in keeping with the generally elevated stylistic level of 19-22.

naualia: Rome had dockyards on the left bank of the Tiber.

22. **rudis:** the wooden sword given to gladiators to mark the end of their career.

23. **sub Amore †puellae†:** for Ovid to describe himself as one who has 'served so often under love of a girl' makes little sense either in itself or in the context of the poem. The issue has been presented throughout as one between Ovid the soldier and Cupid his commanding officer; no *puella* has ever come into it. *puellae* looks like a simple error resulting from the copyist's eye straying to the end of v. 15. If it is, the palaeographically-based conjectures *puella*, *periclis*, and *periclo* (see apparatus on p. 96 and cf. Goold (1965a) 37) are not worth much, and I doubt in any case whether what has been lost is an ablative linked to *defunctum* in v. 24, since the absolute use of that word there facilitates a neat *double entendre* (see next n.). Professor Kenney once suggested *magistro* to me as the missing word; with *Amore*, not *amore*, this would fit well. For *merere sub* + personal name and noun in apposition cf. Liv. xxi. 4. 10 *sub Hasdrubale imperatore meruit*, and for *magister* of a military commander, see *OLD* s.v. 2.

24. **defunctum:** *defunctus* used absolutely can mean not only 'having completed one's task' (cf. Verg. *A*. ix. 98 *ubi defunctae (carinae) finem ... tenebunt*) but also 'having died' (cf. *Am*. i. 8. 108 *ut mea defunctae molliter ossa cubent*), and suggestion of the second meaning here as well as the first is strengthened by the juxtaposition with *placide*, which, though it goes with *uiuere* in this instance, is a word often used with reference to the eternal peace of death (see e.g. Tib. ii. 4. 49-50, *CLE* 541. 12). The hint of ambiguity is no oversight: Ovid will have wanted us to imagine him realising, as he articulated this line, that a life of peaceful retirement, i.e. a life without love, would be as bad as being dead (cf. 9B. 41-2). My translation 'bowing out' is an attempt to render the double meaning.

tempus erat: an idiomatic use of the imperfect, probably without past temporal significance (see Nisbet-Hubbard I. 412), though some understand 'it was time long ago', i.e. 'it is now high time'.

Poem 9B (10)

25-6. **uiue ... deprecer:** a scenario probably directly inspired by Hor. *S*. i. 1. 15-19, though the motif may be Hellenistic in origin; see N. Rudd, *The Satires of Horace* (Cambridge, 1966), 20-21. For the general sentiment see 10. 15-22n.

25. **'uiue' ... 'posito' ... 'amore':** Ovid is fond of dividing short pieces of direct speech into three or more fragments; cf. *Am*. i. 1. 24, *Ars* iii. 697-8. J. Marouzeau collects more examples at *Ovidiana* 103-5.

26. **deprecer:** a nice paradox; Ovid rejects what is ostensibly a boon with a word appropriate to begging himself off a punishment (cf. Verg. *A*. xii. 931).

dulce puella malum est: an ancient oxymoron; for the 'sweet bitterness' of love cf. Sapph. fr. 130 Lobel-Page, Mel. *AP* v. 163. 3-4, 177. 3, Catul. 68. 18 with Kroll's note.

27-34. The constant tendency of love to return when once it has departed is a stock motif which first appears in Greek lyric; see e.g. Alcm. fr. 59a Page and further Nisbet-Hubbard I. 238.

27. **bene pertaesum est:** *bene* = *ualde* is colloquial (see Hofmann 74), and *pertaedet* without the usual accusative of person or genitive of thing involved (cf. Verg. *A*. iv. 18, Liv. iii. 67. 7) is also perhaps suggestive of the casual manner of everyday speech.

animoque relanguit ardor: cf. *Am*. i. 10. 9 *animique resanuit error*, whence the corruption in *PY* (see apparatus on p. 96).

28. **turbine:** 'whirlwind', not 'spinning top' as at Tib. i. 5. 3 *namque agor ut per plana citus sola uerbere turben*; Ovid's image nevertheless seems to owe something to the Tibullan line.

29-32. A pair of similes in which Ovid compares himself with two things often compared with each other – a bolting horse and a ship at the mercy of the winds; cf. *Tr*. i. 4. 13-16 with Luck's note for further examples. The Roman poets readily use the bolting horse simile in the context of anything going out of control (cf. Verg. *G*. i. 512-15, J. A. Washietl, *De similitudinibus imaginibusque Ouidianis* (Diss. Vienna, 1883) 43, 140-41), but nautical imagery is especially common in description of the vicissitudes of love (cf. *Am*. ii. 4. 8, 10. 9, Prop. ii. 12. 7, and see La Penna 195, n. 1, 202-3), and the ship coming into port is a favourite symbol of release from amatory sufferings (cf. *Rem*. 609-10, Prop. iii. 24. 15

with Fedeli's note, and see further C. Bonner, 'Desired haven', *Harv. Theol. Rev.* 34 (1941), 49-68).

29. **spumantia:** a stock epithet of *frena*; cf. Verg. *A.* iv. 135 with Pease's note.

30. **durior oris:** i.e. self-willed. The defining genitive with adjectives is popular in Augustan poetry and post-Augustan prose (see Kühner-Stegmann II. i. 443-6).

31-2. **carinam / tangentem portus:** a stock poetic turn of phrase; cf. Prop. iii. 24. 15, Verg. *G.* i. 303.

33. **incerta Cupidinis aura:** cf. Eur. *IA* 69 πνοαὶ Ἀφροδίτης ('the breezes of Aphrodite'), Prop. ii. 12. 8 *nostra ... non ullis permanet aura locis*, 25. 27, Hor. *Carm.* i. 5. 11-12.

34. **purpureus ... Amor:** see 1. 38n.

35. **fige, puer ...:** while recalling the words of Posidippus (*AP* xii. 45. 1) and Asclepiades (*AP* xii. 166. 5) ναί, ναί, βάλλετ' Ἔρωτες ('Yes, yes, shoot, Loves'), Ovid reverses their sentiments; for Posidippus is defying the Loves to conquer him and Asclepiades begging them to kill him and have done with it, but Ovid invites Cupid's attack because he enjoys what it brings him. Cf. 9A. 5-6, 13-14.

nudus: 'unarmed'; cf. *Ars* iii. 5 with Brandt's note.

praebeor: the passive is metrically convenient here; for the more usual active construction cf. *Ars* i. 16.

36. **hic ... facit:** not *hac ... facit* (so G. Luck, *RhM* n.s. 105 (1962), 351 with some subsequent support; full apparatus on p. 96). This would mean 'is active on this side', i.e. 'is working for me' (cf. Pl. *St.* 463 *augurium hac facit*), whereas Ovid surely intends to say 'is effective in this quarter'. For the absolute use of *facere* cf. *Ep.* 2. 39 *nimium ... facientia tela*, *Tr.* iii. 8. 23 *nec caelum nec aquae faciunt*.

38. Cf. Mel. *AP* v. 198, 5-6 οὐκέτι σοὶ φαρέτρη ... πτερόεντας ὀϊστοὺς / κρύπτει, Ἔρως. ἐν μοὶ πάντα γάρ ἐστι βέλη ('Your quiver has no winged arrows left hidden, Love, for all your darts are in me').

prae: see 4. 19n.

39-46. Ovid points the standard elegiac contrast between the lot of the loveless and his own life of amatory activity; cf. *Am.* ii. 10. 15-22, 31-8, and for the contrast motif in general see E. Bréguet, 'Le thème *alius ... ego* chez les poètes latins', *REL* 40 (1962), 128-36.

39-40. Cf. *Am.* ii. 10. 17-18.

39. **tota ... nocte:** the ablative of duration of time replaces the accusative with increasing frequency from the late republic onwards; cf. Catul. 109. 5 *tota ... uita* with Fordyce's note, and see further Kühner-Stegmann II. i. 360-61.

quiescere: this is regularly used not only as a synonym for *dormire* but also with specific reference to the eternal 'sleep' of death (e.g. Verg. *A.* vi. 371, Tib. ii. 4. 49); it thus anticipates the sentiments of 41-2.

41. **quid est somnus ...?:** Sleep (Hypnos) and Death (Thanatos) were twin brothers in Greek mythology; for the frequent literary association of the two see Nisbet-Hubbard I. 284. For Ovid's expression here cf. Cic. *Tusc.* i. 38. 2 *habes somnum imaginem mortis*.

gelidae: death is conventionally 'cold'; cf. Verg. *A.* iv. 385 with Pease's note.

42. Cf. Mosch. 3. 103-4 ὁππότε πρᾶτα θάνωμες ... / εὕδομες εὖ μάλα μακρὸν ἀτέρμονα νήγρετον ὕπνον ('when once we are dead ... we sleep a sleep which is sound and long, without end or waking'), Catul. 5. 6.

43-6. Cf. *Am.* ii. 19. 5-6, and see p. 90.

amicae ... domina: see 1. 17n.

44. **gaudia:** see 5. 29n.

45. **blanditias:** see 1. 21n.

iurgia nectat: cf. *Am.* ii. 2. 35.

46. **fruar:** a euphemism for sexual intercourse; cf. *Rem.* 537, and see Adams (1982) 198.

repulsus eam: the *exclusus amator* comes to mind (see 1. 17n.).

47-8. Not 'like father, like son', but 'like (step)son, like (step)father'; an amusingly absurd and cheeky variation on the sentiment of *Am.* i. 9. 29 *Mars dubius, nec certa Venus.*

priuigne ... uitricus: Mars/Ares, most often thought of as Venus/Aphrodite's paramour, sometimes replaces Vulcan/Hephaistos as her husband in post-Homeric myth and can thus be described here and at *Rem.* 27 (contrast *Am.* i. 2. 34) as the stepfather of Cupid. Eros was allegedly already identified as the son of the love-goddess in Sappho (see fr. 198 Lobel-Page). The identity of his father was a popular matter for speculation; see e.g. Mel. *AP* v. 177. 5-6, 180 and further D. L. Page, *Sappho and Alcaeus* (Oxford, 1955), 271.

47. **quod:** see 6. 7n.

48. **mouet arma:** for the *double entendre* see 3. 7n.

49. **uentosior alis:** Ovid caps Propertius' exploitation of the double meaning of *uentosus* (both 'nimble' and 'fickle') at ii. 12. 5 *idem* (i.e. *qui pinxit Amorem*) *nonfrustra uentosas addidit alas*. Cupid is traditionally winged in literature and art; cf. *Met.* i. 466 with Bömer's note.

50. **dasque negasque:** erotic euphemisms; cf. *Ars* i. 345. *-que ... -que* is an epic turn of phrase (see Norden on Verg. *A.* vi. 336) doubtless introduced for mock-solemnity; cf. *Am.* i. 2. 35, ii. 11. 7, and see Wills 372-7.

51. **Cupido:** many prefer the variant *rogantem* (see apparatus on p. 96), believing *Cupido* to emanate from *Am.* i. 6. 11. But *rogantem* would most naturally go with *pulchra cum matre* (i.e. *rogantem pulchra cum matre rogante*) and is probably no more than the attempted emendation of a scribe suspicious of the repetition of *Cupido* so soon after its appearance in v. 47. For the absolute use of *exaudire* cf. *Met.* iv. 144, Sen. *Ep.* 95. 2.

52. **indeserta:** a word coined by Ovid and used only here. Its arresting three long syllables at the beginning of the pentameter reinforce the message that Ovid wants Cupid to hold sway in his heart *eternally* (see further p. 13, with n. 96).

meo ... pectore: for the absence of preposition see p. 13.

52-3. **regna ... regno:** *regna* = 'sway' (cf. *Rem.* 15 *si quis male fert indignae regna puellae*, Hor. *Carm.* iv. 1. 4 *qualis eram bonae sub regno Cinarae*, and cf. *Am.* ii. 19. 33); *regno* = 'kingdom' (cf. *Am.* i. 1. 13 *sunt tibi magna, puer, nimiumque potentia regna*). The word-play and the construction with *gerere* in v. 52 recall Tib. i. 9. 80 *et geret in regno regna superba tuo*; see further Murgatroyd *ad loc.* For the ending of the line with short *e* see Platnauer 64-5.

53-4. Ovid's promise of general veneration for Cupid here contrasts well with his abuse of him at the beginning of 9A, but it is probably not as innocent as it at first seems. For it is obviously to Ovid's advantage no less than Cupid's if wayward young women (*nimium uaga turba*) can be brought under his power too, and the manner in which 'both sexes' (*ambobus populis* – a unique use of *populus*) will subsequently make due obeisance to the god of love can only too easily be imagined.

accedant ... eris: see 3. 12n.

53. **uaga:** cf. Prop. i. 5. 7 with Fedeli's note, Thgn. 581 West.

turba: see 2. 30n.

Poem 10 (11)

1. **tu ... tu:** the epanalepsis (see p. 14) reinforces Ovid's favourite parenthetical *memini* (see 1. 11-16n.) in this humorous attempt to authenticate a palpably fictitious statement.

Graecine: this could be C. Pomponius Graecinus, *consul suffectus* in A.D. 16 (cf. *Pont.* i. 6. 3, ii. 6. 1, iv. 9. 1); if it is, this poem can hardly have belonged to the first edition of the *Amores* (see Syme (1978) 74-5, and cf. pp 2-4). Horace, in his lyric, and Propertius are particularly fond of introducing a specific, but occasionally redundant addressee: Ovid does so only here and in *Am.* i. 9.

2-14. Showpiece lines for Ovid's elaborate verbal artistry and wit; see my detailed analysis at *G & R* n.s. 25 (1978), 128-9.

3. **deprensus inermis:** cf. *Am.* iii. 7. 71, *Rem.* 347.

4. **ecce:** often used by Ovid to express indignation at things not being as they ought to be; cf. *Am.* ii. 6. 27, 7, 17, iii. 7. 67, 8. 9. The usage is basically colloquial (see Hofmann 33-5, Tränkle 146-9).

turpis: very arch in view of vv. 19ff.

5-7. **formosa .... pulchrior:** there is no clear difference in stylistic level between these two adjectives (see A. Ernout *RPh* 21 (1947), 65 [= *id.*, *Philologica* II (Paris, 1957), 80], Watson 440-41), nor is the difference in meaning suggested by Catul. 86 (i.e. *pulcher* = 'beautiful in appearance', *formosus* = 'beautiful in appearance *and* disposition') rigidly observed in the rest of Latin poetry. Ovid uses them quite interchangeably for the sake of variation; cf. *Ars* iii. 255ff.

5. **operosae:** see 7. 23n.

cultibus: see 4. 37n.

6. **artibus:** see 4. 25-6n.

8. For the sentiment cf. Phld. *AP* xii. 173. 4.

placet: see 4. 17-18n.

9. **erro, uelut:** see apparatus on p. 96. W.A. Camps' conjecture (*CR* n.s. 4 (1954), 203-4) neatly supplies the first person verb so urgently required by the context (cf. *Am.* ii. 4. 8). R. Führer (*Hermes* 100 (1972), 408-10), troubled by the lack of parallels in Augustan poetry for the shortening of the first person singular *-o* so early in the line, suggests *erramus*. Palaeographically this is as plausible as *erro uelut*, and the ellipse of the particle of comparison is easily paralleled (*Pont.* ii. 1. 15-16), but the plural is harsh in conjunction with the singular *diuiduum* in 10. For the imagery see 9B. 29-32n.

uentis discordibus: see 11. 17n.

phaselos: literally 'bean-pod'; a word first used of the papyrus vessels on the Nile, because of their distinctive shape, and then of any smallish, light boat. Cf. Catul. 4. 1 with Fordyce's note.

10. For the sentiment cf. Anon. *AP* xii. 89. 1.

alter et alter: see 1. 30n.

11. **Erycina:** a name given to Venus after a temple of her worship at Mt. Eryx in Sicily; cf. Hor. *Carm.* i. 2. 33 with Nisbet-Hubbard's note.

sine fine: i.e. *assiduos*. Ovid is fond of replacing an adjective with *sine* + noun. *sine fine* is one of the most common collocations (Zingerle collects many examples at I. 18-19).

12. Cf. Prop. ii. 25. 48 *una sat est cuiuis femina multa mala.*

in curas ... satis: for the construction cf. *Ep.* 2. 44 *in poenas non satis unus eris*. *cura* is one of the stock elegiac words for the sorrow of love.

13-14. 'Why carry coals to Newcastle?'; Ovid's words derive a proverbial ring of much this kind from his use of the standard *exempla* of proliferation. For *folia* cf. *Pont.* iv. 2. 13, for *sidera*, *Ars* i. 59, and for *aquae*, *Am.* iii. 2. 34.

15-22. The notion that a life without love is a life not worth living dates back to Mimn. fr. 1. 1-3 West: τίς δὲ βίος, τί δὲ τερπνὸν ἄτερ χρυσῆς Ἀφροδίτης; / τεθναίην, ὅτε μοι μηκέτι ταῦτα μέλοι, / κρυπταδίη φιλότης και μείλιχα δῶρα και εὐνή ('What life, what joy would there be without golden Aphrodite? May I die when I no longer care for these things – clandestine love, sweet gifts and a couch.'). Cf. *Am.* ii. 9B. 25-6, 39-46 (with n. *ad loc.*), Prop. i. 6. 25ff., Hor. Carm. iii. 12. 1, Alph. *AP* xii. 18.

15. **iacerem:** this suggests not only 'lie in bed' but also 'lie dead' (see 6. 20n.), and hence the notion that a loveless life = death; cf. 9A. 24, 9B. 41nn.

16-18. An elegiac commonplace: cf. *Ep.* 15 (16). 217-18, Prop. iii. 8. 20 with Fedeli's note.

16. **seuera:** see 1. 3n.

17-18. Cf. *Am.* ii. 9B. 39-40.

17. **uiduo ... cubili:** i.e. a bed whose occupant has no-one sleeping with him. *uiduus* is normally used of the bed of someone deserted by lover, husband or wife, and *uacuus* of the bed of one who sleeps alone by choice. Even so, I opt for *uiduo* (= *PYς*), for if Ovid could use *uiduus* for *uacuus* at *Met.* xi. 471, he could obviously do the converse here; cf. also Stat. *Silv.* iii. v. 60.

18. **medio ... toro:** for the solitariness implied cf. *Am.* i. 5. 2, and for the lack of preposition see p. 13.

laxe: better than the variant *late* in that it suggests a body not only comfortably spread out in bed, but totally relaxed too; cf. Verg. *A.* v. 857 *quies laxauerat artus.*

19. **somnos ... inertes:** as sleep = disgraceful idleness, so love = honourable activity in Ovid's scheme of things; cf. *Am.* i. 9. 31-2, 41-6, *Ars* ii. 229, and contrast Tib. i. 1. 5, 57.

21. **nullo prohibente:** cf. *Rem.* 537. Ovid is fond of this type of ablative absolute with *nullo*; see Bömer on *Met.* ii. 202.

disperdat: an uncommon compound in classical Latin (cf. p. 13, with n. 97); it is stronger than the simple verb.

22. **si minus:** = *si non*; a basically colloquial usage (see Hofmann 146).

23-4. Cf. Prop. ii. 22. 21-2 *sed tibi si exilis uideor tenuatus in artus, / falleris: haud umquam est culta labore Venus.* See also 9A. 13-14n.

23. **graciles, non sunt ...:** Kenney's punctuation, adopted here, makes *graciles* predicative (i.e. understand *sunt*). The pentameter then echoes this rhythm and emphasis.

24. **neruis:** not only 'bodily strength' but also 'penis' (see Adams (1982) 38).

25. Literally 'pleasure will give to my *latus* food to produce strength'; for the metaphor cf. Prop. iii. 21. 4 with Fedeli's note. In other words, sex (*uoluptas*) is meat and drink to Ovid. Cf. also *Am.* ii. 19. 24.

lateri: this denotes not only 'the seat of physical strength and vigour' (*OLD* s.v. 2) but also (imprecisely) 'the sexual organs', and it is 'used particularly often to express the general site of the exhaustion which might follow intercourse' (Adams (1982) 49).

in uires: for *in* + accusative with final or consecutive force cf. *Am.* i. 13. 46 *conumisit noctes in sua uota duas*, and see further Kühner-Stegmann II. i. 567-8.

26. Cf. Prop. ii. 22. 23-4.

decepta: cf. Petr. 129 *si libidinosa essem, quererer decepta.*

opera: 'performance', 'service' of a sexual kind; cf. *Ars* ii. 673, and see Adams (1982) 157.

27. **lasciue:** this and its cognates are suggestive of sexual licentiousness and are among the elegists' favourite words for describing their own activities.

28. A single Ovidian line does duty for all Propertius' mythological *exempla* at ii. 22. 29-34.

utilis ... forti corpore: see 3. 7n.

29-30. Propertius expresses the same sentiment more sedately at i. 6. 25-8.

29. **felix, quem ...:** see 5. 9n.

certamina: 'contests', either military or sporting; probably Ovid has the wrestling bout in mind, for this regularly provided Greek and Roman writers with metaphors for sexual intercourse (see Adams (1982) 157-8).

30. **di faciant, leti:** an amusing juxtaposition of the colloquial (*di faciant*; see Tränkle 151) and the elevated (*letum* is largely confined to epic and tragedy and is generally used with some gravity when it does occur in elegy; cf. *Am.* ii. 11. 26).

31-8. See 9B. 39-46n.

31-4. Generally it is the soldier's and merchant's *life* which is unfavourably compared with the lover's (see e.g Tib. i. 1. 1-6, Prop. iii. 5. 1-6 and further Burck 173-4; Fränkel 186, n. 53 points out that the comparison is already found in the archaic Greek elegist Semonides of Amorgos at fr. 1. 15ff. West): here it is their *death*.

31. **induat ... pectora telis:** 'run his breast on to the weapons'; Kenney ((1958a) 62) supports this interpretation with Sen. *Her. F.* 1028 *pectus in tela indue* and other telling parallels.

33. **lassarit:** for the form see 9A. 17n. *lassare* is contemptuous in tone; cf. Stat. *Theb.* v. 413, ix. 723.

arando: cf. *Tr.* i. 2. 76 *latum ... aequor aro*, and for more examples of 'ploughing' words applied to sailing see Nisbet-Hubbard I. 108.

34. **aequora .... bibat:** an expression used of both drowning men (cf. *Ep.* 7. 62, Prop. ii. 24. 27) and sinking ships (cf. *Am.* ii. 11. 6, Sen. *Her. F.* 777). For *aequora* see 11. 1n.

periuro ... ore: merchants were less than honest in the eyes of the Roman poets (see Nisbet-Hubbard I. 10); *Fast.* v. 675-92 provides a sample of the 'perjury' Ovid has in mind.

35. **Veneris motu:** see 4. 14n.

languescere: a poetic euphemism for approaching death; cf. *Tr.* iii. 3. 39, Catul. 64. 188.

36. **medium soluar ...:** the fate is, of course, common enough and did not go unrecorded in antiquity; see e.g. V. Max. ix. 12. 8 (Brandt supplies further examples).

et: for the position see p. 13, with n. 107.

opus: another euphemism for sexual intercourse (see Adams (1982) 157).

37-8. This mocks his predecessors' self-indulgent melancholy (see e.g. Tib. i. 1. 59-66, Prop. i. 17. 19-24, 19) and especially Propertius' *'Ardoris nostri magne poeta, iaces'* (i. 7. 24). For the Latin poets' fondness for picturing their own funeral see Griffin (1985) 148-9.

Poem 11 (12)

1-6. For censure of sailing in the *propempticon* cf. Hor. *Carm.* i. 3. 9-24, Stat. *Silv.* iii. 2. 61ff., and for the theme in ancient poetry generally see Nisbet-Hubbard I. 43-4. These lines, cursing the *first* ship (cf. Prop. i. 17. 13-14 with Fedeli's note, and see 3. 3-4n.), the Argo, in which the Greek hero Jason sailed in an expedition to carry off the famous golden fleece from Colchis (see *Fast.* iii. 849ff. with Bömer's notes), recall the opening of Ennius' tragedy *Medea Exul* (208-14 Jocelyn):

> utinam ne in nemore Pelio securibus
> caesa accidisset abiegna ad terram trabes
> neue inde nauis inchoandi exordium
> cepisset, quae nunc nominatur nomine
> Argo, quia Argiui in ea delecti uiri
> uecti petebant pellem inauratam arietis
> Colchis, imperio regis Peliae per dolum.

This in turn recalls the opening of Euripides' *Medea.* Ovid's passage shares with these two (and with Catul 64. 1-7, lines which also deal with the voyage of the Argo and echo Ap.

Rhod. iv. 920ff.) high-flown vocabulary, complex, periodic sentence-structure and decorative alliteration – all standard features of the grand style. For the possible significance of the multiple echoes here see R.F. Thomas, 'Catullus and the polemics of poetic reference', *AJPh* 103 (1982), 144-62.

1. **mirantibus ... undis:** ablative absolute; for the sentiment cf. Catul. 64. 15 *Nereides admirantes*.

aequoris: a poetical metonym (see p. 12) for *mare*, particularly common in epic and tragedy. Its essential meaning is 'level surface'.

2. **Peliaco pinus uertice caesa:** cf. Catul. 64. 1 *Peliaco ... prognatae uertice pinus*. The use of the adjective *Peliaco* (of Mt. Pelion in Thessaly) instead of the genitive of the noun 'raises the tone above the commonplace' (Jocelyn on Enn. *trag*. 208; see also Bömer on *Met*. xv. 47); for the local ablative without preposition see p. 13. All but Ennius have the Argo constructed of pine.

3. **concurrentis inter cautes:** i.e. the Symplegades or Kuaneai, a mythical pair of rocks which had to be negotiated by the Argo at the entrance to the Black Sea; they were supposed to move together and crush ships attempting to pass between them. Apollonius Rhodius (iv. 922ff.) distinguishes them from the Planctae (see Hom. *Od*. xii. 59-72) of almost identical repute. For the expression cf. V. Fl. i. 630.

temeraria: rare in poetry before Ovid, but freely used by him (33 instances; see Bömer on *Met*. ii. 616). For the sentiment cf. Antiphil. *AP* ix. 29 where τόλμα ('reckless daring') is called 'the inventor of ships'.

4. **conspicuam:** another (see n. above) previously rare adjective in poetry popularised by Ovid (see Bömer on *Met*. viii. 373).

ouem: feminine gender is normal even where a ram is concerned, as here. Generally only the fleece is alleged to have been carried off by Jason, the ram itself having been sacrificed to Zeus.

5. **o utinam:** see 5. 7n.

freta longa: a favourite Ovidian collocation; cf. *Met*. viii. 67 with Bömer's note.

6. **pressa:** this suggests both 'sunk' (cf. Tac. *Hist*. iii. 77 *nimio ruentium onere pressas (nauis) mare hausit*), and 'squeezed' (by the Symplegades; see 3n.). A more choice word here than the compounds *deprimere* and *supprimere*.

bibisset aquas: see 10. 34n.

7. **ecce:** see 10. 4n.

notumque torum sociosque Penates: *notum* and *Penates* (the latter from Virgil onwards a dignified metonym (see p. 12) for 'home') contrast with *fallacis* and *uias* in 8, indicating that Corinna is proposing to exchange the safely familiar and domestic for the dangerously unfamiliar and foreign. And at the same time *torum* and *socios* intimate that she is not just leaving home, but also deserting a lover, the 'couch' being an essential adjunct of the amatory life and *socius* and its cognates frequently being used of things 'shared' in love or marriage (cf. *Am*. iii. 6. 82, *Ep*. 5. 126, and see Bömer on *Met*. vii. 800). These words also have an amusingly incongruous Virgilian resonance (cf. *A*. iv. 648-9 *postquam (Dido) Iliacas uestes notumque cubile / conspexit*, iii. 15 (of Thrace) *hospitium antiquum Troiae sociique penates*, and see J. Diggle, *PCPhS* n.s. 29 (1983), 21-2).

-que ... -que: see 9B. 50n.

8. **fallacis:** 'treacherous' both in exposing Corinna to hidden danger and in causing her to be unfaithful to Ovid.

uias ire: cf. Prop. i. 8B. 30 *destitit ire nouas Cynthia nostra uias*.

9. **quam ... timebo:** cf. Prop. ii. 26. 7 *quam timui, ne forte tuum mare nomen haberet*. The vulgate *quid ... timebo?* (see apparatus on p. 96), 'Why should I fear ...', i.e. 'I shall have no reason to fear ...' is obviously senseless here; see further Goold (1965a) 37-8). The speaker's expression of anxiety is intended to be deterrent; cf. Prop. i. 8A. 1 *nec te mea*

cura moratur. For the motif in other *propemptica* cf. Hor. *Carm*. iii. 27. 7ff., Stat. *Silv*. iii. 2. 51-3, 83-4.

10. This was reputedly adjudged by Ovid's friends one of his three worst lines, and by him one of his three best; for the full story see Sen. *Con*. ii. 2. 12.

egelidum: 'with the chill taken off'; *iam ver egelidos refert tepores* says Catullus (46. 1) as he prepares to visit the *claras Asiae urbes* (46. 6). Recollection of this may have prompted Ovid's *urbes* in 11.

11. A mocking reminiscence, perhaps, of the 'traveller's guide' type of *propempticon* apparently attempted by Parthenius and Catullus' friend Cinna (see Quinn 240, n. 2). Notice the incongruously portentous anaphora (see p. 14).

12. **una:** 'unvarying'; cf. Sal. *Jug*. 79. 3 *ager ... harenosus, una specie*, Catul. 6. 6 *nox est perpetua una dormienda*.

iniusti: conventional of the sea; cf. Prop. i. 15. 12 *iniusto ... salo* with Fedeli's note.

caerula: a stock poetic epithet of the sea and its adjuncts (see Bömer on *Met*. ii. 8). The form *caeruleus* is more common, but *caerulus* is often metrically convenient in dactylic verse (see André 162).

13-14. The provocative implication seems to be that 'little things please little, i.e. female, minds'; Ovid says exactly that at *Ars* i. 159: *parua leuis capiunt animos* (sc. *puellarum*). Certainly both *conchae* and *lapilli* are regarded as suitable love-gifts for women at *Met*. x. 260. The shorescape recalls Lucr. ii. 374-6: *concharumque genus ... uidemus / pingere telluris gremium, qua mollibus undis / litoris incurui bibulam pauit aequor harenam*.

14. **bibuli:** a picturesque evocation of the curious absorbency of sand; cf. Lucr. ii. 376 (cited in previous n.), Verg. *G*. i. 114.

mora: 'reason for delay' and hence 'distraction'; cf. Prop. iv. 8. 4 *tam rarae non perit hora morae*, Sil. xii. 535-6 *muros, / haud dignam inter tanta moram*.

15-26. The ease with which Ovid is diverted into a mischievously patronising aside to 'girls' in general shows how little he is concerned with his supposed personal misery.

15. **signate:** an obvious correction (see apparatus on p. 96), given the second person plurals in vv. 17 and 21.

marmoreis: i.e. 'glittering white'. *marmoreus* is a conventional complimentary epithet of parts of the female body (cf. *Met*. xiii. 746 *marmoreo ... pollice* with Bömer's note, Nemes. *Ecl*. 2. 21-2 *marmoreo pede Naiades uda secantes / litora*), but probably Ovid is specifically thinking here of girls' bare feet glistening with sea-water as they dance playfully on the beach. And could there be also, as Brandt suggests, a reminiscence of the Homeric μαρμαρυγὰς ποδῶν ('flashing of feet', i.e. of boy-dancers) at *Od*. viii. 265?

16. **caeca:** 'unseeing', and hence often 'unseen'; a stock poetic adjective of any uncharted or unlit regions or paths therein (cf. *Met*. xiv. 370 *caecis ... limitibus,* Verg. *G*. ii. 503 *freta caeca*). But see also 16. 32n.

17-22. The implication here is that women will believe anything, but see 49-52n. Cf. also Tib. i. 2. 55-60.

17. **uentorum proelia:** the idea, which dates back to Homer (*Il*. xvi. 765), is of the winds blowing from all quarters at once; cf. Verg. *G*. i. 318 *omnia uentorum concurrere proelia uidi,* and see further Nisbet-Hubbard I. 50.

18-20. **quas ... quasue ... quibus ... quo:** not 'which' but 'what kind of'; it is the *nature*, not the location, of a very standard clutch of maritime hazards (see E. de St-Denis, *Le rôle de la mer dans la poésie latine* (Paris, 1935), 401-2, n. 13), both real and fictitious (cf. 16. 21-6n.), that Ovid wishes to stress.

18. **Scylla ... Charybdis:** the fabled twin terrors of the barking (and in Homer six-headed) monster on the one hand (see also 16. 23n.) and the 'whirlpool' (see 16. 25-6n.) on the other, each waiting to devour the ships forced to sail between the two cliffs which sheltered them (see *Od.* xii. 85ff, 245ff.). Homer locates these hazards vaguely in the vicinity of Sicily, and later writers more precisely in the Straits of Messina between Sicily and Italy.

infestet: the first attestation of this word in poetry; cf. *Met.* xiii. 730-31 *Scylla latus dextrum, laeuum inrequieta Charybdis / infestat*, *Ciris* 57 with Lyne's note, Man. iv. 669, v. 706.

-ue: 'and'; see 1. 31n.

19. **quibus emineant ... Ceraunia saxis:** I take the ablative to be instrumental: 'with what sort of rocks the *Ceraunia*' (i.e. the promontory in Epirus, opposite Brundisium, formed by the northernmost tip of the Ceraunian mountains) 'project', either upwards (from the sea) or, perhaps better, outwards (from the general line of the coast); for *eminere* of horizontal projection cf. *Ars* i. 591 *nihil ... emineant ungues*. There are no exact parallels for this construction, however, and some take the ablative to be local: 'on what sort of rocks the *Ceraunia* tower' (the promontory is over 2,000 ft. high). The destructive record of the Ceraunian promontory (see e.g. Caes. *Civ.* iii. 6. 3, Suet. *Aug.* 17. 3) – also called *Ceraunum saxum* (Prop. ii. 16. 3) and, *pace* Nisbet-Hubbard I. 53, *Acroceraunia* (see Plin. *Nat.* ii. 97 *sinus ... Acroceraunio Epiri finitus promonturio*) – made it a natural item in any list of maritime hazards (cf. *Rem.* 739-40) and doubtless also won it a regular mention in *propemptica*; no exclusive reminiscence of Prop. i. 8A. 19 need be assumed here.

uiolenta: the adjective (striking in its application to something as motionless as rock) alludes to the frequent thunderstorms in the vicinity of the Ceraunian range, which took its name from the Greek κεραύνιος ('thunderstricken').

20. **Syrtes magna minorque:** two notorious areas of sandbanks, each in a bay (*sinu*) off the coast of north Africa: *Syrtis magna* (or more usually *maior*) was identified with the Gulf of Sidra, and *Syrtis minor* with the Gulf of Gabes; see further Sal. *Jug.* 78, Bömer on *Met.* viii. 120, and cf. *Am.* ii. 16. 21.

21. **at:** See apparatus on p. 96. *at* (= *Y*ω) produces a more Ovidian line than *PS*'s *ad* (the two are often confused in *P*; see Kenney (1962) 8, n. 5). Ovid's normal construction with *referre* = 'recount' is not *ad* + accusative, but dative of person; he is fond of the coincidence of strong caesura and strong sense-pause in the third foot of the hexameter (see Platnauer 24-6); and he frequently uses *at* + personal (or demonstrative) pronoun to mark a strong contrast (see e.g. *Am.* i. 7. 63, ii. 5. 33, 10. 19, 35, 19. 2). Admittedly, the contrast 'Let *others tell* of these things, but *you believe* what they all say' is not an altogether satisfying one, but the pentameter makes it easy enough to see what Ovid meant: 'Let others tell of these dangers, but do not let that prompt *you* to sample them for yourselves instead of just taking their word for it'.

21-2. **quod quisque loquetur /credite:** perhaps a consciously humorous reversal of the proverbial *nil temere credideris*; see further Otto 97, and cf. *Ars* iii. 685.

22. **credite: credenti:** the striking polyptoton (see p. 16) underlines Ovid's irony.

23. **fune soluto:** nautical language; cf. Prop. i. 8A. 11 *nec tibi Tyrrhena soluatur funis harena.*

24. **currit:** frequently used of ships; cf. *Tr.* iii. 9. 8, Prop. i. 14. 3, Verg. *A.* v. 862, and see further *ThLL* iv. 1515. 25ff.

panda carina: conventional and grandiose; cf. *Ars* ii. 430, *Ep.* 15 (16) 112, Verg. *G.* ii. 445 with Conington's note.

salum: the *open* sea; an early borrowing (see Acc. *trag.* 10 Ribbeck, Enn. *trag.* 179 Jocelyn) from the Greek σάλος ('swell').

25. **nauita:** an archaic form often metrically convenient. In the first foot of the hexameter Ovid always prefers it to *nauta*; see further Bömer on *Met.* i. 133.

cum: for the position see p. 13, with n.107.

iniquos: conventional of inclement elements and circumstances; cf. *Tr*. i. 10. *Met*. x. 172.

26. **prope tam ... quam prope:** the repetition of the adverb with *tam* ... *quam* is idiomatic; cf. Cic. *ad Brut*. 1. 3. 1 *tam facile ... quam facile*. For the anastrophe see p. 13, with n. 108.

letum: see 10. 30n.

27-30. Cf. Hor. *Epod*. 10. 9-10, 15-20.

27. **quod si:** 'so, if ...'; the phrase is connective, here spelling out to Corinna the relevance of vv. 23-6 to her own situation.

concussas ... undas: cf. *Met*. viii. 604 *concussit* (*aequoreus rex*) ... *omnes* ... *undas*.

Triton: a merman who has the power to arouse or calm the sea with a blast on his conch-bugle; see *Met*. i. 330-42 with Bömer's notes, and cf. *Ep*. 7. 49-50, Verg. *A*. vi. 171.

exasperet: a variation of the commoner *asperare* (cf. especially Verg. *A*. iii. 285 *glacialis hiems Aquilonibus asperat undas*) confined to prose before Ovid; cf. *Met*. v. 7 *uentorum rabies motis exasperat undis* with Bömer's note. See also p. 13, with n. 98.

28. Cf. *Med. Fac*. 98 *haerebit toto nullus in ore color*.

29. **generosa ... fecundae sidera Ledae:** i.e. the twins, Castor and Pollux (the Dioscuri), traditionally believed to protect seafarers (see Nisbet-Hubbard I. 153-4) and to manifest themselves as St. Elmo's fire, the luminous electrical discharge sometimes seen around ships in a storm, *quasi stellae ... uelo insidentes* (Sen. *Nat*. i. 1. 13), and taken to be a good omen. *sidera* here probably refers to this phenomenon (cf. 16. 13n.), which seems to have been a common ingredient of *propemptica*; cf. Hor. *Carm*. i. 3. 2 *fratres Helenae, lucida sidera*, with Nisbet-Hubbard's note. Cf. 16. 13-14n.

The homage apparently paid by *generosa* to the high status won by the Dioscuri through their exploits (see Hom. *Od*. xi. 300-304, and cf. Hor. *Carm*. i. 12. 25-7: *puerosque Ledae, / hunc equis, illum superare pugnis / nobilem*) is immediately undermined by the untimely reminder (*fecundae*) of their mother's somewhat grotesque fertility. Leda is variously alleged to have conceived on the same night Pollux and Helen by Zeus (disguised as a swan) and Castor by Tyndareus (Apollod. iii. 126), to have laid an egg from which Helen hatched (Eur. *Hel*. 257-9), and to have been the mother also of Clytemnestra and two other daughters (Eur. *IA* 49-50, Apollod. iii. 127).

30. **felix ... quem:** generalising masculine; for the expression see 5. 9n.

sua terra: 'his native earth', i.e. the dry land, which is his natural element, as opposed to the sea, which is not; cf. *Am*. iii. 2. 48 *nil mihi cum pelago; me mea terra capit*, Prop. iii. 7. 33-4 *ancora te teneat, quem non tenuere Penates? / quid meritum dicas, cui sua terra parum est?*

31-2. I.e. it is safer to stick to the traditional pursuits of the cultured elegiac mistress: making love (for *torum* see 7n.), reading books of poetry (cf. *Am*. ii. 4. 19-21, and for *libelli* of Ovid's own love elegies see *Am. Epigr*. 1, ii. 17. 33, iii. 8. 5, 12. 7, *Ep*. 1. 1) and playing the lyre (see 4. 25-6n.). For the expression cf. *Ep*. 3. 117-18 *tutius est iacuisse toro, tenuisse puellam, / Threiciam digitis increpuisse lyram*, and for the infinitives see 4. 22n.

32. **Threiciam:** purely ornamental; the lyre was associated with the Thracian singer Orpheus.

increpuisse lyram: *Phoebus ... increpuit lyra* says Horace (*Carm*. iv. 15. 1-2) of Apollo warning him off an ambitious poetic voyage on the sea of epic. The verb describes loud, and usually unpleasant, noises; cf. *Met*. xii. 52, Prop. iv. 3. 66, 7. 12.

33. **si uana ferunt ...:** see 6. 44n., and cf. 16. 46n. *uana* is proleptic.

uolucres: i.e. swift. A conventional epithet of the wind; cf. *Met*. xiii. 807 *uolucri ... aura*, Verg. *A*. v. 503, xi. 795.

34. **Galatea:** a Nereid (sea-nymph), most famous for being the unwilling object of the Cyclops Polyphemus' desire (Theoc. 11, *Met*. xiii. 750ff.). She may have been conventionally involved in *propemptica* of all types (see Quinn 248), but Ovid names her here in direct imitation of Prop. i. 8A. 18. She might, of course, be expected to sympathise with a runaway girl-friend, and Horace even gives her name to the one favoured with the vestigial love-*propempticon* (see p. 60) in *Carm.* iii. 27.

35. For the expression cf. Prop. ii. 28. 2 *tam formosa tuum mortua crimen erit*, *Tr.* iii. 10. 42, [Ov.] *Ep. Sapph.* 180.

36. **-que ... -que:** see 9B. 50n.

Nereidesque deae: Homer mentions 33 Nereids (*Il.* xviii. 39ff.), Hesiod 50 (*Th.* 243ff.). Like their father Nereus, a wise 'old man of the sea', they were supposedly benevolent deities (see Hes. *Th.* 233ff. with West's note).

37. **uade memor nostri:** cf. Hor. *Carm.* iii. 27. 14 *memor nostri ... uiuas*.

reditura: this marks a vital turning-point; see p. 61.

38. **fortior:** i.e. 'stronger' than that on the outward voyage.

39. **mare ... magnus proclinet ... Nereus:** I think Ovid is envisaging Nereus (see 36n.) making Corinna's homeward journey *downhill* by obligingly tilting the sea, as if it were a solid sheet, towards the shores of Italy (cf. Leander's feeling that his return swim across the Hellespont is *uphill* at *Ep.* 17 (18). 122 *cliuus inertis aquae*). Nereus was supposed to live under the sea and could therefore perhaps be thought able to lift it up. *magnus* would point to the strength required for such an operation (otherwise it has little force here). If I am right, the fanciful idea (cf. 16. 51-2n.) is itself as novel as the use of *proclinare* (elsewhere this occurs only in the passive, and in classical poetry only at *Tr.* ii. 84); Burman cites the mediaeval imitation by Joseph of Exeter (*Bellum Troianum* i. 106-7), *hic faciles proclinat aquas, hic euocat antro, / qui uela impraegnet, Zephyrum*). Some alternatively understand 'let Nereus make the (waves of the) sea run this way' (cf. *Met.* xi. 208), but this would be tautologous with *huc agat aestus aquas* in 40.

40. **huc uenti spectent:** the winds are often portrayed in Greek and Roman art and sculpture as human figures with their breath representing the blast itself; e.g. Boreas is shown blowing into a shell on the 'Tower of the Winds' in Athens (see J. N. Travlos, *A Pictorial Dictionary of Ancient Athens* (London, 1971), 285, fig. 368), and on the sarcophagus of Prometheus in Naples the wind is depicted as a small child with blown-out cheeks and a puff of breath coming from his lips (see A. Baumeister, *Denkmäler des klassischen Altertums* (Munich-Leipzig, 1884-8), III. 2115ff., Daremberg and Saglio V. 717ff.). So Ovid could have written not at all obscurely 'let the winds *face* this way', when he meant 'let the winds *blow* this way'. Such a picturesque notion would nicely complement that which I see in the hexameter. Heinsius' *spirent* is certainly much easier, but for that very reason all the more unlikely to have become corrupted to the striking *spectent* (full apparatus on p. 96).

aestus: not *Eurus* (= *PSYς*; see apparatus on p. 96), because 'it would be excessively feeble to say "let the winds blow hither and Eurus too" ' and 'a gratuitous piece of carelessness to follow *Eurus* here with *Zephyri ueniant in lintea soli* in the next verse' (Kenney (1958a) 62). *aestus* will mean 'swell', and not 'tide' – the Mediterranean is virtually tideless – and in conjunction with this I imagine the preceding *uenti* will refer to the wind as a force affecting the movement of the sea rather than as an agent of propulsion as in vv. 37-8 and 41-2 (Kenney cites parallels for the 'co-operation of wind and wave', and for the opposite cf. Luc. iii. 549-50 *ut, quotiens aestus Zephyris Eurisque repugnat, / huc abeunt fluctus, illo mare ...*, 'just as, when the swell conflicts with winds from west and east, the waves run in one direction and the body of the sea in another ...').

41-2. **ipsa ... ipsa tua:** not merely formulaic here (cf. 6. 55n.): Ovid wants to see evidence of Corinna's own desire to expedite her return.

41. **Zephyri:** the mild and gentle, and essentially benevolent, westerlies of spring (see *Met.* i. 64 with Bömer's note). These would obviously assist any vessel returning from the west to Rome, where Ovid is presumably waiting.

43. **primus ego ...:** for the speaker's claim to special status in the 'welcome home' poem cf. Catul. 9. 1-2, Hor. *Carm.* ii. 7. 5, Stat. *Silv.* iii. 2. 133.

44. **nostros ... deos:** Ovid is mischievously referring not, as the masculine plural would at first suggest, to the tutelary images of the gods normally carried on a ship's stern (see Nisbet-Hubbard I. 185), but to his own personal god*dess*, Corinna (the deification of the beloved is common in Latin poetry; see Lyne (1980) 308, n. 20). To extract the sense of *nostram ... deam* from *nostros deos* is easy: Latin masculine includes feminine, and plural often stands for singular (cf. especially *amores, deliciae* = 'sweetheart'; see further La Penna 199-201). But I cannot reproduce the pun in English.

45. **excipiamque umeris:** Ovid apparently envisages not waiting for Corinna's ship to be moored to a quay and gangplanks deployed in the usual way (see L. Casson, *Ships and Seamanship in the Ancient World* (Princeton, 1971), figs. 141, 144, 174), but wading out to the vessel from the shore (not impossible, given the shallow draught of the beamy commercial ships of the time) and bearing Corinna directly back to the beach on his shoulders. Of course, this is a practical enough method of transport through chest-high water, but it is one which has an incongruously pious resonance in Latin, for it was allegedly 'on his shoulders' that Aeneas bore his father Anchises out of the doomed city of Troy (see Verg. *A.* ii. 707-8 with Austin's note). See also 47-8n., *Am.* ii. 16. 29-30.
sine ordine ...: 'indiscriminately'; Ovid seems to be picturing himself hungrily kissing whatever parts of Corinna he can – her hands and legs, perhaps – as he carries her on his back. For demonstrative reception of the traveller cf. Catul. 9. 8-9, Hor. *Carm.* i. 36. 6, Stat. *Silv.* iii. 2. 132-4.

46. **uictima uota cadet:** 'the victim vowed' (i.e. at the outset of the journey) 'will fall'; a reference to the ritual sacrifice performed by returning travellers (often on board ship) as a thank-offering to the gods for their safety. Cf. Hor. *Carm.* i. 36. 1ff., ii. 7. 17, *Epod.* 10. 21-4 (a macabre inversion of the motif), and see further D. Wachsmuth, ΠΟΜΠΙΜΟΣ 'Ο ΔΑΙΜΩΝ: *Untersuchung zu den antiken Sakralhandlungen bei Seereisen* (Diss. Berlin, 1967), 131-3, Nisbet-Hubbard I. 401-2. The line-ending echoes Prop. i. 17. 4 *omniaque ingrato litore uota cadunt*, perhaps pointing an ironic contrast with the loveless situation Propertius is describing.

47-9. More Virgilian resonance: the imagined backcloth for Ovid's amatory self-indulgence – a makeshift meal on the beach – is the same as for Aeneas' dutiful self-suppression in hiding his own gloom and anxiety as he makes a rousing speech to his comrades (*A.* i. 198-202). For the *ad hoc* furniture cf. Tib. ii. 5. 99-100, and for the celebratory feast in the 'welcome home' poem cf. Hor. *Carm.* i. 36. 10ff., ii. 7. 21ff.

47. **tori ... molles:** in the context these words are mischievously suggestive of love-making to come (see 7n. above, 4. 14n.) rather than mere eating and drinking.

48. See apparatus on p. 96. Kenney's defence of *PSY*'s reading ((1958a) 62-3) is persuasive: *cumulus* is a more appropriate word for the kind of 'heap' of sand which might be scraped up (contrast *sternentur* in 47) to do duty for a table than *tumulus*, which normally designates something much bigger (a 'small hill' or a 'grave mound'), and *mensae* is perfectly intelligible as a dative of purpose (these are more frequently abstract nouns, but cf. Prop. ii. 26. 31-2 *unum litus erit sopitis unaque tecto / arbor*, Cic. *Tusc.* v. 90 *mihi amictui est Scythicum tegimen*). I cannot parallel *posse* + infinitive = future indicative, but it is a common enough periphrasis for the future infinitive passive when the sense is potential, as here; see e.g. Sal. *Cat.* 40. 1 *existumans facile eos ad tale consilium adduci posse*, Caes. *Gal.* i. 3. 8 *sese potiri posse sperant*, and further Hofmann-Szantyr 313-4.

49-52. An amusing reversal of the scenario Ovid sketches in vv. 17-22. For travellers' tales in the 'welcome home' poem cf. Catul. 9. 6-8, Stat. *Silv*. iii. 2. 135-41.

49. **apposito ... Lyaeo:** cf. *Am*. ii. 5. 14. *Lyaeus*, 'loosener', was a cult-title of the Greek wine-god Dionysus and a common poetic metonym (see p. 12) for 'wine'; see Nisbet-Hubbard I. 104, Bömer on *Met*. iv. 11.

50. **ut:** 'how'; for the position see p. 13, with n. 107.

51. **dum ... properas:** the retention of the indicative after *dum* in *oratio obliqua* is rare before Tacitus. It seems to suggest that the person whose speech is reported and the reporter share the same sentiment; cf. Cic. *Tusc*. 1. 101 (a Latin rendering of Simonides' famous epigram on the Spartan dead at Thermopylae) *dic, hospes, Spartae, nos te hic uidisse iacentes / dum sanctis patriae legibus obsequimur*, and see further Kühner-Stegmann II. ii. 542-4.

iniquae: see 25n.

52. **praecipites ... Notos:** cf. Hor. *Carm*. i. 3. 12 *nec timuit praecipitem Africum*, and see 6. 44n.

extimuisse: for the uncommon construction with direct object cf. *Met*. ii. 503 with Bömer's note.

53-54. One of Ovid's most explicit commendations of self-deception in love (see further p. 9). The unusually spondaic nature of the hexameter lends the outrageous statement an appropriate air of mock-solemnity.

53. **omnia pro ueris credam:** = *omnia credam uera*; cf. *Fast*. iv. 204 *pro magno teste uetustas creditur*, Sal. *Cat*. 51. 36 *potest ... falsum aliquid pro uero credi*.

54. **blandiar:** the 'repudiating' deliberative subjunctive, which here conveys a certain defensiveness on the part of the speaker; cf. Pl. *Mil*. 1311 *quid ego ni fleam?*, and see further Woodcock 130-32.

ipse meis: formulaic; cf. 6. 55n.

55-6. Cf. Tib. i. 3. 93-4 *hoc precor, hunc illum nobis Aurora nitentem / Luciferum roseis candida portet equis*. Tibullus' prayer is essentially the same as Ovid's, but the day Tibullus is looking forward to is that which will return *him* from a journey overseas, faithful as ever to his (he hopes) faithfully waiting Delia. For the expression cf. also *Tr*. iii. 5. 55.

56. **Lucifer:** the Morning Star (i.e. the planet Venus) of legendary radiance; cf. *Tr*. i. 3. 71-2 *caelo nitidissimus alto / ... Lucifer*, *Met*. iv. 664-5 *caelo clarissimus alto / Lucifer*.

equo: see 5. 38n.

Poem 12 (13)

1. **ite triumphales ...:** the laurel garland had both solemn poetic and military associations, being conventionally worn by Apollo, patron god of poets, and his devotees (see e.g. Hor. *Carm*. iii. 30. 15-16, iv. 2. 9, Tib. ii. 5. 5, Prop. iii. 1. 9-12, and see Nisbet-Hubbard II. 118) and by a Roman general in his triumphal procession (see e.g. *Met*. i. 559-60 with Bömer's note). But Ovid is laying claim to it because he has successfully seduced his girl-friend! For a similarly disrespectful use of triumphal imagery cf. *Am*. i. 7. 35-40 and see further Galinsky (1969) 91-102.

ite ... circum: 'encircle'; cf. *Ars* iii. 274 *angustum circa fascia pectus eat*, Verg. *A*. v. 558-9 *it ... / ... per collum circulus auri*.

laurus: Ovid prefers second declension forms of *laurus* in the singular for both the garland and the bay-tree (cf. Nisbet-Hubbard II. 118 on Horace's usage), and all the MSS give a second declension plural form at *Ars* iii. 690. But fourth declension plurals exclusively are attested at *Fast.* iv. 953 and almost exclusively at *Am.* ii. 13. 18 (McKeown reports *lauros* in a few *recc.*). Since certainty here is thus impossible, it seems best to follow the generally more reliable *PY* (see apparatus on p. 97).

2. **uicimus:** see p. 64, and cf. also Lucil. fr. 1323 Marx *uicimus, o socii, et magnam pugnauimus pugnam*, which Donatus on Ter. *Eu.* 899 tells us is a reference to an amatory 'fight'.

in nostro est ... sinu: hardly to be taken literally in view of all the self-congratulation which follows. For *sinu* cf. 15. 14n.

ecce: here an exclamation of pure exuberance (cf. 10. 4n.). For the postponement to third (or later) place in the sentence cf. *Met.* ii. 93 with Bömer's note, xi. 693, *Fast.* iii. 250, vi. 676, *Ep.* 14. 110.

3. Ovid mentions all the traditional obstacles faced by the elegiac lover wanting to make love to his mistress; the anaphora (see p. 14) contributes to the excited tone. For the *uir* see p. 6; for the *custos*, p. 31; and for the *ianua firma*, 1. 17n. Cf. also the general situation in *Am.* i. 4 and 6, ii. 2, 3 and 19, and iii. 4.

tot hostes: this (the only sensible reading; see apparatus on p. 96) refers collectively to what has gone before. I have adopted Kenney's punctuation, which helpfully points the ironic hyperbole.

4. **ab arte:** see 4. 30n.

5. **praecipuo:** a 'special' triumph; this suggests both an altogether better one than the usual military kind and one to be exclusively (and irregularly) available to Ovid; see pp. 64-5.

6. **quaecumque est:** this is depreciatory in tone and relates not to *praeda*, which would be gratuitously uncomplimentary to Corinna, but to *uictoria*.

7-8. Here Ovid simply belittles the storming of citadels (note the disparaging *humiles* and *paruis*) in comparison with his own 'capture' of a girl; the climactic *puella* is strategically postponed. In later Greek literature, however, the first operation is often used as a metaphor for the second (see e.g. Lucian, *DMeretr.* 11. 1, Alciphr. 16. 3, Agath. *AP* v. 294, especially vv. 19-23).

8. **ductu:** 'command', 'leadership'; prosaic and technical, especially in the phrase *ductu auspicioque* and in inscriptional language. In the Augustan period it indicated the authority still enjoyed by a general now forced to operate *auspicio Principis* (see e.g. V. Ehrenberg & A. H. M. Jones, *Documents illustrating the reigns of Augustus and Tiberius* (2nd edn., Oxford, 1976), 63, no. 43). The audacity of the word here is thus plain.

9-10. Perhaps initially inspired by Propertius' comparison of himself with Agamemnon at ii. 14. 1-2, but in spirit closer to Pl. *Bac.* 925ff.:

> Atridae duo fratres cluent fecisse facinus maxumum,
> quom Priami patriam Pergamum diuina moenitum manu
> armis equis exercitu atque eximiis bellatoribus
> mille cum numero nauium decumo anno post subegerunt.
> non pedibus termento fuit, praeut ego erum expugnabo meum
> sine classe sineque exercitu et tanto numero militum.

Ovid's phraseology, too, perhaps owes something to v. 930; see Barsby 150.

9. **Pergama:** properly 'the citadel of Troy', but from the earliest times a popular poetic metonym (see p. 12) for Troy itself; cf. *Met.* xii. 445 with Bömer's note.

bilustri: the only classical instance of this word; see further p. 13, with n. 96. Cf. *Am.* iii. 6. 27 *Troia lustris obsessa duobus*, Sidon. Apoll. *Carm.* 299 *clausa ad Pergama dat bilustre bellum*.

10. **ex tot:** 'among so many' sc. *homines*. For the substantival use of *tot* cf. *Am.* iii. 3. 37 *tot meruere peti*.

in Atridis ... erat: 'belonged to the Atridae' (i.e. Agamemnon and Menelaus). *in* + ablative here seems to be an unusual, and perhaps metrically necessitated, alternative to the dative of possession (see further p. 13).
pars quota: 'how much?' in proportion to the total, implying 'a small amount'; cf. *Met.* ix. 69 and, as an exclamation rather than a rhetorical question, *Met.* vii. 522 with Bömer's note.

11. **seposita:** 'set apart (from all other)', 'exclusive'. This sense is found only here, and its very rarity underlines the boldness of Ovid's claim (see next n. and p. 13, with n. 97). Ovid may have been prompted to the word by Tibullus' use of it also in a triumphal context at ii. 5. 8 (to Apollo) *indue uestem / sepositam.*
ab milite dissors: this is the only occurrence of *dissors*, probably an Ovidian coinage (cf. previous n.). The implication is that the equivalent of the humble but (in war proper) essential ranker (*milite*) does not exist in Ovid's field of operations (cf. 13-14n.).

12. **gloria:** the honour and distinction, both military and civil, traditionally sought by a Roman aristocrat (see e.g. Cic. *Arch.* 26). The enjambement (see p. 15) heightens the word's impudence here.
titulum muneris: 'entitlement to the tribute', i.e. for having achieved *gloria*; for the defining genitive cf. *Fast.* iv. 115 *titulo mensis ... secundi*. Ovid's expression subtly keeps the triumphal scenario in the reader's mind, for *titulus* was also the term for the inscription at the base of the *statuae triumphales* in the Forum (see Eck 142-3).

13-14. A slight variation of the idea in v. 9 (perhaps prompted by Tib. i. 1. 75 *hic ego dux milesque bonus*): in the battle for Corinna, Ovid played *both* ranker *and* general (and all other military parts) himself. *dux* was a regular term for the famous generals of the republic and for Octavian himself up to Actium (see Syme (1939) 311).

13. **hanc ... finem:** *finis* is occasionally feminine in both poetry and prose; cf. Verg. *A.* ii. 554 with Austin's note, and see further Neue and Wagener I. 672, 674.

14. Cf. *Am.* iii. 11. 18 *ipse tuus custos, ipse uir, ipse comes*, *Ep.* 17 (18). 148, Musaeus 255 (see Fränkel 196, n. 7).
signifer: see 3. 10n.

15. **meis ... actis:** dative, as normally with *immiscere*.

16. **huc ades:** 'come hither'; normally a deferential request to a deity for presence or favour (cf. *Am.* iii. 2. 46, *Met.* viii. 598 with Bömer's note), and absurdly hymnic here.
o: see 9A. 1-2n.

17-26. See p. 65.

17. **belli ... causa:** cf. *Fast.* i. 520 *causa noui femina Martis erit*, *Am.* i. 10. 2, Hor. *S.* i. 3. 107.

17-18. **rapta fuisset ... foret:** a mixture of tenses in a past unreal condition common up to Livy (numerous examples at Woodcock 155, Kühner-Stegmann II. 397). The imperfect subjunctive arguably conveys better than the pluperfect the idea of a continuous state, rather than an event, but metrical convenience may be the chief reason for the choice here. For the sentiment cf. Prop. ii. 3. 35-6 *tanti ad Pergama belli / Europae atque Asiae causa puella fuit.*

18. **Tyndaris:** Helen, daughter of Tyndareus and wife of Menelaus of Sparta, abducted by the Trojan Paris.
Europae ... Asiaeque: the division between the two was traditionally thought to be marked by the R. Don and the Bosporus. Hence the oft-mentioned intercontinental nature of the clash between Greece and Troy (cf. Catul. 68. 89, Verg. *A.* vii. 223-4, x. 91, Prop. ii. 3. 35-6, and see Hardie 311-13). For the delayed *-que* see p. 13, with n. 107.

19-26. In the traditional versions of the stories to which Ovid alludes in 19-24 (see nn. below) the women concerned – particularly Lavinia as portrayed by Virgil – played almost notoriously passive roles, but here the insistent anaphora (see p. 14) involving the subject *femina*, together with a string of active verbs (*uertit, impulit, immisit, dedit*), mischievously suggests otherwise. Even the heifer in 26 is cast as an egger-on. Emotive vocabulary (*turpiter, iuste, soceros*) also suggests that female malevolence upset the normal relationships of a decent world.

19-20. The Centaurs, fabled half-man, half-horse creatures (*biformem*; cf. *Met.* ii. 664, ix. 121, xii. 456), invited to the marriage of Pirithous, king of the Lapiths (a Thessalian tribe), to Hippodamia, reputedly became drunk and disgraced themselves by brawling with their hosts for possession of the beautiful bride; cf. Hom. *Il.* i. 263ff., *Met.* xii. 210ff. with Bömer's notes.

19. **siluestris:** cf. *Am.* i. 4. 9. The adjective implies primitive savagery; cf. Hor. *Ars* 391.

21-2. Legend had it that Aeneas, after landing in Italy with his fellow survivors of the sack of Troy and being granted the hand of Lavinia, daughter of Latinus, ruler of the Latins, had to fight a full-scale war for her with Turnus, the Rutulian chieftain to whom she had formerly been betrothed; in Livy's version the Latins fought with Aeneas, but in Cato's and Virgil's against him (see further Ogilvie on Livy i. 1-3).

21. **iterum:** this goes with *femina*: a woman *for the second time* was the cause of the Trojans' warring (the first time it was Helen); cf. Verg. *A.* vi. 94-5 *causa mali tanti coniunx iterum hospita Teucris / externique iterum thalami.*

noua bella mouere: cf. Verg. *A.* vi. 820 *natos noua bella mouentis.* The infinitive with *impellere* is also Virgilian; see Austin on *A.* ii. 55.

22. **iuste:** a conventional epithet of Latinus, perhaps based rather loosely on the picture of him in *Aeneid* vii, where he is pious and gentle. For the apostrophe (see p. 14) cf. *Fast.* ii. 544.

23-4. The reference is to the so-called 'Rape of the Sabine women', when Romulus, in need of females in the newly established Rome, allegedly invited the neighbouring Sabines to games at which the Romans carried off their women (cf. *Ars* i. 101-34 with Hollis' notes). War between the Romans and the Sabines reputedly followed, stirred up, according to Livy (i. 9), not by the women themselves, who, though initially indignant were eventually appeased, but by their parents (cf. *Fast.* iii. 199-229).

23. **femina:** here collective singular.

Romanis: the dative replaces the more normal *in* + accusative with *immittere*; cf. 2. 23-4n.

24. **soceros:** the 'fathers-in-law' of the young Roman men, i.e. the fathers of the Sabine women: cf. *Fast.* iii. 202 *tum primum generis intulit arma socer.*

dedit: 'caused'; cf. Verg. *A.* viii. 570-71 *saeua dedisset / funera* with Fordyce's note.

25-6. Despite Ovid's claim to personal observation (see 2. 47n.), a bookish illustration, doubtless known to him from both Sophocles (*Tr.* 507ff.) and, especially, Virgil (*A.* xii. 715ff.). Cf. also *Met.* ix. 46ff., and see further F. Bömer, 'Der Kampf der Stiere', *Gymnasium* 81 (1974), 503-13.

25. **niuea:** a standard ornamental epithet of cattle and other animals; cf. *Met.* i. 652, v. 330, x. 272, and see further Bömer on *Met.* i. 852. Cf. also 1. 24n.

26. **spectatrix animos ... dabat:** cf. *Ep.* 17 (18). 93-4 (Leander to Hero) *protinus addis / spectatrix animos. spectatrix* is a rare word which finds favour for the first time with Ovid; see Bömer on *Met.* ix. 359. For the attributive use of the noun see 6. 1n. The plural *animos* is both metrically convenient and (with *dare*) idiomatic; see Bömer on *Met.* v. 47.

27-8. Cf. Propertius' conclusion of *his* mythological catalogue at ii. 6. 22: *per te* (*Romulum*) *nunc Romae quidlibet audet Amor.* Though more provocative and personal than Propertius' statement, Ovid's coheres less well with what precedes: *qui multos* is a transparently mechanical connection with 19-26, and in replacing Propertius' conveniently ambiguous *Amor* (cf. 1. 3n.) with *Cupido*, Ovid undermines all his previous claims about the motivating role of females. The word-order shows mild hyperbaton (see p. 16).

28. **signa mouere:** 'move the standards'; this is a technical military term normally = 'begin a march' (cf. *Fast.* vi. 764), but here the meaning seems closer to that of *signa ferre*, 'carry the standards', i.e. 'go to war'. Cf. Hor. *Carm.* iv. 1. 16 *signa feret militiae tuae* (i.e. *Veneris*). See also 3. 10n.

Poem 13 (14)

1. Unusual syntax and vocabulary help to underline the novelty of the subject. The causal *dum* ('through', 'as a result of') + present indicative (without temporal significance) is first attested here (cf. Mart. vii. 13. 1-3); *onus* is used of the foetus for the first time (cf. *Met.* x. 481 with Bömer's note), and the collocation *grauidus uenter* (only in Ovid) makes its first appearance (cf. *Ep.* 15 (16). 44, *Met.* x. 505 with Bömer's note); for *temeraria* see 11. 3n.

2. **uitae:** genitive of respect, regular with both substantival and adjectival uses of *dubius*; cf. Apul. *Met.* v. 28 *filium dubium salutis iacere*, and see Bömer on *Met.* xv. 438.
lassa: sc. from illness; cf. *Am.* iii. 11. 8, Ter. *Hec.* 238. See also 9A. 19n.

3. **illa quidem:** this adds an emphatic rider; cf. Verg. *G.* iii. 217, 501.
clam me: *me* is probably ablative; the prepositional *clam* also takes the accusative, but the ablative is clearly attested with the only two other instances of it in elevated poetry (Acc. *trag.* 654 Ribbeck, Lucr. i. 476). The unusualness of the preposition helps to highlight this important phrase (see p. 71). R. Verdière ('Ovide, *Amores* ii. 13. 2-4', *Latomus* 48 (1989), 190-92), however, argues for emendation to *clamat*.

4-5. Some see an admission of moral responsibility in *sed tamen aut ex me conceperat* (e.g. Due 142), but I take the train of thought to be: 'I ought to be angry with her, but fear stops me; all the same (i.e. 'despite my fear, I ought still to be angry because ...'; for the corrective force of *sed tamen* cf. *Am.* ii. 2. 35, 10. 15), the child was (I think) mine'. Ovid implies that he is put out at not being given the chance to dissuade his beloved from endangering her life (how he would have coped with her pregnancy's effects on his love-life, had he been successful, he significantly does not say), but he is apparently at least as much aggrieved at Corinna's infringement of what he feels are his paternal rights. In 14, however, he censures her on this count only in the most indirect way (see 14. 33-4n.); to do otherwise would draw attention to his psychological weak-spot and the absurdity of his traditionally patriarchal reaction to the loss of an *illegitimate* child.

4. **digna:** sc. *est*; some *recc.* include this, perhaps rightly.

5-6. **aut ego credo ...:** the uncertainty seems puzzling, but see p. 71. The wittiness of the pentameter is perhaps a hint that the situation is not after all to be viewed too solemnly.

5. **conceperat:** the pluperfect, 'she *had* conceived', suggests that the child is no longer viable at this stage, but the appeal to Ilithyia, goddess of childbirth (v. 21), that Corinna may still be labouring to deliver the aborted foetus or placenta.

7-26. A formal prayer replete with conventional elements (also found in hymns): invocation of the deity with a solemn vocative, and cult-titles or cult-centres mentioned in a relative clause (7-10, 19-21); a 'bargaining' clause introduced by *sic* (12-14); request for favour or presence (15-16, 21-2); citation of services rendered by the person prayed for (17-18); vows by the petitioner (23-5); *tu* in address (16, 19, 26); anaphora (11); and elevated style (7-8). See further E. Norden, *Agnostos Theos*: *Untersuchungen zur Formengeschichte religiöser Rede*, (Leipzig-Berlin, 1913), 143ff., Williams (1968) 132ff. For a catalogue of other Ovidian elegiac specimens see M. Swoboda, 'De Ouidii carminum elegiacorum fragmentis hymnico-precatoriis', *Eos* 66 (1978), 73-90.

7. **Isi:** for the invocatory vocative cf. *Met.* ix. 773. The cult of the Egyptian goddess Isis, saviour, healer, mother-figure, benefactress and protectress extraordinary, though officially banned within the city of Rome from 21 B.C. (see Dio Cass. liii. 2. 4, liv. 6. 6), was especially popular in the Augustan period with women, to whom she was believed to be particularly well-disposed. It is a measure of Ovid's concern that he brings himself to supplicate a goddess whose cult the elegiac lover traditionally regarded with deep suspicion (see 2. 25n.). For a convenient synopsis of the Isiac religion's position see Pomeroy 217-26, and for more detailed studies of its intellectual and psychological appeal, Heyob *passim*, F. Solmsen, *Isis among the Greeks and Romans* (Cambridge Mass.-London, 1979), 67-85, Witt *passim*.

7-10. **Paraetonium ... quae colis ...:** for the relative clause with mention of alternative cult-centres in a hymn or prayer cf. Hor. *Carm.* i. 30. 1 with Nisbet-Hubbard's note. Apparently more intent on poetic colour than religious exactitude, Ovid lumps together (a) known centres of Isiac worship (Memphis and Pharos), (b) places more generally evocative of Egypt and the Nile delta (Paraetonium and Canopus) and (c) the Nile itself, whose annual flooding Isis was thought to control; cf. *Met.* ix. 773-4 *Isi, Paraetonium Mareoticaque arua Pharonque / quae colis et septem digestum in cornua Nilum.* Notice also in vv. 7-8 the contrived word-order of the high style, with a balancing pair of nouns + noun phrase enclosing the relative pronoun and verb which governs them.

7. **Paraetonium:** a port on the border of Egypt and Libya; see Str. xvii. 1. 16. 799.

genialia: sc. 'fertile'; cf. *Ep.* 18 (19). 9 *rus geniale* and the common similar use of *laetus* (*OLD* s.v. 1).

Canopi: a port and island at the most westerly mouth of the Nile.

8. **colis:** = *incolis*; see Bömer on *Met.* ix. 276 and futher p. 13.

Memphin: a city in Lower Egypt; for its Isiac associations see Witt 100-103. For the Greek accusative ending spelled *-in*, rather than *-im*, see Kenney (1958a) 60.

palmiferam: cf. *Met.* x. 478. Propertius may have coined the word at iv. 5. 25 *palmiferae ... Thebae*. Ovid is fond of compound adjectives in *-fer*, with their high-flown, poetic ring (see Leumann 131, Tränkle 58, Bömer on *Fast.* i. 125), to ornament geographical references; cf. *Am.* ii. 17. 32, *Met.* xv. 713, 753.

Pharon: the island off Alexandria famed for its lighthouse and a centre of the cult of Isis, who is called *Pharia* at *Ars* iii. 635 (cf. *Fast.* v. 619, Tib. i. 3. 32). See further Bömer on *Met.* ix. 773.

9. **celer:** the Nile is unusually swift-flowing for a large river in its lower reaches.

lato delapsus in alueo: only the generally greater reliability of *PSY* gives this reading the edge over *lato dilapsus ab alueo*, the combination of MS variants (see apparatus on p. 97) favoured by Burman, which yields equally good sense ('having broken up from its broad channel', i.e. into the delta branches). For the disyllabic scansion of *alueo* cf. Verg. *A.* vi. 412, vii. 33, 303, ix. 32.

10. **per septem portus:** cf. *Ep.* 14. 107 *per septem Nilus portus emissus in aequor*. For the seven branches of the Nile delta (nowadays reduced to two) see Hdt. ii. 17 with Lloyd's note.

in maris ... aquas: for the word-order see p. 13, with n. 109

11. **per ... per:** a frequent form of anaphora (see p. 14) in prayer and entreaty; cf. *Am.* iii. 11. 45-8, *Met.* vii. 853-4, Verg. *A.* iv. 314-15, Stat. *Theb.* ii. 649.

sistra: horseshoe-shaped, metal rattles used in Isiac ritual; see Witt, plate 39, and for a full description and bibliography see Bömer on *Met.* ix. 693.

Anubidis ora: the dog-headed Anubis (Virgil calls him *latrator* at *A.* viii. 698; cf. Prop. iii. 11. 41 with Fedeli's note), an Egyptian god of death and resurrection and allegedly the offspring of Osiris' adulterous union with Nephthys (sister of himself and Isis), was in

Greco-Roman religion the constant companion and guardian of Isis and a participant in her ritual procession; see further Witt 198ff., Griffiths on Apul. *Met.* xi. 274. 15, Bömer on *Met.* ix. 690.

12-14. The 'bargaining clause' so common in formal prayers; cf. *Am.* ii. 6. 20, Hor. *Carm.* i. 3. 1 with Nisbet-Hubbard's note. In return for Isis' favour Ovid wishes her rites to continue flourishing.

12. **pius ... Osiris:** brother-husband of Isis and, together with their son, Horus, one of the chief figures in the cult. Re-enactment of Isis' tireless search for Osiris after his murder by another brother, Seth (or Typhon), and of her mourning for him and eventual discovery of his dismembered body and revival of it took place at the Roman festival of the *Isia* from 28 October to 1 or 3 November. *pius* will refer either to Osiris' world tour before his death, spent preaching goodness and respect for the laws of god and man, or to the family devotion with which Osiris, as part of the Isiac trinity, became identified. See further Witt 36ff., Heyob 53ff.

13. **labatur circa donaria serpens:** *donarium* properly = 'a place where gifts are deposited and kept', and the word denotes the 'treasure-chamber(s)' of a temple at Luc. ix. 516 and Apul. *Met.* ix. 10, but Virgil uses the plural more loosely for 'temple' itself at *G.* iii. 533 and Ovid more loosely still for 'altar' at *Fast.* i. 335. Any one of these three meanings is possible here, though visual imagination most easily accommodates the last. Snakes were variously associated with Isiac religion (see Bömer on *Met.* ix. 694, and for further bibliography Courtney on Juv. 6. 538), and on murals and altars were frequently depicted coiled around the sacred box or basket (*cista mystica*) which allegedly contained the cult's secrets (see V. Tran Tam Tinh, *Essai sur le culte d'Isis à Pompéi* (Paris, 1964), pl. 10. 1, *CIL* VI. 34776), but *donaria* can hardly refer to this object.

14. **corniger Apis:** the sacred bull of Memphis worshipped by the Egyptians and sometimes conceived of as the offspring of a boviform Isis (Griffiths on Apul. *Met.* xi. 274. 18). Probably Ovid alludes to the carrying of an image of the Apis bull in one or more of the Isiac cult's many processions (*pompae*; see Witt 165-84), but parallels are to seek.

15. **huc:** common in prayerful requests; cf. *Fast.* iii. 789, and see also 12. 16n.
adhibe uultus: a uniquely Ovidian alternative to the more common *animum adhibere*; cf. *Am.* ii. 1. 37.

15-16. **in una parce ...:** cf. especially Prop. ii. 28. 41-2 *si non unius, quaeso, miserere duorum! / uiuam, si uiuet; si cadet illa, cadam*, [Tib.] iii. 10. 19-20 *laus magna tibi tribuetur in uno / corpore seruato restituisse duo*. The sentiment is a variation of the cliché which regards a friend as a second self; for further references and bibliography see E. Bréguet, '*In una parce duobus*. Thème et clichés'. *Hommages à L. Hermann. Collection Latomus* 44 (Brussels, 1960), 205-14, Bömer on *Met.* xi. 388.

17-18. A highly problematical couplet; see apparatus on p. 97. The hexameter (with the universally accepted *sedit*) apparently refers, appropriately enough, to Corinna's dutiful incubation (i.e. ritual residence) in the temple of Isis at the times prescribed for her devotees; for the expression cf. *Ars* iii. 635 *cum sedeat Phariae sistris operata iuuencae*, *Tr.* ii. 297, *Pont.* i. i. 52; Tib. i. 3. 30, Prop. ii. 28. 45; for *operata* see also 7. 25n., and for incubation 2. 25n.). But no combination of the MS readings seems to produce a satisfying pentameter. For no 'Gallic troop' (*turma*) or 'group' (*turba*), as far as we know, 'wet' (*tingit*), 'touched' (*tangit*) 'encircled' (*cingit*) or otherwise encountered laurel in any Isiac connection, nor did the laurel have any function so specific to the cult as to justify calling it the goddess' own (see Griffiths' note on the conjecture *laureis* Apul. *Met.* xi. 10). Yet *qua tingit laurus*, at least, could well be right, Ovid's claim being that Corinna has often incubated 'where [?] wets [?its] laurel'. Laurel branches were used generally for sprinkling lustral water (cf. especially Juv. 2. 157-8 with Courtney's note), and *suas* would be an easy correction of *tuas* (for MS confusion of these possessives see e.g. apparatus for 4. 18, 6. 8 and 9. 38); the chief difficulty lies with the subject of *tingit*.

R. P. Oliver ((1969) 152-3) explains the vulgate *Gallica turma* as a reference to the eunuch priests of Cybele known as *Galli* and suggests that she, Cybele, was addressed in this poem along with Isis and Ilithyia, vv. 17-18 being all that remains of the appeal to her, following the loss of a portion of text after v. 16 in the common ancestor of all our surviving MSS. But such an interpretation of *Gallica turma* is totally unsupported by any linguistic parallels or other evidence, and this alone disables Oliver's explanation (as well as those of Brandt and Lenz in their commentaries and that of Due at 143, n. 27). A lacuna of some sort, however, remains a distinct possibility. For the couplet 17-18 is, as Oliver perceived, emotionally anti-climactic after vv. 15-16, and it is also curiously jejune as a conventional recitation of 'services rendered' to Isis (cf. Tibullus' list of his Delia's Isiac observances at i. 3. 23-32, and see Nisbet-Hubbard I. 360); furthermore, since ancient deities were thought to be jealous beings, Ovid is arguably dangerously remiss in not promising to Isis commemoration and thank-offerings comparable with those promised to Ilithyia in vv. 22-6 (see also 23-4n.); and finally, while the two poems of an Ovidian dramatic diptych are generally roughly even in length (see p. 30), this piece as it stands is 16 lines shorter than its sequel, 14.

If some lines (though not necessarily as many as 16) *have* been lost after, rather than before, vv. 17-18, I wonder whether the enigmatic *Gallica turma* could have come from one of them – and indeed have prompted the entire omission, if an absent-minded copyist accidentally substituted it for a phrase containing the look-alike *turba*, 'congregation' (cf. *Met.* i. 677) in v. 18 and left out all the intervening lines (the presence of *turba* in ς is more likely to be due to scribal corruption of *turma* than to tradition, for, if the common *turba* had stood in the archetype, it would have been unlikely to have been corrupted to the much rarer *turma*). Assuming *turba* to be right, however, what could *Gallica* have displaced? I suggest *dedita*, 'dedicated' (for the absolute use cf. Sen. *Ben.* iii. 5. 2, Juv. 6. 181), which could have prompted the erroneous *dedit* in v. 17.

In sum, then, I suspect a lacuna of two or more couplets after v. 18 and tentatively suggest for that line *qua tingit laurus dedita turba suas*, 'where the dedicated congregation wets its laurel'. *candida*, conjectured for *Gallica* by A. Ramírez de Verger ('The text of Ovid, *Amores* ii. 13. 17-18', *AJPh* 109 (1988), 86-91), is also in itself attractive, but the sequence of corruption Ramírez postulates is improbable and his complete reading, i.e. *quis tangit laurus candida turba tuas*, unconvincing. I argue more fully against him and for my own solution (with some speculation on the context in which *Gallica turma* may have appeared in the putative lost passage) in 'Ovid, *Amores* ii. 13. 17-18: "Quae Oedipum requirant interpretem" ', *CPh* 87 (1992), 241-6. Yet another alternative, *qua tangit laurus Gallica tura tua*, is suggested by K. Morgan, 'Ovid, *Amores* ii. 13. 18. A solution', *CW* 85 (1991), 95-100.

17. **certis ... diebus:** cf. *Fast.* ii. 512.

18. **laurus:** for the form see 12. 1n.

19. **tuque:** this in Ovid always signifies a change of addressee (cf. *Met.* vii. 194, x. 69, xiii. 130, xv. 234), which discountenances the notion that *Ilithyia* in v. 21 is no more than a cult-title of Isis.

laborantes utero ... puellas: cf. Hor. *Carm.* iii. 22. 2-3 (to Diana) *laborantes utero puellas / ... audis*, Catul. 34. 13-14.

miserata: i.e. *quae misereris*; cf. Verg. *A.* i. 597 *o sola infandos Troiae miserata labores.* The perfect participle of deponent verbs is often used in a 'timeless' sense; see further Woodcock 81.

20. **tarda ... tendit onus:** a perceptive evocation of the discomfort of pregnancy and childbirth; cf. Prop. iv. 1. 100 *uteri pondera lenta.* For *onus* see 1n.

latens: i.e. 'lying beneath the surface', though not, of course, here undetected. The word frequently implies danger; cf. Verg. *A.* i. 108 *saxa latentia.*

21. **lenis ades:** a standard form of appeal for divine favour; cf. Hor. *Carm.* iii. 18. 3, and see further Nisbet-Hubbard I. 243. The plea for *lenitas* (literally 'gentleness') is usually especially apposite for the goddess called upon to ease the pangs of labour (cf. Hor. *Saec.* 13-14 *rite maturos aperire partus / lenis, Ilithyia, tuere matres*), but here, when not normal labour but the self-inflicted pain of an induced abortion is in point, it is almost grotesque; cf. Stroh (1979) 343-4.

Ilithyia: the Greek goddess of childbirth. Her name (Εἰλείθυια, literally 'she who comes (to aid)') was sometimes used as a cult-title of both Hera and Artemis, and she was often identified with the Roman Juno-Lucina; see further Bömer on *Met.* ix. 273-323. For the spondaic scansion cf. *Met.* ix. 283, *Ciris* 326. Greek proper names bulk large among the rare fifth-foot spondees (generally with hiatus at the end of the fourth foot) in Augustan hexameters (see Platnauer 38-9); here the lingering over the long syllables is particularly appropriate to the pleading tone (cf. *Orithyiae* at *Am.* i. 6. 53).

22. **quam iubeas:** for the relative + generic subjunctive with *digna* cf. *Fast.* iv. 270, Verg. *A.* vii. 653.

muneris esse tui: 'live (*esse*) by your favour', i.e. 'owe her life to you'; cf. *Met.* xiv. 125. *muneris* is a type of partitive genitive; see further Kühner-Stegmann II. 1. 453.

23-4. **ipse ego ... ipse:** the emphasis on personal action seems purely mechanical – unless it was meant to balance a promise made to Isis on Corinna's behalf in a lost portion of text (see 17-18n.); cf. Prop. ii. 28. 43-6, Tib. i. 3. 29-32.

23. **candidus:** white clothing, signifying ritual purity, was *de rigueur* for participants in a wide range of religious ceremonies; cf. *Fast.* ii. 654, iv. 906, Tib. ii. 1. 16, and see further Bömer on *Fast.* i. 70.

24. **ante ... tuos pedes:** a standard phrase of suppliants and worshippers; cf. *Ep.* 12. 186, Prop. ii. 28. 45.

25. **SERVATA NASO CORINNA:** *SERVATA CORINNA* is ablative absolute and *NASO* the subject of a suppressed verb such as *dedit.* For the citation of a proposed commemorative inscription (*titulus*) cf. *Am.* i. 11. 27-8, *Ars* ii. 744, iii. 812, Tib. i. 9. 83-4, Prop. iv. 3. 72, and for the sentiment, Prop. ii. 28. 44. For the name *NASO* see 1. 2n.

26. **tu:** see 2. 25n.

locum: 'opportunity', not 'space'; Ilithyia is not to be imagined hurriedly clearing the display areas for new stock.

27-8. Cf. 14. 43-4n. These lines are perhaps addressed to an unconscious Corinna.

27. **monuisse:** a metrically convenient perfect; see 4. 22n.

28. **hac ... pugna dimicuisse:** the military metaphor conveys Ovid's disapproval of Corinna's action (cf. 14. 1-6n.). *dimicuisse* (see 7. 2n.) is a true perfect: the deed is irrevocably done.

Poem 14 (15)

1-6. The military imagery's provision of a link with 13 only gradually becomes apparent, for not until vv. 5-6 is it revealed that the subject under discussion is (still) abortion; see also p. 71. The same range of imagery characterises abortion as an act of violence in the language of the later Roman laws relating to it (see Watts 94).

These opening lines could well serve as a retort to Euripides' feministic Medea, who declares at *Med.* 251-2 ὡς τρὶς ἂν παρ' ἀσπίδα / στῆναι θέλοιμ' ἂν μᾶλλον ἢ τεκεῖν ἅπαξ ('I'd rather stand in the battle-line three times than bear one child'): 'And you women deserve to, too', implies Ovid, 'when you adopt battlefield methods to *avoid* bearing one'. He uses a military image of abortion again at *Ep.* 11. 43-4, *nimium uiuax admotis restitit infans / artibus, et tecto tutus ab hoste fuit*, and of childbirth itself a few lines later (47-8): *nescia quae faceret subitos mihi causa dolores, / et rudis ad partus et noua miles eram.*

1. **Quid iuuat:** see 6. 17-19n.
immunes belli: cf. Verg. *A.* xii. 559-60 *urbem / immunem tanti belli*; Ovid is the first to use *immunis* + genitive freely (see Bömer on *Met.* iii. 11).
cessare: see 18. 3n.

2. **peltatas:** i.e. equipped with the light, lunate shield (*pelta*) used by the Amazons, the fabled race of female warriors from the banks of the R. Thermodon (see Verg. *A.* i. 490-91, Prop. iii. 14. 13, D. von Bothmer, *Amazons in Greek Art* (Oxford, 1957), plates lxxv, lxxxii. 4, lxxxiv. 2); the allusion to them is meant to conjure up an image of unfemininity. *peltatus* in Latin poetry is first recorded in Ovid; cf. *Ep.* 20 (21). 117-18, Sen. *Ag.* 218, Mart. ix. 101. 5.

3-4. **si sine ... suis ... sua:** the sibilation (thought disagreeable by ancient authors; see Wilkinson (1963) 13) well conveys Ovid's professed distaste. Note the bitter emphasis on *self*-mutilation.

3. **Marte:** for the metonymy (see p. 12) cf. *Am.* i. 9. 29, *Met.* iii. 123 with Bömer's note, Hor. *Carm.* ii. 14. 13.
telis: causal ablative.

4. **caecas:** doubly suggestive: the abortionist probes where she cannot see (Ovid is obviously thinking of a surgical abortion here; cf. 27-8n.), and does it without heed. Cf. *Fast.* i. 623-4 *neue daret partus, ictu temeraria caeco, / uisceribus crescens excutiebat onus.*
in sua fata manus: a stock pentameter-ending: cf. *Am.* i. 6. 14, *Tr.* v. 2. 30, *Pont.* i. 9. 22 (*mea fata*), Prop. iii. 9. 56 (*sua fata*), 16. 6 (*mea membra*).

5-6. See 3. 3-4n. The inventor of abortion is assumed to be female; cf. *dig.* xlviii. 8. 3. 2.

5. **conuellere:** this implies violence; cf. *Met.* xi. 123, *Ep.* 16 (17). 111. Contrast with the somewhat gentler *labefactat* at 13. 1.

6. **fuerat:** for the tense see 1. 11n.

7. **rugarum:** either the loose folds of skin left immediately after childbirth or the more permanent 'stretch-marks' (cf. Mart. iii. 42, 72. 4). Fear of disfigurement is regularly alleged to be the reason for women's reluctance to tolerate pregnancy; cf. Sen. *Dial.* xii. 16. 3, Gel. xii. 1. 8. The implicit suggestion that it is a trivial one is patent humbug from the man who offered a libidinous appreciation of Corinna's *planus uenter* at *Am.* i. 5. 21. Cf. also *Ars* iii. 785-6.

8. **sternetur ... harena:** sand was spread in the gladiatorial arena before contests to absorb the resulting gore, and Ovid's grim metaphor for 'setting about' the process of abortion simultaneously suggests the violence, the bloodiness and the unwomanliness of it (the aspiring *gladiatrix* epitomises the 'butch' female at Juv. 6. 246-68). For the 'potential' future (*sternetur*) expressing a suspicion, cf. *Ars* i. 224 *Tigris erit*, 'that will be the Tigris' = 'I suspect that that is the Tigris', *Am.* i. 2. 7 *sic erit*, and see Hofmann-Szantyr 311, Kühner-Stegmann II. i. 142.
tuae ... pugnae: the foetus itself is the antagonist. *pugna* links the gladiatorial metaphor with the foregoing military one and with 13. 28. *tuae* is the first clear indication that Corinna is present in 14.
tristis: cf. *Ars* i. 164 *sparsaque sollicito tristis harena foro.*

9-12. An argument whose unassailable, yet simplistic, logic smacks of popular wisdom, where it may have originated (Wilhelm (137) notes its use also to condemn homosexual practices at [Lucian] *Am.* 22), but rhetorical exercises are another likely source (cf. 15-16n.).

The population-level in a particular section of society was in fact a matter of real concern in Ovid's time. Augustus' *lex Iulia de maritandis ordinibus* of 18 B.C. (reinforced by the *lex Papia Poppaea* in A.D. 9) penalised childlessness and offered financial incentives to the propertied classes to produce more legitimate children (for what purpose is not entirely clear, though safeguarding the inheritance of property and creating a propertied class exemplary in traditional domestic virtue have both been suggested; see respectively A. Wallace-Hadrill, 'Family and inheritance in the Augustan marriage laws', *PCPhS* n.s. 27 (1981), 58-80, G. K. Galinsky, 'Augustus' legislation on morals and marriage', *Philologus* 125 (1981), 126-44). Ovid's poem in itself is no more reliable a pointer to the contemporary abortion-rate than the highly rhetorical claims at [Ov.] *Nux* 24 (*raraque in hoc aeuo est quae uelit esse parens*) and Juv. 6. 594 (*iacet aurato uix ulla puerpera lecto*), but a high incidence of abortion-attempts, which would have resulted in the death or sterility of many women of child-bearing age as well as the loss of the children conceived, may have contributed to the apparently unsatisfactorily low birth-rate (see M. K. Hopkins, 'A textual emendation in a fragment of Musonius Rufus: a note on contraception', *CQ* n.s. 15 (1965), 72-4, *id.* 'Contraception in the Roman Empire', *CSSH* 8 (1965), 124-51, *id. Death and Renewal* (Cambridge, 1983), 94-7). With no reliable form of contraception, and even full-term confinement hazardous, Augustan wives faced with an unwanted pregnancy may well have considered the risks of abortion acceptable and the procedure emotionally less traumatic than exposing the newborn infant, the alternative method of family limitation. If so, reduction of the abortion-rate may have been one of the indirect aims of the Augustan legislation. But whatever the precise thinking behind it, its general principle is invoked with amusing inappropriateness here, when Ovid lectures the woman who has aborted what he believed to be his own *illegitimate* child on the dire demographic consequences of failure to reproduce.

10. **gens hominum:** an apparently unique alternative to *gens humana* or *genus hominum* = 'the human race'.

uitio: understand *earum*, i.e. the *matribus ... antiquis* of v. 9; for the possessive with *uitio* cf. Cic. *Har.* 56, *Att.* xi. 9. 1. 'Through human fault', from *hominum* taken 'apo koinou' with *uitio* as well as *gens* (so Kenney (1958a) 63 and Lenz, following Burman), seems feeble, when specifically *women's* fault is at issue.

deperitura fuit: the indicative is regular when the 'potential' future participle + *esse* is used in the apodosis of an unreal condition; cf. vv. 16 and 18 below, and see further Woodcock 156, Kühner-Stegmann II. ii. 402. Apart from Horace (at *Ep.* ii. 1. 40), Ovid is the only Augustan poet to admit the prosaic *deperire* (also at *Am.* i. 15. 32, *Ars* iii. 90, *Ep.* 5. 104, *Met.* xv. 168); see further p. 13, with n. 97. The prefix *de-* implies 'perish *completely*'.

11-12. I.e. *parandus erat qui iaceret lapides, primordia generis nostri, in uacuo orbe*; violent hyperbaton (see p. 16). Deucalion and Pyrrha, sole human survivors of a divinely imposed flood, threw stones over their shoulders to repopulate the world; for the story see *Met.* i. 367-414, with Lee's brief discussion in his note on 318.

11. **generis primordia:** the identical phrase at *Met.* xv. 391. There must be a touch of irony in its Lucretian ring (see e.g. Lucr. i. 55 *rerum primordia pandam*), given Lucretius' own contempt for non-scientific accounts of the origin of the species.

12. **parandus erat:** the indicative is regular in the apodosis of unreal conditions involving a sense of obligation or necessity (cf. 10n.).

13-22. 'All manner of outstanding people would never have seen the light of day, if their mothers had aborted them.' A perennially popular argument with anti-abortionists (see Watts 93), though Ovid's specific examples and impudent sequence trivialise it here (see p. 71). Note the artistic variation of word- and clause-order in the string of conditional sentences.

13-18. A sea-nymph, a Vestal Virgin and a goddess are hardly to be compared with a worldly elegiac girl-friend (cf. the comically inapposite *exempla* at *Am.* ii. 8. 11-14). But, with two of them (Thetis and Venus) pregnant by mortals and one (Ilia) raped by a god, all arguably had better reason than Corinna to resort to abortion!

13. **numen aquarum:** here = the sea-nymph Thetis, mother of Achilles; at *Met.* iv. 532 = Neptune.

14. **iusta ... pondera:** of the unborn child also at *Ep.* 15 (16). 44 (cited at 13. 1n). The collocation is uniquely Ovidian; see Bömer on *Met.* ii. 163.

15-16. A variation of the same illustration at Sen. *Con.* x. 4. 8 suggests that it belonged to the stock-in-trade of rhetoric.

15. **Ilia:** the Vestal Virgin who was the mother of Romulus and Remus, in some versions of the legend called Rhea Silvia (see Nisbet-Hubbard I. 26, Bömer on *Fast.* ii. 283). The use of the name *Ilia* here provides a link with the story of *Ilium* (Troy) alluded to in the previous couplet.

necasset: the repeated use of this word (see also vv. 22 and 38) is not, as some suppose, indicative of Ovid's moral outrage or revulsion at the idea of abortion. For *necare* does not only or primarily mean 'murder'. It is in fact a remarkably wide-ranging and basically neutral term covering all non-heroic and non-military killing. It is used legalistically of judicial execution, and technically with reference to exposure of unwanted babies (e.g. *Met.* ix .679, *Fast.* ii 385), destruction of animal and plant life and annihilation of natural forces and phenomena (e.g. *Rem.* 808). Significantly, it is used quite blandly of terminating the life of a human foetus at Pl. *Truc.* 202 and also in medico-scientific contexts totally unencumbered with moral considerations (e.g. Plin, *Nat.* xx.143); only Juvenal, by the crucial addition of *homines* (cf. 29-34n.) makes the word suggestive of culpable homicide in the context of abortion at 6. 595-6 *homines in uentre necandos / conducit.* For a detailed study of the word and copious illustration of all the above-mentioned categories see Adams (1973) 280-90 and *id.*, 'The uses of *neco*', Part I, *Glotta* 68 (1990), 230-55, Part II, *Glotta* 69 (1991), 94-123 (I am grateful to Dr Adams for correspondence on this point). Ovid's general liking for words with legalistic colour (see p. 12, with n. 91) may be a factor in his greater readiness to admit *necare* than any other poet (Bömer on *Met.* ix. 679 gives statistics).

16. **dominae ... Vrbis:** both 'the ruling city' (the identical expression for 'Rome' at *Rem.* 291, *Pont.* iv. 5. 7 and *Met.* xv. 444-7; see further Bömer *ad loc.*), and 'the mistressy city', i.e. the city full of *dominae*? The same play seems possible at *Rem.* 291. Mention of *Vrbs* (*Roma*) is often synonymous with mischief in Ovid's elegy; cf. *Am.* i. 8. 42, ii. 4. 47, 4. 47, 9A. 15-16, 12. 23-4, *Ars* i. 60, iii. 633. For the adjectival use of *dominus* see also 5. 30n.

17-18. A joke at the expense of Augustus' claimed descent of himself and the Julian *gens* from Aeneas and his son Iulus (reverently reflected at e.g. Verg. *A.* i. 267-88; see further Nisbet-Hubbard I. 13, Zanker 36 with figs. 27a, 193-5, 201-10); cf. *Am.* i. 2. 51.

17. **grauida temerasset:** for the verbal echo of 13. 1 see p. 70. *temerare* means 'to violate anything protected by religious sanctions' (*OLD* s.v. 1), in this case a foetus destined for divinely ordained greatness, and it is nicely piquant here in that the hypothetical violator is herself divine.

aluo: like *uenter* (see 13. 1n.), commonly used of the womb (cf. Lucr. iii. 346, Hor. *Carm.* iv. 6. 20.).

18. **Caesaribus:** i.e. both Julius and his adopted son, Augustus.
futura fuit: see 10n.

19-21. **cum posses nasci ... cum fuerim periturus:** *cum* is concessive and the subjunctive potential in both clauses. In the first the imperfect confines the potentiality to the past: 'although/when you could have been born' – there is no longer any possibility of this, because she is alive already (cf. Nep. *Phoc.* 1. 2 *fuit perpetuo pauper, cum diuitissimus esse posset*, and see further Kühner-Stegmann II. ii. 348). In the second the perfect (+ future participle) extends it to the future: 'although/when I may have been destined to die' – the possibility remains open, since he is not yet dead. The perfect subjunctive with periphrastic future is generally uncommon, and I have found no exact parallels for the construction here.

20. I.e. *si tua mater temptasset opus quod tu temptauisti*; hyperbaton (see p. 16).

21. **periturus amando:** does Ovid mean being mortally afflicted by the emotion (cf. 7. 10n.) or dropping dead in the act (cf. 10. 35n.)? In either case he significantly avoids saying that the love in question is for Corinna! For the ablative of the gerund see 1. 31n.

22. **uidissem ... dies:** unparalleled in Latin as a metaphor for 'be born', 'come into existence', despite the frequency of *dies* = 'the light of day'.

23-6. Ovid indirectly likens aborting a foetus to picking unripe fruit (ironically, an image also used often of erotic desire for a virgin's immature body; see e.g. Hor. *Carm.* ii. 5. 9-10 with Nisbet-Hubbard's note). Both actions involve interfering with the course of nature and traumatically wrenching away something which would come forth readily in the fullness of time (note the contrast between *fraudas* (23), *crudeli ... manu* and *uellis* (24) on the one hand and *sponte ... sua* and *fluant* (24) on the other), but one who picks fruit unripe normally does so out of impatience to have it, whereas Corinna has acted out of impatience to be *rid* of the unborn child. Presumably, therefore, Ovid wishes to imply that it is the inconvenience and discomfort of the pregnancy she does not want rather than the child itself – otherwise, to promise her a live child, as a reward (*pretium*) for waiting would make little sense: ripe fruit is no more welcome than sour to one who does not want it.

23-4. Closely echoed by 'Lygdamus' (see 5. 36-8n.) as a protest against premature death at [Tib.] iii. 5. 19-20 *quid fraudare iuuat uitem crescentibus uuis / et modo nata mala uellere poma manu?*

24. For the artistic word-order see p. 15.

25. **matura fluant:** the erroneous readings of some *recc.* (see apparatus on p. 97) feebly relate *matura* to *poma* in v. 24; despite the appropriateness of the expression as a whole to the 'dropping' of 'ripe' fruit (cf. *Am.* iii. 7. 34 *nullo poma mouente fluunt*), the reference is obviously to letting 'things' in general 'come forth' when they are 'ready'. *fluere* (used of the menstrual flow at Plin. *Nat.* vii. 66) suggests the physical process of childbirth.
nata: things which have 'started' to develop; the word is used of embryonic plants and fruit (cf. *Met.* i. 108 *flores sine semine natos*, [Tib.] iii. 5. 20 (cited at 23-4n.) as well as here, by implication, the human foetus, obviously not yet 'born' in the strict sense (cf. v. 28).

26. **uita:** the postponement of the subject gives it unexpected emphasis.

27-34. For the 2nd person plurals see pp. 71-2.

27-8. **subiectis ... telis ... dira uenena:** two of the commonest methods of abortion in antiquity (for a comprehensive list see Krenkel 446-8). *telis* revives the emotive military metaphor of vv. 1-6. The use of abortifacients (cf. *Ep.* 11. 39), though not in itself illegal, could be penalised under the law of poisons in the Roman Empire, if the woman to whom these potions were administered suffered harm (*dig.* xlviii. 19. 38. 5). The absolute interdict on them in the Hippocratic *Oath* is probably rooted in medical concern for the mother rather than in ethical concern for the foetus.

27. **uestra ... effoditis uiscera:** contrast the gruesome expression with 13. 1. For *uestra uiscera* = 'your own flesh and blood' cf. *Rem.* 59 *nec dolor armasset contra sua uiscera matrem* (where *matrem* = Medea) with Henderson's note.

29-34. Medea (see next n.) and Philomela (or Procne; see 6. 7-10n.) both killed their own children to take vengeance on their caddish, adulterous husbands, Jason and Tereus respectively.

Abortion was not equated with murder either in Roman law, which explicitly stated that the unborn child was *nondum homo* (*dig.* xxxv. 2. 9. 1) or in pre-Christian moral philosophy (the Stoics even claimed that life did not begin until the moment of birth; see Waszink on Tertull. 25. 5, 37. 2). Juvenal, however, does equate the two, be it out of conviction or for rhetorical effect, at 6. 595-6 (see 15n. *necasset*), and Ovid's comparison of aborting mothers with the notorious infanticides here has often been taken as an indication of his determination to do the same. But the comparison follows on the condemnation of abortion as an offence against Nature in 23-6 (see also p. 71), and I think its purpose – like that of the comparison with wild animals in vv. 35-6 – is not so much to suggest that abortion is criminal killing as that a mother's destroying the fruit of her own womb, whether before birth or after, is killing of the most *unnatural* kind. This also seems to be the point of unfavourable comparison of an aborting mother with Medea in the later Greek prose writers Theophylactus (*Ep.* 30. 7-12) and Chariton (ii. 9. 15-20), and there too, as in vv. 31-2 below, Jason's treatment of Medea is cited in mitigation; Yardley ((1977) 398-9) suggests that the pervasiveness of the comparison may point to its origin, and perhaps that of Ovid's anti-abortion arguments in general, in school rhetoric.

29. **Colchida:** a common mode of reference (first at Hor. *Epod.* 16. 58) to Medea, daughter of the King of Colchis, a country at the eastern end of the Black Sea; see further Bömer on *Met.* vii. 296.

respersam puerorum sanguine: for the expression cf. *Met.* vii. 396 *sanguine natorum perfunditur*, Verg. *Ecl.* 8. 47-8 *saeuos Amor docuit natorum sanguine matrem / commaculare manus.*

30. **aque:** much to be preferred to the *atque* of the vast majority of MSS (see apparatus on p. 97), (i) because the unelided *atque*, generally rare in elegiac poetry, is unparalleled in the *Amores*, and (ii) because no support is offered by any of the few Ovidian instances of ablative of agent without *a/ab* (see 4. 35n.); see further Kenney (1958a) 58-9, Nisbet-Hubbard II. 322. For *aque* cf. *Tr.* iv. 4. 85.

caesum: appropriately of Itys (see *Met.* vi. 636-45), 'carved up' rather than merely 'killed'; *caedere* = 'kill' is normally 'confined to the military, sacral and legal languages, and to descriptions of the slaughter of animals' (Adams (1973) 291).

queruntur: a suggestion, perhaps, of the nightingale's fabled lament for Itys (see 6. 7-10n.).

Ityn: for the spelling of the Greek accusative *-yn* (not *-ym*) see Kenney (1958a) 60.

32. Cf. *Rem.* 60 *socii damno sanguinis ulta uirum est* (also of Medea). *iactura* here = 'sacrifice', i.e. a loss voluntarily sustained in order to gain something else; cf. Verg. *A.* ii. 646. For *socii* see 11. 7n.

33-4. Ovid's rhetorical question is cunningly addressed to 'girls' in general, but is an oblique way of saying to Corinna: 'It's not as if you had the excuse that *I'm* an unfaithful husband you could hurt by destroying my offspring, is it?'. Only the reader who has been privy to 13. 5 knows how nearly the cap fits: unfaithful Ovid may well have been (see *Am.* ii. 4), husband he is not; but he has felt precisely a husband's hurt at Corinna's aborting of his (putative) child; see 13. 4-5n. and cf. *Fast.* i. 619-24.

33. **quis:** like other Latin authors, Ovid observes no consistent distinction between interrogative *quis* and *qui. quis* is used adjectivally especially often in rhetorical questions; cf. *Am.* ii. 2. 28, and see further Bömer on *Met.* i. 248.

Iason: for the spelling see 2. 45n.

34. **sollicita:** 'troubled', 'agitated', i.e. in the way of one driven to a *crime passionel*.

35-6. Lions and tigers conventionally typify savage animals (cf. *Met*. xv. 86 with Bömer's note for further examples and bibliography), and the perfects *fecere* and *ausa* (sc. *est*) are accordingly gnomic. Ovid's claim is more rhetorically effective than accurate, since animal mothers do sometimes kill their young (it is, of course, to this notion that *hoc* in v. 35 refers, and not *figere ... corpora* in 34). Ovid's illustration varies the claim, much used as a Stoic *exemplum*, that animals of the same species refrain from attacking each other (see Wilhelm 137, Courtney on Juv. 15. 159-64).

35. **in Armeniis ... latebris:** tigers are first called 'Armenian' by Virgil (*Ecl*. 5. 29), possibly with some contemporary geographical accuracy (see Pease on *A*. iv. 367, where they are called 'Hyrcanian'), but the epithet became conventional (cf. *Met*. viii. 21, xv. 86, with Bömer's notes) and may owe something to the fact that the *River* Tigris rises in Armenia. Varro claims (*L*. v. 100) that *tigris*, of both the river and the animal, is an Armenian word, but *Tigris* of the river, which seems more likely to have taken its name from the animal than vice versa, is already attested in Akkadian (I am grateful to Professor A. B. Lloyd for information on this point).

36. **nec:** for the position see p. 13, with n. 107.

37. **tenerae:** the irony of the word here (see 1. 4n.) is underlined by its prominent position and separation from *puellae*.

non impune: a common and colloquial expression; see Bömer on *Met*. ii. 474.

38-9. **ipsa perit / ipsa perit:** the witty repetition (cf. *Am*. ii. 5. 2-3) undermines the gravity of the words. Domitian's niece Julia allegedly died as a result of abortion; see Suet. *Dom*. 22, Plin. *Ep*. iv. 11. 6.

39. **ferturque:** = *efferturque*; cf. *Ars* iii. 20, *Fast*. ii. 847, and see p. 13.

rogo: dative of end of motion; cf. Prop. iv. 3. 71, and see Hau 58.

resoluta capillos: the loose hair normal for female mourners (cf. Tib. i. 1. 67 *solutis crinibus* with Murgatroyd's note) is here transferred to the corpse.

40. The climax of Ovid's harangue, perhaps inspired by Tib. i. 6. 81-2 (of a once unfaithful woman now old and poor) *hanc animo gaudente uident iuuenumque cateruae / commemorant merito tot mala ferre senem*.

qui ... cumque: the only Ovidian instance of *quicumque* in tmesis; this is generally common in poetry.

41-3. Ovid's words seem to imply that a relapse for Corinna is not yet out of the question.

41-2. Cf. Hom. *Od*. viii. 408-9 ἔπος δ' εἴ πέρ τι βέβακται / δεινόν, ἄφαρ τὸ φέροιεν ἀναρπάξασαι ἄελλαι ('If any unlucky word has been spoken, may the winds immediately snatch it up and whisk it away'). For the role of the winds see 6. 44n.

42. **sint ominibus pondera nulla:** cf. *Ep*. 7. 65 *nullum sit in omine pondus*, 13. 133, *Am*. i. 14. 41. *omen* is the mere mention of an awful possibility, which the speaker considers unlucky.

43-4. Cf. 13. 27-8, and see p. 70. Cf. also Tibullus' plea for the unfaithful Marathus at i. 9. 5-6: *parcite, caelestes; aequum est impune licere / numina formosis laedere uestra semel*.

peccasse ... culpa: these words, used so often of amatory infidelity (see e.g. *Am*. ii. 7. 11, 8. 26), perhaps betray Ovid's conception of Corinna's abortion more as a breach of faith with him than as a moral offence.

43. **faciles:** the sense 'indulgent' or 'favourable' (of gods) is a poetic usage; cf. *Met*. v. 559 with Bömer's note.

44. **poenam:** deliberately vague; it would hardly be appropriate for Ovid to appear to be wishing *death* upon Corinna (cf. vv. 37-40), whatever the circumstances.

Poem 15 (16)

1. **anule:** address to the gift is much less common than address to the recipient in the gift-poem, but cf. Theoc. *Id.* 28, Mart. iii. 2.
formosae: see 10. 5-7n.
uincture: see 6. 36n.

2. **in quo censendum ...:** this is not to suggest that the ring is cheap, but rather that its monetary value is of no consequence in comparison with its sentimental worth. For *censere* + ablative = 'value' or 'measure by' cf. *Pont.* i. 2. 138, Juv. 8. 2, 74; the word is avoided altogether by all the Augustans except Horace (in his *Epistles*) and Ovid (see Axelson 64).

3. **eas:** this virtually = *sis* (cf. 2. 56n.), but is also suggestive of the physical process of delivery; cf. *Ep.* 3. 20.

4. **articulis induat:** *induere* + dative of a part of the body is the normal expression for 'putting on' a piece of jewellery (cf. Plin. *Nat.* xxxiii. 1 *anulum induit digitis, Med. Fac.* 21), but this verb construed with accusative and dative also has the meaning 'run (something) on to' or 'up against (something else)' (see 10. 31n.); here, therefore, with *articulis*, 'knuckles' (cf. *Met.* viii. 807), it perhaps conveys something of the pleasurable friction involved in drawing on a ring and so paves the way for the sexual innuendo of the following two couplets.

5. **tam bene conuenias ...:** *illi* must be understood with both the personal *conuenias* and the impersonal *conuenit*: literally 'May you fit her as well there is a fit for her with me'. For the construction with *conuenit* (though not the sense) cf. *Fast.* iii. 95-6 *et tibi cum proauis ... Sabinis / conuenit,* Ter. Ad. 59 *haec fratri mecum non conueniunt.* Here the play on *conuenire*'s two meanings of 'suit' in a general and 'fit' in a specifically physical sense gives a novel twist to the traditional motif of the gift's suitability for the recipient (cf. Crin. *AP* vi. 227. 5-6, ix. 239, Leonid. *AP* ix. 355. 3-4): the ring is to accommodate the mistress' finger as well as her vagina accommodates Ovid's penis (cf. the play on *apta* at *Am.* ii. 8. 4, and for innuendo involving *conuenire*, Pl. *Ps.* 1181 *conueniebatne in uaginam tuam machaera militis?*; note also the punning use of 'ring' for 'vagina' at Shakespeare, *Merchant of Venice* V. 1. 307 to conclude a passage which shows considerable Ovidian influence). Thus Ovid moots the suggestion of sexual role reversal, with the woman playing the active, normally male, part, and the ring, the man's token, the female, passive one (see also on *teras*, v. 6, and *tractaberis*, v. 7).

6. **iusto:** used of anything of ideal proportion; cf. Caes. *Civ.* i. 23. 5 *iustum iter conficit.*
teras: this word and its cognates may refer to the friction associated with all manner of sexual activity (see Adams (1982) 183). When *terere* is used of normal heterosexual intercourse, it is usually with reference to the man's 'rubbing' of the woman, (see e.g. Pl. *Capt.* 888, Prop. iii. 11. 30), but so vague is the word, as Adams remarks, that Ovid could well have used it with the vaginal action on the penis in mind here (see 5n.).

7. **felix:** I take this with *anule* ('you lucky ring!'; cf. *Met.* viii. 36-7 *felix iaculum, quod tangeret ille, / quaeque manu premeret, felicia frena uocabat*); alternatively construe with *tractaberis* ('you will have the luck to be handled'; cf. *Met.* viii. 486 *an felix Oeneus nato uictore fruetur?*).
domina: see 1. 17n. *amica.*
tractaberis: on the face of it, simply 'you (the ring) will be handled' or 'drawn on', but this word may well, like *teras* (v. 6), be sexually suggestive, for its compounds and cognates are used of the man's action in heterosexual intercourse; see e.g. Suet. *Dom.* 1. 3

contractatis multorum uxoribus, Petr. 139. 1 *torum frequenti tractatione uexaui*, and further Adams (1982) 186.

8. **inuideo donis ... meis:** a variation on the commonplace of envy of a rival (cf. *Am*. i. 4, ii. 5, Hor. *Carm*. i. 13). For envy of an inanimate object close to the beloved cf. Mel. *AP* v. 171 (of a wine-cup), and see further Murgatroyd (1984) 53, n. 12). *donis* (like *munera* in v. 9) is poetic plural.

miser ipse: wittily counterpoints *felix ... anule* in v. 7.

ipse meis: see 6. 55n.

9. **o utinam:** for the hiatus see 5. 7n.

fieri ... possem: 'Would that I could (now) be turned into ...'; the imperfect subjunctive to express an unfulfilled wish for the present is standard in classical Latin; further examples at Woodcock 88-9.

10. **artibus:** sc. *magicis*; this is generally specified (see e.g. *Am*. iii. 7. 35, and further *ThLL* II. 665, 34ff.), but for *ars* alone = 'magic' cf. *Am*. i. 8. 6, *Met*. vii. 176.

Aeaeae Carpathiiue senis: two fabled experts in metamorphosis: (i) Circe, the witch on the island of Aeaea who turned Odysseus' companions into swine (Hom. *Od*. x. 210ff.); cf. Verg. *A*. iii. 386 *Aeaeaeque insula Circae*, and see further Bömer on *Met*. iv. 205); (ii) Proteus, an 'old man of the sea', capable of changing himself into an infinite variety of shapes (Hom. *Od*. iv. 351ff.). Ovid follows Virgil (*G*. iv. 387) in locating Proteus in the Carpathian Sea (i.e. between Rhodes and Crete; cf. *Met*. xi. 249 *Carpathius uates*); Homer places him in Egyptian waters. Note the artistic juxtaposition of the two learned epithets.

11. **cum libeat dominae:** the text remains uncertain (see apparatus on p. 97), but this radical conjecture at least has the merit of allowing vv. 11-14 to fit the pattern of the rest of Ovid's fantasy in vv. 15-26, where he imagines a series of everyday actions on his mistress' part, which will, unbeknown to her, give him, in his ring form, an erotic thrill or opportunity (for the impersonal *libet* + dative in Ovid cf. *Met*. xiii. 766, *Ep*. 17 (18). 92). A scribe misconstruing *libeat* with a suppressed *mihi* rather than the expressed *dominae* could well have glossed with *cupiam*, and this subsequently displaced *libeat*. *si dominae libeat* was Bentley's conjecture; this gives the desirable sense, but it is hard to account for the loss or corruption of *si* in all but one 12th-13th century MS (*F*). The omission of a subordinating *cum* by haplography after the putative corruption of *libeat* to *cupiam* (i.e.*<CV>CVPIAM*) and the subsequent scribal importation of *te* (amongst other things) is palaeographically more plausible, and, if the mood may be explained as the result of attraction by the subjunctives *elabar* and *cadam* in vv. 12-13 (these forms are ambiguous, but a switch to the more vivid future has better effect later in v. 19, as Ovid's excitement mounts, and the sudden urgent proviso in v.18 eases the transition), *cum libeat* gives good sense: 'then, *when my mistress felt the urge* to touch her breasts' (sc. to relieve some momentary discomfort – an itch, perhaps?) 'and slip her left hand inside her dress ...' (an easy enough 'hysteron proteron' construction; see p. 13). The attraction is not easily paralleled, but cf. perhaps Cic. *Leg*. ii. 2 *quis non, cum haec uideat, irriserit?*.

Madvig's *te cupiam, domina, et* also gives basically good sense, but (i) nowhere else does Ovid address his mistress directly as *domina*, and a change to direct address is also arguably more effective later (*tuos*, v. 20); (ii) the double *et* seems ponderous; and (iii) the asyndeton between vv. 12 and 13 is harsh. *cum cupiam* (Oliver (1958) 103-5, supported by Goold at (1965a) 38-9), which is a refinement of the *si cupiam* favoured by most modern editors, is even less convincing. If 'I' is assumed to be Ovid-the-ring speaking (so Oliver), the *manum* in 12 must itself be the ring's, which is hard to understand without foreknowledge of vv. 25-6, and, in any case, to endow the ring with human parts at the outset would be to detract from the carefully contrived climax of the fantasy. Nor is it natural or easy to understand Ovid-the-man to be speaking in vv. 11-12 and Ovid-the-ring in vv. 13-14 and the rest (thus Goold). Moreover, both these interpretations, doubtless influenced by *Am.* i. 4. 37, 5. 20, necessitate special pleading for *laeuam* (see 12n.), and both fail to explain how the ring would be in a *position* to slip into the mistress' bosom (cf. vv. 15-18).

11-12. **tetigisse ... inseruisse:** for the tense see 4. 22n.

12. **laeuam:** the hand on which the Romans usually wore rings (see Plin. *Nat.* xxviii. 57, Petr. 32, 74). Those who believe that the *manus* in question is not the mistress', but the ring's or Ovid's (see 11n. above), explain *laeuam* as the hand used in erotic fondling. But except where the action of *laeua* is contrasted with that of *dextera manus* (see e.g. *anth.* I. 2. 724. 84 Riese), fondling of the genitals is normally what mention of *laeua manus* implies (see e.g. *Ars* ii. 706 and further Adams (1982) 209).

tunicis: the *tunica* was properly a chemise-like garment worn by both sexes, but the word is often used as a general term for 'clothes'. For the poetic plural, cf. *Am.* iii. 14. 17, *Ars* iii. 109.

13. **elabar digito:** for the ablative without preposition see p. 13, and cf. Mart. xiv. 123. 1.

14. **sinum:** the space between the breasts, where, in the case of a woman wearing a belted garment, the fallen ring could easily nestle, and also, suggestively, the place where a beloved was conventionally held (see e.g. *Am.* ii. 12. 2, *Ars* ii. 360, *Ep.* 3. 114).

mira ... ab arte: cf. 10n. For *ab arte* see 4. 30n.

15-18. The general sentiment of these lines is fairly closely paralleled in an elegiac distich scribbled on a tomb in Pompei: *uellem essem gemma (h)ora non amplius una / ut tibi signanti oscula pressa darem* (*CIL* IV, Suppl. 3, fasc. 4, 10241; *pressa* is H. Solin's correction for the mis-reading *missa*); it also features, complete or in part, in two other Pompeian graffiti (see H. Solin in *Neue Forschungen in Pompeji*, edd. B. Andreae and H. Kyrieleis (Recklinghausen, 1975), 266, no. 61 and *CIL* IV. 1698). It is tempting to assume the distich-writer to have been influenced by Ovid (see e.g. A. W. van Buren, 'A Pompeian Distich', *AJPh* 80 (1959), 380-82, L. Pepe, 'Un distico Pompeiano e Ovidio', *Univ. di Genova Fac. di Lettere, Ist. di Filol. class. e mediev.* 39 (1974), 223-234.), and, certainly, attempts to prove the opposite (see O. Hiltbrunner, 'Ovids Gedicht vom Siegelring und ein anonymes Epigramm aus Pompei', *Gymnasium* 77 (1970), 283-9 and *id.*, 'Die neue Lesung des pompeianischen Epigramms vom Siegelring', *Gymnasium* 88 (1981), 45-53) are totally unconvincing; but in the absence of any precise verbal similarities, the possibility of completely independent composition cannot be ruled out (see W. D. Lebek, 'Ein lateinisches Epigram aus Pompei und Ovids Gedicht vom Siegelring (*Am.* ii. 15)', *ZPE* 23 (1976), 21-40).

Ovid varies the general sentiment in these lines at *Ep.* 17 (18). 15-18.

15. **arcanas ... tabellas:** love-letters. For *tabellae* see 5. 5n.

16. **tenax ... siccaque:** 'hysteron proteron' (see p. 13): the seal-stone (probably of sardonyx; see Plin. *Nat.* xvii. 88, R. A. Higgins, *Greek and Roman Jewellery* (London, 1961), 38) would stick *because* it was dry. For the postponement of *-que* see p. 13, with n. 107.

ceram: the blob of wax securing the thread tied around the closed *tabellae*; see Pl. *Bacch.* 748, Bömer on *Met.* ix. 566.

17. **umida:** strictly this is redundant, but it neatly counterpoints *sicca* in v. 16 and contributes to the artistic symmetry of its own line (see p. 15). For the moistening of seals, normally with the tongue, cf. *Met.* ix. 568, *Tr.* v. 4. 4-5, Juv. 1. 68.

18. **tantum:** = *dummodo*. A favourite Ovidian usage; cf. *Am.* iii. 8. 59, *Rem.* 714.

scripta dolenda mihi: i.e. by refusing a request for an assignation (cf. *Am.* i. 12. 1-2) or by granting one to a rival (cf. *Am.* ii. 5. 5).

19. **si dabor ut condar loculis:** = *si dabor loculis* (dative) *condendus*; cf. *Fast.* iii. 375-6 *iuuenca / quae dederat nulli colla premenda iugo*, and for further examples see Goold (1965a) 39 (cf. Oliver (1958) 104). For *loculi* = 'jewel case', cf. Juv. 13. 138-9 *gemmaque princeps / sardonychum, loculis quae custoditur eburnis* with Courtney's note.
exire: 'to come off (your finger)'; apparently a unique usage.

20. **digitos:** poetic plural, for metrical convenience.

21. **non ego dedecori ...:** sc. by being a large and vulgar bauble? Cf. Juv. 1. 28-30.
sum ... futurus: = *ero*. Most editors read *sim* with *PSY* (see apparatus on p. 97), but consistency in vv. 19-26 (cf. 11n.) demands the equivalent of the future indicative (see further Oliver (1958) 104).
mea uita: a colloquial term of endearment, common in both prose and verse; cf. Catul. 45. 13, 109. 1, Prop. i. 2. 1 with Fedeli's note, Cic. *Fam.* xiv. 2. 3, 4. 1, and see further La Penna 209, Hofmann 195. It is less popular with Ovid, the most detached of the elegists, than with Catullus and Propertius, and is avoided altogether by Tibullus, linguistically the most fastidious.

22. I.e. *onusue quod tener digitus ferre recuset;* mild hyperbaton (see p. 16).
tener: see 1. 4n.

23. **perfundes imbribus artus:** *perfundere* (generally passive or reflexive) + ablative is a semi-technical term for 'bathe' (cf. Verg. *A.* xi. 495); the retained accusative is exclusive to Ovid (cf. *Met.* iii. 163-4 *solebat / uirgineos artus liquido perfundere rore*, and see Oliver (1958) 105). For *imber* of an artificial shower cf. Verg. *G.* iv. 115, where the reference is to watering plants. For rings being removed while washing, cf. Ter. *Hau.* 653-5; for them being kept on cf. Mart. xi. 59.

24. **damnaque sub gemmam ...:** most women instinctively remove a stone-set ring before washing for fear – perhaps irrational – of the stone being dislodged by water getting between it and its metal setting. This is surely the *damna* ('damage') *sub gemmam* (not *gemma*; see apparatus on p. 97) *euntis aquae* (for the genitive of cause cf. *Ars* i. 186 *ignauae ... damna morae*). Other explanations are laboured and far-fetched (see Oliver (1958) 103-4 and Munari's references *ad loc.*). There is nothing to be said for the transposition *fer pereuntis* (Douza, with considerable later support; see e.g. Goold (1965a) 40-41). Ovid's normal imperative for 'endure' is *perfer*, not *fer*, which he only ever uses to mean 'bring' (usually *opem*), and *aqua periens* is water which runs *away* or leaks *out of* something, not *into* it (see e.g. Hor. *Carm.* iii. 11. 27).

25. **puto:** this, like the parenthetical *memini* (see 1. 11-16, 10. 1nn.), is sometimes in Ovid a pointer to the falsity or absurdity of the stance adopted or claim made; cf. *Am.* i. 2. 5, 12. 9, iii. 1. 8, 11. 34. The use of the device twice in *Am.* iii. 7 (vv. 2 and 55) helps to link that poem, where Ovid reflects on the erection which never was, with the present couplet, where he anticipates the one which never can be. For the scansion *pŭtŏ* see 5. 53-4n.
membra: poetic plural; cf. *Am.* iii. 7. 13, and see Adams (1982) 46.
libidine surgent: a direct but relatively modest description of erection; contrast Catul. 32. 11, Hor. *Epod.* 12. 19-20, Marc. Arg. *AP* v. 104. 4-5.

26. **peragam partes ... uiri:** *partes peragere* = 'to play a role', but *peragere* may also mean 'to carry (something) through to the finish' and is so used by Ovid in a sexual context at *Ars* ii. 480: *arte Venus nulla dulce peregit opus* (cf. also *Am.* i. 4. 47-8). There is in Ovid's words here, therefore, the clear suggestion of intercourse following the erection imagined in v. 25.

27-8. **paruum, proficiscere, munus ...:** the gift-poem format provides a convenient formal ending after the abrupt deflation of the fantasy.

28. **fidem:** positioned with ironic prominence, given the carnality of what has gone before.

Poem 16 (17)

1-10. Ovid's description of his native land draws upon three interrelated literary traditions: (i) the *locus amoenus* set-piece (see 6. 49-50n.); (ii) the 'panegyric of places' theme, which often encompasses (i) and includes comment on physical features, flora and fauna, and climate (see further Nisbet-Hubbard II. 95-6); (iii) the wider 'ethnographical' tradition, which often encompasses both (i) and (ii) (see R. F. Thomas, *Lands and Peoples in Roman Poetry. The Ethnographical Tradition*, *Cambridge Philol. Soc. Suppl. 7* (Cambridge, 1982), especially 2-7).

1. Cf. Tib. ii. 3. 1 *rura meam, Cornute, tenent uillaeque puellam*, and (the same situation from the woman's point of view) [Tib.] iii. 14; see further p. 78. *tenet* appropriately suggests an enforced sojourn, but it is also a metrically convenient alternative to *habet* (cf. v. 34).

Pars ... tertia: the other two Paelignian 'ridings' were Corfinium and Superaequum (see Plin. *Nat.* iii. 106).

Sulmo: modern Sulmona in the Abruzzi (see next n.), the birthplace of Ovid (see *Tr.* iv. 10. 3 *Sulmo mihi patria est* with Luck's note). A statue of him still stands in its main piazza.

Paeligni ... ruris: the ancient Paeligni inhabited a fertile valley in the wild hills of the Abruzzi 100 miles east of Rome. They were noted for a spirited secession in the Social War (91-87 B.C.; see *Am.* iii. 15. 9-10, E. T. Salmon, 'S. M. P. E.', *Ovidiana* 10-20), but Ovid's interest in them is confined to the reflected glory he thinks his poetry will bring them (*Am.* iii. 15. 8 *Paeligni dicar gloria gentis ego*); cf. 1. 1n., and see further M. Bonjour, *Terre Natale* (Paris, 1975), 210ff. For the region see M. Besnier 'Sulmo, Patrie d'Ovide' in *Mélanges Boissier* (Paris, 1903), 57-63, G. Highet, *Poets in a Landscape* (London, 1957), 177-80, 193-4, F. van Wontergehm, *Formae Italiae, Regio IV,* Vol. I, *Superaequum, Corfinium, Sulmo* (Florence, 1984).

2. **parua:** cf. *Fast.* iv. 685-6 *Paelignos, natalia rura, petebam, / parua*, *Am.* iii. 15. 11-12.

irriguis ... aquis: Ovid's native valley has three rivers, which, unlike many in Italy, do not dry up in summer. The abundance of water on which he insists in vv. 5-6, 9-10, and 34-5 (cf. *Am.* ii. 1. 1, iii. 15. 11 *Sulmonis aquosi*, *Fast,* iv. 685-6 *natalia rura... / ... assiduis uuida semper aquis*, *Tr.* iv. 10. 3 *gelidis uberrimus undis*) is thus more than just a standard feature of the *locus amoenus* (see 1-10n.). *irriguis* perhaps = 'refreshing' (cf. the metaphorical use of the cognate verb at Verg. *A.* iii. 511 *fessos sopor irrigat artus*) rather than 'irrigating' (cf. Verg. *G.* iv. 32, Tib. ii. 1. 44), for Ovid seems to have in mind the generally healthy (*salubris*) atmosphere created by the constant presence of cool, running water in a hot climate and not, at this stage, the beneficial effect of that water on the land.

3. **sol ... tellurem ... findat:** a conventional description of the worst summer heat; cf. *Met.* iii. 152, Catul. 68. 62, Verg. *G.* ii. 353, Tib. i. 7. 21-2, [Ov.] *Nux* 118 (cited 4n.).

admoto ... sidere: literally 'with its beam brought close', i.e. at midsummer, when the distance between the earth and the sun is shortest (cf. [Tib.] iii. 7. 160 *propior (Phoebus) terris aestiuum fertur in orbem*). For *sidus* in this sense cf. Sen. *Her. O.* 1286-8 *sic arctoas laxare niues / quamuis tepido sidere Titan / non audet*, Stat. *Theb.* i. 159 *quasque procul terras obliquo sidere tangit* (*Sol*) and (pl.) *Met.* xiv. 172 with Bömer's note.

4. **Icarii stella ... canis:** i.e. Sirius, the greater dog-star, whose rising towards the end of July marks the hottest days of the year (cf. *Fast.* iv. 939-40 *est Canis, Icarium dicunt, quo sidere moto / tosta sitit tellus*, [Ov.] *Nux* 118 *finditur Icario cum cane terra*, Verg. *G.* iv. 425-8, *A.* x. 273-5, Tib. i. 1. 27 with Smith's note). Icarius was a legendary Athenian who received the gift of wine from Dionysus but was killed by his neighbours when he offered it to them, because they mistook it for poison. Icarius' daughter, Erigone, was eventually led to her father's body by the barking of his faithful dog, Maera. Dionysus rewarded all three of them with catasterism, Icarius becoming the constellation Boötes, Erigone becoming Virgo and Maera becoming Sirius (see Bömer on *Fast.* iv. 939).

5. **arua pererrantur:** a standard Ovidian expression; cf. *Met.* xii. 209 *arua pererrat,* vii. 534-5 *per agros / errasse*, and for a collection of further variations see Goold (1965a) 24.
liquentibus undis: see 2n.

6. **tenero:** i.e. easily workable; cf. *Fast.* i. 351 *teneris ... sulcis.*
herba: this includes any kind of springing vegetation and here evokes a generally 'green and pleasant land' rather than specifically luxuriant growth of grass (dealt with in 9-10); cf. Lucr. v. 783-4 *principio genus herbarum uiridemque nitorem / terra dedit circum collis camposque per omnis.* Verdancy is a standard feature of the *locus amoenus* (see 1-10n.).

7. **ferax Cereris ... feracior uuis:** *ferax* with the genitive is relatively common (first at Hor. *Epod.* 5. 21-2 and in Ovid probably also at *Met.* vii. 470 *nitidaeque ferax ... oliuae*; cf. *ThLL* VI. 488. 73ff.). With the dative or ablative it is much rarer (only 6 instances in all, and most of them ambiguous, but the ablative is clearly attested at Stat. *Theb.* vii. 307 and the dative at *Aetna* 262). The case-variation presented by all our MSS (see apparatus on p. 97) here is thus possible, but it seems oddly gratuitous. Heinsius' *uuae* (genitive) for *uuis* (corrupted under the influence of *undis* in v. 5?) may be right, but more attractive is Lee's tentative *Cereri*, easily corrupted by a scribe more familiar with the genitive construction; *uuis* then would be dative (cf. *Aetna* 262 *fertilis haec (gleba) segetique feracior, altera uiti*). Grain (see next n.) and grape are conventionally paired; cf. Lucr. v. 14-15, Verg. *G.* ii. 228-9.

7-8. **Cereris ... Pallada:** the names of Ceres, goddess of arable crops, and Pallas Athene, giver of the olive to men, are here used as highly poetical metonyms (see p. 12) for 'grain' (cf. Verg. *G.* ii. 229 *(fauet terra) densa magis Cereri*) and 'olive trees' (cf., with Luck's note, *Tr.* iv. 5. 4 *infusa Pallade*, where *Pallade* = 'olive oil', Sil i. 237-8 *nec Cereri terra indocilis, nec inhospita Baccho, / nullaque Palladia sese magis arbore tollit*).

8. **quoque:** in Ovid and other poets this not infrequently precedes the word it qualifies; cf. *Met.* iii. 456 with Bömer's note.
baciferam: the first appearance of this word in extant Latin (afterwards in poetry at Sen. *Oed.* 415 (of ivy) and, again of the olive tree in metonymy, at Sil. iii. 596 *gens bacifero nutrita Sabino*). Its appearance at Plin. *Nat.* xvi. 50, *ex omnibus sola bacifera (taxus)*, suggests that it may have originated in technical prose, but the high-flown ring it shares with other compounds in *-fer* (see 13. 10n. *palmiferam* and cf. p. 13) contributes to the couplet's mannered style (a standard feature of the poetic *locus amoenus*; see 1-10n.).

9. **resurgentes:** *resurgere* is virtually a technical term for new plant growth; cf. Plin. *Nat.* xvi. 132, and see *OLD* s.v. 3a.
riuis labentibus: causal ablative. *labi* is conventionally used of running water, especially in the *locus amoenus* (see 1-10n.); cf. *Am.* ii. 17. 31, *Met.* ii. 406, 455 with Bömer's notes.
herbas: here (cf. 6n.) 'meadows'; cf. Lucr. vi. 785, Hor. *Carm.* iii. 23. 11.

10. Note the mannered arrangement of adjectives and nouns; cf. 8n. *baciferam*, and see p. 15.
gramineus ... caespes: a standard and highly poetic collocation cf. *Tr.* v. 5. 9, Verg. *A.* xi. 566, and see further *ThLL* VI. 2169. 26ff.
obumbrat: one of Ovid's uncommon compounds (see p. 13, with n. 97). There are 4 more instances of it in his work (cf. *Met.* xiii. 845, xiv. 837, *Ep.* 16 (17). 48, *Pont.* iii. 3. 75) and 2 in Virgil, but it is avoided altogether by the other Augustans.

11-12. Ovid plays (a) on the two meanings of *ignis* – 'love' (*ardor*; cf. 1. 8n.) and 'the beloved' (*quae mouet ardores;* cf. *Am.* iii. 9. 56 *dum tuus ignis eram*, *Ep.* 17 (18). 85, Verg. *Ecl.* 3. 66, Hor. *Epod.* 14. 13) – and (b) on the difference between *abest* and *adest*. The 'fire' of love (which here contrasts effectively with the coolness of the countryside) was a fruitful subject for the ingenuity of the Hellenistic and early Latin epigrammatists (see e.g. Mel. *AP* v. 96, xii. 127, Philod. *AP* v. 124, 131, Diosc. *AP* v. 138, Anon. *AP* ix. 15, Aed. *poet.* fr. 2 Büchner, Porc. *poet.* fr. 6 Büchner), but (*pace* L. Alfonsi, *Latomus* 18 (1959), 800-1) Ovid shows no direct debt to any of them. His playfully pedantic self-correction hints that what follows is not to be taken altogether seriously (cf. 11. 10n.).

12. **ardores:** an idiomatic plural; see 4. 9n. *amores.*

13-14. The gods Castor and Pollux were identified with the constellation Gemini. After Castor, who was born mortal (see 11. 29n.), had been killed while fighting alongside his divine twin Pollux to retain possession of the daughters of Leucippus whom they had abducted, he was allowed to share his brother's immortality on condition that they lived by turns in heaven and in Hades (see *Fast.* v. 699-719 with Bömer's note). Thus, their celestial existence was only part-time and also inevitably separated them from their beloveds. No wonder Ovid did not want to join them! For the general sentiment cf. *CLE* 937. 2 *a peream sine te si deus esse uelim*; *Ep.* 17 (18). 169-170 and Tib. ii. 3. 31-6 offer further variations.

Castor and Pollux were believed to be the special protectors of seafarers (see 11. 29n.), and so the reference to them here obliquely prepares for the shipwreck theme which emerges in vv. 22-32 (establishing at the same time one of the poem's many links with poem 11; see p. 81).

13. **medius Polluce et Castore:** the only clear instance of a double ablative construction with *medius* (cf. the ambiguous *Corintho Athenisque urbem* at Vell. i. 1. 2).

14. **in ... parte fuisse:** 'to have a share (in)'; cf. *Tr.* v. 14. 9 *nostrorum cum sis in parte malorum*, *Pont.* ii. 2. 102 *et nos in turbae parte fuisse tuae*. For the tense of *fuisse* see 4. 22n.

15-18. A humorous variation of the 'inventor' motif (see 3. 3-4n.). First (15-16) comes a malediction inverting the conventional *sit tibi terra leuis* (see Lattimore 65-74, and for the inversion cf. Crin. *AP* vii. 401. 6-7, Prop. ii. 6. 31, iv. 5. 76). But then (17-18) Ovid backs down slightly, as well he might, since it is *he*, and not his mistress, who has used the invention of roads (contrast *Am.* ii. 11. 5-8). And what he wants was, in a sense, already common practice; for poetic *puellae* regularly did follow *iuuenes* on lengthy journeys (e.g. Gallus' Lycoris at Verg. *Ecl.* 10. 21-2, 46-9, Propertius' Cynthia in i. 8A, and – we may infer – Corinna herself in *Am.* ii. 11): the trouble was that these *iuuenes* were never their devoted *poetae.*

15. **iaceant:** see 6. 20, 10. 15nn.

iniqua: i.e. excessive in weight; cf. Verg. *G.* i. 164 *iniquo pondere rastri.*

16. An adaptation of the much commoner disapproval of the pioneers of sailing; cf. Tib. i. 3. 35-6 *priusquam / tellus in longas est patefacta uias* with Murgatroyd's note.

in longas ... secuere uias: a unique conflation (under the influence of Tib. i. 3. 35-6, cited in previous n.) of the expressions *uiam secare*, 'to open up a path' (cf. Verg. *G.* i. 238) and (*orbem/terram*) *in uiam patefacere*, 'to open up for journeys'.

17. **iussissent:** a subjunctive of wish sometimes called the 'past jussive': 'they should have bidden', i.e. 'I wish that they had ...'; cf. Verg. *A.* iv. 678, viii. 643, and see further Kenney (1958a) 66, Kühner-Stegmann II. i. 187.

18. **in longas ... secanda uias:** the close echo of 16 underlines the absurdity of Ovid's suggested compromise.

19-20. Here Ovid debunks the apparent altruism of the familiar 'willingness to travel with friends' motif (see e.g. Hor. *Carm.* ii. 6. 1-4 with Nisbet-Hubbard's note on v. 1, Prop. i. 6. 3-4). *His* line is not 'I'd be prepared to suffer any hardships out of devotion to her' (see e.g. Prop. ii. 26. 29-30, 35-6, and cf. *Am.* i. 9. 9-14, Prop. iv. 3. 45-6), but 'I'd be prepared to suffer *on condition that she were with me*'.

19. **si premerem ... fuisset:** for the mixture of tenses cf. Ter. *Hau.* 230-31 *si mihi secundae res de amore meo essent, iam dudum, scio, / uenissent.* When the imperfect is preferred to the pluperfect in a past unreal condition, 'the sense "was destined to", "was likely to" can still usually be seen' (Woodcock 155).

uentosas ... Alpes: for the harshness of the Alpine climate cf. Verg. *Ecl.* 10. 47, Liv. xxi. 31. 8, and see Bömer on *Met.* ii. 226. The Alps represent the northerly limit conventionally mentioned in the travel motif (see 19-20n.), and the Syrtes (v. 21) the southerly one; see further Pöschl 16-17.

horridus: i.e. shaking with cold; cf. *Met.* xv. 212 *hiems ... horrida,* Mart. iii. 36. 3.

20. **dummodo cum domina:** for the ellipse of the verb cf. *Am.* i. 9. 47, *Fast.* v. 242, and see further Hofmann-Szantyr 421-2. The prosaic *dummodo,* which is almost entirely avoided by the other Augustans, is in tune with the subsequent thought of down-to-earth pleasure (see next n.). For *domina* see 1. 17n.

molle: ostensibly a reference to the diminished hardships of the Alpine terrain and climate (see 19n.). But the word also hints at the personal comfort the mistress could offer *en route*; see 4. 14n.

21-6. See p. 81.

21. **Libycas ausim perrumpere Syrtes:** word-order reflects sense, with *ausim perrumpere* bisecting *Libycas Syrtes* (cf. p. 16). For the Syrtes see 11. 20n. and 19n. above on *uentosas ... Alpes.* For *ausim* see 4. 1n.

22. **dare ... uela Notis:** *dare uela* = 'expose one's sails to the winds' (cf. *Ep.* 15 (16). 122). For *Notis* see 6. 44n.

non aequis: litotes (see p. 13).

23. **quae uirgineo portenta ...:** i.e. the raging dogs which in post-Homeric myth (see Bömer on *Met.* vii. 65) sprouted from the pubic area of the sea-monster Scylla's body (erroneous etymologising perhaps suggested this conception, since σκύλαξ means 'puppy'). Ovid tells the story of why and how she acquired her fabled form at *Met.* xiii. 730 - xiv. 67. His allusion to Scylla here is stereotyped (see nn. below) and doubtless owes something to ancient art (see Kenney (1958a) 66, n. 2, Bömer on *Met.* xiv. 66-7). See also 11.18n.

uirgineo: this has possessive force; Scylla was often thought to have the form of a young woman above the waist. Cf. *Met.* xiii. 793 *uirginis ora gerens,* [Tib.] iii. 4. 89 *Scylla uirgineam canibus succincta figuram.*

sub inguine latrant: *sub* is here a metrically convenient alternative to *ab*; cf. *Pont.* iv. 10. 25 *Scylla feris trunco quod latret ab inguine monstris. inguine* = the area between her legs, deformed to accommodate the dogs; cf. *Met.* xiv. 60-61 *cum sua foedari latrantibus inguina monstris / aspicit,* Verg. *Ecl.* 6. 75 *candida succinctam latrantibus inguina monstris,* Prop. iv. 4. 40 *candidaque in saeuos inguine uersa canes* with Fedeli's note.

24. **uestros, ... Malea, sinus:** the waters around Cape Malea, the promontory at the southernmost tip of the Peloponnese (now Cape Matapan), were proverbially dangerous; cf. Verg. *A.* v. 193, Prop. iii. 19. 8 with Fedeli's note. Pomponius Mela mentions two other promontories which form *sinus* with Cape Malea (ii. 3. 50 *inter Scyllaeon et Malean sinus Argolicus dicitur, inter Malean et Taenaron Laconicus*), but it is difficult to accept that Ovid was thinking of these when he wrote *uestros* here, i.e. that he meant 'I should not fear the bays of you (three) promontories, Cape Malea' (thus Goold (1965a) 41-2). To say nothing of the linguistic awkwardness, never elsewhere are these other capes mentioned in

connection with the fabled hazards of Malea, and a hidden reference to them in *uestros* would have been as obscure to Ovid's public as it is to us. Housman's conclusion (*CQ* 3 (1909), 247-8 [= *Classical Papers* 793-94]) that this is one of only four classical instances of *uester* = *tuus* (the others he identifies are Catul. 39. 20, 99. 6 and Sen. *H. Oet.* 1513) thus seems inescapable, and the motivation of mere metrical convenience cannot be ruled out. If, however, Ovid was aware of a Peloponnesian Cape Scyllaeon, this could well explain, as Goold suggests, his otherwise slightly puzzling insertion of the well-known hazards of the Peloponnesian Cape Malea *between* those of Scylla and Charybdis.
curua: a reference primarily to shape, but perhaps also to reputation; cf. 2. 26n.

25-6. Scylla's partner (see 23n.), Charybdis (not exactly a whirlpool, though traditionally described as such), alternately sucked in and spewed out water, in the process swallowing ships and throwing up the wreckage (see Hom. *Od.* xii. 101-10, 432-41). The unpleasant imagery stems from Homer and is particularly popular with Ovid; cf. *Ep.* 12. 125, *Rem.* 740, *Met.* xiii. 731.

25. **quae ... Charybdis:** *Charybdis* represents the object of *timeam* (v. 24), but it has been attracted into the case of the relative pronoun which is the subject of *fundit* and *receptat* (v. 26); cf. Verg. *A.* i. 71-3 *sunt mihi bis septem .... Nymphae, / quarum quae forma pulcherrima Deiopea, / conubio iungam*, *Am.* ii. 2. 4 with n., and see further Kühner-Stegmann II. ii. 289.
saturata: 'glutted', 'gorged'; this reinforces the digestive imagery.

26. **fundit ... effusas:** there is no appreciable difference between the two verbs here, and the variation is probably metrically motivated; cf. *Met.* xiii. 731, and see p. 13.
ore: this cleverly works with both the preceding *effusas* (as ablative of origin) and with the following *receptat* (as local ablative).
receptat: a frequentative form appropriate to the unceasing cycle of Charybdis' activity.

27-8. **si ... uincat et ... auferat:** a protasis eventually answered by *feremus* in v. 30. This combination of moods and tenses, which well represents a remote fancy becoming more vivid, is normal in Ovid (see 3. 12n.), but all our oldest MSS have corrupted the present subjunctives (see apparatus on p. 97), perhaps because of the 'complication here, introduced by the extra protasis in the imperative mood' (Kenney (1958a) 63), i.e. *impone* (v. 29) = *si impones*. Cf. the construction at *Am.* ii. 2. 40.

27. **Neptuni uentosa potentia:** for the concerted action of wind and sea see 11. 40n. *aestus*.

28. **subuenturos ... deos:** i.e. the images carried on a ship's stern; see 11. 44n. *subuenturos* = *qui subueniant* (generic); see 6. 36n.

29-30. Cf. *Am.* ii. 11. 45 with n., and see p. 81.

29. The word-order splendidly reflects the physical interlocking which Ovid envisages; cf. p. 16.

30. **corpore ... facili:** cf. *Ars* i. 160 *puluinum facili composuisse manu.*

31-2. Leander of Abydos was in the habit of swimming the Hellespont at night to join his beloved, Hero, in Sestos on the opposite shore. She held up a lamp to act as a beacon for him, until one stormy night the lamp blew out and he was drowned. Cf. *Ars* ii. 249 *saepe tua poteras, Leandre, carere puella; / tranabas, animum nosset ut illa tuum*, *Ep.* 17 (18) and 18 (19). The significance of Ovid's allusion to the story (for its structural function see p. 79) may lie in a hidden pun on *caeca* in v. 32 (see n.).
Hero: for the spelling see 2. 45n. *Io*.
iuuenis: the same word obliquely alludes to Leander at Verg. *G.* iii. 258.

32. **tum:** i.e. 'on the famous occasion when he drowned'; laconic, perhaps, but not at all obscure, in view of the evident popularity of the story in Ovid's time. This was perhaps due to the Augustans' 'discovery' of a Hellenistic poem on the subject, a fragment of which has now come to light (Lloyd-Jones and Parsons 901A; see further Thomas on Verg. *G.* iii. 258-63).

caeca: = 'unlit', and on the face of it just a reference to the lack of Hero's lamp on Leander's last journey (see 31-2n.), but I think *caeca* may suggest *sine igne*, and hence the pun which provides a satisfying contrast between Ovid's (imagined) situation and Leander's: Leander failed, where Ovid will succeed, because he lacked not just the 'flame' of his beloved's lamp (cf. *Ep.* 18 (19). 153), but also the 'flame' identifiable with the beloved herself (cf. vv. 11-12, and notice the puns on both *ignis* and *lumen* in Leander's own words at *Ep.* 17 (18). 85-6: *ut procul aspexi lumen, 'meus ignis in illo est: / illa meum' dixi 'litora lumen habent'*). That this would make nonsense of Leander's story – he would never have needed to cross the Hellespont anyway, if he *had* had with him the 'flame' I believe Ovid is thinking of – would simply add to the fun. But could Ovid's contemporary readers have been expected to 'see through' *caeca* to a hidden pun on *ignis*? Probably yes, if the Hellenistic poem on the Leander story which apparently became fashionable at this time (see previous n.) also contained such cleverness, and the *Hero and Leander* of the 5th century A.D. Greek poet Musaeus, who is thought to have used it extensively, suggests that it did; note especially vv. 239-41: ἀναπτομένοιο δὲ λύχνου / θυμὸν Ἔρως ἔφλεξεν ἐπειγομένοιο Λεάνδρου / λύχνῳ καιομένῳ συνεκαίετο ('when the lamp was set alight, Love inflamed the heart of Leander as he approached; he burned along with the burning lamp') – Musaeus did not use Ovid (see K. Kost, *Musaios: Hero und Leander* (Bonn, 1971), 19ff.). Virgil's allusion to Leander's exploit at *G.* iii. 258-63, with *nocte natat caeca ... freta* at 260, may have inspired Ovid to exploit *caeca* here. If I am right about its hidden double meaning, it retrospectively casts an interesting new light on Ovid's comment *cetera caeca uia est* at *Am.* ii. 11. 16: Corinna might not find the open sea *caeca* at all, if she had an *ignis* with her!

For the general notion of the disastrous consequences of isolation for the lover cf. *Rem.* 591-2.

33-8 The return to Sulmo is a timely reminder to the reader that all Ovid's heroic travelling is being contemplated from an armchair.

33. **operosi:** this is used here and at *Ars* i. 399 (*operosa ... arua)* of that which demands and receives much *opera*, at *Am.* ii. 7. 23 and 10. 5 of one who provides it.

34. **me teneant:** Ovid's inability to get away from Sulmo is reflected in the 'trapping' of this phrase (cf. 1n.) between the two *quamuis* clauses describing the area (see p. 16).

natent: the metaphor (cf. Verg. *G.* i. 372-2 *omnia plenis / rura natant fossis*) provides a link with the shipwreck motif which has preceded.

35. **riuos:** here = 'irrigation channels' but at Verg. *G.* i. 106 *satis fluuium inducit riuosque sequentis*, 'rivulets'.

rusticus: unlike Tibullus (see e.g. i. 8. 7-8, ii. 3. 5-10), Ovid is content to see the *work* of the countryside left to others.

36. Cooling breezes are a stock feature of the *locus amoenus*; see 1-10n.

mulceat: a favourite poetic word for the action of a beneficial breeze; cf. *Met.* 108 with Bömer's note.

comas: a very common poeticism for 'leaves'; cf. Prop. iii. 16. 28 with Fedeli's note.

37. **Paelignos:** for the plural see 1. 1n.

celebrare: 'inhabit'; the verb's implication of *regular* contact with a place or person is very much weakened in Ovid; cf. *Met.* x. 703 and (with a poignant echo of the present passage) *Tr.* iv. 8. 9-10 *et paruam celebrare domum* (*deberem*) *ueteresque Penates / et quae nunc domino rura paterna carent.*

38. **rura paterna:** not just Ovid's father's land, but land which has been in the family for generations; cf. *Tr.* iv. 8. 10 (cited 37n.), Hor. *Epod.* 2. 3). Note how the phrase is emotively 'embraced' by *natalem ... locum*; for such enclosed phrases in apposition see J. Solodow, '*Raucae, tua cura, palumbes*; study of a poetic word order', *HSPh* 90 (1986), 129-53, and cf. v. 44.

39. **Scythiam Cilicas ... Britannos:** all proverbially remote and uncivilised. Scythia, a region to the north-east of the Black Sea, was supposed to be intensely cold (see e.g. *Met.* i. 64 with Bömer's note, *Tr.* i. 3. 61 with Luck's note) and its people exceptionally warlike (see Curt. iv. 6. 3); Cilicia, a Roman province of Asia Minor, was synonymous with piracy (see e.g. Cic. *Ver.* 4. 21, Luc. iii. 228); and Britain was at the ends of the earth (see e.g. Hor. *Carm.* i. 35. 29 *ultimos orbis Britannos*, iv. 14. 47, Catul. 11. 11-12, 29. 4, Verg. *Ecl.* i. 66).

uiridesque: i.e. painted with woad; cf. Caes. *Gal.* v. 14. 3 *omnes uero se Britanni uitro inficiunt, quod caeruleum efficit colorem*, Mart. xi. 53. 1 *caerulei Britanni*.

40. An oblique reference to the Caucasus mountains, where Prometheus was chained by Zeus for an eagle to peck away his liver as a punishment for his restoration of fire to mankind (Aes. *PV* 7ff.). The allusion to his ghastly fate here highlights the proverbially barbaric nature of the Caucasus region (cf. Hor. *Carm.* i. 22. 6-7 with Nisbet-Hubbard's note). It also recalls Propertius' assertion at ii. 25. 14 that it might be easier to endure *Caucasias ... aues* than put up with his mistress: Ovid's answer is that *doing without* his mistress has made him feel as if he is keeping Prometheus company already. For the structural function of the mythological reference see p. 79.

saxa: cf. the prominence of 'rocks' in Propertius' unspecified place of isolation at i. 18. 4, 27, 32.

41. **amat ... non deserit:** a variation on the marriage language regularly used, both in poetry and in technical prose, of the training of vines on supports of elm; cf. Cato *Agr.* 32, Verg. *G.* i. 2 *ulmisque adiungere uitis* (with Thomas' note) and, in a simile illustrating marriage itself, Catul. 62. 54 (*uitis*) *ulmo coniuncta marito* (see further Nisbet-Hubbard II. 245). Ovid's artistic arrangement of words brings a little new life to the cliché here.

42. **saepe:** emphatic because of its position. All blame for the separation is now transferred to Ovid's mistress.

43. **at:** this expresses indignation; cf. *Ep.* 2. 45, and for the variously emotive use of the particle see Hand I. 440-42.

44. **oculos:** commonly invoked in oaths and entreaties; cf. *Am.* iii. 3. 9-10, 13-14, 11. 48, Prop. i. 15. 33-4. For lovers' oaths in particular see 8. 18-19n.

sidera nostra: cf. *Am.* iii. 3. 9 *radiant ut sidus ocelli*, *Ep.* 19 (20). 55-6 *oculique tui, quibus ignea cedunt / sidera*, Prop. ii. 3. 14 *oculi, geminae, sidera nostra, faces*, [Plat.] *AP* vii. 669. 1. Perhaps we are meant to recall the emphasis on lack of illumination in vv. 31-2: deprived of his 'stars', Ovid is emotionally as vulnerable as Leander was physically. For the enclosing of the phrase by *oculos tuos* see 37n. *rura paterna*.

45-6. **uerba puellarum ... uentus et unda ferunt:** cf. Prop. ii. 28. 8 *quidquid iurarunt* (*puellae*) *uentus et unda rapit*, and for the general sentiment, Catul. 70. 4, Call. *Epigr.* 25 (= *AP* v. 6), Soph. fr. 811 Radt; see also 6. 44n.

45. **foliis leuiora caducis:** this brings a welcome variation to the 'wind and water' motif (see previous n.); cf. *Ep.* 5. 109-10 *tu leuior foliis, tum cum sine pondere suci / mobilibus uentis arida facta uolant*, and see further Otto 140.

46. **irrita:** i.e. 'so that they become null and void'; cf. Catul. 30. 10 (with Kroll's note) and the parallel proleptic use of *uana* at *Am.* ii. 11. 32.

47. **mei ... relicti:** literally 'for me abandoned' (as, of course, Ovid has not been; *he* is the one who has gone away!); cf. *Pont.* ii. 7. 4 *si ... sit tibi cura mei*, [Tib.] iii. 17. 1 *estne tibi, Cerinthe, tuae pia cura puellae?*.

48. **pollicitis addere facta:** cf. *Ep.* 17 (18). 192 (Leander to Hero) *pignora polliciti non tibi tarda dabo.*

49-52. A skilful variation of Prop. iv. 8. 15-22 (see Neumann 14-17); cf. also Alciphr. iv. 18. 17 (see further p. 79).
esseda: poetic plural; the *essedum* was a two-wheeled carriage adapted from the war-chariot of the Gauls and Britons, and obviously suited to gadabout women; cf. Prop. ii. 32. 5.
mannis: Gallic ponies, specified not just to match the ethnic origin of Ovid's mistress' conveyance, but also because they were noted for their speed; cf. Lucr. iii. 1063, Prop. iv. 8. 15.

50. **ipsa:** see 11. 41-2n.
per admissas ... iubas: *per* is generally translated 'over', but the idea is perhaps of the violently shaken reins actually being brushed by the horses' streaming manes (for *admissas* cf. *Am.* i. 8. 50, ii. 11. 56). The unusual use of the preposition may have been prompted by Propertius' *ausa per impuros frena mouere locos* at iv. 8. 22.

51-2. The road to Sulmo must indeed have been dangerous because of steep gradients and numerous bends. As at *Am.* ii. 11. 39-40, therefore, Ovid calls for the physical world to ease his beloved's passage – only here it must even manage without any divine assistance, the mountains spontaneously flattening themselves and the roads co-operating (by straightening themselves out?) as she approaches.

52. **faciles:** both 'easily negotiable' and 'kind' (cf. 14. 43n.).
curuis uallibus: local ablative.

Poem 17 (18)

1. **turpe ... seruire puellae:** for the expression cf. *Am.* i. 3. 5 *accipe per longos tibi qui deseruiat annos* (and see p. 83), Tib. ii. 3. 33-4, Prop. iii. 15. 21. For the slavery metaphor see p. 82.

2. **illo conuincar iudice:** the phrase has the legalistic colour which appealed to Ovid (see p. 12, with n. 91); he is the only elevated poet other than Lucretius to admit *conuincere.*

3. **infamis:** this word, though not used technically here, also has legalistic colour (cf. previous n.), *infamia* being official 'disgrace', which incurred certain penalties (see Courtney on Juv. 1. 48, Berger s.v.). Ovid's equable acceptance of his notoriety here and pride in it at *Am.* iii. 1. 17-22 contrast sharply with Propertius' professed anxiety about *his* reputation at ii. 24. 1-10 and his fear that his love is to be compared with the *infamis amor* of Antony at ii. 16. 39.

3-6. For the plea for reasonable treatment and the sympathy of Venus cf. *Am.* i. 3. 1-4 (and see p. 83.).
moderatius urat: cf. *Ars* iii. 253 *Phyllida Demophoon praesens moderatius ussit.* Ovid found *moderatius* useful for hexameter-endings (6 of its 8 appearances in his work occupy the same position in the line as here); other poets avoid the adverb altogether. *urat* in the context of slavery perhaps suggests not only the usual 'burning' of love (see 1. 8n.) but also 'branding'; cf. Tib. i. 5. 5, and see Lyne (1979) 128.

4. **Paphon ... Cythera:** both Paphos, a city in S.W. Cyprus, and Cythera (neuter plural), an island in the Aegean S.W. of Cape Malea (see 16. 24n.), were both credited with being the birthplace of Venus/Aphrodite and were centres of her cult (see *Met.* x. 529-30 with Bömer's note, Hor. *Carm.* i. 30. 1 with Nisbet-Hubbard's note). The coupling of the two centres is a cliché; cf. Posidipp. (or Asclep.) *AP* v. 209 Παφίη Κυθέρεια ('Paphian lady of Cythera').

fluctu pulsa: this recalls Venus' supposed birth from the foam.

5. **dominae ... praeda:** here these words sustain the metaphor of slavery (cf. especially *Am.* i. 3. 1 *quae me nuper praedata puella est*, and see p. 83), but for *domina* in general see 1. 17n.

mitis: cf. Prop. ii. 20. 20 *posset seruitium mite tenere tuum.*

6. **formosae:** see 10. 5-7n.

7-9. **dat facies animos ... :** for the frequent haughtiness (*animos ... fastus*) of attractive women directly attributed to their awareness of their physical beauty (*facies*; see 3. 13n.) cf. *Ars* iii. 103, Prop. iii. 8. 35-6; for a variation see Prop. iii. 25. 11-16.

uiolenta: probably 'cruel' or 'callous' in general (cf. *Ep.* 3. 61 *cui me, uiolente, reliquis?*), though physical aggression may be in Ovid's mind (cf. *Am.* ii. 7. 7).

8. The rhythm and sentence structure echo *Am.* ii. 5. 8; cf. also *Ep.* 16 (17). 37. The elegiac poet himself must bear some responsibility for a girl's consciousnessness or over-estimation of her good looks; see e.g. Prop. iii. 24. 1-8.

10. **compositam:** i.e. having completed her toilette; for the expression cf. *Met.* iv. 317-18 *nec tamen ante adiit ... / quam se composuit*, and for the underlying sentiment, *Ars* iii. 105 *cura dabit faciem.* Coiffure rather than make-up is probably what Ovid has in mind, for *componere* is frequently attested of the former (though usually with *capillos, crines* etc.; see *ThLL* III. 2114. 65ff.), but never of the latter.

11. **regni:** here 'power' in general (cf. *Met.* xiv. 20 *siue aliquid regni est in carmine*), not 'sway' over a lover (see 9B. 52-3n.).

12. **o facies ... nata:** a parenthetical exclamation (not an 'extended vocative'; so Goold (1965a) 32), closely echoed at [Ov.] *Ep. Sapph.* 22 *o facies oculis insidiosa meis*. For *nata* cf. Prop. ii. 22. 4 *o nimis exitio nata theatra meo*, and see 5. 4n.

13. **idcirco:** a somewhat prosaic word (see Bömer on *Met.* xi. 449, Axelson 80, n. 67) in keeping with the poem's analytical veneer.

14. A variation on the proverbial likening of small to great (see e.g. *Met.* v. 416-17 *quodsi componere magnis / parua mihi fas est*, with Bömer's note, Otto 204-5). The juxtaposition of *magnis* and *inferiora* (which reflects that of *tibi* and *me* in the hexameter) is paralleled in many of the other examples of the motif (see also p. 16, with n. 125).

15-20. Cf. *Am.* ii. 8. 11-14, where heroic *exempla* are used to justify *Ovid's* condescension.

15-17. **traditur ... creditur:** no distinction is intended.

15. **nymphe:** this (= Greek nominative νύμφη) is often a metrically convenient alternative to *nympha* and is preferred by Ovid; cf. *Met.* i. 744 with Bömer's note.

15-16. **Calypso ... recusantem uirum:** the nymph Calypso was so smitten with Odysseus that she kept him on her island of Ogygia (Hom. *Od.* i. 13-15) for 7 years; all to no avail, however, since Odysseus remained unseduced by her condescension, and on Zeus' orders she had to release him (*Od.* v. 1-261).

16. **detinuisse:** Ovid makes Odysseus' detention sound agreeably diverting at *Ars* ii. 125-42.

17. The interwoven word-order wittily reflects the coupling of the goddess and the mortal; cf. p. 16.

aequoream ... Nereida: i.e. Thetis. The expression echoes Catullus in his poem on Thetis' marriage to Peleus (64. 15); for Thetis' condescension cf. especially Catul. 64. 20 *tum Thetis humanos non despexit hymenaeos*. For the Nereids see 11. 36n.

Pthio ... regi: P(h)thia was a city in Thessaly, where Peleus settled after being banished from his native Aegina because of his murder of his half-brother Phocus (see Apollod. iii. 160); Homer speaks of it as his home (see e.g. *Il.* ix. 393-400). The non-aspirated spelling *Pthio* is authenticated by W. Schulze, *Orthographica* (Marburg, 1894), 49-52; see also U. Knoche, *Gnomon* 8 (1932), 520.

18. **Egeriam ... Numae:** Numa Pompilius, the second legendary king of Rome, was reputedly advised on legal and constitutional matters by the nymph Egeria, whom he used to meet by night in a wood (see Liv. i. 21. 3). According to some accounts she became his wife or mistress (*Fast.* iii. 275, *Met.* xv. 482 with Bömer's note, Juv 3. 12-16).

iusto: Numa was credited with enlightened religious and legal reforms; see Liv. i. 18. 1 *incluta iustitia religioque ea tempestate Numae Pompilii erat.*

concubuisse: see 8. 6n. For the construction with the dative cf. *Fast.* vi. 574, Prop. ii. 15. 16.

19-20. Venus/Aphrodite's marriage to Vulcan/Hephaistos, the blacksmith-god, was less than idyllic: despising his lameness (apparently a congenital deformity; see Hom. *Il.* xviii. 394-7), she cuckolded him, but he caught her in a specially designed net *in flagrante delicto* with Mars (see *Ars* ii. 561-94, Hom. *Od.* viii. 266ff.).

incude relicta / turpiter ... claudicet: Ovid's words recall Hom. *Il.* xviii. 410-11 ἦ καὶ ἀπ' ἀκμυθέτοιο πέλωρ αἴετον ἀνέστη / χωλεύων ('And he raised his outlandish bulk from the anvil-block, limping').

pede: mention of Vulcan's odd foot leads easily to the odd numbers of metrical feet in the two lines of the elegiac couplet (see next n.).

21. **impar:** the unmatched nature of elegiac lines is Ovid's favourite mode of oblique reference to the genre (cf. *Am.* i. 1. 1-2, iii. 1. 37, 66 *Ars* i. 264, *Tr.* ii. 220, and see J. C. Thibault, 'A difference of metaphor between Propertius and Ovid' in *Classical Studies presented to B. E. Perry* (Urbana, 1969), 31-7). This points to Ovid's preoccupation with technique rather than emotion.

21-2. **apte / iungitur:** cf. *Am.* iii. 1, where Ovid says of the personified Elegy *pes illi longior alter erat* (v. 7) and *pedibus uitium causa decoris erat* (v. 10). Enjambement (see p. 15) neatly reflects the notion of 'coupling'.

22. **herous:** sc. *modus*, i.e. the hexameter; cf. *Fast* ii. 125-6 *quid uolui ... elegis imponere tantum / ponderis? heroi res erat ista pedis.*

23. **mea lux:** a standard elegiac term of endearment (but avoided by Tibullus); cf. *Am.* i. 4. 25, Catul. 68. 132, 160, Prop. ii. 14. 29; Pichon collects further references s.v. (cf. 15. 21n. *mea uita*).

in quaslibet ... leges: for the construction cf. Pl. *As.* 234-5 (a young man buying a prostitute) *in leges meas / dabo* (*quod poscis*), *ut scire possis, perpetuom annum hunc mihi uti seruiat,* and for the *leges* of *seruitium amoris* imposed by the elegiac mistress on her lover cf. *Am.* i. 8. 70 *captos legibus ure tuis*, Prop. iv. 7. 74-81.

accipe: cf. *Am.* i. 3. 5 (and see p. 83).

24. **iura:** here virtually synonymous with *leges*: 'rules', 'conditions'. For the *iura* of servitude proper cf. *Met.* xv. 596-7 *quem uobis indicat augur /... / famularia iura daturum*, and of *seruitium amoris*, *Am.* i. 2. 20, iii. 11. 2, *Ep.* 15 (16).. 322, Prop. i. 9. 3, iii. 11. 2.

te deceat ... dedisse: literally 'let it be proper for you to impose ...', i.e. I concede that it is your place to impose ...'; for the tense see 4. 22n..

medio ... foro: 'in public'; cf. *Pont.* i. 7. 30, Tib. i. 2. 96, Prop. iii. 9. 24. The phrase apparently reaffirms Ovid's indifference to notoriety as one *qui seruit puellae* (cf. vv. 1-3), but see pp. 82-3. *medio ... toro*, the variant which some prefer (see apparatus on p. 98), is at first sight easier, but lacks point.

25-6. For the ambiguous reference of this couplet see p. 82.

25. **non tibi crimen ero:** for *crimen* of a person = 'a (source of) disgrace' cf. *Am.* ii. 18. 37, iii. 7. 4, Prop. iii. 19. 15. Ovid's claim (cf. *Am.* i. 3. 13 *sine crimine mores)* is utterly disingenuous in respect of his amatory behaviour (see especially *Am.* ii. 4), more reasonable in respect of his poetry (cf. *Am.* i. 3. 20 *prouenient causa carmina digna sua*, Gallus fr. 4. 1-2 Büchner *c[ar]mina .../quae possem domina deicere digna mea*).

nec quo laetere remoto: contrast Propertius' explicit threat to use his elegy to vilify Cynthia at ii. 5. 17-30.

26. **infitiandus:** a legalistic word = 'deny', 'repudiate'; see Berger s.v., Courtney on Juv. 13. 60. Ovid, who is the only Augustan poet to admit it (10 instances in all), was perhaps prompted to it here (where it is non-technical) by the loosely juristic imagery of vv. 1-3 (see further p. 12, with n. 91).

27. **sunt mihi ... felicia carmina:** the trump card of the proverbially 'poor' elegiac poet; cf. *Am.* i. 3. 7-12, 10. 59-60, Prop. iii. 2. 11-16. *felicia* suggests both abundance and appropriateness, and echoes *Am.* i. 3. 19 *te mihi materiem felicem in carmina praebe* (see p. 83).

censu: 'material wealth'; cf. *Ars* iii. 55 *dat census honores*, *Fast.* i. 217 with Bömer's note.

28. **per me nomen habere:** there is a play here on *nomen* = 'fame' and = 'name': what *multae* want (but will never get!) is the 'fame' of being recognised as the real woman behind the 'name' in Ovid's poetry. For the elegiac poet's awareness of his special form of power cf. *Am.* i. 10. 60 *quam uolui nota fit arte mea*, i. 3. 25-6, 15. 29-30, Tib. i. 4. 65-6, Prop. ii. 5. 5-6, 25. 3-4, 34. 93-4, iii. 2. 17-18. It can, of course, work to his disadvantage: see e.g. *Am.* iii. 11. 19-20, 12. 5-8.

29-30. Cf. *Ars* iii. 538 *et multi quae sit nostra Corinna rogant*, *Tr.* iv. 10. 60 (cited 34n.), and see p. 83. The pentameter's spondaic opening well conveys the note of longing.

29. **circumferat:** prosaic in this sense; see *ThLL* III. 1142. 53ff.

30. **quid non ... dedisse uelit:** no doubt Ovid has something special in mind: if 'praising a girl's beauty' often brings the poet 'the girl herself' (*Am.* ii. 1. 33-4), might not the *prospect* of his doing so prove equally efficacious (cf. Prop. ii. 34. 55-8)? For the tense of *dedisse* see 4. 22n.

31-4. It is just as impossible for any other girl besides Corinna to be celebrated in Ovid's love-poetry as it is for two rivers, widely separated and completely different in character, to run in the same bed. The comparison was no doubt prompted by the common use of river, stream and spring imagery to represent the source from which Greek and Roman poets draw their inspiration or subject-matter; see e.g. Call. *Ap.* 107-12, Prop. iii. 1. 3, 6, 3. 5-6, 13-16, 51-2 with Fedeli's notes.

nec ... nec: the most common formulation of comparative *adynaton* ('impossibility'; cf. 1. 26n.) is 'Sooner will X (which is contrary to nature) happen than Y materialise' (more examples in Brandt's note on *Ars* i. 271), and Ovid's double negative formulation is both unusual and artistically engineered: note the separation of *diuersi* from *eadem* in v. 31 followed by the close coupling of the two rivers in v. 32, and the embellishment of the second with the high-flown and alliterating *populifer* (cf. 13. 10n.).

31. **ripa ... eadem:** local ablative; *ripa* is collective singular and therefore = 'bed'.

labuntur: see 16. 9n.

32. **frigidus Eurotas:** the river on which Sparta stood. It was said, presumably because of its invigorating quality, to toughen up Spartan youth (see Sen. *Suas.* ii. 5).

populifer: this adjective appears only in Ovid (for the formation see p. 13). Poplars do indeed adorn the Po valley (Ovid tells the story of their provenance at *Met.* ii. 340ff.), but their association with rivers is an Ovidian cliché; see *Met.* i. 579 *populifer Sperchios*, *Rem.* 141, *Fast.* ii. 465.

33. **cantabitur:** the standard term for celebration in verse; cf. *Am.* i. 3. 25, 15. 13, iii. 11. 19, *Tr.* ii. 427.

libellis: see 11. 31-2n.

34. The elegiac poet's claim that his *puella* is his inspiration is conventional (cf. *Am.* i. 3. 19, *Tr.* iv. 10. 59-60 *mouerat ingenium totam cantata per urbem / nomine non uero dicta Corinna mihi,* Tib. ii. 5. 111-12, Prop. ii. 1. 4, 30. 40), but Ovid is unusual in insisting on assigning this role to one girl for all time; cf. *Am.* iii. 12. 16 *ingenium mouit sola Corinna meum.* For *ingenium* see 18. 11n.

Poem 18 (19)

1-4. Cf. Prop. i. 7. 1-6 *Dum tibi Cadmeae dicuntur, Pontice, Thebae / armaque fraternae tristia militiae, / ... / ... / nos, ut consuemus, nostros agitamus amores, / atque aliquid duram quaerimus in dominam.* See further p. 87.

1-2. The *carmen* in question was obviously an epic dealing with the beginnings of the Trojan War (*prima ... arma*) and its conduct up to the point at which the *Iliad* starts (*ad iratum ... Achillem*; cf. Hom. *Il.* i. 1 Μῆνιν ἄειδε, θεά, ...' Ἀχιλῆος / οὐλομένην, 'Sing, Muse, of the destructive wrath of Achilles'). See also 37-8n., Hinds (1998), 115-16.

1. **perducis:** 'take as far as'; for this sense cf. Quint. *Inst.* i. pr. 6.

Achillem: the most common accusative form of *Achilles*, though *Achillen* is also found. See further Housman *JPh* 31 (1910), 259-60 [= *Classical Papers* 834-5].

2. **iuratis:** either (a) the oath sworn by the supporters of Agamemnon not to return home until Troy had been sacked (Hom. *Il.* ii. 286-8; cf. *Ars* i. 687-8, Verg. *A.* iv. 425, Hor. *Carm.* i. 15. 7 with Nisbet-Hubbard's note), or (b) the oath extracted from Helen's suitors by her father Tyndareus binding them to assist and defend the conjugal rights of whichever of them was chosen to be her husband (see e.g. Eur. *IA* 51ff., and see further Bömer on *Met.* xii. 6).

induis arma uiris: Ovid identifies Macer with the cause which is his theme (cf. his own stance at *Am.* ii. 1. 11-18). *induere arma alicui* may also be used purely figuratively for 'bring someone to go to war'; see e.g. Liv. xxx. 31. 4.

3. **Macer:** the poet who is called *Iliacus ... Macer* at *Pont.* iv. 16. 6, and whose epic on the Trojan War is mentioned again at *Pont.* ii. 10. 13-14. Ovid names him as a relative of his third wife (*Pont.* ii. 10. 10) and a friend with whom he travelled to Asia Minor and Sicily in his youth (*ibid.* 21-8). Almost certainly he was Pompeius Macer, the son of Theophanes of Mytilene, author of two epigrams in the *Greek Anthology* (*AP* vii. 219, ix. 28) and reputedly appointed procurator of Asia and overseer of libraries in Rome by Augustus (see further Syme (1978) 73 and Bertini's note on the present line; Green (26-8) challenges this identification, as does P. White, ' "Pompeius Macer" and Ovid', *CQ* n.s. 42 (1992), 210-18). Perhaps it is the same Macer whose desertion of *Amor* for *castra* (i.e. 'love-poetry for epic'?) Tibullus regrets at ii. 6. 1 (cf. 39-40n., and see Bright 217ff.). See also p. 87.

ignaua Veneris ... in umbra: *umbra* is regularly connected with the poetic as opposed to the civil or military life (cf. *Ars* iii. 542 *contempto colitur* (sc. *a poetis*) *lectus et umbra foro*, Hor. *Ep.* ii. 2. 77-8, Mart. ix. 84. 3), and see P. L. Smith, '*Lentus in umbra*: a symbolic pattern in Virgil's *Eclogues*, *Phoenix* 19 (1965), 298-304. At *Am.* i. 9. 42, *mollierant animos lectus et umbra meos*, Ovid connects it also with the life of love, and here, coupling it with *Veneris* and contrasting it with Macer's sphere of activity, he further associates it with love-*poetry* (elegy) as opposed to war-poetry (epic). The word also suggests avoidance of the limelight (cf. Prop. iii. 9. 29 (to Maecenas) *in tenuis humilem te colligis umbram*) and hence Ovid's shunning of the more ambitious poetic genres. For the love-poet's alleged *ignauia* cf. *Am.* i. 15. 1, Prop. ii. 30. 25.

cessamus: 'relax, do nothing'; *cessare* is also used of dalliance with elegy at *Am* iii. 1. 24: *cessatum satis est; incipe maius opus!* (i.e. a tragedy). The word conjures up the elegiac lover's life of *otium,* with all its pejorative social and moral connotations; cf. Prop. iii. 23. 15-16, and see L. Alfonsi, 'Otium e uita d'amore negli elegiaci augustei', *Studi Calderini e Paribeni* I (Milan, 1956), 187-209, Fränkel 8-10).

4. A *recusatio* (see p. 24) in brief; new slants on the full-blown motif come in the next 14 lines.

tener: a conventional epithet of *Amor*; cf. 19 below, *Am.* iii. 15. 1, *Ars* i. 7, Tib. ii. 6. 1, and see 1. 4n.

ausuros grandia: a deliberately imprecise expression, intended to cover both attempts at high-flown poetry described in vv. 5-18.

frangit: cf. *Tr.* iii. 14. 33 *ingenium fregere meum mala,* with Luck's note, Prop. ii. 34. 34, iii. 21. 33.

Amor: both the god (recalling especially *Am.* i. 1), and the emotion (recalling more loosely *Am.* ii. 1); see also 15n.

5. For the fragmented direct speech cf. 9B. 25n.

tandem: an idiomatic expression of impatience; cf. Cic. *Catil.* i. 1 *quo usque tandem abutere, Catilina, patientia nostra?.*

6. **in gremio sedit:** cf. 2. 62n.

7-8. **pudet ... amare pudet:** Ovid leaves the cause of his shame unspecified, but his girl-friend mischievously suggests one which she knows will strike at his Achilles' heel of susceptibility to her charms.

me miseram: this, beginning the line on 39 other occasions, is one of Ovid's favourite exclamations, and is probably to be taken as an exclamation here too (cf. *Tr.* iv. 3. 52 *me miseram, si te iam pudet esse meam*), though it is tempting to understand it as the object of *amare* (so e.g. Lee and Green in their respective translations); perhaps we should not rule out a two-way construction (this phenomenon in Latin poetry may often be obscured by the conventions of modern punctuation; see G. B. Townend, 'Virgil Unpunctuated' in *Meminisse iuuabit*, ed. F. Robertson (Bristol, 1988), 128-39).

9-10. Cf. Catul. 35. 8-10: 'Tell Caecilius to come to Verona', says Catullus '*quamuis candida milies puella / euntem reuocet, manusque collo / ambas iniciens roget morari*'.

10. **oscula mille dedit:** the exaggeration recalls the famous Catul. 5. 7-9 (*da mi basia mille...*). For Ovid's appreciation of kiss-treatment cf. *Am.* ii. 5. 51ff., 19. 18.

11-12. **uincor ... reuocatur ... cano:** all historic presents (rare in the *Amores*; see M. von Albrecht, '*Qua arte narrandi Ouidius in Amoribus usus sit*' in *Ouidianum. Acta conuentus omnium gentium Ouidianis studiis fouendis*, edd. N. Barbu, E. Dobroiu and M. Nasta (Bucharest, 1976), 57-63). They indicate that Ovid returned to love-poetry under the influence of his mistress *on numerous separate occasions in the past* (note *saepe* in vv. 5 and 7). In the real present (or thereabouts; see 19n.), as he tells us in vv. 19-26, he is writing amatory didactic (see 19-20n.) and elegiac love-letters – not poems about his 'personal wars'. The military metaphor is sustained in both *uincor* and *reuocatur*, the latter being regularly used of recalling troops from battle.

sumptis ... armis: for *arma* symbolising the epic genre cf. *Am.* i. 1. 1-2 *arma ... uiolentaque bella parabam / edere,* Prop. iii. 1. 7 with Fedeli's note. The expression here suggests that Ovid had actually begun an epic, rather than merely thought about beginning one, when he was distracted. But if he had, it probably did not amount to much (see 1. 11-16n.).

ingenium: 'genius', 'poetic talent'; cf. *Am.* ii. 17. 34.

12. **resque domi gestas:** i.e. *res amatorias*. The phrase is mischievously full of respectable resonance; cf. *Met*. xv. 748 (with Bömer's note), where it is used of the civil as opposed to military achievements of Julius Caesar.

bella: sc. *amoris*; cf. *Am*. i. 9. 45 *nocturna ... bella*, and see pp. 53-4. We may be meant to recall the *bella* proper intended for poetic treatment at *Am*. i. 1. 1 (cited 11n. above).

13. **sceptra:** poetic plural; the *sceptrum* here stands for the subject-matter of tragedy (royal houses and their sagas), just as *arma* stands for epic (see 11n.). Cf. *Am*. iii. 1. 13, 63.

13-14. **tragoedia ... creuit:** the exact meaning of this is not certain. However, we may observe: (a) that Ovid regularly uses the perfect active of *crescere* in an absolute sense with reference to things which have grown up (i.e. come into being) or grown bigger, but have not necessarily stopped growing; Fränkel (77) cites *Met*. i. 304 *ubi creuerunt* (of stones *in the process of* being transformed into human beings), and cf. also *Met*. i. 419-21 *semina rerum / uiuaci nutrita solo ceu matris in aluo / creuerunt*, iii. 415 *sitis altera creuit*, *Fast*. i. 211 *creuerunt et opes et opum furiosa cupido*, iii. 446 (*farra*) *quae male creuerunt*, *Tr*. iv. 2. 9 *creuit et aucta mora est*; (b) that the high-flown poems referred to in any sort of *recusatio* (and vv. 15-18 have much in common with that motif; see p. 24), are always – naturally – incomplete; and (c) that there are no parallels for *crescere* being used of literary composition other than with reference to a single work or part thereof (see e.g. *Tr*. v. 9. 3-4 *inque libellis / creuisset sine te pagina nulla meis,* with Luck's note, Stat. *Silv*. iii. 5. 6 *cumque tuis creuit mea Thebais annis*, Plin. *Ep*. ii. 5. 3 *liber creuit*). These factors make it more likely that Ovid is pointing to a single, substantially-advanced, but still incomplete, play (cf. Cameron 332, Luck (1970) 477-8, Sabot 73, with n. 92; Jacobson (308, with n. 24) heads those who argue for a *finished* work) rather than to the genre of tragedy, enhanced by his own (necessarily complete) contribution (Sabot documents support for the latter view at 72, nn. 90, 91). There is a chance that the said play is largely fictitious, but more probably it is the lost *Medea* (see pp. 86-7). And, whatever the truth, a claim here to have ventured into tragedy contributes to the maze of problems concerning the dating and arrangement of the *Amores*; see further pp. 2-4.

13. **curaque ... nostra:** causal ablative and an agricultural metaphor which complements *creuit* (*cura* is the attention required by crops and stock; see Verg. *G*. i. 3, iii. 124, 138 and 157 with Thomas' notes). *nostra*, between the singulars *sumpsi* and *eram* is merely a metrically convenient poetic plural.

14. **operi:** 'genre'; cf. Hor. *S*. ii. 1. 1-2 *sunt quibus in satira uidear nimis acer et ultra / legem tendere opus*, Quint. *Inst*. x. 1. 69 *hunc* (i.e. *Euripidem*) *... secutus, quamquam in opere diuerso*.

quamlibet aptus: literally 'suited as much as you like', i.e. 'ever so much suited'; cf. Plin. *Nat*. xxxvi. 22. 45 *specularis lapis finditur in quamlibet tenues crustas*. *quamlibet* intensifies Ovid's customary claim to unlimited poetic ability (see p. 25), and on the evidence of his *Medea* Tacitus (*Dial*. 12) and Quintilian (*Inst*. x. 1. 98) confirm his flair for tragedy. Ovid is the first extant writer to use *quamlibet* adverbially with any freedom (18 times), but, like his successors, he does so mostly in a concessive sense, i.e. 'no matter how (much)'.

15. **risit Amor:** this recalls Love's laughter in the similar circumstances of *Am*. i. 1. 3 (*risisse Cupido dicitur*). It does not necessarily imply mockery of Ovid's writing in itself, but of his belief that he is free to write what he likes; it indicates that 'I'll show you!' is Love's intention. *Amor* here = the god, but in v. 18 both the god and the emotion. Cf. vv. 4, 19, 36nn., and see also 1. 3n.

pallam ... cothurnos: the floor-length cloak (σύρμα) and built-up boots which were regarded as the conventional, dignifying garb of the tragic actor (though there is doubt about when they were actually introduced to the stage; see Brink's notes on Hor. *Ars* 278 and 280). Here they are attributed (together with the sceptre) to the tragic playwright as symbols of his status (cf. *Am.* iii. 1. 63), and at *Am.* iii. 1. 12-14 and 31 to the personified figure of Tragedy herself.

pictosque: nowhere else except at *Am.* iii. 1. 31 is the *tragic* buskin described as 'painted' or 'coloured', and Ovid may be unconsciously thinking of the red or purple *cothurni* apparently worn for hunting; see Verg. *Ecl.* 7. 32, *A.* i. 337.

15-16. **- que ... -que ... -que:** see 9B. 50n.

16. **sceptraque priuata ... sumpta manu:** as kingly accoutrements symbolise tragedy, so the status of private citizen symbolises love-elegy. This (unique) image is a nod in the direction of the traditional hierarchy of the genres, in which tragedy (with epic) is at the top and elegy lower down (the juxtaposition of *sceptra* and *priuata* paradoxically draws attention to the artistic gap between the two; cf. p. 16), but it is not an admission of effrontery, for Ovid has already said that he has what it takes to write tragedy. See also next n.

cito: not 'early' in Ovid's poetic career (so Munari, Bertini and others), but 'easily', 'with little trouble' (cf. *Ep.* 12. 92, *Pont.* ii. 4. 25). The poet's very facility for changing genres has alerted Love of the need to recapture him for elegy. The variant *bene* (see apparatus on p. 98), which gives good sense, may have originated as a scribal gloss.

17. **hinc quoque:** i.e. from tragedy as well as from epic (vv. 11-12).

dominae: see 1. 17n.

numen: 'divine power'; this, here uniquely attributed to a human being, helps to identify *Amor* with *amor* (cf. 4n.) – the mocking god with a disgruntled mistress' source of power.

iniquae: i.e. 'unsympathetic' towards Ovid's flirtation with non-erotic poetry (cf. vv. 5-8 and *Am.* ii. 1. 11-18). For *iniquus* in this sense cf. *Met.* ix. 476, *Fast.* ii. 626.

18. **de ... uate triumphat Amor:** this recalls Cupid's deflation of the self-styled *uates* (see 1. 34n.) at *Am.* i. 1. 21-6 (cf. 4n.). For *Amor* see 15n. For the expression cf. Prop. ii. 8. 40 *si de me iure triumphat Amor.*

cothurnato: the adjective is first attested in Ovid; cf. *Fast.* v. 348 with Bömer's note.

19-20. Coming from a poet who wrote an *Ars Amatoria*, who uses the terms *ars* and *artes* frequently to refer to it (or to the related *Remedia Amoris*) and who elsewhere uses *praecepta* and its cognates only within and of the eroto-didactic poems (see Jacobson 309-10), the present couplet looks like the clearest possible reference to the *Ars*. And if it does refer to that work – or part of it (see 19n. *profitemur*) – then this poem was almost certainly written specially for the second edition of the *Amores* (see pp. 2-4). Some argue that the reference here is not to the *Ars* but to the *Amores*, on the grounds that they too contain erotic *praecepta* and elements of *ars* (see e.g. D'Elia 215-16, Cameron (1968) 332, Sabot 74-6, and for slightly different grounds Holzberg (1997b) 13). The very next poem, 19, is in fact a good example of this, but erotodidaxis is a relatively minor aspect of the *Amores* as a whole, and it is hard to see why Ovid should choose to characterise the entire collection by referring to it.

quod licet: literally '(that) which is allowed'; this covers the two alternatives (*aut ... profitemur ... aut ... scribimus)* spelled out in 19-26.

19. **teneri ... Amoris:** the adjective suggests the god, the context the emotion; cf. 15n.

profitemur: the word implies that Ovid is a professional instructor; cf. Cic. *Brut.* 48 *Lysiam primo profiteri solitum artem esse dicendi.* The present tense here (and in *scribimus*, v. 22) need not be taken absolutely literally: 'now' for a writer often relates not strictly to the present time, but more loosely to his latest period of composition (e.g. 'Now I'm writing novels' may well mean 'The last thing I wrote was a novel, and I intend to go on writing novels'). So Ovid could well be at a point where he has written *Ars* i and ii and some or all of the 'single' *Epistles*, and has more of each (*Ars* iii and either more 'single' or the 'double' *Epistles)* planned or under way; see further pp. 3-4.

20. I think this must be intended, like the announcement of Sabinus' replies to some of the 'single' *Epistles* in vv. 27-34, to show that poetry of Ovid's already in circulation (almost certainly a part of the *Ars*; see 19-20n.) had been 'taken up' in some way by its readers (probably he means that the young bloods 'instructed' by him are now beating him at his own game; for the general notion cf. *Am.* i. 4. 46, Tib. i. 6. 10 and see p. 38). Otherwise the complaint seems pointless here. *Am.* ii. 19. 34, given its clearer contextual relevance, was probably the model for this line (excessive 'love of neatness' has tempted some copyists at both points to rationalise the choice of verb; see apparatus on p. 98), but the effect of having Ovid's complaint here that he *is* suffering from his own advice closely echoed in the following poem by the wish that he may not do so is rather odd (despite the probably different sense at 19. 34; see n. *ad loc.* and p. 11). For *urgere* = 'cause pain' in an amatory context cf. *Am.* i. 2. 17, *Met.* ix. 624, Tib. ii. 1. 79.

ei mihi: see 3. 1n.

ipse meis: formulaic; see 6. 55n.

21-34. See p. 86.

21. This refers to *Ep.* 1, written by Penelope *(Penelopes* is genitive = Πηνελόπης).

reddatur: a word regularly used of 'delivering' letters or parcels (cf. *Tr.* iv. 7. 10), which encapsulates the genre of the *Heroides.*

22. This refers to *Ep.* 2, from the Thracian princess Phyllis, to Demophoon, son of Theseus, who fell in love with her on his way back from Troy, promising, on his departure for Cyprus, to return and marry her. Phyllis, after waiting long in vain (but cf. 32n.), finally despaired and hanged herself. Her story had been treated by Callimachus (fr. 556; see further E. Rohde, *Der griechische Roman und seine Vorlaüfer* (3rd edn., Leipzig, 1914) 39, n. 3, 504, n. 2), and it particularly appealed to Ovid (cf. *Ars* ii. 353, iii. 37-8, *Rem.* 591-608).

23. **Paris:** the addressee of *Ep.* 5, from the Idan nymph Oenone, and also of *Ep.* 16 (17), from Helen; but 5 is what Ovid has in mind here, for 16 (17) belongs to the collection of 'double' *Epistles* and answers 15 (16), a letter from Paris himself. After abandoning Oenone for the escapade with Helen, Paris was wounded by the poisoned arrow of the Greek hero Philoctetes and sought Oenone's help; but she could not give it in time to prevent his death (see Apollod. iii. 154-5).

Macareus: son of Aeolus, king of the winds, and the addressee of *Ep.* 11, from his sister Canace, with whom he committed incest. In Ovid's epistle Canace never charges him with desertion, but it is clear that she is the one who is bearing the brunt of their father's rage, for, having forced her to surrender her child by Macareus to a horrible death, he has ordered her to kill herself. The story was treated in Euripides' lost *Aeolus*; cf. *Tr.* ii. 384 with Luck's note.

male gratus Iason: Jason (for the spelling *Iason* see 2. 45n.), leader of the Argonauts (see 11. 1-6n.), is the addressee of both *Ep.* 6, from Hypsipyle, Queen of Lemnos, and *Ep.* 12, from the witch Medea, daughter of the king of Colchis. Line 33 makes it clear that Ovid is here referring to *Ep.* 6, where Hypsipyle condemns Jason's desertion of her for Medea as poor return for the hospitable reception and sexual gratification she gave him (he fathered twin sons by her) when the Argonauts landed on Lemnos – and certainly he did unexpectedly well, given that the Lemnian women had just murdered all their own menfolk, with the exception of Hypsipyle's father, whom she had secretly saved (see Ap. Rhod. i. 609-909, Prop. i. 15. 17-20; the story also seems to have featured in some lost Greek tragedies, including a *Hypsipyle* by Euripides and a *Lemniae* by Sophocles). Mention of Jason's ingratitude, however, suggests that Ovid is also thinking of his infamous behaviour towards Medea, who sacrificed the affection and company of her family for love of him (see especially *Ep.* 12. 105-12), only to be in her turn abandoned by him for a rival. But this does not necessarily indicate that *Ep.* 12 was already in existence.

24. For the phraseology cf. *Am.* ii. 11. 36.

Hippolytique parens: i.e. Theseus, the addressee of *Ep.* 10, from the Cretan princess Ariadne, whom, according to some versions of the myth, he abandoned on the island of Naxos after she, like Medea, had helped her lover at the expense of her kin (see especially Catul. 64. 52-250, and cf: *Ars* iii. 35-6, *Fast.* iii. 459 with Bömer's note).

Hippolytus: the addressee of *Ep.* 4, from his stepmother Phaedra, whose love for him appals him, both as her stepson and as a devotee of the virgin goddess Artemis (cf. *Am.* ii. 4. 32, *Met.* xv. 497-9 with Bömer's note; the fullest surviving treatments of the story are Euripides' *Hippolytus* and Seneca's *Phaedra*).

25. Dido, victim of the most celebrated desertion in Latin literature (in Verg. *A.* iv) and the one non-Greek correspondent in the *Heroides*, is the writer of *Ep.* 7. Ovid logically reserves *his* Dido's pleading for a stage in the story at which Virgil's has relatively little to say: the point at which she holds Aeneas' sword, ready to kill herself (*A.* iv. 645-62).

tenens ... ensem: possibly understand *in gremio*, as Ovid specifies at *Ep.* 7. 184, rather than *manu*; however, the phrase is perhaps not to be taken literally at all, but simply as an indication that Dido's letter is a suicide note (so Goold (1965a) 42; see also 26n.).

miserabilis: a significant departure from the awesome Virgilian *infelix*, 'ill-starred', characterising the Ovidian Dido (also at *Fast.* iii. 545) as a woman simply unhappy in love (cf. *Ars* i. 737 *ut uoto potiare tuo, miserabilis esto*) rather than the tragic victim of god and circumstance. The adjective has close associations with the elegiac genre (see Thomas on Verg. *G.* iv. 514), and, interestingly, the bereaved singer Orpheus is the only person of whom Virgil uses it (*G.* iv. 454).

26. **Aoniam Lesbis †amata† lyram:** almost certainly the unacceptable readings offered by the MSS (full apparatus on p. 98) have their ultimate origin in the accidental substitution, at a pre-archetypal stage in the tradition, of the ending of v. 34 (which also concerns 'the Lesbian', i.e. the 7th-century B.C. Greek lyric poetess Sappho) for the probably very similar pentameter-ending here. Bornecque's conjectured *Aoniam* (see next n.) *amata lyram* seems to be on the right lines. For it allows the phrase relating to 'the Lesbian' (*Lesbis* is used as both feminine noun and adjective; cf. [Ov.] *Ep. Sapph.* 100) to parallel exactly that relating to Dido, which is what the rhythm of the couplet seems to require; and it could also indicate that Sappho's letter, like Dido's, was written as she contemplated suicide. According to a tradition probably originating in Greek comedy, Sappho killed herself by leaping off the cliff of Leucas, when Phaon, a boatman of Mytilene, spurned her love, and in ancient art she is shown doing so lyre in hand (see Goold (1965a) 41-2;). *amata*, however, still looks like a senseless importation from v. 34, and the variant *amica*, which Goold favours, is scarcely more satisfactory. For (a) *amica* in the *Epistles* is a pejorative term, used by the heroines of their rivals (the one understandable and witty exception is Briseis' application of it to herself at *Ep.* 3. 50), and so would be quite inappropriate of Sappho here. And (b) it does not provide a satisfying contrast with *amata* in v. 34: something indicating Sappho's rejection or frustration is required. *omissa*, 'forsaken', is perhaps worth considering; for this sense cf. Turpilius *com.* 160 Ribbeck *quaeso omitte ac desere hanc meretricem*, Tac. *Ann.* xiii. 44. 1 *ut omitteret maritum emereatur, tuum matrimonium promittens*, and for Ovid's admission of this prosaic word see *Am.* ii. 1. 17.

R. J. Tarrant ('The authenticity of the letter of Sappho to Phaon (*Heroides* 15)', *HSPh* 85 (1981), 133-53) has argued convincingly on stylistic grounds that the surviving *Epistula Sapphus*, assigned by Daniel Heinsius to the final place (15) in the collection of single *Epistles* despite being transmitted separately from the rest of the collection, is spurious (*contra*, Jacobson 277-8, with copious bibliography). But the present line indicates that Ovid did write a letter from Sappho to Phaon, even if it has now been lost (Tarrant's contention that vv. 26 and 34 are interpolated is unpersuasive).

Aoniam: 'Boeotian', and hence 'belonging to the Muses', since their reputed home, Mt Helicon, was situated in Boeotia; cf. *Am.* i. 1. 12 *Aoniam ... lyram, Ars* iii. 547, *Fast.* iv. 245.

27. **cito:** here perhaps 'quickly', though the 'easily' of v. 16 (see n.) is not out of the question.

Sabinus: he is not positively identifiable (see Syme (1978) 75) but was evidently also the author of an epic and a *Fasti*-type poem (see *Pont.* iv. 16. 13-16). See also p. 86.

de toto ... orbe: i.e. all the places in the *Greek and Roman* world where the deserting husbands or lovers are supposedly to be found.

27-8. **rediit ... rettulit:** was Sabinus' a real 'world tour' or an arm chair one, made only in his poetic imagination? At all events, Ovid's wording facetiously sustains his pose as a kind of mythological courier.

28. **diuersis ... locis:** I take this to be ablative of origin with *rettulit*, but others see it as local ablative with *scripta*.

29. **candida:** probably an allusion to Penelope's famous wifely chastity; cf. *Ep.* 4. 31-2 *si tamen ille prior, quo me sine crimine gessi, / candor ab insolita labe notandus erat*, [Tib.] iii. 10. 17-18 (of Sulpicia) *at nunc tota tua est, te solum candida secum / cogitat.*

30. **suo:** an ironic use of the affectionate possessive (cf. 5. 28n.); Hippolytus never will be Phaedra's in the sense she wishes.

31. **pius:** this is an oblique indication that there is no joy for Dido in Aeneas' letter; he is just as *pius* now as when, obedient to his destiny, he failed to respond to her distress at Verg. *A.* iv. 393-6: *at pius Aeneas, quamquam lenire dolentem / solando cupit ... / ... / iussa tamen diuum exsequitur classemque reuisit.* Virgil's use of *pius* at this point poignantly highlights the conflict between the demands of love and those of proto-Roman duty: Ovid's is almost an open sneer at all that Aeneas stands for.

Elissae: Dido's original Phoenician name (according to Servius on Verg. *A.* i. 340; see further Bömer on *Fast.* iii. 553), which is often metrically convenient in dactylic verse.

32. **si modo uiuit:** this reminds the reader of the traditional outcome of the Phyllis story (see 27n.), but perhaps also reflects Demophoon's anxiety and renewed promise of return (in some versions of the story he did come back, though too late) as expressed in the letter by Sabinus.

33. **tristis:** 'grim' because, presumably, it confirmed his desertion of Hypsipyle in favour of Medea (see 23n.).

littera: singular for the more usual plural, which is intractable in the hexameter; cf. *Ep.* 6. 9, 17 (18), 15, *Met.* ix. 516.

34. **dat uotam Phoebo ... lyram:** i.e. as a thank-offering for Phaon's love (see 26n.), which Sappho is perhaps to be understood to have won in the end through her lyric poetry; for the vow of her lyre to Phoebus cf. [Ov.] *Ep. Sapph.* 181-4.

amata: i.e., presumably, discovering from Phaon's letter that her love is requited after all (cf. 26n.). The happy ending is not, however, traditional.

35. **qua tutum uati:** gentle irony, again centred on *uates* (cf. 18n.): the poet of martial epic *risks his reputation*, if he shows too much readiness to bring love-themes into his heroic verse.

36. **aureus ... Amor:** like his mother, χρυσέη 'Αφροδίτη (see 10. 15-22n.), Love is conventionally 'golden' (as in v. 19, the adjective suggests the god, but the context the emotion; see 15n.); cf. *Am.* i. 2. 42 (of Cupid the *triumphator*) *ibis in auratis aureus ipse rotis, Rem.* 39 with Henderson's note.

Marte: metonymy; see 14. 3n.

37-8. The lovers here mentioned all belong to the pre-Iliadic part of the Trojan saga; cf. 1-2n.

37. **nobile crimen:** *crimen* probably = Helen herself rather than her *affaire* (see 17. 25n.). She is a celebrity among (scandalous) amatory characters because *her* adultery caused the Trojan war; the allusion to it here provides a link with v. 2. For *nobilis* of *ill* fame cf. *Tr.* ii. 384 *nobilis est Canace fratris amore sui*, and for *crimen* see 17. 25n.

38. After his death at Troy, Protesilaus (see 6. 41n.) was briefly allowed leave of absence from the Underworld to visit his wife Laodamia (for the spelling see G.P. Goold, *Phoenix* 12 (1958), 113, and cf. apparatus on p. 98). When it was time for him to return, she killed herself. Cf. *Ars* iii. 17-18 *respice Phylaciden, et quae comes isse marito / fertur et ante annos occubuisse suos*, *Tr.* i. 6. 20 (the same phraseology as here), *Pont.* iii. 1. 109-10, Catul. 68. 80. Here Laodamia, the paragon of conjugal love, is ironically coupled with Helen, the most infamous of faithless wives. Laodamia is the writer of *Ep.* 13, but the present line gives no indication of whether that poem was already in existence at this point.

39. **si bene te noui:** i.e. 'if you are the man I think you are'; cf. *Ars* iii. 51, *Pont.* i. 6. 4, ii. 3. 49.

istis: see 1. 20n.

39-40. **non bella libentius istis / dicis:** this has more point if Macer has *already* written some elegy; see 3n. For *istis* see 1. 20n.

40. **uestris:** sc. 'of all you epic poets'.

castra: this is also used as a metaphor for the genre elegy at Prop. iv. 1. 135 *at tu finge elegos ... haec tua castra*.

Poem 19 (20)

1-2. **seruata ... serues:** *seruare* is virtually a technical term in the *custodia* motif: cf. vv. 19 and 50, *Am.* i. 6. 63, ii. 2. 1, 3. 1, 12. 4, Tib. i. 6. 16, 34, 37.

1. **stulte:** cf. Tib. i. 6. 15 *coniunx incaute,* and contrast *dure ... uir* of the man who does *not* guard his *puella* at *Am.* iii. 4. 1.

2. **puella:** this reflects her status from Ovid's point of view, even though she is probably the other man's *wife* (see p. 91).

at: 'at least':; this sense is common after negative conditional clauses; see Kühner-Stegmann II. ii. 83.

fac serues: a colloquial construction, which Ovid uses 41 times in the elegies but in the *Metamorphoses* only at iii. 13 (see Bömer *ad loc.*).

3. *Leitmotiv* (i); see pp. 91-2, and cf. *Am.* iii. 4. 17 *nitimur in uetitum semper cupimusque negata* and 31 (cited 52n.).

4. I.e. *si quis amat quod sinit alter* (*amare*), *ferreus est*; a combination of hyperbaton (see p. 16) and ellipse; cf. 4. 16n.

ferreus: i.e. 'totally insensitive' (cf. Juv. 1. 31). This is a perversion of the word's normal elegiac associations; cf. especially its application to the door-keeper who stands between Ovid and his beloved at *Am.* i. 6. 27.

quod: see 2. 14n.

5-8. *Leitmotiv* (ii); see pp. 91-2, and cf. *Am.* ii. 9B. 43-6, *Ars* iii. 579-80 *quod datur ex facili, longum male nutrit amorem: / miscenda est laetis rara repulsa iocis*.

7. **quo mihi fortunam:** the ellipse of a verb (*uelim*, or similar: 'to what purpose would I want ...') is easily paralleled: see *Am.* iii. 4. 41 *quo tibi formosam, si non nisi casta placebat?*, iii. 7. 49 *quo mihi fortunae tantum? quo regna sine usu?*, Hor. *Ep.* i. 5. 12 *quo mihi fortunam, si non conceditur uti?*, with Wickham's note. It is clear from *Am.* iii. 7. 49

that amatory *fortuna* for Ovid in large part = *formosa puella*, and this perhaps explains why he speaks of *fortuna* which never *'bothers* to deceive' him (*curet* very strongly suggests a personal agent). Lee's conjecture *formosam* points the sense, but it is probably unnecessary.

8. **laedat:** cf. *Ars* iii. 598 *non nisi laesus amo*. For the general sentiment cf. also Prop. iii. 8. 34.

9-10. **uiderat ... uitium uersuta ... Corinna ... capi ... callida:** the striking alliteration helps to highlight the two adjectives, which both point to Corinna's cleverness. But while *callidus* is relatively common (Ovid's use of it here recalls especially Tib. i. 6. 6, where it applies to Delia, and he himself uses it again at *Tr.* ii. 500 to characterise the faithless wives of the Adultery Mime (see 5. 13-22n.)), *uersutus* is very uncommon, at least in extant poetry (in Ovid again at *Met.* xi. 312 and in Propertius at iv. 7. 37, but avoided by the other Augustans). It is most memorable as the word Livius Andronicus used to translate πολύτροπος ('many-wiled') in the opening line of Homer's *Odyssey*.

10. **capi:** see 4. 13n.
opem: = 'ruse'; cf. *Met.* iii. 633, *Am.* iii. 7. 56, *Ep.* 6. 98. This sense is first attested in comedy; see Pl. *Epid.* 152 (cf. 9-10n.).

11-13. **a, quotiens ... a, quotiens:** Ovid is especially fond of the anaphoric repetition (see p. 14) of this common pathetic exclamation; cf. *Met.* ii. 489-91, *Ep.* 5. 49-51, 15 (16). 241-3, *Tr.* i. 3. 51-3.

11. **sani capitis mentita dolores:** a favourite female ploy; cf. *Am.* i. 8. 73 (the *lena* to her 'pupil') *capitis modo finge dolorem*, iii. 11. 25, Pl. *Truc.* 632, Tib. i. 6. 36.

12. **cunctantem tardo:** the completely spondaic first half of the pentameter wittily reflects the situation. For the lover's reluctance to depart cf. Asclep. *AP* v. 189. 2.

13. **finxit culpam:** i.e. she pretended to have been unfaithful. For *culpa* see 14. 43-4n., and for the ruse cf. *Ars* iii. 593-4, *Rem.* 769-70; the boot is on the other foot at *Ars* ii. 445-6.

14. **speciem praebuit esse nocens:** the construction is analogous to *uisa est esse nocens*, but I have found no exact parallels for it.

15. Cf. *Ars* ii. 439ff., and for fire imagery in general 8. 1n.
ubi uexarat ... refoueratque: the pluperfect instead of the perfect with *ubi* here indicates repeated action; see Woodcock 174-5. With *uexarat* understand *me* (cf. *Tr.* iii. 8. 27). The compound *refouere* is first attested in Ovid; cf. *Ep.* 11. 58, *Met.* viii. 537, x. 187 (and see p. 13 with n. 96).
tepidos: see 2. 53n. *tepet*, and *Ars* ii. 445.

16. **apta:** a *double entendre* is no doubt intended; cf. 8. 4n..

17. **blanditias:** virtually synonymous with *dulcia uerba*; cf. 1. 21n. Munari points to the verbal echo at Maximian 5. 101 *nil tibi blanditias, nil dulcia carmina prosunt*.

18. **oscula, di magni, ...:** cf. *Ep.* 17(18). 102 *oscula, di magni, trans mare digna peti*. For *oscula* see 18. 10n.; for the colloquial *di magni* cf. Pl. *Cist.* 522, Catul. 14. 12, 53. 5, and see Hofmann 30.

19. **rapuisti ... ocellos:** a cliché; cf. *Am.* iii. 11. 48, *perque tuos oculos qui rapuere meos*, *Ep.* 12. 36, Prop. iii. 10. 15, [Ov.] *Ep. Sapph.* 22, Ap. Rhod. iii. 1019.

20. **time insidias:** 'fear traps'. Goold ((1965a) 44, and *HSPh* 71 (1966), 105) insists that *'pretend to* fear traps' is the sense required and wishes to emend (see apparatus on p. 98). But Ovid is simply seeing the situation from the point of view of the girl herself who will say 'I fear traps', sc. 'set by my husband to catch me' (cf. *Am.* iii. 4. 32 *sola placet, 'timeo' dicere si qua potest*, 8. 63 *me prohibet custos, in me timet illa maritum*, *Ars* iii. 604, Tib. ii. 6. 50, Prop. ii. 23. 18). The only oddity is the elision of a word of iambic form before a long syllable (which made Lachmann scent corruption here). But it is paralleled in Ovid at

Ep. 16 (17). 97 *disce meo exemplo formosis posse carere*; Palmer's conjecture *ex exemplo*, which conveniently removes the parallel for Goold, is ugly and un-Ovidian.
rogata nega: see 3. 5, 9B. 50nn.

21-2. **proiectum in limine ... frigora .. pati:** the classic lot of the *exclusus amator* (see 1. 17n.) Cf. [Call.] *Epigr.* 63 (= *AP* v. 23). 1-2, Asclep. *AP* v. 189. 1-2, Hor. *Carm.* iii. 10. 1-8, 19-20, Prop. i. 16. 21-4.

22. **pruinosa ... nocte:** for the ablative see 9B. 39n. Frostiness is regularly associated with the time just before dawn (cf. *Am.* i. 6. 65, 13. 2, Prop. ii. 9. 41, and see further Bömer on *Fast.* vi. 730), but here Ovid seems to be applying it to the whole night. *pruinosus* is first attested in his work (7 instances). The adjectives in *-osus* defy classification as poetic, prosaic, colloquial etc., and seem to be admitted or avoided largely according to authors' personal taste. Ovid is more liberal with them than the linguistically fastidious Tibullus, but less so than the bold Propertius. See further Axelson 60-61, Tränkle 59-60, A. Ernout, *Les adjectifs latins en -osus et -ulentus* (Paris, 1949).

23. **sic mihi durat amor:** cf. *Am.* i. 8. 96 *non bene, si tollas proelia, durat amor.*
adolescit: cf. *Ars* ii. 594 *has artes tolle, senescit amor.*

24. **alimenta:** this heralds the dietary metaphor in vv. 25-6. Cf. *Am.* ii. 10. 25.

25-6. A rich and over-generous diet of love gives Ovid emotional indigestion. The implications of *pinguis* in the context of food are clear from Catul. 62. 3 *iam tempus iam pinguis linquere mensas*, where the reference is to the (obviously lavish) catering of a wedding feast, while *patens* connotes sexual accessibility; cf. *Met.* xiv. 133 *si mea uirginitas Phoebo patuisset amanti*, *Priap.* 52. 3, 83. 21 Bücheler, Solinus (3rd century A.D., cited by Heinsius) 31 *feminas suas primis noctibus nuptiarum adulteriis cogunt patere.* Both words have been alleged to have programmatic significance, but see p. 92.

25. **nobis:** dative of the person judging, 'to my mind'; it should also be understood 'apo koinou' with *nocet* (26).

26. **dulcis ... esca, nocet:** Cf. Cic. *de Orat.* iii. 99 *quis potione uti aut cibo dulci diutius potest?*, Apul. *Met.* ii. 10 (to a sex-hungry admirer) *caue ne nimia mellis dulcedine diutinam bilis amaritudinem contrahas*, Anon. *AP* xvi. 16. 2 καὶ τοῦ μέλιτος τὸ πλεόν ἐστι χολή ('Even too much honey is gall').

27-30. The *exempla* return to the *custodia* motif, illustrating the supposedly beneficial effects of strict confinement or surveillance from the *girl's* point of view. If pressed, the analogies suggest that Ovid must see himself as the arch-philanderer Jupiter. The two myths are coupled again at *Am.* iii. 4. 19-22, and both were favourite subjects of ancient art (for Danae see Daremberg and Saglio III, 706, fig. 4229 and n. 14, and for Io, *ibid.* I. 418-19, L. Curtius, *Die Wandmalerei Pompejis* (Hildesheim, 1960), 258ff, 278f., J. M. C. Toynbee, *The Art of the Romans* (London, 1965), 116, 256 with Plate 65).

27-8. Danae was confined in a tower by her father Acrisius, king of Argos, to preserve her virginity, because it had been predicted that a son of hers would kill him. But Jupiter turned himself into a shower of gold to reach her and fathered Perseus; cf. *Am.* iii. 4. 21-2, 12. 33-4, *Ars* iii. 631-2, *Met.* iv. 611 with Bömer's note (the story is often rationalised to account for the power of bribery; see e.g. *Am.* iii. 8. 29-34, Hor. *Carm.* iii. 16, *AP* v. 31 (Antip. Thess.), 33, 34 (Parmenio), 217 (Paul. Sil.)). The pentameter's opening verbal and rhythmical echo of the hexameter perhaps helps to point the irony of the *exemplum* (see previous n.).

27. **aenea:** a prison of bronze here (cf. Hor. *Carm.* iii. 16. 1), but of iron at *Am.* iii. 4. 21, and of both bronze and iron at *Am.* iii. 8. 32.

28. **de Ioue:** *de* rather than the more common *ex* is first used to denote parentage in Ovid; cf. *Met.* iii. 214 *de ... lupo concepta Nape*, and for poetic preference for *de* over *ex* in general see Bömer on *Met.* iii. 116.

28-29. For the story and the spelling *Io* (accusative) see 2. 45n.

30. I.e. *illa facta est Ioui gratior quam fuerat*; mild hyperbaton (see p. 16).

31. **quod licet et facile est:** object of *quisquis cupit*. For *quod licet* and the general sentiment see 3n., and for the sexual nuances of *facile* see 3. 5n.

31-2. **arbore frondes / carpat:** a variation on the proverbial sentiment at *Am.* ii. 10. 13 (see n. *ad loc.*); cf. also *Ib.* 195-6 *inde ego pauca* (sc. *e poenis tuis*) *canam, frondes ut siquis ab Ida / aut summam Libyco de mare carpat aquam.* Kenney ((1962) 11, n. 1) suggests that *e* from v. 32 is to be understood 'apo koinou' with *arbore*, but the plain ablative is perfectly intelligible, and the presence of the preposition in 32 (the only certain instance of *e* with *potare* recorded in *ThLL*) probably a matter of metrical convenience (see p. 13).

32. **e magno flumine potet aquam:** cf. Call. *Epigr.* 28 (= *A P* xii. 43). 3-4 μισῶ καὶ περίφοιτον ἐρώμενον, οὐδ' ἀπὸ κρήνης / πίνω, ('I dislike a lover who does the rounds, and I do not drink from a (public) well'). Callimachus, however, is expressing distaste for anything which has to be shared with others, and Ovid for a beloved who is too readily available to him. Horace uses a variation of the same illustration to ridicule human acquisitiveness at *S.* i. 1. 54-6: *ut tibi si sit opus liquidi non amplius urna / uel cyatho, et dicas 'magno de flumine mallem / quam ex hoc fonticulo tantundem sumere.* A programmatic interpretation of Ovid's Callimachean reminiscence seems to me hardly justified; see p. 92.

33-4. See 5-8n.

33. **regnare:** see 9B. 52-3n..
deludat amantem: cf. *Am.* ii. 9B. 43, and see p. 90. *deludere* = 'trick' or 'fool' rather than simply 'deceive'; Ovid wants his beloved to *pretend* to be unfaithful rather than *actually* to be so (see next n.). He is the first extant poet to use *deludere* in this sense; see Bömer on *Met.* iii. 366.

34. **ne monitis torquear ...:** here Ovid is not so much concerned about specific ruses he has taught being used against him (cf. 18. 20n.), as about the danger of his mistress failing to make the distinction between pretence and actuality (see previous n.). Lee captures the sense well with 'Perhaps I'll live to regret that advice'.

35. **quidlibet eueniat:** literally 'let anything you like happen'.
indulgentia: cf. *Ars* ii. 435 (of girls) *sunt quibus ingrate timida indulgentia seruit.*

36. Note the witty chiasmus, and for the sentiment see 3n. For *quod* see 2. 14n.

37. **at:** resumptive; see 8. 17n.
formosae: see 10. 5-7n.
secure: 'negligent'; cf. [Tib.] iii. 16. 1.

38-9. **incipe ... incipe:** the repetition sounds a note of exasperation and implies that Ovid has been loving unhindered for some time.

38. **prima claudere nocte forem:** cf. Hor. *Carm.* iii. 7. 29 (to a lover with a rival) *prima nocte domum claude.*

39. **furtim:** cf. 8. 8n. *furtiuae*.
limina: poetic plural, and here, as often, 'gate' or 'door', not 'threshold' (see *ThLL* VII. 1409. 17ff., 29ff.); the collocation *limen pulsare* first appears in Ovid and then several times in Silver Latin poetry.

40. **canes:** an occupational hazard for the clandestine lover; cf. *Tr.* ii. 549, Tib. i. 6. 31 with Murgatroyd's note, Prop. iv. 5. 73-4, Hor. *S.* i. 2. 126.

41. Nape in *Am.* i. 11 and 12 immediately comes to mind; cf. also *Am.* iii. 14. 31, *Ars* i. 383, iii. 470, Tib. i. 2. 93-4 with Murgatroyd's note for further examples. For *tabellae* see 5. 5n.

42. **uacuo secubet ... toro:** *secubare* is virtually a technical term for the sexual abstinence demanded by religious observance, which elegiac *puellae* often use as an excuse for keeping a lover at bay; cf. *Am.* iii. 10. 1-2 *Annua uenerunt Cerealis tempora sacri: /*

secubat in uacuo sola puella toro, Tib. i. 3. 26 (with Murgatroyd's note), 6. 11, and cf. 2. 25n. For *uacuo ... toro* see 10. 17n.

ipsa: i.e. 'the mistress' (cf. Irish 'himself', 'herself').

43. Cf. Catul. 66. 23 *quam penitus maestas exedit cura medullas!*

aliquando: 'at last', as at *Fast*. iv. 39, *Met*. ii. 391 and Verg. *A*. viii. 200; the word's central position in the line and rarity in hexameter poetry (see *ThLL* I. 1599. 28ff.) make it very emphatic.

44. **materiam:** 'substantial reason'; cf. *Ars* ii. 34 *materiam, qua sis ingeniosus, habes* (more examples at *ThLL* VIII. 464. 53ff.).

dolis: for a selection of the sort of thing Ovid has in mind see *Ars* ii. 240ff., and for the thrill of success see *Am*. ii. 12. 3-4.

45. **uacuo furari litore harenas:** for sand as an example of infinite number see e.g. *Tr*. iv. 1. 55, Otto 159, *ThLL* VI. 3. 2528. 60ff. The expression here sounds as if it ought to be proverbial, but classical parallels are to seek. *uacuo* either means 'devoid of observers' or 'without a legal owner' (see Stroh (1979) 397, n. 64). In either case it emphasises the tameness of the action: stealing when 'the coast is clear', or from what amounts to 'common property', requires no great daring or ingenuity.

46. **uxorem:** though this word *can* be used of the female partner in any stable relationship (see Stroh (1979) 344, n. 49, and cf. 2. 47-60n. for a similar situation with *maritus*), its standard meaning is 'wife', and Ovid relies on it being so understood, as he builds up to the climax of v. 57 (see n. and further p. 91).

stulti: a shorthand reference to Ovid's basic complaint in v. 1.

47-50. Ovid outrageously implies that the *maritus* will be the loser if he refuses to participate in *his* game. *mea* amusingly replaces the expected *tua* at the end of v. 48, and witty word-play contributes to the humorous effect; notice the polyptoton (see p. 16) *incipis, incipiet*, the juxtaposition of opposites *incipiet* and *desinere* (cf. p. 16), and the repetition with contrast, *bene seruasses ... bene uerba darem*.

47. **praemoneo:** a largely prosaic word (see Bömer on *Met*. xv. 785), whose 'no nonsense' tone is immediately undercut by the subsequent absurdity.

49. **multa diuque tuli:** the same expression in a more conventional elegiac situation at *Am*. iii. 11. 1

49-50. **speraui ... futurum ... ut darem:** a cumbersome and uncommon use of the periphrastic *futurum esse / fore ut* + subjunctive to compensate for the lack of a future infinitive from *posse* (see Kühner-Stegmann II. i. 689-90).

51. **lentus:** here 'over-tolerant' and also 'slow on the uptake' (a link with *stulte* in v. 1 and *stulti* in v. 45), but at *Am*. i. 6. 41 'inflexible'. For the word's unusual range see *OLD* s.v.

nulli patienda marito: those very things, in fact, which the Augustan husband was forbidden to tolerate *by law* (see 2. 47-60n) – as if Ovid were on the side of legality!

52. **at mihi:** *mihi* is dative of reference, and not dative with *concessi* (see next n.). Combined with *at* it marks a strong contrast with the (understood) *tu* of the hexameter; cf. *Am*. ii. 10. 19.

concessi finis amoris erit: cf. *Am*. iii. 4. 31 *iuuat inconcessa uoluptas* (offered as a reason for *not* confining a desirable girl). This is one instance, I think, where the easier reading (see apparatus on p. 98) is also the better one, for *concessa* (= *PYH*), which some prefer, as ablative absolute with *puella* understood (see Goold (1965a) 45), seems to me to have nothing to recommend it but its difficulty (and therefore theoretically greater liability to corruption); *Am*. iii. 7. 55 as interpreted by Goold is certainly no convincing parallel.

53. Contrast Prop. ii. 23. 12 *a pereant, si quos ianua clausa iuuet!*

scilicet: this conveys outraged disbelief; cf. Verg. *A*. ii. 577 with Austin's note.

infelix: here ironically applied to the *un*troubled lover or his lot; cf. *Am.* ii. 5. 53, Prop. ii. 23. 19-20.

54. **nox:** = sexual satisfaction; cf. *Am.* i. 8. 67, Prop. ii. 23. 11 (more examples at *OLD* s.v. 3c).

sub nullo uindice: 'subject to no claimant', (so Henderson on *Rem.* 145, where the same phrase occurs in a different context). *uindex* is one of the legalistic terms which Ovid admits fairly frequently (26 instances), but Catullus, Lucretius and the other Augustans exclude almost entirely (see Kenney (1969) 253-6). It is properly a term connected with the process of *manus iniectio* (Berger s.v. offers a technical definition; see also 5. 29-32n.), but outside the legal context denotes anyone who 'lays claim' to any rights or property or who 'takes vengeance' for a wrong. And since a cuckolded husband would normally be expected to do exactly that, the word is highly appropriate here; moreover, its legalistic tone particularly suits a context where a real law is being brought to mind (see p. 91).

55. **traham suspiria:** for sighing in one's sleep as a sign of amatory anxiety cf. Prop. ii. 22. 47, iii. 8. 27 with Fedeli's note, [Tib.] iii. 6. 61.

56. **perisse uelim:** cf. *Am.* ii. 2. 10.

57. **quid mihi cum ...:** Ovid is fond of this expression; see G. R. Stanton, *RhM* 116 (1973), 85.

facili: cf. *Am.* ii. 3. 5.

lenone marito: with this juxtaposition Ovid confirms that he has in mind the *lenocinium* ('connivance') clause of the *lex Iulia de adulteriis coercendis* (see 2. 27-60n.). For the opposite, but equally scandalous, viewpoint cf. *Am.* iii. 4. 37-8 *rusticus est nimium quem laedit adultera coniunx, / et notos mores non satis Vrbis habet.*

58. **gaudia:** see 5. 29n.

59. Cf. *Am.* iii. 11. 27-8 (to the unfaithful mistress) *his et quae taceo duraui saepe ferendis: / quaere alium pro me quid uelit ista pati.*

quin: an exasperated 'why not?'; cf. *Am.* iii. 7. 69.

60. **me:** emphatic. Since the man is going to have rivals anyway, he may as well have the one most worth having – viz. Ovid.

ueta: the postponement of the main verb, combined with the unusual sense pause before the last word of the pentameter, ensures that both the poem and the book end with (literally) a bang, not a whimper.

GENERAL INDEX

Only items of general literary and linguistic interest are included here; readers seeking information about a specific poem, passage or expression should refer to the discussions and commentary.